STATEMAKING AND SOCIAL MOVEMENTS

STATEMAKING AND SOCIAL MOVEMENTS

Essays in History and Theory

Edited by Charles Bright and Susan Harding

Ann Arbor
The University of Michigan Press

1987 1986 1985 1984 4 3 2 1

Library of Congress Cataloging in Publication Data
Main entry under title:

Statemaking and social movements.

 Includes bibliographical references.
 1. State, The—Addresses, essays, lectures. 2. Social
movements—Addresses, essays, lectures. I. Bright,
Charles, 1943–   II. Harding, Susan Friend.
JC325.S7354 1984   306'.2 84-7430
ISBN 0-472-10050-5

ACKNOWLEDGMENTS

Many people helped us prepare this volume. All the authors contributed more than their essays; they helped to create and shape the whole. Sam Bowles, Lynn Eden, Michael Geyer, and Theda Skocpol were especially helpful with advice and suggestions. Isabel Hull, Rayna Rapp, and William Rosenberg read the entire manuscript very carefully and gave us, and each of the authors, invaluable suggestions. The volume has been greatly improved because of their helpful criticism.

We would particularly like to thank Charles Tilly, who gave us the theoretical compass for thinking about states and offered much encouragement and advice as we carried out the project.

The book would never have been completed without the help of John Mersereau, Razelle Brooks, Alita Mitchell, and Margaret Marz of the Residential College of the University of Michigan. Our students and teaching colleagues also contributed to the conceptual evolution of the volume. It is, in many ways, a product of the unique atmosphere of the Residential College, where an emphasis on undergraduate teaching is combined with the cultivation of an intellectual environment unconstrained by disciplinary boundaries.

We would also like to thank the College of Literature, Science and the Arts and Alfred Sussman and Eugene Feingold of the Horace H. Rackham School of Graduate Studies at the University of Michigan for providing us with financial support at critical moments and, in particular, for helping us bring the authors together for a weekend of discussion.

Charles Bright
Susan Harding

CONTENTS

PROCESSES OF STATEMAKING
AND POPULAR PROTEST
An Introduction

Charles Bright and Susan Harding

In the past decade, scholarship on the state has reached a watershed as scholars in various disciplines have stretched their analytic frameworks to the point of collapse. In the United States, the political crisis of the 1960s and 1970s produced a critical rethinking of the state and the political organization of power. The faltering of postwar economic growth, the unraveling of the political accord between capital and labor, and the political mobilizations of the right during the 1970s challenged not only the authority of the American state but also basic assumptions about the nature of the state and its relationship with society. These currents of reassessment reinforced the ongoing theoretical debate over the state that had arisen, especially among Europeans, in the wake of the Nazi disaster and revelations about Stalinism, and they gave support to scholars working within an emerging neo-Marxist tradition who were beginning to reexamine the structuring of state power under capitalism. Broadly speaking, such crosscurrents of discussion have produced a critique of existing theoretical perspectives and a more critical attitude toward the state itself, one which recognizes not only the tremendous power of the modern state and its capacity to inflict suffering, but also the serious limitations of the state's ability to achieve economic equality or social justice.

Nonspecialists are often in a better position to rethink a theoretical perspective than are specialists. While a number of political scientists, such as Lindblom, Wolfe, and Offe, have made important contributions,[1] much of the critical new work on the state and the political organization of power has come from historians, anthropologists, sociologists, and economists working on specific problems within their respective disciplines. This volume gathers some of the work of these social scientists. It is a sampler of current discourse on states and politics and does not pretend to be historically or theoretically comprehensive—the current rethinking has only begun and a new paradigm has not emerged. Each essay is in itself an act of rethinking in which the author reworks one or more received assumptions about the state in his or her field. There are considerable differences among the authors gathered here, but, because we exchanged essays as they were taking shape and then gathered to discuss them for two days, we were able to develop some common lines of criticism and reconceptualization. The collection as a whole, and to varying degrees each of the essays, departs from prevailing perspectives in several respects and offers some guidelines for a way of thinking about states, politics, movements, and the relationship between states and social formations that joins history and theory.

— An Exchange between Marx and Weber

Most current thinking about the state is grounded in the distinct conceptions of the state cast by Karl Marx and Max Weber and developed by their respective intellectual progeny.[2] Both traditions portray the state as the apparatus of governance, administration, and coercion within a society, but they diverge sharply on how they conceive the relationship between state and society. The Marxist tradition is distinguished by its assumption that the state and its actions are in some manner epiphenomena of economic or class forces. This assumption generates powerful causal links, but lends itself to reductionism, to reducing states and statemaking to the operation of economic and class interests. The distinguishing assumption of the Weberian tradition is, by contrast, the irreducibility of the state to extrapolitical processes. The state in the modern era is treated as a rationalized bureaucratic organization operating according to legal and procedural guidelines which the state itself establishes. This perspective tends toward reification, toward treating the state as a "thing in itself," a self-contained, independently constituted force for domination acting on its own behalf. The essays gathered here work within both Marxist and Weberian traditions, but also against their tendencies toward reductionism and reification. The result is a fruitful exchange between the two traditions and a number of interesting departures from them.

Within Marxism, this volume derives from a debate over the nature and degree of the autonomy of states from economic forces under capitalism. Are states under capitalism "capitalist states"? Are they tools of the capitalist class? Do they invariably contribute to the reproduction and well-being of a capitalist social order or class domination? And if so, why? In this debate, Nicos Poulantzas made a major conceptual break from the reductionist assumption of classical Marxism. Responding to Ralph Miliband's attempt to analyze state institutions and practices as instruments of the capitalist class, Poulantzas advanced a more complex argument for the "relative autonomy" of the state from capitalism.[3] The state was not the mere product or tool of a ruling class, since the interests of that class were often competitive and contradictory. Rather, the state was itself embroiled in the contradictions and conflicts of a class society and, indeed, could act against the interests of specific capitalists. The productive mode still shaped politics within the state, according to Poulantzas, but only in the "very complex sense" that political struggles between classes transformed class domination under capitalism in ways that insured its reproduction and legitimized the accumulation process.

Much subsequent work within the Marxist tradition has dealt, directly or indirectly, with what "relative autonomy" means. The autonomy of the state can mean many things: that the state is governed by its own laws; that it is not reducible to something else; that it is not causally dependent on something else; that it is self-regulating; that it is self-contained and not affected by external influences. These meanings are not necessarily incompatible, and they all crop up in the discussion of "relative autonomy." But the root difficulty remains: if this autonomy is, in fact, only relative, then the state must still be reducible to something else, and the analytic task is to determine the admittedly complex mediations through which economic and social imperatives are translated into political forms and actions. If, on the other hand, the autonomy is considered in some sense to be absolute, then the state must be treated as not fully reducible to other imperatives, but rather as a specific terrain with a history, language, and practice quite distinct from the economy or class relations.[4] It is this latter position, which breaks clear of reductionist assumptions, that is explored by a number of essays in this volume, most explicitly by Herbert Gintis and Samuel Bowles, Elizabeth Brumfiel, Kenneth Finegold and Theda Skocpol.

Max Weber's writings on politics and the state were more extensive than Marx's and have, consequently, been very influential in recent discussions of the state and statemaking. Weber's basic characterization of the state as a legally established bureaucratic order that administers jurisdiction and monopolizes legitimate means of coercion within a bounded territory was effectively used by the contributors to Charles Tilly's edited volume, *The Formation of National States in Western Europe*.[5] These influential essays explore the major processes—war, taxation, fiscal policy, judicial centralization, and so on—by which the relatively decentralized and institutionally modest polities of early modern Europe were turned into modern nation-states. In Tilly's volume, the stress is on the processes by which stately institutions were built, rather than on the institutions themselves, upon politically manifest social struggles, rather than on relentless bureaucratization. The essays in the present volume follow this lead. The state remains an autonomous, irreducible set of institutions, but the view of the state as an internally rationalized bureaucracy immune to popular influences or governed by self-generated rules gives way to a view of the state as the arena of routinized political com-

petition in which class, status, and political conflicts, representing both
elite and popular interests, are played out. These are open-ended and
contingent processes that do not lead in a historically predetermined
direction. The essays in this collection go beyond the contributors to
Tilly's in suggesting that statemaking does not end once stately institutions emerge, but is continuous. Moreover, the focus here is not exclusively on statemaking processes that build up and support centralized
institutions of state, but also on processes that dismantle stately institutions or arrest the centralization of power. These directions are explored
most fully in the essays by Rod Aya, Charles Bright, and Michael Geyer.

The analysis of the state that emerges here steers between reductionism and reification by centering analysis on the structured political
processes that make, remake, and unmake states continuously—in other
words, on statemaking—rather than on extrapolitical determinants or institutional outcomes. The state *is* autonomous in the sense that it is not
reducible to economic and social struggles and is not causally dependent
upon dominant social classes. The state *is not* autonomous in the sense of
being self-contained or self-directing, since it is continuously penetrated
by social and economic struggles that insure that no political process is
purely political and that the logic by which bureaucracies develop is
never simply rational. States are neither static givens lording over society
nor subservient by-products of other social forces; they are the institutional and ideological products of historically specific processes structuring power relations in a society. They are institutions of governance, as in
Weber, and they are central agents of social order and reproduction, as in
Marx, but such characterizations pale before the fantastic diversity and
fluidity of form, function, and malfunction that current studies of states
and political processes reveal. Nor do they do justice to the extent to
which all states are internally divided and subject to penetration by conflicting and usually contradictory social forces. Such complexity and dynamism yield to analysis when we focus on statemaking processes.

In seeking a conception of the state that accords it neither too much,
nor too little, autonomy from other social forces, and by focusing on
statemaking as a continuous process, we arrive at an understanding of the
state as a distinct realm of structured political relations that is defined by
contention along its boundaries and among politicians and bureaucrats
who, in competing for office and influence, rework social and economic
conflict into political terms. These contentious processes both define the
state vis-à-vis other social and economic institutions and continually remake the state itself. Thus, while the authors gathered here see the state
as the organized apparatus of governance and coercion, attention has
shifted from stately institutions to the structured relations between the
state and other spheres of society, and to the ways in which politicians and

bureaucrats import social and economic conflict into the state and reproduce it as politics.

As contests over state activities, boundaries, and structures, popular protests, social movements, and ultimately revolutions must be included as statemaking processes. State authorities distinguish sharply between routine politics and insurgent movements, treating the latter as if they were "outside" the state, unruly and illegitimate. Yet, in fact, popular protests and movements, revolutions, party and electoral politics, and policy making and policy implementation are all statemaking processes. That is, they are all mechanisms through which politicians and state managers, social and economic elites, and popular groups contest—and in contesting, alter—what the state is, what it shall do, and who shall have access to its resources.

Taken together, these essays propose that the structures, activities, and ideologies of states, as well as statemaking processes themselves, are the historically contingent subjects of contention. Although participation in these processes is highly stratified and all states serve elite interests far better than popular ones, access to statemaking processes is itself subject to contention and is thus contingent. We expect these realities to vary over time and from state to state. Without surrendering to the theoretical chaos of historical particularism, therefore, we recommend historically well-informed theorizing about states and statemaking processes. All but one of the essays in this volume treat a specific problem in the history of European or American states, yet the assumptions in question affect the discussion of states generally, and to make this point, we have included an essay on Aztec statemaking. While there is, inevitably, some intellectual tension in the simultaneous call for a general way of thinking about states and social movements and for historically specific treatments of statemaking, it is useful, for precisely this reason, to assemble in one place essays that address a wide variety of historical problems and a range of theoretical concerns, yet share and overlap enough that they begin to yield new terms of discourse on the state. Analytically, the essays divide between studies that focus on statemaking and consider social and economic struggles from the vantage point of the state, and studies that focus on social movements and consider the impact of such movements upon state action as well as upon the shape of the state itself. We review them here in this order.

Statemaking Processes

Herbert Gintis and Samuel Bowles, in their essay on the emergence of the postfeudal social order in Europe, express most clearly the new directions in Marxist thinking about the state. They directly take issue with the classic tendency to reduce states and statemaking processes to economic or class forces. They also reject the view that early modern states in Europe were the by-products of the transition from a feudal to a capitalist mode of production, or a kind of signature of new forces at work in the economy. Instead, they treat states in early modern Europe as major agents or motors of the economic transition. Moreover, they describe this transition as one from a feudal to a "state commercial" (rather than capitalist) "social formation" (rather than mode of production). They thus emphasize the autonomous role of the state and the importance of the articulation among social, political, and economic spheres, none reducible to the others, in comprising a social system. In this way, they construct a distinct chronology for the political realm and refuse to treat political change as the effect of economic change. Instead, they make a strong case for understanding society as a contradictory totality in which shifts in the articulation among separately constituted spheres—economic, social, religious, political, familial—account for changes in the whole.

While Gintis and Bowles are primarily interested in the relations among social spheres, their analysis of the feudal state underscores the need to see politics as a realm of contestation for itself, distinct, uniquely constituted, and therefore capable of generating transformational dynamics independent of changes in productive relations. Elizabeth Brumfiel goes around the world from medieval Europe to study Aztec statemaking in Mesoamerica during the same period. Through a similar process of critical reevaluation, she has arrived at essentially the same way of thinking about non-Western statemaking as other contributors have about Western statemaking.

Most anthropological literature on the state offers two possible approaches to answering the question, why did states arise? One is a structuralist, or Marxist, approach that sees states as coercive institutions arising out of class conflict and hence ultimately reducible to economic relations, and the other is an ecological approach that sees states as managerial systems arising in response to ecological problems such as population pressure. Brumfiel departs from both approaches and, directing our attention instead to the prestate political dynamics in the Valley of Mexico, she argues that the process of Aztec statemaking arose out of contradictions within the structure of rulership which continually generated warfare among paramount rulers and political instability in the pre-Aztec petty kingdoms. She identifies the moment of Aztec state formation in the alliance of three paramounts and their reorganization of tribute relations—a shift in political relations that permitted the creation of a bureaucracy some thirty years later. Brumfiel does not banish extrapolitical processes or ecological factors from her explanation of state origins; they affect the statemaking process, but they are not its determinants. In arguing that states are the outcomes of essentially political processes, Brumfiel shows how the emergence of the Aztec state wrought changes in social and economic spheres, and she makes a powerful case for the autonomy of political relations in generating those transformational pressures.

The autonomy of the political is nowhere more forcefully argued than by Kenneth Finegold and Theda Skocpol in their essay on the National Industrial Recovery Act and the New Deal American state. Analyzing the origins of the NIRA, the authors show that, while social and economic interests continuously infringed upon the political process, they did not directly shape policy but were mediated by politicians, who in competing for offices and influence, took up, reshaped, and adapted exogenous pressures to serve their political ends. At the same time, however, the implementation of policies thus formed did not directly express the intentions of the politicians who made them. In the case of the NIRA, the weakness of the American state's capacity coupled with fierce bureaucratic struggles within the implementing agencies distorted the consequences of policy. A program designed to foster business recovery became, instead, a source of heightened class tension, promoting the mobilization of labor and the alienation of business from the Roosevelt administration. The unintended consequences of state policies and programs such as these cannot be explained within either rationalist or functionalist conceptions of the state. Instead, Finegold and Skocpol make the structured processes of policy-making and implementation the pivot of their analysis. In this way, they can show how politicians, in attempting to conciliate both popular and elite imperatives and constraints in ways that would give them advantage in their competition with one another, devise policies that reflect neither the interests of any single constituency nor their own intentions. The authors develop a framework which assumes both the autonomy of the political realm and its continuous penetration by both elite and popular interests, a framework in which unintended consequences are expected rather than problematic.

This perspective is also adopted by Lynn Eden in her essay on American policy formation in the early cold war period. Eden takes us deep inside the American state to examine the individual rationales and discrete choices of politicians, military officials, and state bureaucrats as they formulated some of the military and foreign policies that launched the cold war. Implicitly, this essay is a test of Miliband's instrumentalist conception of the state. Eden argues that the class backgrounds of policymakers and the class interests represented by them did shape their specific prescriptions for the future, but she does not find the ruling class consensus that Miliband claims exists. Rather, she finds a significant split among the representatives of capitalist interests and finds that class factors did not directly determine the policies that emerged. Instead, policy was the outcome of a decidedly contradictory process in which a variety of interests were bargained and thrown into competition in the political arena. Eden impresses us with the unpredictability of outcomes and the discrepancy between the imperatives of political competition within the state—the stuff of everyday politics—and the enormity of the issues at stake in the formulation of policy. Overall she shows how politicians and state managers translate social, economic, and global concerns into political terms and how essentially political maneuvers for influence and power reshape the direction of the state.

States are constantly penetrated by social and economic conflicts, yet not reducible to those conflicts, so the interactions between the state and other social spheres, and the shifting, continuously contested terms of their articulation become the focus of analytic attention. Raymond Grew, in his essay on the nineteenth-century state in Europe, focuses on how boundaries between states and their societies were established and maintained. He sees a paradox in the fact that, as national bureaucracies were consolidated and the capacity of states for social intervention increased, liberal theorists were busy elaborating laissez-faire doctrines of nonintervention and state neutrality, while politicians conducted a general retreat from social intervention, limiting themselves to those areas where they could act, or appear to act, neutrally. In this process of retreat, state managers sought to deploy rules for the regulation of social competition, and it is this effort that leads Grew to the central contradiction of the nineteenth-century laissez-faire state. In asserting its authority to enforce impartial rules upon economic and social conflicts which it did not, in fact, control, state authorities were increasingly compelled to intervene in conflicts between capital and labor, producer and consumer, believer and nonbeliever, thus undermining the myth of neutrality and reducing the political flexibility of the state. Working with an essentially Weberian focus on legitimacy and legal domination, Grew arrives at an understanding of how nineteenth-century European statemakers sought to maintain distance from other social spheres, how important ideology was in this effort, and how ultimately fragile the boundaries thus established proved to be.

Charles Bright, in his essay on the American state in the nineteenth century, approaches the problem of relations between political and economic spheres from a different angle. He seeks to account historically for the extreme decentralization of power in the federal system after about 1830 by showing how the state failed to defend its boundaries and was penetrated and neutralized by social and economic antagonisms. In his argument, politicians, mediating social and economic conflict politically, reached a stalemate at the federal level over the role the state should play in the promotion of economic and social development. This stalemate produced a progressive weakening of the federal state. Efforts to break the stalemate, especially through political mobilizations and party building, not only failed, but worked against further centralization of power—promoting, indeed, a deconstruction of the state administration on the federal level. Politically paralyzed, the state was penetrated from several sides and milked for resources. It was able to promote a general economic expansion through the distribution of partible resources without, however, being able to direct or control that expansion. The American state could not, therefore, contain the transformational pressures generated by economic growth nor control increasing sectional animosities and the drift toward civil war. The paralysis of the state was the direct outgrowth of political impasse within the state. What broke that impasse, at least partially, was not the economic imperatives for change that built up in the late nineteenth century so much as actions by political challengers who managed by the 1890s to undercut the existing political parties and, by challenging their control over the electorate, to reshape the terms of survival for politicians. Bright thus sees the nineteenth-century American state unmade and remade by the same political processes.

The idea that statemaking processes do not always work toward stronger, more coherent state institutions is dramatically illustrated by Michael Geyer's essay on the Nazi state. Here the boundaries between social spheres collapsed entirely; indeed, in order to "find" the state under National Socialism, Geyer must abandon the idea of a state as an autonomous political realm or a centralized, rational bureaucratic apparatus. For the Nazis not only accelerated a process of political fragmentation already begun under the Weimar Republic, they actively politicized economic and social life. Geyer shows that, as the Nazis parceled out political authority and the instruments of domination, they sought to reconstruct German society and politics on an entirely new, racist basis. The National Socialist party, as carrier of racist ideology, was to dominate all aspects of German social, economic, and political life. In this respect, war and domestic terror were not incidental aberrations of rulers gone mad, but the necessary instruments for making racist ideology concrete and the means of reassembling the mechanisms of social reproduction and economic production on a new foundation, one grounded in violence and dedicated to conquest. While primarily concerned with Germany in the Third Reich, Geyer suggests that the institutional incoherence and political fragmentation of the Nazi state may, in fact, be an extreme expression of a condition common in most twentieth-century states.

Social Movements and the State

The emphasis upon the processes of statemaking provides a bridge between the problem of states as structures or institutions and the growing scholarly literature on social movements. A concept of statemaking involves not only state initiatives and the reactions of social groups to them, but also social mobilizations which target the state and trigger responses by its governors. The latter would like us to believe that state actions are the outcome of such formal procedures as elections, legislative deliberation, and executive decrees. But the boundaries between legitimate state politics and the activities of challengers, dissidents, and rebels "outside" the sphere of the state is defined and redefined by contestatory actions. Several authors in this collection focus on popular protest and upon the ways the interactions between legitimate authorities and social groups beyond the pale of accepted political processes define—or redefine—the state itself.

In his essay on the duel in early modern France, Robert Schneider provides a subtle discussion of the interaction between the state, or the king's managers, on the one hand, and traditional social elites, on the other. That the French nobility often opposed the expansion of the state is well known, and statemaking in France is often treated as the process whereby the monarchy defeated and encapsulated recalcitrant lords. Schneider shows us a more complex process in which the nobles were not simply objects of state action but, as it were, antagonistic partners of the state in an ideological redefinition of the social role and status of the aristocracy. Focusing on the duel, Schneider shows that the increasing amount of violence between nobles in the sixteenth and seventeenth centuries was an unintended effect of state formation, as the old aristocracy responded to the creation of new nobles by the state and the dilution of their status. His discussion of the dueler's mind-set shows the state caught between its need to impose order and its need to uphold the noble estate. In its campaign to suppress the duel, moreover, the state had cooperation from many aristocrats who were prepared to adapt their codes of honor to the competition for place and favor in the state. Many nobles collaborated in their own domestication, and the encapsulation of the nobility in this instance becomes a matter not only of state initiatives, but also of a movement among the nobility for access to place and preferment in the state. Thus the French state and its most powerful opponents negotiated terms of coexistence in the regulation of dueling that converted a warrior class outside the state into servants and wards of the state. As Schneider shows us, the process produced a number of unintended and unwelcome consequences for the rulers of the French absolute state.

Charles Tilly's contribution traces the emergence of "national social movements" in nineteenth-century Europe. The early modern state was forged by tremendous contention, not only in the countless wars fought between various emergent states, but in the struggles between state managers and the populations they were in the process of subjugating.

Popular uprisings in the early modern period were largely defensive efforts to resist taxes and the loss of local control over food and food prices. During the eighteenth and nineteenth centuries, as state structures were nationalized and electoral politics evolved, popular agitation also underwent profound changes. In place of rebellion, deliberately constituted groups came to make claims upon the state, presenting organized, sustained, self-conscious challenges to state authorities. Tilly's point is that these challenges—national movements—became routine ways of doing political business during the nineteenth century. Movements were less defensive responses to state initiatives than open-ended mobilizations for access to and control over resources. The outcome of these contests was determined by the historical profile of both the challengers and the authorities. As movements managed to gain access to and control over state resources, they also reshaped the political arena and altered the activities of the state itself.

This point is amplified in Daniel Fusfeld's discussion of the challenge that the radical American labor movement posed for local, state, and federal government in the late nineteenth century. Fusfeld rejects the prevailing historical interpretation that radical labor was "bought off" by higher wages or demobilized by a shift from "class consciousness" to "job consciousness" among workers. Instead, by scrutinizing the historical record of interactions between radical labor and authorities in business and government, Fusfeld concludes that the demise of the radical labor movement was the result of an increasingly systematic repression carried out by those authorities. In response to the challenges of radical labor, corporate leaders in business and government forged alliances with labor moderates to create the grounds for repression. This alliance, while violently reshaping the American labor movement, also promoted a restructuring of power relations at the national level of the American state, producing, in Fusfeld's view, the modern corporate state. The challenge mounted by radical labor and the response it provoked thus remade the American state while unmaking the radical labor movement.

State-serving views of revolution reduce them to chaotic eruptions of popular frustrations or the well-laid plans of manipulative leaders. Rod Aya, in his essay, elaborates a contrasting view of revolution, a political model that enables us to see both how revolutions happen and what role lower-class groups and popular uprisings play in them. In his argument, a revolution is not the outcome of a situation, but the situation itself—the historical moment when two or more political contenders are able to make effective claims to sovereignty within a territory. To understand popular interventions in these situations, we must ask how social changes altered the interests and options of contending groups, supplying them with common grievances and amplifying their bases of solidarity and tactical power. Revolutions are by definition disorderly events, rife with illegitimate political activity, but they are not categorically distinct from normal political processes. Instead, in Aya's view, they are normal political processes carried to the extreme—moments of ultimate statemaking, of the most massive restructuring of power relations in a society.

Susan Harding takes us inside the civil rights movement in the American South to show us how both popular and official perceptions were challenged and recast in the course of movement actions. Specifically, Harding shows how white hegemony—the prevailing ideas about power relations between blacks and whites—was reorganized by sustained and escalating conflicts between black challengers and white authorities in Greensboro, North Carolina, and through the social process surrounding the indictment and trial of Klansmen who murdered the three civil rights workers in Philadelphia, Mississippi. The essay also reveals something of why ordinary people may risk and sacrifice so much to participate in political conflicts. In those contests, world views—hence personal identities, the nature of social experience, and the meaning of lives—are to an extraordinary degree in the collective hands of movement participants. Harding's larger point is that a social movement not only brings about institutional changes in society and the state, but that a movement also *is* a process of change which alters the participants' and opponents' experience of social power relations. In the case of the civil rights movement, blacks changed the hegemonic southern worldview from one in which blacks were invisible and visibly subordinated to whites to one in which blacks could claim equality and act with the knowledge that that claim had been publicly validated.

Some Divisions and Further Revisions

It remains to acknowledge some of the ways in which the thinking of these authors diverges. Some of them are more comfortable, relatively, with Weberian or with Marxist conceptions of the state. Charles Tilly, Rod Aya, Raymond Grew, and Kenneth Finegold and Theda Skocpol would attribute to the state more autonomy from economic elites than would Daniel Fusfeld or Lynn Eden. Actually Lynn Eden gives a divided opinion—some politicians and state managers are captives of identifiable economic interests, while others are not. Herbert Gintis and Samuel Bowles break with Marxist reductionism, but they still argue that who gets the surplus of production is the central political fact of a society, and thus they remain within the Marxist tradition. Charles Bright and Daniel Fusfeld present different visions of the nineteenth-century American state—the one of a ramshackle, stalemated system, the other of a fairly monolithic, coherent institution dominated by capitalist elites. Charles Tilly reads the historical record of Europe over the past five centuries as one of building increasingly centralized, internally differentiated, sovereign states, while Michael Geyer argues that statemaking in twentieth-century Germany was decidedly decentralizing, and Finegold and Skocpol describe the American state in the same period as institutionally incapable of carrying through its economic policies for recovery. Indeed, the essays on the twentieth-century state in this collection suggest that, though institutionally more vast and imposing, the modern state has become paradoxically more fragmented and internally contradictory.

While Rod Aya and Elizabeth Brumfiel portray revolutionary situations as the outcomes of essentially political processes, Gintis and Bowles explain revolutionary developments in terms of contradictory tensions between distinct spheres of social relations. Fusfeld, Tilly, and Aya describe movements in terms of specific actions and institutional effects, while Robert Schneider and Susan Harding probe the edges of the concept to investigate the cultural dynamics and ideological effects of social conflict. The latter also join Michael Geyer in conceiving the state as an ideological as well as an institutional system, as an expression and arbiter of how we think and who we are, as well as of what we have and do.

The essays divide rather evenly between treatments of European states and the American state, and there are some rather striking contrasts between them. The essays on European statemaking are more abstract and conceptual as their authors move through familiar issues of theoretical dispute. They proceed from the assumption that state structures and the general nature of state activities are recognized by all. By contrast, the essays on the American state are theoretically more cautious as their authors navigate in a political universe scarcely mapped by discourse on the state. They are less certain of the benchmarks, more skeptical of broad generalizations, and more inclined to forgo theory in favor of pursuing the state descriptively. While all the contributors recognize some autonomous realm of the state, most of the authors of the American essays are more reluctant to treat the state as a force, separately derived, which confronts society. There is also less apparent sense of the state as a serious threat to individuals or an effective constraint upon social activity.

Such contrasts reflect partly the distinct traditions of scholarship that the authors draw on as they examine the history of states on either side of the Atlantic. They also reflect striking differences in the histories themselves.

Political crisis promotes serious thinking about states. The historical experience of continental Europe has repeatedly promoted, indeed necessitated, rethinking the issues of power, authority, governance, and legitimacy. The transitional states of the early modern period were the products of violent processes in which there were far more losers than winners. Many of the triumphant absolute states were, in turn, shattered by revolutions. In the nineteenth and twentieth centuries, acute political crises in Europe have repeatedly generated reassessments of the state among intellectuals and the public at large. The terrain of state discourse has thus been well plowed, and European thinking has been characterized by a deep sense of the fragility, impermanence, and problematic nature of political institutions. History itself poses, inescapably, the problem of the state in Europe.

Americans, by contrast, have generally viewed their political institutions as uniquely capable of avoiding systemic crisis. Despite the experience of civil war, class conflict, economic depression, and political stalemate, Americans have persisted in the conviction that their stately system is a "success" and not in need of serious reappraisal. The way American history is often written, there were no moments of social revolution that called basic structures of state or society into question, nor any moments of class upheaval or political impasse that shattered basic institutions and loyalties. In this context, a comprehensive theory of politics that could interpret or even anticipate acute crisis in the political system has seemed unnecessary.

As this vision of unique political success began to unravel in the crises of recent decades, American scholars turned to the more developed European discourse on the state for guidance in a period of political uncertainty. The incorporation of continental perspectives in a critical reappraisal of the capacities and practices of the American state has just begun. In this volume, we hope to contribute to that process and to a fuller understanding of the complex, fluid, and chimerical processes of statemaking generally.

NOTES

1. Charles Lindblom, *Politics and Markets: The World's Political-Economic Systems* (New York: Basic Books, 1977); Alan Wolfe, *The Limits of Legitimacy: Political Contradictions of Contemporary Capitalism* (New York: Free Press, 1977); Claus Offe, "Structural Problems of the Capitalist State," *German Political Studies* 1 (1974) and *Strukturprobleme des kapitalistischen Staates* (Frankfurt a.M.: Suhrkamp, 1972).
2. Two useful anthologies of readings are Reinhard Bendix, ed., *State and Society* (Berkeley: University of California Press, 1966) and Anthony Giddens and David Held, eds., *Classes, Power, and Conflict: Classical and Contemporary Debates* (Berkeley: University of California Press, 1982).
3. For the exchange between Miliband and Poulantzas, see Robin Blackburn, ed., *Ideology in the Social Sciences* (New York: Fontana, 1972). For a fuller

statement from each, see Ralph Miliband, *The State in Capitalist Society* (New York: Basic Books, 1969) and Nicos Poulantzas, *State, Power, Socialism* (London: New Left Books, 1978).

4. This point is developed by David Plotke in "The United States in Transition: Towards a New Order," *Socialist Review* 54 (November-December, 1980): 71–123, esp. 87–88.

5. Charles Tilly, *The Formation of National States in Western Europe* (Princeton: Princeton University Press, 1975). Other studies in this vein include Theda Skocpol, *States and Social Revolutions* (New York: Cambridge University Press, 1979) and Gianfranco Poggi, *The Development of the Modern State* (Stanford: Stanford University Press, 1978).

States and Statemaking

STATE AND CLASS
IN EUROPEAN FEUDALISM

Herbert Gintis and Samuel Bowles

Recent studies of the state have drawn nearly exclusively upon contemporary history for theory building and empirical support.[1] In this essay we shall apply an approach to the relationship between state and economy which we have developed in the context of liberal democratic capitalism[2] to an earlier social dynamic: the consolidation and decay of feudalism in western and central Europe between the eleventh and sixteenth centuries.

We share with Marxist historical materialism the notion that social formations are in general contradictory systems whose social dynamics can be captured only by understanding both their dominant structures of surplus extraction and the forms of social contestation to which they give rise. Yet our conception differs from the Marxist view in key respects, two of which will be explored in this essay.

First, we do not believe that the social relations governing surplus extraction are exclusively class relations. Nor can they be explained fully in terms of class relations. Feudal society, in particular, can be understood only by treating the state as an independent social force. The changing patterns of alliance and opposition between state- and class-based groupings over the extraction and control of surplus labor time thus play a central part in our account of feudal dynamics.[3]

Second, we reject the conception of history as a succession of epoch-defining institutions which serve the interests of the dominant class, punctuated by relatively brief periods of revolutionary transition to a wholly new, yet equally functional, set of institutions. Rather, there is no simple mapping from social institutions to class interest, and virtually all social systems exhibit institutions allowing the successful contestation of power and the pursuit of political and other projects by the subordinate classes. In consequence, social struggles normally involve projects toward strengthening versus weakening such structured bases of power. Specifically, European feudalism is distinguished by a structure of peasant power built directly into manorial organization and the constitution of village communities.

In short, we shall here develop a view of feudalism as supporting a *heterogeneity of power*, by virtue of its constitution as a system of *struc-*

19

tured oppositions between distinct mechanisms of surplus labor extraction, and between dominant and subordinate groups within them.

By *surplus labor time* we mean the total time worked by the producers (in all their pursuits, on demesnal lands as well as their own plots) minus the direct and indirect labor time devoted to the production of the goods and services which constitute the standard of living of the producers. By *surplus product* we mean the total output of the society minus the amounts which constitute the producers' average living standard. Surplus labor time is thus a summary index of the heterogeneous collection of luxury goods and personal services, military provisions, investment in the production, and the like, of which the surplus product is comprised. Neither concept is without conceptual difficulty, of course, but much like the concepts of national product and per capita income, they are essential theoretical tools.

The centrality of surplus extraction to our analysis of the dynamics of feudalism is justified by its key role in the reproduction and expansion of diverse forms of social organization, whether they be states, manorial systems, or urban communities. Put very simply, those social forms which reliably conferred upon an elite control over a sizable surplus product permit its undertaking military, cultural, organizational, and productive projects which promote its survival and expansion in competition with other social forms less adept at extracting and controlling surplus labor time.

If the emphasis upon the heterogeneity of power distances our approach from the Marxist, our insistence upon the centrality of surplus extraction distinguishes our analysis from non-Marxist alternatives, as exemplified by Douglass North and Robert Thomas's *The Rise of the Western World*, and John Hicks's *A Theory of Economic History*.[4] Whereas we focus upon the size and distribution of the controllable surplus in explaining institutional change, these authors stress either the natural tendency toward the spontaneous emergence of commodity forms through voluntary contract, or the structural accommodation to economic forms enjoying superior allocational efficiency.[5]

The Concept of Feudalism

European feudalism may be represented as (*a*) a form of property-based production and extraction, (*b*) a form of state, and (*c*) a specific articulation of the two. These institutions of course coexist with other social forms, notably the family and the church, which are less central to our argument. Property-based production included three related but contrasting sets of social relations whose relative strength varied across time and space: the manor, the village community, and the urban economy.

The feudal state included two strongly competitive institutional forms whose defining rules were sharply contrasting and incompatible. The intense jurisdictional competition between them was mitigated only by their necessarily mutual dependence within a stable feudal order. Royal sovereignty, the first of these competing forms of state, exhibited in prototypical form the modern system of unitary administration, justice, and military organization. Feudal suzerainty, the second of these forms, was marked by the liege-vassal relationship, fragmented jurisdiction, and the hierarchical layering of authority. The unity of the feudal state lay precisely, we shall suggest, in the dynamic underlying the contrast of sovereign and suzerain principles of concentrating power and distributing the prerogatives of office.

We shall suggest that the unique character of feudalism lay in its pattern of *separation* and *fusion* of power. Feudalism involved a separation of powers by virtue of its constitution as a system of *oppositional structures:* within the state, between sovereign and suzerain administration, and within the economy between urban, manorial, and village community production. Yet feudalism no less involved a strong fusion of power, in the form of a structural unity of feudal suzerainty as a form of state and manorial production as a form of economy: the basic unit of agrarian production (the manorial system) coincided with the elemental unit of suzerain jurisdiction (the fief), and the same individual (or individuals in the case of overlapping jurisdictions)—the lord of the manor—occupied the position of dominance in both.[6]

Our conception of feudalism diverges considerably from that of traditional liberal theory which, until recent years, has treated feudalism as a system of social relations among free men, as exemplified by Ganshof.

"Feudalism" may be regarded as a body of institutions creating and regulating the obligations of obedience and service . . . on the part of a freeman (the vassal) towards another free man (the lord), and the obligations of protection and maintenance on the part of the lord with regard to his vassal.[7]

This conception abstracts from the conditions of production and expropriation of the surplus product produced by labor. Yet as we shall see, by ignoring the issue of the distribution of the surplus among "free men," and between free men and a subject peasantry, the commitment to a juridical conception of feudalism renders much of feudal social development quite incomprehensible. .

By contrast, Marxist theorists have formulated definitions directly related to the organization of the productive apparatus, while affording juridical and state relationships a distinctly subordinate status. Thus we are offered the "coercive sanction" conception summarized by Rodney Hilton, "The essence of the feudal mode of production in the Marxist sense is the exploitative relationship between landowners and subordinated peasants, in which the surplus . . . is transferred under coercive sanction of the former."[8]

In the Marxist treatment, the lord-serf replaces the liege-homage relationship as the essence of feudalism. Moreover, the juridical elements of serfdom are themselves ignored by treating the servile condition as merely "an obligation laid on the producer by force and independently of his own volition," to cite Maurice Dobb's well-known definition.[9]

This Marxist conception suffers from an excessive generality: it is unable to distinguish feudalism from any agriculturally based society with a dominant landlord class. As a result, as Perry Anderson has noted, "no term has undergone such an indiscriminate and pervasive diffusion [in Marxist theory] as that of feudalism, which has often in practice been applied to any social formation between tribal and capitalist poles of identity, unstamped by slavery."[10]

Anderson responds to this lack of specificity by augmenting the traditional Marxist definition with specific institutional aspects of the feudal state and church, together with a sensitive analysis of feudal "variational forms" whose interactions account for the dynamics of European feudalism as a whole. In particular, he rejects the possibility of characterizing a social formation in terms of its economic relations alone.

> pre-capitalist modes of production cannot be defined *except* via their political, legal and ideological superstructures, since these are what determine the type of extra-economic coercion that specifies them. The precise form of juridicial dependence, property, and sovereignty that characterize a pre-capitalist social formation . . . [are] . . . the central indices of the determinate mode of production dominant within it.[11]

While an important step forward, this conception remains flawed. Anderson accepts a notion of "economic" and "extra-economic" essentially equivalent to "market" and "nonmarket" and hence inadequately distinguishes among noncapitalist societies in which market production is relatively unimportant. The feudal state is thus vaulted to the key position in his account of the specificity of feudal society. Yet to remain faithful to the traditional notion of property-based extraction as an essential core, with respect to which surrounding social forms are but embellishments and instruments of reproduction, Anderson is impelled to consider the feudal state as "superstructural," and hence derivative of class relations. This inconsistency disappears, we believe, when the feudal state is treated as an integral aspect of feudalism, an axis of power distinct from yet related to that of feudal production.

A distinct attempt to define feudalism without regard for its characteristic form of state is the "natural economy" conception of Henri Pirenne. According to this conception, accepted by Paul Sweezy and other Marxist theorists, feudalism can be characterized by the absence of markets and trade, and its demise can be directly linked to the resumption and growth of trade in the later Middle Ages. In this view, the rise of towns engaging in regional trade and guild production represents a foreign element introduced into an essentially stable system through external shock.[12] Yet Maurice Dobb's early research questioned the adequacy of this assumption: "It seems probable, if one may venture a tentative judgment, that a majority of towns originated on the initiative of some feudal institution, or in some way as an element of feudal society, rather than as entirely alien bodies."[13]

Subsequent research demonstrated convincingly that such was the case.[14] Thus Hilton could confidently assert that "town life developed, as a consequence of the development of economic and social forces, *within* feudal society, *not* . . . as a result of the external impact of itinerant traders."[15]

Lacking the space to address other attempts to characterize feudalism independent from its specific manner of articulating the state-economy relationship, we must rest content with the general observation that none appears devoid of serious conceptual errors or explanatory deficiencies. We shall thus proceed to a sketch of the nature of the feudal articulation.

The key characteristic of the feudal state is its constitution as a structured opposition between the institutions of sovereignty and suzerainty. While the sovereign presence in this totality was in many regions and periods less than fully salient, the principle of suzerainty itself was always complemented by a web of royal institutions operating under the aegis of the highest among the feudal suzerains—the monarch—and his administrative staff. The cultural and technical raw materials of the sovereign state were legacies of the Roman Empire, available throughout Europe, and incorporated in the structure of the Hapsburg branch of the empire, as well as the church as a temporal entity—not to mention the major European monarchies.

The state in medieval Europe was fragmented, but incompletely fragmented. The first fully developed feudal system, the Carolingian, involved a clear interpenetration of decentralized suzerainty and centralized monarchical administration. The latter elements, however, quickly atrophied in the decades following the death of Charlemagne, under external pressure from east and north. But their juridical forms were conserved, to be redeployed in the thirteenth and once again in the sixteenth centuries.

England, incompletely feudalized under Anglo-Saxon rule, developed a genuine balance of monarchy and infeudation after the Norman invasion. William I set the tradition of king as direct overlord to all lords, and reserved the administration of high justice for the king's courts. Thus through the greater part of English history, the struggle between monarch and feudal aristocracy was distinctly less jurisdictional than representational.

In the German principalities, despite the advanced disintegration of the institutions of empire, the Hapsburg dynasty provided a more than nominal counterweight to feudal decentralization. Finally, as V. G. Kiernan, Otto Hintze, Perry Anderson, and others have stressed,[16] the church itself maintained the traditions of the centralized state throughout the Middle Ages. In Anderson's words,

> It was no accident, in fact, that the one medieval monarchy which had achieved complete emancipation from any representative or corporate restraints was the Papacy, which had been the first political system of feudal Europe to utilize Roman law wholesale, with the codification of canon law in the twelfth and thirteenth centuries.[17]

Moreover, it was often in attempting to neutralize the territorial ambitions of the church that medieval states were forced to resort to similar organization practices. The medieval church, notes Kiernan, "which often collided with and seemed to injure the feudal State, in the long run, and by a complex process of interaction, doubled and trebled its strength. The absence alike from China, from India, from Islam, of a Church of this order . . . is of an importance that scarcely can be overestimated."[18]

It is often held that the monarchy in the feudal period represented little but a level of suzerainty; that the relationship of the king to his barons was in principle no different from the relationship of the barons to their knights, or any lord to his vassal. Thus, in the words of Anderson, "in principle, the highest superordinate level of the feudal hierarchy . . . was necessarily different not in kind, but only in degree, from the subordinate levels of lordship beneath it. The monarch, in other words, was a feudal suzerain of his vassals . . . not a supreme sovereign set above his subjects."[19]

In one respect, this characterization is not only accurate, but central to the character of feudalism: there was little movement of the surplus from the base of the apex of the feudal hierarchy. At least prior to the thirteenth century in England, and even later elsewhere, a monarch strengthened his position by becoming a stronger overlord rather than by becoming a stronger sovereign. Rents, labor services, and feudal levies from royal lands easily eclipsed taxes, duties, and other sovereign extractions from vassals and state subjects as forms of access to surplus labor time.

The capacity of the state to impose taxes depended closely upon the monarch's ability to obtain the consent of his major vassals, "Down to the end of the Middle Ages . . . few Estates ever yielded to royal rulers the right to raise permanent or general taxation without the consent of their subjects."[20]

Yet in other respects this characterization of the feudal monarchy is quite misleading, especially in those areas, such as England and France, which were to stand in the forefront of the transition to capitalism. England has often been treated as something of an "exception," due to the nature of the Norman conquest which instituted its feudal institutions: the English state was always more unified than indicated by the feudal principle of fragmented sovereignty.[21] France, on the other hand, never fully relinquished its Carolingian past.

Another indication of the presence of the sovereign state can be traced in the course of development of private property from the ninth to fourteenth centuries. The transition from the suzerain principle of the inalienability of the fief, based on the pledge of vassal to his lord, to the seemingly more modern principle of private and alienable property, took place within the dynamic of the feudal social formation. Yet private property achieves its legal substance only on the basis of royal law and courts, which were thus woven into the very fabric of feudal society.

Similarly, while the sovereign state had no direct power to extract surpluses, its juridical presence vis-à-vis the peasantry was not negligible. In England, at least, free peasants were protected by the jurisdiction of the king's court,[22] and in addition even the serf was free against anyone except his own lord.[23] Nor was it impossible for the dependent serf to sustain an action against his lord—from the earliest times for issues concerning life and limb as well as deprivation of waynage (plow and team), and later in cases of land tenure itself.[24]

Turning to the manorial system, it is common to assert the unity of the political structures underlying the lord's control. Thus Robert Brenner notes that "it is precisely the interrelated characteristics of arbitrary exactions by the lords from the peasants and control by landlords over peasant mobility that gave the medieval serf-economy its special traits."[25] Yet in the same study Brenner, in countering the argument that success of the "second serfdom" in Eastern Europe lay in the latter's lack of towns, points to the *structure of village communities* in explaining the superior power of the peasantry in the West.

> Through much of western Germany by the later middle ages the peasantry had succeeded, through protracted struggle on a piecemeal vil-

lage-by-village basis, in constituting for itself an impressive network of village institutions for economic regulation and political self-development. These provided a powerful line of defence against the incursions of landlords.[26]

M. M. Postan makes the same point in his description of English conditions in the twelfth century: "The village communes could be as active and as effective a vehicle of local authority as the manorial organization itself."[27] Perhaps Paul Vinogradoff stresses the importance of the village community in the feudal social formation most generally.

> The village is legally recognized as a unit, separated from the manor although existing within it. . . . Indeed, the rural settlement appears in our records as a "juridical person." . . . We see no traces of the rightless condition of villains which is supposed to be their legal lot, and a powerful community is recognized by the lord in a form which bears all the traits of legal definition. . . . The manorial courts were really meetings of the village community under the presidency of the lord or of his stewards.[28]

In addition, the very division of labor in agriculture, the organization of peasant plots, and even the practices of crop rotation are comprehensible only with a clear understanding of the role of village community and the interest of the subject peasantry in maintaining its power. Marc Bloch consistently stressed that the demographic incidence of the various "types of agrarian civilization" (enclosure, open-field, and individual holdings) in medieval France could not be understood in terms of agricultural technology alone.

> Communal grazing . . . was [not] made inevitable by the shape of the fields. . . . without communal habits of cultivation the wheeled plough could never have been adopted. . . . The truth is that communal grazing arose first and foremost from an attitude of mind. . . . the wheeled plough . . . and a collective habit of cultivation are the twin characteristics of one very distinct type of agrarian civilization.[29]

This communal "attitude of mind" was not, however, simply a cultural accident. It was rather an aspect of the structured opposition between the manors and the village communities over which they exerted their control. Vinogradoff, in expressing his findings from the manorial court rolls, makes this point clear. "The superior right of the community found expression in the fact that the fields were open to common use as pasture after the harvest. . . . Even the lord himself had to conform to the customs and rules set up by the community."[30]

Our understanding of the origins and persistence of the open field system is still too murky to state clearly its connection to class struggles. Yet as Vinogradoff makes clear, its tenacity appears incompatible with the standard notion of the manorial apparatus as an undifferentiated system of domination of lord over peasant. "The intermixture of strips in the open fields . . . was therefore a system particularly adapted to bring home the superior right of the community as a whole, and the inferior, derivative character of individual rights. . . . The feudal theory of the lord's grant is insufficient to explain the different aspects assumed by rights of common."[31] As we shall later stress, the strength and cohesiveness of the village community appears to have played a critical role in determining the character of the transition from feudalism.[32]

The structured opposition of manorial and village communal production is neatly contrasted with the structured confluence of political power in suzerain state and manorial economy. Feudal suzerainty involved a series of hierarchical and overlapping juridical regions specified by the creation of fiefs according to the principles of liege-homage. At the base of the feudal state hierarchy the fief tended in general to coincide with the manor (or a union of manors), the site of the direct confrontation of lord and subordinate peasantry. This particular articulation of feudal state with feudal agricultural production gave rise to the most critical of the specific defining characteristics of the feudal social formation: the *fusion of the elementary unit of the suzerain state and the basic unit of agrarian production.*

This fusion can be understood only by recognizing that in feudalism, as in other social formations, class relations possess a political structure distinct from the state. The feudal fusion is in fact expressed by two unities, one institutional and the other political. First, the basic unit of state (the fief) coincides with the basic unit of production (the manor). Second, the apex of the political structure of the basic unit of state coincides with the apex of the political structure of the unit of production, as incarnated in the person of the lord of the manor.

This underlying unity by no means contradicts the structured opposition of manorial and village community systems of production. Clearly the lord's power was far greater in demesnal production than in that falling under the jurisdiction of the village community, despite the former's extensive use of an administrative apparatus (bailiffs and haywards have their counterparts in all feudal systems) to protect their interests in the management of communal plots. And as Postan makes clear, even in demesnal production the lord's position of dominance was contingent and could be turned against him.

> The purely administrative difficulty of running a demesne economy efficiently were those of supervision and control . . . remote and intermit-

tent [control] . . . offered great opportunities to dishonest bailiffs and reeves. . . . Landlords therefore tried from time to time to relieve themselves of their managerial risks by letting out the demesnes as going concerns, or else by dissolving them altogether into peasant tenancies.[33]

In brief, the balance of power among the lord, the administrative structure he instituted to protect his interests, and the village community, represented a central locus of class struggle in the feudal period.

The feudal social formation, in short, can be portrayed as an articulation of several distinct sites, the overall pattern exhibiting the character of a contradictory system based on the fusion of fief and manor, and the oppositions of town to manor, of manorial administration to village community, and of suzerainty to sovereignty. In the next section we shall describe the evolution of forms of surplus extraction and argue that our approach allows a consistent explanation of social struggle in the feudal social formation.

The Feudal Extraction Process

The unique character of feudalism lies in its specific manner of juxtaposing a variety of forms of extraction based on both proprietary and state exploitation. In this section we shall discuss the ways in which the dynamics of feudalism depend upon the particular patterns of group alliance and contestation generated by these varied forms of extraction.

Feudal extraction is not only heterogeneous, but distinctly political. Neither attribute is peculiar to feudalism, of course, as extraction processes are often quite heterogeneous[34] and are normally mediated by the direct exercise of political power.[35] Feudal lords obtained surplus labor time by virtue of three distinct yet interpenetrating social positions they held: control of the process of production on the manorial demesne, claims on the produce of peasant holdings, and rights of feudal suzerainty. Corresponding to each was a distinct form of surplus: labor services, rents, and taxes, respectively. The relative contribution of these varied widely over time and space. In each of the lord's positions of power, moreover, his capacity to extract surpluses from producers depended upon the efficacy of his political organs, and their power in counterposition to those of peasant communities.

A portion of feudal production regularly occurred on the lord's demesne and under his direct administration. Control of the demesne was regularly supplemented by the lord's enjoyment of a monopoly of essential resources complementary to land (water, mills, and roads), and his preferred access to lines of transport and commerce. This aspect of feudal production corresponds to extraction of surpluses through the application of direct peasant labor services.

The level of labor services depended upon the extent of the lord's dominance within the political organization of manorial production. Indeed, the efficacy of this mechanism depended directly upon the contingent ability of the lord to control the demesnal production process. Historical evidence indicates that the lord's access to such forms of demesnal extraction was often, and for extended periods, significantly circumscribed by his inability to supervise and control the delegation of his powers. Postan, for instance, notes that "direct management . . . was easiest in periods when the legal and political regime was so stable and so well ordered that lords could easily exercise their control over their local officials."[36] In times of civil or international war, as well as during Crusades, the natural feudal movement was toward the expansion of individual holdings and stronger village organization of production.

Traditionally the extent of recourse to extraction through labor services is considered as dependent upon the degree of market penetration and monetization of economic relations, or the extent of labor scarcity in the feudal economy.[37] We agree with Robert Brenner, however, whose research has demonstrated the lack of correspondence between the commutation of labor services and either the degree of market penetration or population density. In defending the centrality of class struggle against the standard demographic and commercial theories of changes in the distribution of income in thirteenth- to fifteenth-century Europe, Brenner concludes that "it is the structure of class relations, of class power, which will determine the manner and degree to which particular demographic and commercial changes will affect long-run trends in the distribution of income and economic growth—and not *vice-versa*."[38] His conclusions hold as well, we believe, for the organization of production as for the resulting distribution of income.

The contribution to lordly income of the second form of feudal extraction, rents and dues on lands directly worked by the peasantry, was just as variable across time and space as that of labor services. Since independent peasant production represented the only feasible agrarian alternative to demesnal production in the feudal period, the above analysis implies that the extent of peasant production depended inversely upon the effective power of the lord at the apex of the political structure of manorial production. The level of rents, moreover, reflected in general the relative power of the lord's political and coercive apparatus in counterposition to the power of peasant communities.

The importance of the structured relations of power between lord and peasant is virtually ignored in most interpretations of the level of rents, which regularly refer to notions of "custom" and "subsistence" for their explanation.[39] Yet as Bloch stresses, "custom" in the cultural discourse of a feudalism which lacked a tradition of written law was in fact "one of the most flexible [forms of law] ever known. . . . Because its efforts to imitate the past were inevitably based only on an inaccurate picture of it, the first feudal age changed very quickly and very profoundly."[40]

Custom served two roles in the feudal period. First, it registered and ratified the resultant of class and other social forces through which the level of rents were determined. Second, the perceived violation of customary practices could serve to alter a given balance of social forces by increasing the solidarity and resolve of the injured parties. Thus the oft-noted "inertial" force of custom was itself quite consistently mediated by and dependent upon the socially structured distribution of power. The view that the level of rents was regulated by the subsistence needs of the peasantry is at variance with the observation of wide variations in peasant income over time. Moreover, it depends on the romantic fiction of the absolute power of the lord over his serfs. In the manorial system both tenure and feudal obligations were subject to strict regulation. Certainly the obligations of the lord to his tenants were not limited to that of free men alone. Bloch notes, for instance, "as a tenant the serf had exactly the same duties and the same rights as anyone else; his possession of his holding was no longer [in the Frankish period] precarious, and his labour, once rents and services had been paid, was his own."[41]

The condition is general. Vinogradoff cites many cases where the rights of the tenants are upheld by manorial courts.[42] The reciprocal obligations of lord and tenant, in short, were subject to transformation over time according to the balance of class pressures. And as we shall stress later, the stronger the institutions of the sovereign state, and the greater the independent power of this state against the pressures of the landed elites, the more capable were peasant communities of protecting their interests.[43] The "custom of the manor" and its transformation over time is but an expression of this complex of political relations.

The third form of lordly extraction involved taxes, tallages, judicial levies, and related transfers. These levies represent *state extractions*, accruing to the lord by virtue of his position at the apex of the suzerain state, and involve seigneurial burdens imposed on serf and free peasantry alike. These transfers cannot be assimilated to property-based extractions, for the mechanisms governing their exaction were independent from conditions of land tenure.

Neither can their quantitative importance be minimized. Indeed, to quote Rodney Hilton's general observation regarding feudal England,

> by the twelfth century, peasant surplus was transferred to the landed aristocracy less in the form of rent calculated on the size of the peasant hold, whether in labor, kind, or money, than in seigneurial taxation (tallage) and in the profits of jurisdiction. . . . The sum total . . . , it has

been calculated, considerably exceeded the previous landlord income which had been based on the yield from the demesnes and the rents from the holdings.[44]

Succeeding centuries witnessed the reversal of this trend, and then its reappearance. Similar conditions held in many other regions of medieval Europe.[45]

In addition many of the observed rental payments accruing to the lord were merely accounting mechanisms for the control of tax exactions, quite removed from a logic of property and production. Such, for instance, were the servile burdens associated with the use of the lord's oven, mill, and brewery.

If feudal production embodies the structured opposition of the lord's manorial administration and the village community, a parallel system of opposition is incorporated into legal and judicial actions themselves. In the words of Vinogradoff, "When the reeve and the four men attend the sheriff's tourn or the eyre, they do not represent the lord only, but also the village community. . . . Indeed, the rural settlement appears in our records as a 'juridical person.' "[46]

Nor can this legal position be understood simply as imposing burdens upon the subject peasantry.

> An action committed against the interests of the lord is not punished by any one-sided act of his will, or by the command of his steward. . . . The negligent ploughman . . . is presented as an offender by his fellow-peasants, and according to strict legal formality . . . the whole court with its free and unfree suitors participates materially in the administration of justice, and its office is extended to questions of law as well as to issues of fact.[47]

This is of course not to say that lords always acted through legal channels, or the balance of "justice" was not predominantly on their side. Feudal legal forms do, however, exhibit a system of structured oppositions rendering the extractive capacity of the lord contingent upon the reproduction of an always problematic balance of power vis-à-vis the peasant community.

This discussion of feudal suzerainty and the agrarian economy does not exhaust the major relations of surplus extraction in the feudal social formation. We must deal in addition with the global interrelation among these units—in particular the competition among manors for labor services—and the position of the sovereign state.

As Brenner has emphasized, labor surpluses, while tending to augment the potential power of the landed classes, could be offset by strong peasant communities. On the other hand, labor shortages tended to redound to the benefit of the dependent class. Thus in general, the feudal land/labor ratio must be taken as a *condition* affecting the balance of class forces.[48]

But how is this condition of labor surplus/labor scarcity structurally integrated into feudalism? It is traditionally held that the legal binding of the peasant to the soil circumvents the forces of supply and demand.[49] Yet the fusion of feudal suzerainty and manorial production renders this mechanism ineffective. The fragmented nature of feudal suzerainty ensured, over the long term, a surrogate market in labor, in the dual sense that competition among manorial units could not be avoided, and the material dependence of a peasant producer on his particular lord could not be guaranteed.[50]

Given the weakness of the sovereign state, the customary prohibitions upon peasant flight were structurally incapable of enforcement. "Every page of the documents," says Vinogradoff, "testifies to frequent migrations from the manors in opposition to the express will of the landowners. The surveys tell of serfs who settle on strange land even in the vicinity of their former home. It is by no means exceptional to find mention of enterprising landlords drawing away the population from their neighbors' manors."[51] In the French case, Bloch agrees. "The departure of a serf was so little a crime against his condition that it was sometimes expressly catered for."[52]

Indeed, Hilton notes that competition among landlords often lay at the basis of village enfranchisements,[53] frequently the central instrument of peasant power in contestation with the lord. The French situation was again in line with the English. "Once enfranchisement had been introduced into a given region it usually spread with great rapidity . . . because of seigneurial anxiety over the loss of tenants."[54]

Thus while the feudal economy gives the *appearance* of "control by landlords over peasant mobility,"[55] and indeed whole theories have been developed on this basis,[56] reality was quite otherwise.[57]

It may be argued that the poverty of the peasantry, together with the difficulties and dangers of travel, effectively ensured the laborer's attachment to the soil. No doubt this was an important consideration in the short run; but were it so over the long term, we would expect that the possession of tenants would itself represent a form of feudal wealth, as it appears to have in Russia, where estates were measured in "souls" rather than in hectares. While there were structural constraints against the marketing of landed wealth, these did not apply to serfs. Thus the lack of effective seigneurial control over servile mobility is suggested by the absence of a market in peasant dependents. "Serfs could be bought and sold legally," Vinogradoff reports, "but this occurred rarely (apart from their tentaments). There was no 'market' in villains . . . it was all but impossible for the lord to treat his man as a transferable chattel."[58]

As result of this structural weakness in the articulation of feudal state and feudal agrarian production, in times of labor shortage, the landlord class was impelled to significantly strengthen the sovereign state apparatus, preferring to vie with it for a share of the peasant surplus rather than face a general decline in the surplus itself.

As is well known, the sovereign state (the monarchy), while initially quite weak, gathered strength in the general course of social development in the feudal core of Europe and in time supplanted feudal suzerainty. Indeed we shall see that the decline of feudalism did not lead to the shift of social surplus to an emerging class, as the traditional Marxist view would expect, but rather facilitated the growth of the sovereign state apparatus. This growth in general did not benefit the landlord class, and as often as not served to undermine lordly power. At the same time, as Marxist interpretations have always stressed, the sovereign state throughout the feudal period held a central position in the reproduction of feudal class relations and the structure of surplus extraction.

But the sovereign state suffered a severe structural weakness in the feudal period: it lacked direct access to surpluses generated through agrarian production, and with few exceptions could tax the peasantry directly only insofar as its judicial and administrative power supplanted that of feudal suzerains. The latter, moreover, could be taxed in general only with their consent, and for purposes subject to their will.

The monarchy thus had a double interest in preserving the economic hegemony of the feudal lords. On the one hand, it was precisely as feudal overlord in his own right that the monarch could most conveniently tap the surpluses of peasant producers. On the other hand, its success in taxing the landlord class was predicated upon the latter's ability to extract surpluses from its dependents. While the global project of the sovereign state apparatus was the control of the landed nobility, the principle of limited sovereign extraction ensured that this project could be accomplished only within the framework of the continued domination of the landlord class over a subservient peasantry. The sovereign states, even as late as the sixteenth and seventeenth centuries, lacked the administrative and military capacity adequately to control the dependent classes from which it drew its surpluses. Conversely, the aristocracy on balance had little interest in weakening the sovereign state, given the structural weaknesses of feudalism to which it was a response.

To increase its extractive power, however, it was clearly in the interest of dominant groups in the sovereign state apparatus to change the rules of the game. In administrative terms this involved expanding the jurisdiction of royal courts. In economic terms it involved protecting and fostering the development of alienable private property, and promoting commercial relations in urban and international spheres as a secure basis of taxation outside the sphere of feudal relations.

The organic relationship of trade centers to the feudal system is well expressed by Perry Anderson. "Feudalism as a mode of production," he argues, ". . . was the first in history to render possible a dynamic *opposition* between town and country; the parcellization of sovereignty inherent in its structure permitted autonomous urban enclaves to grow as centres of production within an overwhelmingly rural economy, rather than as privileged or parasitic centres of consumption or administration."[59]

Parcellized sovereignty, however, permitted nothing of the kind. Towns were chartered and protected by sovereigns or strong regional princes, and where this process was for one reason or another circumvented, the towns either attained hegemony over the rural areas, thus undermining the feudal dynamic (as in parts of Italy, Germany, and the Low Countries), or they were strangled by predatory lords (as in East Elbian Europe).

The crown's role in creating and protecting international trade routes, sheltering commercial capital from the predation of feudal lords, and ensuring a flow of exportable goods paralleled its role in fostering the autonomy of cities. Thus even in the earliest period of sovereign state development, there was an objective conflation of interests between commercial, urban, and trade interests on the one hand, and the sovereign state on the other. This conflation was to be characteristic of the whole period of European state development.

The mutual attraction of sovereignty and commerce may be traced to two interrelated sources. First, the exigencies of surplus extraction through taxation led monarchies to prefer private property to feudal seisin, and hence Roman to feudal law.[60] Thus the institution of alienable property was consolidated well *before* the transition to capitalism. Similarly, the possibility of a flexible administration and collection of tax revenue is predicated upon a sufficiently widespread system of generalized exchange. In the words of Gabriel Ardant, "an analysis of the system of taxation in contemporary times as well as in the past shows that *tax collection and assessment are indissolubly linked to an exchange economy*."[61]

Second, through the selective control of market relations, the state could gain from the granting of trade monopolies, in a manner quite out of the reach of decentralized feudal suzerainties. The feudal lord not only lacked the military power to control urban communities; he also could not prevent traders from moving their activities outside his jurisdiction. In this sense the mobility of trade as well as labor represented an insuperable structural weakness of the feudal social formation to which the sovereign state was considerably immune. Thus in the absolutist period not only were towns chartered and protected by royal sanction, but a direct link between crown and artisanal producers was created through the granting of guild privileges and the regulation of pricing and production.[62] This royal strategy was supplemented by granting controlled access to international markets and domestic natural resources, rendering mercantilist economic policy a central tool of surplus extraction.[63]

Fernand Braudel has often stressed that the extension of commercial relations is a consequence (and in turn a cause) of the consolidation of the sovereign state. Even the Marxist historian Georges Lefebvre has noted that "the merchant community and the State furnished each other with mutual assistance: the former as creditor and supplier of public contracts . . . the latter as distributor of privileges, prizes, monopolies. . . . it is impossible to deny that the collusion between commerce and the State promoted the development of capitalism."[64]

Yet generally this central point is ignored. Accounts of the rise of commercial forces generally attribute their growth either to *exogenous* shocks, or to relations *endogenous* to the feudal economy.[65] The notion of a social formation as an articulation of distinct forms of surplus extraction affords an explanation of this phenomenon both theoretically coherent and in better harmony with the historical evidence.

The Decline of Feudalism in Europe

Feudalism is an articulation of state and economy. Its transformation must then involve a qualitative change in one or more of the following: the structure of the state, the structure of the economy, and the characteristic articulation of the two. The changes in each of these three spheres accompanying the transformation of the feudal core of Europe in the fourteenth to seventeenth centuries may be outlined as follows.

The major changes in economic organization included (*a*) the withdrawal of the landed classes from the production process, and their transformation into a rentier class; (*b*) the rise of independent petty commodity producers in the agrarian sector, often technically dynamic and linked by commercial ties; (*c*) the growth of merchant capital engaged in vigorously expanding maritime trade; and (*d*) the integration of urban and commercial elites into the system of land ownership and agricultural production for profit. The old feudal aristocracy persisted throughout the period, but was pressed on all sides by an economically resurgent peasantry and a buoyant commercial class eager to usurp the cultural accoutrements of nobility.

In the state sphere, the key changes included (*a*) a shift in the monopoly of the means of coercion to the sovereign state, and a corresponding decline in the military role of the feudal lords; (*b*) the transformation of the sovereign state into a *direct* extractor of surplus, its juridical and administrative arms reaching to the very base of the dependent producing classes; and (*c*) its increased potential to behave as an *independent actor* vis-à-vis social classes in the political and distributional struggles of the age.[66]

The major development in the articulation of state and economy in this period involved the dissolution of the fusion of suzerain state and manorial economy characteristic of fully developed feudalism: feudal suzerainty became dissociated from agrarian production per se, and the financing of the sovereign state was separated from the feudal exploitation of a dependent peasantry.

The effect was by no means the laissez-faire articulation idealized in the nineteenth century, but rather what might be termed a "mercantile" articulation: the state closely regulated trade and market-oriented production, while allying with the rising commercial classes by protecting their sources of supply, offering monopolies over the exploitation of natural resources and subject colonies, and guaranteeing the safety of trade routes and access to foreign markets. The newly empowered sovereign state protected its basic source of social surplus, the dependent peasantry, from excessive feudal exploitation through the juridical arm of its administrative apparatus. Finally the feudal aristocracy was increasingly integrated into the military arm of the state apparatus.

The emerging social formation was neither capitalist nor feudal, and is rather characterized by an alliance of commercial interests and the absolute state within the framework of an economic system in which the landed aristocracy, however weakened, remained dominant. Its appellation as "state commercialism" is thus apt.

Why the feudal dissolution? The critical development in the feudal decline, according to our account, was the growing capacity of state elites to gain control of a sizable surplus product, and the superior military and administrative capacities of the sovereign state apparatus thereby made possible.[67] This view may be contrasted both with the traditional Marxist view which—in one or more ways—sees the feudal demise as an effect of economic developments, relatively narrowly defined, and with the equally common view which postpones the demise of feudalism to the eve of the French Revolution, defining the relevant dynamics as a "transition from feudalism to capitalism."

Marx and Engels, in the *Communist Manifesto* and the *German Ideology*, treat the feudal transition as a process of endogenously developing forces of production recasting the social relations of production into a pattern more conducive to their efficient application, through the medium of class struggle. This explanation has been questioned by modern authors.[68] For one thing, the collapse of classical feudalism in the fourteenth century involved the exhaustion of old, rather than the pressure of new forces of production.[69] For another, neither the peasantry nor the commercial classes held a position of economic dominance in the succeeding period.

Another account, the "production for use" theory of feudalism, has been put forward by Paul Sweezy in his notable exchange with Maurice Dobb. According to this view the development of commercial relations outside the nexus of feudal relations acted as "solvents" to feudal relations, revealing the inefficiency of manorial production, and creating a class whose ultimate opposition to feudal hegemony was to be decisive.

However, the development of market relations as often as not involved the *tightening* or even the *imposition* of feudal ties (in Poland, Prussia, Russia, parts of England and France).[70] Hilton's treatment of feudal England is on this point quite in agreement with Brenner's comparative analysis. Merchant capital, notes Hilton, "was never applied either to agricultural or industrial production in any innovative fashion. The so-called commercial revolution in no way altered the feudal model of production. . . . If anything, it was the declining cash incomes of the feudal aristocracy which was the first symptom of the end of the feudal mode of production."[71]

This debate over the transition from feudalism is the backdrop for Perry Anderson's erudite and insightful *Passages from Antiquity to Feudalism.* Anderson accounts for the commercial character of the succeeding period by abandoning the attempt to capture the specificity of feudal dynamics in terms of an ideal-type feudal mode of production in favor of viewing feudalism as a spatially diverse social formation, the complementary structure of its various parts interacting to produce the conditions for the development and eventual dissolution of the whole, its laws of motion "governed by a complex unity of its different regions, not by any simple predominance of the manor."[72]

Following Marx's discussion in the *Grundrisse*, Anderson locates the specific character of European feudalism in its birth as a synthesis of Germanic and Roman elements. "The catastrophic collision of two dissolving anterior modes of production—primitive and ancient," he observes, "eventually produced the feudal order which spread throughout medieval Europe."[73] Central to the dynamic tension of feudal Europe, he asserts, were the distinct proportions according to which these two elements were combined as we pass from northern to central, and then to southern Europe. The northern variant, always close to the Germanic gentile organization, received a weak contribution from the ancient Roman Empire. Serfdom was weak, seigneurial justice unknown, and the monarchy always remained feeble. By contrast the southern variant, in Italy and surrounding regions, retained its urban civilization and municipal political organization, and preserved its universalistically minded ecclesiastical power. Only in the central region did a "balanced" fusion of these modes of production produce the classical feudal order.

The tension among the variants in the feudal synthesis accounts both for its development and later for its specific capacity to generate capitalist activity. The Roman contribution to the feudal social formation, embodied in the "southern variant," served as a uniquely corrosive agent in the dissolution of feudal particularism. Roman law and administration provided the concept of private property and the raw material for mercantile practice in the towns. But of greatest importance,

> *politically,* the revival of Roman law corresponded to the constitutional exigencies of the reorganized feudal States of the epoch. . . . the *primary* determinant of the adoption of Roman jurisprudence lay in the drive of royal governments for increased central powers. . . . The juridically unconditional character of private property . . . found its counterpart in the formally absolute nature of the imperial sovereignty.[74]

Anderson's is a sophisticated attempt to come to grips with the anomalies generated in the traditional Marxist theory of modes of production confronted with the complexities of feudalism. He allows the form of state to materially affect the logic of development of the social formation as a whole while broadening the concept of feudalism to include the period from the Black Death to the industrial revolution, through his treatment of the feudal economy as a dynamic opposition between manorial and urban social relations of production.

Anderson thus solves the "transition problem" by denying the existence of any such transition in the period under consideration. Trade relations being integral to feudalism, the rise of commerce defines no fundamentally novel element in the later period. Moreover, he suggests that no fundamental change in economic relations occurred.

> so long as aristocratic agrarian property blocked a free market in land and factual mobility of manpower—in other words, as long as labor was not separated from the social conditions of its existence to become "labour-power"—rural relations of production remained feudal.[75]

Finally, despite extensive changes in state forms, the landed class remained dominant. "The nobility underwent profound metamorphoses in the centuries after the close of the Middle Ages; but from the beginning to the end of the history of Absolutism, it was never dislodged from its command of political power."[76]

Yet neither of these assessments can go unquestioned. On the one hand, a developed market in land was well established in many parts of Europe by the fifteenth century, although with some restrictions on ownership. Moreover, we cannot accept the economic relations of the period as "feudal" merely because they are not "capitalist." On the other hand, dislodgment of the nobility is precisely what often transpired. Beginning in the thirteenth century, the process of consolidation of sovereignty proceeded rapidly in several regions, stalled through the cataclysmic economic downturn of the fourteenth century, and regained its pace in the mid-fifteenth. Having abandoned by this time the effort to contain the direct extractive capacity of the sovereign state, the landed classes throughout fought to control taxation through representative bodies. This battle was generally unsuccessful in western Europe, the low point coming in the seventeenth century.

Anderson is of course well aware of this movement; indeed much of *Lineages* is devoted to its chronicles. His interpretation, however, is quite different, "Feudal coercion was displaced upwards, to a centralized monarchy; and the aristocracy typically had to exchange its estates representation for bureaucratic office, within the renovated structures of the state."[77]

The aristocracy was indeed successful in insinuating itself into positions of power within the state apparatus—administration, military, and tax farming. Such a move, from a system perspective, involves a transformation in the structure of exploitation. Anderson conflates one of the structural characteristics of a system (which *did* change) with the patterns of recruitment into elite positions (which did not). The resulting system dynamics will thus be distinct, even if the individual or family recipients of the surplus in some sense remain the same. The relative success of the aristocracy in insinuating itself into the state apparatus no doubt partly explains its continued social eminence, but it cannot be interpreted as evidence of the sovereign state as an instrument of feudal class rule.

Moreover, this success was anything but complete. Venality in its various forms certainly reduced the power of the state to move confidently against aristocratic interests, and limited its overall effectiveness in achieving its own projects.[78] But these projects were never determined by state functionaries, and monarchs often succeeded in staffing positions of highest power with individuals not beholden to indigenous aristocratic interests.[79]

Compared with structural aspects of the emerging social order, such as the extent to which the aristocracy was transformed into a commercial agrarian class and the character of the renovated military apparatus, the form of state recruitment was of relatively limited importance. This fact can be gleaned from the pattern of "constitutional" and "absolute" states in the sixteenth and later centuries. The constitutional states (e.g., England, Holland) remained substantively beholden to their leading classes, and relied on taxation only with their consent, while the absolute states (France, Spain, the German principalities) did not. In addition, the constitutional states depended on naval rather than land-based military power. In both cases the leading classes were inserted into the military apparatus, but the land-based powers clearly possessed a superior coercive arm in their dealings with local feudal forces.[80]

Anderson is thus correct in his critique of theories of the rise of the absolute state as either capitalist or a mediator between aristocratic and capitalist interests, "the Absolute State was never an arbiter between the aristocracy and the bourgeoisie, still less an instrument of the nascent bourgeoisie against the aristocracy."[81] However, he concludes from the fact that the growth of the sovereign state was a condition of existence of the aristocracy in this later period, that it therefore must be a functional instrument toward its reproduction: "Absolutism is just this: *a redeployed and recharged apparatus of feudal domination*, designed to clamp the peasant masses back into their traditional social position. . . . it was the new political carapace of a threatened nobility."[82]

There are several problems with this argument. First, if the fundamental form of surplus extraction is no longer feudal, the state cannot be considered an agent of feudal reproduction, whatever its role in sustaining the preeminence of aristocratic families. Second, even the validity of this account of the origins of the sovereign state would not imply that emergent state power need remain securely within the orbit of aristocratic power. Whether accepted by the landed classes to offset internecine rivalries, to combat external threat, to counter the power of a nascent bourgeoisie, or to more effectively suppress an increasingly restive peasantry, the sovereign state acquired a life of its own. Thus Brustein and Hechter note:

> Once the state gained power at the expense of its constituents it was free to pursue its own interests, subject, as always, to existing constraints. At first the modern state enacted policies on behalf of the landed aristocracy. . . . But gradually thereafter, modern western European history tells the story of how the state slowly deprived the landed aristocracy of its prerogatives.[83]

In addition, it is misleading to say that a centralized state was needed as a more efficient instrument of peasant repression because the first period of sovereign state formation occurred in the thirteenth century prior to the major peasant uprisings.[84] Moreover, the peasant movements of the fourteenth and fifteenth centuries—which occurred predominantly in regions of strong state formation (southeastern England, the Paris basin, Flanders, Lombardy, the Rhine basin, Catalonia) were *reactions* to royal taxation, and did not persist into the later, and stronger, period of state formation.[85] It would have taken a quite socially aware aristocracy to continue to promote the consolidation of royal power over centuries during which the peasantry was not only relatively quiescent but, when provoked, directed its ire more frequently against the tax collector than the landlord.

Anderson's explanation, moreover, obscures the central weakness of the feudal social formation: its inability, after the atrophy of its protective military function, to control the extraction of surpluses under conditions of labor shortage. The sovereign state, in point of fact, possessed the global means of surplus extraction to a degree never attainable by the decentralized manorial system.

The explanation of the absolute state's emergence as a functional response to the new requirements for the reproduction of feudal exploitation after the fourteenth century thus fails. The structural weakness of the feudal articulation of state and economy, together with the superior extractive capacity of the sovereign state and its heightened effectiveness as a military machine in the context of the emerging nation-state organization of Europe are all comprehensible within the conception of the social formation as an articulation of sites of domination. The emergence of the absolute state does represent a transition involving a new logic of social contestation, but it is not reasonable to treat the "transitional" period as feudal, even within an extended conception of the term.

The State Commercial Social Formation

In this section we will outline the dynamic of the state commercial social formation, limiting ourselves to a discussion of the forms of social contestation generated by this social formation by virtue of its particular structure of exploitation and domination.

First, the break in the fusion of suzerain state and manorial economy effectively withdrew from the hands of the landlord class its traditional means of ensuring the reproduction of its position of social dominance. The first step in this direction was the commutation of services, which deprived the lord of political leadership at the site of feudal production. The refusal of traditional Marxist theory to recognize a political structure *within* the site of production has led to a general underestimation of the importance of this change. But as Bloch has noted, through commutation

the lord had abdicated from his position as head of a large agrarian and

semi-industrial undertaking. . . . Politically speaking, the lord was still a
leader to his men, he remained their military commander, their judge,
their born protector. But his economic leadership had gone—and all the
rest could easily follow. He had become a "stockholder" in the soil.[86]

But the development of sovereign power proceeded then to increasingly restrict the military and juridical functions of the lords as well.
By the sixteenth century in France, while the greater part of lordly income derived from juridical fees, Bloch indicates that the scope of seigneurial political power had been severely circumscribed.

> seigneurial justice now had a formidable rival in public justice, dis-
> pensed whether by the courts of the great principalities or by those of
> the crown. . . . A large number of cases were removed from the sei-
> gneurial courts altogether. . . . lastly, it was now possible to appeal
> against their judgments.[87]

As a result of this derogation of direct political power of the landed
classes, the new social formation supported a qualitatively distinct relationship of state to aristocracy—a curious admixture of mutual support
and bitter hostility. Unable to dispense with sovereign rule, in this new
period the traditional landed classes fought for the *representative control
of and participation in* the state rather than for its dissolution. Indeed,
the very concept of representative government was a product of the
political project of the traditional nobility of this period.

The position of the state, however, was far more complex, and involved its playing class forces against one another toward consolidating its
extractive capacity. Charles Tilly summarizes the situation as follows.

> The state-makers only imposed their will on the populace through cen-
> turies of effort. . . . In all these efforts . . . the state-makers frequently
> found the traditional authorities allied with the people against them.
> Thus it became a game of shifting coalitions, kings rallying popular
> support by offering guarantees against cruel and arbitrary local magnates
> or by challenging their claims to goods, money, or services. . . . mag-
> nates parading as defenders of local liberties against royal oppression.
> . . . Ultimately the people paid.[88]

From Catalonia and Castile in the fifteenth century right up to the French
Revolution, this dynamic held a central position in European state
development.

A particularly striking confirmation of this novel dynamic of surplus
extraction lies in a widespread stance taken by the absolute state vis-à-vis
the peasantry in this period—a stance involving the *protection* of the
peasantry against lordly extraction. Were the state merely an instrument

of aristocratic economic dominance, we would expect diametrically opposed behavior. However, over the protests of the nobility, the sovereign state often acted to promote village enfranchisements,[89] and often the royal courts promoted structural changes in rural land ownership which was to make the French peasantry among the most independent in Europe.

> the slow-moving advance of French royal justice . . . by a curious historical paradox . . . had proved more beneficial to the peasantry than the daring innovation carried through by the Norman and Angevin kings of England. . . . It was fortunate for the French peasant that although the landlords had captured the judiciary . . . the victory of absolute monarchy kept the "feudal reaction" within bounds.[90]

The German princes applied the same strategy (Bauernschutz) from the thirteenth century onward, and the English state was prevented from doing so only by virtue of its relatively complete dependence on the smaller landlords in its drive for administrative and juridical centralization.[91]

It has often been noted that areas of peasant resistance[92] and village power[93] have tended to coincide with regions of strong towns independent from feudal control. It is possible that the activity of the state rather than the proximity of towns accounts for the increased power of the peasantry in its struggles against feudal exaction in this period. However, a more compelling explanation of the observed correspondence is simply that *both* powerful peasant communities *and* strong independent towns were promoted by a dynamic sovereign state, the extractive efforts of which included the strengthening of these sources of surplus at the expense of the feudal suzerainty. This may indeed have been the case in eastern Europe, Sweden, and England; the general proposition will require a more detailed comparative study than we have either the space or the expertise to undertake.

Yet clearly the sovereign state protected the peasantry only the better to exploit it. A dramatic indication of the centrality of the state in surplus extraction lies in the fact that virtually *all* the major peasant uprisings in the state commercial period were directed in the first instance not against the landlord, but against the tax collector. In the English case, highlighted by the great peasant revolt of 1381, Hilton's *Bond Men Made Free* makes this point quite clear.

> Already towards the end of May 1381, villagers in Essex were resisting the attempts of tax-collectors. . . . general hatred [was] felt by the peasants and artisans for all the king's advisors. . . . The morning of Corpus Christi was spent by the rebels pursuing their London enemies, of

whom the most important were the lawyers and others connected with the judicial system.[94]

Hilton is thus led to call this greatest of English peasant uprisings an "anti-tax riot" (p. 151). Nor, according to Hilton, is this phenomenon limited to England.

> It was the imposition of the indemnity tax by the king of France . . . which pushed the self-assertive, unservile peasants and artisans in the maritime districts of Flanders into rebellion; it was the requisition for the victualling of the castles of the nobility in the region of Paris . . . which provoked the Jacquerie in 1358; it was the insolent taxation imposed by the king's lieutenant . . . which began the . . . Jacquerie of the Tuchins.[95]

It is important to add that both fourteenth- and sixteenth-century peasant revolts occurred in periods of *falling* lordly incomes, though *rising* taxes.[96]

Perhaps the most critical of the new dynamics of surplus extraction in the state commercial social formation—certainly concerning its contribution to the subsequent emergence of capitalism—lay in the heightened importance of the symbiotic relationship between sovereign state and commercial forces to which it gave rise, and through which prodigious surpluses were extracted. The state in this period pursued imperial policies through the logic of its own interests, and promoted commercial capital as an aspect of consolidating its position as an extractor of surpluses; the fortunes of commercial capital thus become complementary to the aggrandizement of the sovereign state.

It may be argued, however, that the most vibrant and progressive commercial regions lay *outside* the core areas of state consolidation, in the Italian peninsula and the Low Countries. Certainly this is the case in the sixteenth and seventeenth centuries, but this fact does not contradict the notion that the general ascendancy of commercial capitalism was in large part the product of the extraction strategies of sovereign state consolidation. The decline of Italian trade hegemony, coincident with the shift from Mediterranean to overseas trade routes, was a precondition of the rise of the Atlantic states, and there is no reason to believe that Holland and the other northern trading areas would not have been swallowed up or marginalized, as prior loci of trade had been, had feudal Europe followed a different logic of social development. The attempts of Charles V and Phillip II to mulct these regions in the interests of consolidation of the empire ultimately failed,[97] but the position of the northern trade areas was tenuous at best.

Moreover, a good deal of the resilience of the independent trading states was derived from their intimate ties with the new monarchies, whose wars and administrative expenses they underwrote in return for access to exploitable trade routes and natural resources.[98] Ultimately, however, the new sovereign states begrudged their dependence upon the foreign traders, and made every effort to supplant them with domestic commercial interests that could be rendered more accessible to state policy. This effort was, of course, ultimately successful.

Conclusion

In our approach to the period, feudal development is explained by the contradictory articulation of feudal social structures. While conserving the Marxist notion of the centrality of the mechanisms of surplus extraction and their contestation, our analysis stresses the complexity and contradictory nature of these mechanisms.

The attractions of this analysis, we believe, are manifold. It permits a clear differentiation of feudalism from other forms of precapitalist agrarian rent extraction exhibiting quite different social dynamics, and explains the bitter struggles among dominant groups in feudal society, the shifting sources of their revenues, and the heterogeneous character of peasant rebellions, in a manner not available to a theory which treats all exploitation as a reflection or redirection of property-based surplus extraction.

The conception of feudalism as a contradictory totality also clearly poses the question of the structural weaknesses of the feudal system. While these weaknesses are in part explicable in purely economic terms, key aspects can be understood only in terms of the inability of feudal suzerainty, as a form of state, to secure lordly control over labor services in a period of labor scarcity and increased mobility, and to exploit the expanding scope of surplus transfer through the establishment of commercial trade routes. By virtue of these weaknesses, the manorial system proved unable to compete with more favorably placed forms of surplus extraction—especially with the sovereign state in league with commercial capital. The future of feudal social formations depended in no small part on the outcome of these structural contradictions.

The concept of feudalism as a particular state-economy relationship allows for a wider range of alternatives in formulating the structural changes involved in the transition process. The proposition that the disintegration of feudalism involved the breakdown of the fusion of feudal suzerainty and manorial production in the face of the increased power (often in alliance) of both sovereign state, village community, and freeholding peasantry is impossible in a conception of the transition as an "economic" process.

Finally, our stress upon the state as a constitutive part of the social formation renders comprehensible the nature of the postfeudal social formation. The key to the period, which we have referred to as "state commercialism," was the position of the absolute state as the linchpin of a complex set of class alliances and antagonisms, involving peasantry, aristocracy, commercial capital, and urban production. The "problem" of the transition from feudalism to capitalism is thus easily resolved: there was none.

Despite its sophistication, the contemporary Marxist theory of the state has failed to question the most critical of the founding assumptions of classical Marxism: the conception of the state as an effect or reflection of class relationships. The ultimate subordination of the state is thus taken for granted, and the research project (whether historical or theoretical) is conceived as a quest for the precise social mechanisms by means of which this subordinate status is stabilized and reproduced. We consider this aspect of Marxism an unwarranted functionalism. The feudal state, while continually engaged in the reproduction of feudal class relations, at the same time was so situated as to undermine these very relations. Functional theory cannot conceive how structurally articulated sites, each of which contains within it the conditions of existence of the other, can serve ultimately as their mutual conditions of destruction. The secret, we believe, lies in the capacity of social struggles to transform the characteristic articulation of sites.

Thus in the case of feudalism the sovereign state, in the persons of the monarch and his administrative and military hierarchy, safeguarded the position of the landed classes over the dependent producers, while attempting to gain direct access to producer surpluses through the capacity of direct tax exactions. The landed classes, by contrast, sought in general to maintain the power of the sovereign state vis-à-vis its external enemies and usurpers among its ranks, yet limit and contain its direct access to producer surpluses. The history and ultimate demise of feudalism consists in part of the playing out of these forces.

NOTES

We would like to thank Robert Brenner, Heide Gerstenberger, David Gordon, William Lazonick, and Stephen Marglin for their insightful comments on this essay.

1. See Ralph Miliband, *The State in Capitalist Society* (London: Weidenfeld and Nicolson, 1969); Claus Offe, *Strukturprobleme des kapitalisticschen Staates* (Frankfurt: Suhrkamp, 1972); Nicos Poulantzas, *State, Power, Socialism* (Paris: Presses Universitaires de France, 1978).
2. Samuel Bowles and Herbert Gintis, "Structure and Practice in the Labor Theory of Value," *Review of Radical Political Economics* 12, no. 4 (Winter,

1981): 1–26; "The Crisis of Liberal Democratic Capitalism," *Politics and Society*, 11, no. 1 (Winter, 1982): 51–93.

3. Thus while we are in complete agreement with the careful attention given to the concept of the economic surplus in Kula's seminal work, we depart considerably from his analysis, which focuses almost entirely on "relations among economic subjects" and which by defining feudalism broadly as an economic system (without reference to state structures) extends the concept of feudalism to virtually any exploitative rent-based society: "Feudalism . . . is in a certain sense a universal fact: in one form or another every society which has left the stage of primitive communism has known it." See Witwold Kula, *Teoria Economica del Sistema Feudale: Proposta di un Modello* (Torino: Einaudi editore, 1970; Warszawa, 1962), p. 6 [translation ours].

4. Douglass C. North and Robert Paul Thomas, *The Rise of the Western World* (Cambridge: Cambridge University Press, 1973); John Hicks, *A Theory of Economic History* (Oxford: Clarendon Press, 1969).

5. For a general critique of this approach, we refer the interested reader to Alexander J. Field, "The Problem with Neoclassical Institutional Economics: A Critique with Special Reference to the North-Thomas Model of pre-1500 Europe," in *Explorations in Economic History* 18 (1981): 174–91. The North-Thomas interpretation is in many respects close to the Marxist model directly critiqued in this essay. Both explain the feudal decline by relying on a notion of institutional change driven by the tendency of productive forces to overcome institutional inertia. They differ in that North and Thomas offer a theory of institutional accommodation and Marx a theory of class struggle and revolution as the means whereby such change is affected.

6. This fusion of course contrasts with ancient, capitalist, and other societies in which there is a formal *separation* between state and economy, in terms both of institutional interpenetration and the staffing of positions of power.

7. F. L. Ganshof, *Feudalism* (New York: Harper and Row, 1961), p. xvi.

8. Rodney Hilton, ed., *The Transition from Feudalism to Capitalism* (London: New Left Books, 1976), p. 30.

9. Maurice Dobb, *Studies in the Development of Capitalism* (New York: International Publishers, 1947), p. 35.

10. Perry Anderson, *Lineages of the Absolutist State* (London: New Left Books, 1974), p. 401.

11. Anderson, *Lineages*, p. 404.

12. Henri Pirenne, *Economic and Social History of Medieval Europe* (London: Routledge and Kegan Paul, 1936); Paul Sweezy, "A Critique," in *The Transition from Feudalism to Capitalism*, ed. Rodney Hilton (London: New Left Books, 1976), pp. 33–56.

13. Dobb, *Studies*, p. 78.

14. A. B. Hibbert, "The Origins of the Medieval Town Patriciate," in *Towns in Societies: Essays in Economic History and Historical Sociology*, ed. Philip Abrams and E. A. Wrigley (Cambridge: Cambridge University Press, 1978), pp. 91–104. See also Susan Reynolds, *English Medieval Towns* (Oxford: Clarendon Press, 1977).

15. Hilton, *Transition*, p. 111.
16. V. G. Kiernan, "Foreign Mercenaries and Absolute Monarchy," *Past and Present* 11 (April, 1957): 66–87; Otto Hintze, *The Historical Essays of Otto Hintze* (New York: Oxford University Press, 1975); Anderson, *Lineages*.
17. Anderson, *Lineages*, p. 28.
18. V. G. Kiernan, "State and Nation in Western Europe," *Past and Present* 31 (July, 1965): 24.
19. Perry Anderson, *Passages from Antiquity to Feudalism* (London: New Left Books, 1974), p. 151.
20. Anderson, *Lineages*, p. 46.
21. H. Mitteis, *The State in the Middle Ages* (Amsterdam: North Holland Publishing Co., 1975); Anderson, *Passages;* Marc Bloch, *French Rural History* (Berkeley: University of California Press, 1973).
22. Paul Vinogradoff, *Villainage in England* (New York: Russell and Russell, 1923), p. 130.
23. Vinogradoff, *Villainage*, p. 70.
24. Vinogradoff, *Villainage*, chap. 2. See also Frederick Pollock and Frederic William Maitland, *The History of English Law Before the Time of Edward I* (Cambridge: Cambridge University Press, 1968).
25. Robert Brenner, "Agrarian Class Structure and Economic Development in Pre-industrial Europe," *Past and Present* 70 (February, 1976): 35.
26. Brenner, "Agrarian Class Structure," p. 56.
27. M. M. Postan, *The Medieval Economy and Society* (London: Weidenfeld and Nicolson, 1972), p. 120.
28. Vinogradoff, *Villainage*, pp. 212–13.
29. Bloch, *French Rural History*, pp. 46–56.
30. Vinogradoff, *Villainage*, p. 230.
31. Vinogradoff, *Villainage*, p. 277.
32. Brenner, "Agrarian Class Structure"; Michael Hechter and William Brustein, "Regional Modes of Production and Patterns of State Formation in Western Europe," *American Journal of Sociology* 85, no. 5 (March, 1980): 1086.
33. Postan, *Medieval Economy and Society*, p. 952.
34. Jeanne Koopman Henn, *Peasants, Workers, and Capital: The Political Economy of Labor and Incomes in Cameroon* (Ph.D. diss., Harvard University, 1978).
35. Bowles and Gintis, "Structure and Practice in the Labor Theory of Value."
36. Postan, *Medieval Economy and Society*, p. 96.
37. Postan, *Medieval Economy and Society;* Dobb, *Studies;* Paul Sweezy, *The Theory of Capitalist Development* (New York: Monthly Review Press, 1946).
38. Brenner, "Agrarian Class Structure," p. 31. See also Hilton's insightful summary of the fourteenth-century English case, in *Transition*, p. 25.
39. Marc Bloch, *Feudal Society*, 2 vols. (Chicago: University of Chicago Press, 1961); Dobb, *Studies;* Sweezy, "A Critique."
40. Bloch, *Feudal Society*, 1:113–14.
41. Bloch, *Feudal Society*, 1:263.
42. See, for example, *Villainage*, pp. 80–81.

43. Bloch, *French Rural History*, chap. 4; *Feudal Society*, chap. 19.
44. Hilton, *Transition*, p. 17. Hilton's description, we should note, does not hold for the following century, when expansion of the demesne resumed.
45. See, for example, Bloch, *French Rural History*, chap. 3.
46. Vinogradoff, *Villainage*, pp. 358–59, 368.
47. Vinogradoff, *Villainage*, p. 378.
48. Karl Marx, *Capital* (New York: International Publishers, 1967), vol. 1, chap. 33.
49. Brenner, "Agrarian Class Structure"; Evsey D. Domar, "The Causes of Slavery or Serfdom: A Hypothesis," *Journal of Economic History* 30, no. 1 (March, 1970): 18–32.
50. By this we do not mean that the wage—the "price of labor power"—is market determined. This is no more true for capitalism (cf. Bowles and Gintis, "Structure and Practice in the Labor Theory of Value") than it is for feudalism.
51. Vinogradoff, *Villainage*, p. 158.
52. Bloch, *French Rural History*, p. 87.
53. Rodney Hilton, *Bond Men Made Free* (London: Methuen and Co., 1973), p. 74.
54. Bloch, *French Rural History*, p. 111.
55. Brenner, "Agrarian Class Structure," p. 35.
56. Domar, "Causes of Slavery or Serfdom."
57. See J. A. Raftis, *Tenure and Mobility: Studies in the Social History of the Medieval English Village* (Toronto: Pontifical Institute of Medieval Studies, 1964), and for an overview on the mobility question Alan MacFarlane, *The Origins of English Individualism* (New York: Cambridge University Press, 1978).
58. Vinogradoff, *Villainage*, pp. 151–52.
59. Anderson, *Lineages*, p. 422.
60. Anderson, *Lineages*, p. 27.
61. Gabriel Ardant, "Financial Policy and Economic Infrastructure of Modern States and Nations," in *The Formation of National States in Western Europe*, ed. Charles Tilly (Princeton: Princeton University Press, 1975).
62. Harry A. Miskimin, *The Economy of Early Renaissance Europe, 1300–1460* (Cambridge: Cambridge University Press, 1975), pp. 107ff.
63. Eli Hechscher, *Mercantilism* (London: George Allen and Unwin, 1955).
64. In *Transition*, ed. Hilton, p. 125.
65. See Hilton, *Transition*, and Robert S. Lopez, *The Commercial Revolution of the Middle Ages* (Cambridge: Cambridge University Press, 1976).
66. By "independent" we mean "irreducible to other social actors or structures." Clearly this is compatible with the state's being significantly influenced by such actors.
67. This approach to the development of the early modern state was proposed by Charles Tilly in *The Formation of National States*.
68. Cf. Hilton, *Transition*, and references therein.
69. Dobb, *Studies*; Anderson, *Lineages*.

70. Brenner, "Agrarian Class Structure." Surprisingly similar issues arise in the interpretation of eighteenth-century France as a "feudal" period. See Alfred Cobban, *The Social Interpretation of the French Revolution* (Cambridge: Cambridge University Press, 1971), and Frank A. Kafker and James M. Laux, *The French Revolution: Conflicting Interpretations* (New York: Random House, 1976).

71. *Transition*, pp. 23–24. Anderson also cites studies showing that the decline in seigneurial incomes, due to declining terms of trade between industry and agriculture, preceded the Black Death in France, and precipitated bitter interaristocratic rivalries. See *Passages*, pp. 200ff.

72. Anderson, *Passages*, p. 151.

73. Anderson, *Passages*, p. 128.

74. Anderson, *Lineages*, p. 27.

75. Anderson, *Lineages*, p. 17.

76. Anderson, *Lineages*, p. 18.

77. Anderson, *Lineages*, p. 429.

78. Franklin L. Ford, *Robe and Sword: The Regrouping of the French Aristocracy after Louis XIV* (Cambridge: Harvard University Press, 1953); Hans Rosenberg, *Bureaucracy, Aristocracy, and Autocracy* (Boston: Beacon Press, 1958).

79. For a contrasting view, see J. F. Bosher, *French Finances: 1770–1795* (Cambridge: Cambridge University Press, 1970), and Theda Skocpol, *States and Social Revolutions* (Cambridge: Cambridge University Press, 1979).

80. Cf. the discussion in Michael Mann, "State and Society, 1130–1815: An Analysis of English State Finances," in *Political Power and Social Theory*, ed. Maurice Zeitlin (Greenwich, Conn.: Jai Press, 1980).

81. Anderson, *Lineages*, p. 18.

82. Anderson, *Lineages*, p. 18.

83. Hechter and Brustein, "Regional Modes of Production," p. 1086.

84. Joseph Strayer, *On the Medieval Origins of the Modern State* (Princeton: Princeton University Press, 1970), pt. 2, pp. 57ff.

85. Hilton, *Bond Men Made Free*.

86. Bloch, *French Rural History*, pp. 100–101. For a similar judgment on the part of Vinogradoff, see his discussion in *Villainage*, p. 182.

87. Bloch, *French Rural History*, p. 103.

88. Tilly, *The Formation of National States*, p. 24

89. Bloch, *French Rural History*, p. 109.

90. Bloch, *French Rural History*, pp. 129, 134.

91. Brenner, "Agrarian Class Structure"; Hilton, *Bond Men Made Free*.

92. Hilton, *Bond Men Made Free*.

93. Hechter and Brustein, "Regional Modes of Production."

94. Pp. 138, 145.

95. Hilton, *Bond Men Made Free*, pp. 114–15.

96. Hilton, *Bond Men Made Free*, p. 153. We might add that the relative success of the English landlords in curbing royal extraction meant that Kett's Re-

bellion and other uprisings of the sixteenth century were more clearly directed against the landlord than in other areas of Europe.

97. Fernand Braudel, *The Mediterranean and the Mediterranean World in the Age of Philip II* (New York: Harper and Row, 1975), pt 4, sect. 1.

98. Violet Barbour, *Capitalism in Amsterdam in the 17th Century* (Ann Arbor: University of Michigan Press, 1963), chap. 6.

AZTEC STATEMAKING
Ecology, Structure, and the Origin of the State

Elizabeth M. Brumfiel

The state is a powerful, complex, permanently instituted system of centralized political administration. It exercises sovereignty in carrying out basic political functions (maintaining territorial rights, maintaining internal order, making and executing decisions regarding group action), and its authority in these matters is buttressed by state sovereignty in the use of force within its jurisdiction. States are characterized by administrative complexity; administrative personnel are hierarchically ordered and specialized by administrative task.[1]

States are, by no means, a universal attribute of human society; in most groups studied by anthropologists, the state is absent. Groups can execute political functions as a whole, making political decisions by consensus and enforcing them through the application of informal sanctions. Political leadership is sometimes supplied by a headman or "big-man," but in such cases, leadership status is a matter of personally acquired prestige, not tied to a permanently instituted office. Offices of leadership sometimes exist in the form of senior positions within kinship groups, but these leaders either lack the right to employ coercion to enforce their directives or the legitimate use of force extends only to members of the leader's own kinship group. In all these cases, political decisions are made and carried out in the absence of a specialized, complex administrative hierarchy.

The numerous attempts to explain why states emerge in some times and places but not others have been dominated by two contrasting approaches: the ecological and the structural. The first, based on the work of Julian Steward, relates state formation to the problems and/or opportunities presented to a human population by its environmental setting. In this approach, population growth and its resulting pressures provide the dynamic for state formation, and at least the initial stages are said to be promoted by the ecological benefits that the state confers upon its general

Reprinted from *American Anthropologist* 85 (June, 1983): 261–84. Copyright © by The American Anthropological Association.

population. The second approach, growing out of the Marx-Engels tradition, regards state formation as a process generated by particular sociocultural orders. Certain types of societies (stratified societies, for example) are said to possess an internal dynamic that exerts pressure for state formation even when the relationship between the human population and its environment is stable. In this approach, the focus is less upon a human population as a whole and more upon social components and their interactions. Of these two approaches, the first has received a greater share of attention and has been elaborated more fully. As a result, some of its difficulties are now evident. The structural approach has been less thoroughly explored.

This essay has three objectives: to discuss the strengths and weaknesses of the ecological approach to state formation in its current form, to suggest how a greater emphasis upon the internal dynamics of political systems might enhance our understanding of state formation, and to illustrate the utility of a structural approach by reviewing the developmental history of the Aztec state.

The Ecological Approach

By definition, the state is a powerful, specialized institution for political administration; therefore, state office holders can function as highly effective problem solvers. They can use the resources of their positions to gather information concerning the problems facing society, they can develop expertise in effective problem solving, and they can mobilize the food, matériel, and manpower needed to effect their solutions. Recognition of the superior managerial capacity of state government has been one of the major insights supplied by the ecological approach. It is also the basis from which the ecological hypothesis of state formation is derived: states arise in socioenvironmental contexts where effective management is either necessary or especially beneficial.

Initially, it was argued that states were a response to the organizational problems of constructing and maintaining large-scale irrigation.[2] This view is no longer accepted as universally valid because archaeological research has revealed instances where states emerged in the absence of large-scale irrigation or where it was utilized only after the state had come into being.[3] But effective problem solving is a widely applicable asset, and numerous variants of the managerial hypothesis have emerged during the past twenty years. For example, it has been suggested that states arose to facilitate internal distribution,[4] to procure essential extralocal raw materials,[5] to coordinate subsistence systems,[6] to defend a population's resources or capture the resources of others,[7] to meet the demands for goods made by potentially dangerous outsiders,[8] to stabilize agricultural productivity,[9] or to perform several of these functions simultaneously.[10] It has been proposed that states emerged for different specific reasons, and that what the developmental histories of states share in common is not a specific set of ecological problems requiring management, but simply some set to which the state is an effective response.[11] Thus, emphasis upon the managerial effectiveness of states has endowed the ecological approach with the capacity to deal with a widely divergent set of specific cases within a single, broad explanatory framework.

However, the wide applicability of the managerial hypothesis has created the need for further theoretical elaboration, because if the state is such an effective response to so many different kinds of problems, then it is necessary to account for the fact that the state emerged only in *some* times and in *some* places. For this, those operating within the ecological paradigm have most often focused on the interaction of population growth and environmental setting.

Population growth and its ensuing problems would explain why, after centuries without the benefits of state organization, a human population might suddenly find a state system either beneficial or necessary.[12] Environmental differences from one region to another would explain why population growth resulted in state formation in some places but not in others. States would emerge only in certain environmental settings where the problems of population growth were particularly severe because growth rate was high or arable land limited or where overpopulation could be accommodated by the application of some managerial strategy (construction of irrigation systems or other means of agricultural intensification, administration of local exchange systems or long-distance trade, etc.).

But the attempt to account for the timing and location of state formation in terms of population growth and environmental suitability has not been very successful. In several cases, states have emerged in the absence of population pressure.[13] And it has proven extremely difficult to differentiate between environments that would foster state formation and those that would not. States have formed in areas where agricultural land is limited geographically (coastal Peru) and in areas where stringent limits are absent (the Southern Maya Lowlands). States have emerged in areas where resources are unevenly distributed (Central Mexico) and where resource distribution is quite homogeneous (the Nile Valley). And while state formation is generally accompanied by some form of agricultural intensification, this can occur in a variety of environmental settings.[14]

Cases of state formation in the absence of population pressure have been particularly vexing. Most ecological models of state formation have relied upon positive feedback through the channels of population growth and recurring population pressure to maintain the system in a state of evolutionary change.[15] But if state formation occurs in the absence of a serious disparity between population and resources, it seems necessary to search for some other source of systemic dynamic. Yoffee has suggested that we look within the system itself.[16]

The Structural Approach: Marx-Engels

A number of anthropologists have argued that certain sociocultural systems, because of their inherent structural properties, are dynamic. Some of these systems might, by their very nature, be impelled along a course of evolutionary change destined to culminate in state formation. Service characterizes the development of the state and civilization as being "orthogenetic" and "self-contained."[17] Friedman and Rowlands speak in terms of "epigenesis": structural transformation over time in which the trajectory of change is determined by the structural properties of the initial system.[18] It is this approach to state formation that is here designated as the structural approach. Various structural properties might generate the dynamic for sociocultural change,[19] but within the literature on state formation, structurally induced social conflict has received the greatest attention.

The first social conflict theory of state formation was set forth by Engels, working from the notes of Marx.[20] Engels argued that the state appeared when new "industrial" techniques (cattle raising, loom weaving, forging metal tools) made feasible an array of economic institutions (private property, money lending at interest, mercantile exchange, and the use of slave labor) destined to divide society into a number of strata (rich and poor, freepeople and slaves), each with differing and mutually antagonistic economic interests. The state, distinguished by its specialized institutions for maintaining internal order (judicial courts, a constabulary, prisons, and other coercive institutions), arose to mediate and, ultimately, to suppress these conflicts.

Although it appears that Engels was mistaken in regarding state formation as a direct consequence of certain technological innovations, the evidence for private property, mercantile exchange, and slave labor within early states has led some contemporary anthropologists to accept conflicts of economic interest as the cause of state formation and to view the early state, as Marx and Engels did, as an institution for suppressing class conflict.[21] Others have demurred. Service has sharply criticized the Marx-Engels theory on two grounds.[22]

First, Service disputes the Marxist conception of economic inequality in early states, arguing that in early states, inequality is rooted first and foremost in political (and not economic) institutions. According to Service, the primary basis of economic inequality is not private property or mercantile exchange or slavery; economic inequality is primarily a consequence of a politically instituted system of tribute, taxation, and corvée that extracts goods and services from the commoner stratum and transfers them to the ruling elite. Here, Service sees a clear parallel to the economic systems of chiefdoms: societies marked by permanent offices of political leadership (held by the seniormost kinsmen), hereditary differences in social status (based on genealogical nearness to the chief), and regular flow of goods and services to the chief (rendered by consensus of the tribute payers since the chief's use of coercion is limited). The early states, Service argues, represent an intensification of the inequalities already present in prestate chiefdoms; Marxists have erred in focusing upon the political implications of economics rather than the economic implications of politics.

Second, Service criticizes the Marxist notion that states arise to suppress conflicts of economic interests. Given the structure of economic inequality in chiefdoms and early states, Marxist theory would anticipate intense conflict developing between tribute-gathering rulers and their tribute-rendering subjects. But according to Service, there is no evidence of violent conflict between rulers and subjects in any of the historical or archaeological records of state formation. The few "civil wars" that were fought, Service suggests, were wars of succession between aristocratic rivals, not wars of class against class.

The Structural Approach Revised

Service's characterization of economic inequality in early states seems accurate.[23] However, his contention that conflicts of economic interest played no role in early state formation and that suppression of conflict was not a primary function of early states is open to debate, as will be discussed below. For the moment, it seems more appropriate to observe that, having rejected the importance of economic conflict in state origins, Service focuses his attention upon the realm of politics and there finds a satisfactory reason for state formation: "The classical civilizations . . . all must have had small beginnings in the simple attempts of primitive leaders to perpetuate their social dominance."[24]

Efforts to perpetuate social dominance imply that the position of leaders in certain types of prestate political systems is not totally secure. The same implication can be read into statements by others who view the state as an organizational mechanism for perpetuating and augmenting the power of prestate leaders.[25] If it can be shown that, in certain types of political systems, threats to the leader's status are regularly generated, then an alternative to the Marxist social conflict theory might be formulated—a theory that explains the state as a consequence of conflicts arising from political, rather than economic, structures.

A review of the ethnographic literature on chiefdoms suggests that the position of these ruling paramounts is quite insecure. Incumbents often faced the specter of popular rebellion led by arisocratic pretenders to the paramount office.[26] The potential for violent competition between political rivals probably exists in any system where leadership is instituted in permanent offices because, as Goody points out, these offices are *unique* social statuses that are filled from a *pool* of socially qualified individuals.[27] But competition will be particularly intense in chiefdoms, where the leader's right to use coercion is limited. In the absence of coercive force, incumbent chiefs seek to enhance their authority by actively promoting the prestige of office.[28] This generates a contradiction: to survive competition, incumbents buttress their authority with prestige, but the prestige of office tempts competitors to vie more diligently to seize office from incumbent leaders.[29]

However, competition for office is not entirely an aristocratic concern divorced from all conflicts of economic interest between rulers and ruled. Civil war in weakly centralized polities often serves as the mechanism by which commoners seek and often find redress against oppressive political elites. Fallers's analysis of civil war among the Soga of precolonial Uganda provides a typical example.

> The sharing by the ruler's brothers of his ascribed fitness to rule . . . provided a ready source of leadership for revolt against what customary norms defined as misrule. Excessive cruelty, burdensome demands for tribute and the like are often spoken of by the Soga as factors contributory to revolt and usurpation.[30]

It appears, then, that structurally induced social conflict in political systems where leadership is instituted in weak, but permanent, offices has both a political and an economic basis. It is a three-party affair where commoners exploit elite rivalries to lighten their tribute demands, while rival elites exploit commoner discontent to gain access to office, and the ruling paramount uses whatever strategies he can devise to secure his own position against both commoners and rival elites. The process of state formation might be nothing more (nor less) than a series of effective strategies designed and implemented by beleaguered rulers to survive these challenges to power.[31]

It is beyond the scope of this essay to designate the full range of strategies which singly or in combination might accomplish state formation, but Webster and Lewis consider state development through warfare, Friedman and Rowlands focus upon state-sponsored craft production and regional exchange, and Brumfiel discusses the manipulation of marital alliances between neighboring elites.[32] Earle provides an excellent case study of how warfare, trade, and the development of irrigated agricultural lands were used by rulers of the incipient Hawaiian state to secure their power.[33]

The specific strategies implemented by individual statemakers would vary according to the specific dimensions of the structurally generated conflict (i.e., the identity of political competitors and the resources at their disposal) and the costs of various centralizing strategies in different technoenvironmental contexts. Thus, the actual process of state formation might differ from case to case, especially in the initial stages where rulers' options were most narrowly constrained by the threat of rebellion and usurpation. But as the centralization of authority proceeded, rulers could be expected to employ the power gained by one means to enhance other means of power. Thus, initial differences in state forms would diminish over time; there would be convergent evolution.[34]

The structural attributes of the prestate system and its technoenvironmental context could also account for the distribution of state formation in time and space. According to the analysis presented above, the pressures for state formation are generated by some sociocultural systems, but in others, such pressures do not exist and state formation will not occur. Identifying the structures that lead to state formation and the conditions determining *their* distribution in time and space constitutes a major task for future research.

Even with the appropriate internal dynamic present, state formation might be contingent upon technoenvironmental conditions.[35] Certainly Friedman's analysis of political development among the Kachin suggests that centralizing trends were cut short by the limited potential of the native agricultural system.[36] The Hawaiian chiefdoms also seem to have been condemned to cycles of centralization and decentralization by the difficulties of interisland transport and communication.[37] Hence, environmental suitability plays a critical role in structural models of state formation as it does in ecological models. But the difficulty of differentiating between technoenvironmental regimes that foster state formation and those that do not will probably diminish as anthropologists augment their interest in population ecology with a special concern for political ecology: how ecological variables present obstacles and opportunities to individuals pursuing their political goals in various structural contexts.

The following sections attempt to illustrate the utility of the structural approach by examining a specific case of state formation: the emergence of the Aztec state in Central Mexico during the fifteenth century. Discussion focuses upon two issues. First, was the warfare that brought the Aztec state into being caused by population growth and a resulting competition for scarce resources, or was it rooted in the internal political dynamics of the prestate polities? Second, did the centralization of authority in Central Mexico occur because political leaders carried out managerial functions, or was it due to new political options suddenly opened by the evolving dynamics of political interaction?

A Case Study: The Aztec State

The choice of the Aztec example deserves some comment. The emergence of the Aztec state clearly is not primary state formation since states already had existed in Central Mexico for fifteen centuries. But neither is the emergence of the Aztec state a case of secondary state formation if this term is reserved for states which arise through trade contacts, warfare, or political alliance with states already in existence. Aztec state formation was the result of interactions among small, autonomous polities within rather narrow geographic confines: the Valley of Mexico and immediately adjoining areas. As I hope to demonstrate, these polities closely resembled developed chiefdoms both in terms of size and internal structure. It is highly probable that the causes and processes which brought the Aztec state into being are analogous to those in operation during cases of primary state formation.

The Aztec case provides an unusually well documented history of the process of state formation. Before Spanish conquest, the Aztecs and their neighbors preserved their political histories through oral transmission and pictorial documents. Many of these histories were recorded in written narratives during the first two centuries after Spanish conquest.[38] They provide the basic data for analysis, but they contain numerous sources of bias. Traditions from one domain tend to inflate the antiquity and splendor of its own past while denigrating all others. Traditions were sometimes revised to cover up the more sordid phases of local history. Those who recorded the histories in postconquest times had their own reasons for doing so: to defend their claims to certain privileges as members of the native nobility or to raise their status in colonial society by extolling the virtues of native civilization. Against all these sources of distortion in the historical record stands the fact that the traditions of several locales have survived, sometimes recorded by more than one individual. Thus, it is often possible to correct the excesses of one source by referring to the others. Together, they provide a fairly coherent outline of the events surrounding Aztec state formation.

The twelfth-century decline of the Toltec state created a vacuum of political power within the Valley of Mexico. This vacuum was filled by a score of small, autonomous, internally unstable and mutually hostile political domains. By the end of the fourteenth century, warfare had resulted in the subordination of some domains to others. Azcapotzalco on the western side of the valley and Texcoco on the eastern side emerged as the two dominant powers (fig. 1), and with the defeat of Texcoco in 1418, Azcapotzalco came to control almost the entire valley. However, Azcapotzalcan hegemony was short-lived. In 1430, a military force assembled by the ruler of Tenochtitlan (a client state of Azcapotzalco) and by the deposed heir of Texcoco defeated Azcapotzalco. In the wake of Azcapotzalco's defeat, the rulers of Tenochtitlan, Texcoco, and Tlacopan (representing the more accommodating nobility of Azcapotzalco) forged a military alliance, quickly consolidated their control over the Valley of Mexico, and began a series of conquests that carried them far beyond the valley. When the Spaniards arrived less than a century later, this Triple Alliance had come to dominate much of Mesoamerica.

The defeat of Azcapotzalco, the formation of the Triple Alliance, and the consolidation of control over the Valley of Mexico together mark the beginning of a new political era. The shifting alliances and endemic warfare that had characterized regional politics previously came to an end. In their place was established a power structure durable enough to withstand severe crop failure, attempted rebellion, and several crises in succession. The birth of the Triple Alliance was accompanied by an acceleration of trends toward the centralization of political authority on the regional level, the widening of the spheres of state concern and regulation, and the expansion of the territory under state control. Thus, the era of Triple Alliance formation is identified as the era of state formation; understanding the events of this era should enhance our ability to understand the forces that bring about major transformations in political structure.

The Valley of Mexico Political System:
The Prestate Structure

Sanders, Parsons, and Santley have characterized the thirteenth and fourteenth centuries in the Valley of Mexico as "a troubled era of struggle and conflict between numerous small polities."[39] It is to the structure of these small polities and their conflicts that I now turn.

By the end of the fourteenth century, as many as fifty small, autonomous domains had been established within the Valley of Mexico.[40] Each contained five thousand to fifty thousand people and covered an area of from eighty to two hundred square kilometers. Each domain was governed by a paramount (*tlatoani*) who ruled by virtue of his membership in the local ruling lineage. Each paramount was surrounded by a group of nobles who assisted in the administration and defense of the domain. This group contained the ruler's own children and the descendants of past

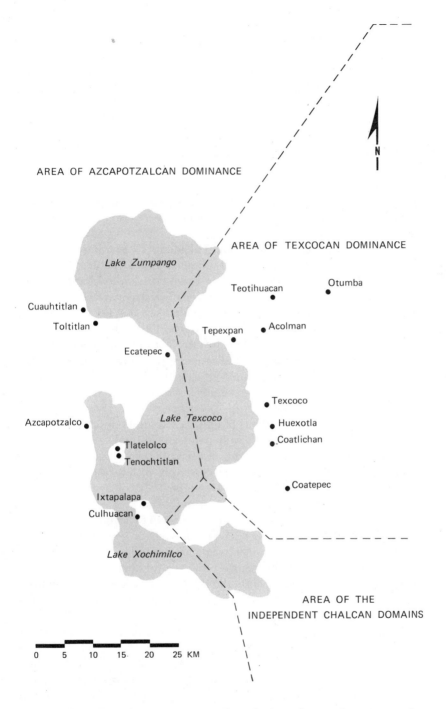

Fig. 1. The Valley of Mexico in 1400 (after Charles Gibson, *The Aztecs Under Spanish Rule* [Stanford: Stanford University Press, 1964], Map 2).

rulers, all of whom were qualified to assume the paramount office, and a number of vassal lords (*teteuctin*) who were ineligible for the paramountcy. Members of the elite stratum probably constituted well under 10 percent of the population in each domain.

The rest of the people were commoners: food producers and craftsmen. In each domain, some commoners resided in close proximity to the ruler's palace in the central town, but others lived in surrounding villages and hamlets. Commoners provided material support to those who governed by laboring in tribute fields and providing domestic service in the palaces and houses of the elite. Commoners were also expected to serve as soldiers in time of war.

These small polities resembled chiefdoms in two important ways. First, each possessed a fairly simple administrative structure. The administrative hierarchy consisted of two or three decision-making levels. The paramount and his noble assistants reached decisions in councils at the highest level; on the lowest level, ward chiefs saw that the decisions were carried out. Vassal lords may have constituted a third (intermediate) level, responsible for the commoners attached to their noble estates. At all levels of administration, specialization of personnal by task was rare. With only minimal horizontal and vertical specialization, the organization of these polities more closely resembles the administrative structure of chiefdoms than states.[41]

Second, like the chiefdoms of eastern Polynesia described by Goldman and Sahlins, these polities were politically unstable.[42] Their histories are marked by numerous incidents of usurpation and regicide. There are also incidents of polities fissioning or simply disintegrating because of internal conflict.[43] This violence is symptomatic of a political system where power is only weakly centralized and authority is easily challenged.

The paramounts of these small polities seem to have used many of the same stratagems employed by Polynesian chiefs to counter the threat of revolt. Paramounts sometimes tried to strengthen political support through the distribution of wealth. In fact, royal liberality seems to have been institutionalized as a part of the ruler's role.[44] Paramounts seem also to have diverted some resources into awesome display. It is hard to say how great an investment was made because not many thirteenth- and fourteenth-century elite residences and temples in the Valley of Mexico have been excavated. But the gradual acceptance of "Toltec" forms of sacrifice, temple building, and royal investiture to replace the less showy "Chichimec" forms may reflect attempts to enhance the authority of office through impressive ritual activity.[45]

Both these stratagems required a ruler to expend wealth from the royal treasury. Hence, the extent to which they could be employed was limited by the size of the ruler's tribute receipts. These could not easily be enlarged because commoners had ways of resisting excessive demands. They might support the efforts of some noble competitor planning revolt. Or, commoners might find relief from a ruler who demanded too much by simply leaving his domain and seeking admittance to another.[46]

Hence, despite the fact that these small Mexican polities were *not* chiefdoms (in the sense that kinship ties between ruler and ruled did not supply the ideological basis for governance), their political instability may have stemmed from similar structural problems. Faced by many noble competitors and restless commoners, paramounts sought to secure their positions by engaging in royal liberality and conspicuous display. But as they increased the tribute burden to finance liberality and display, they also increased the likelihood of popular revolt or desertion and undermined the security they hoped to gain. If anything, the absence of kinship ties between ruler and ruled must have heightened instability in these small polities; if rulers were released from the constraints of the kinship ethic in dealing with commoners so, too, were the commoners in their relations with rulers. Not bound to their rulers by kinship, commoners were free to throw their support to any competitor who gained their confidence. I would argue that the chronic warfare which characterized relations between the small polities in the Valley of Mexico during the thirteenth and fourteenth centuries was rooted in the political quandary rulers faced when dealing with noble competitors and fickle commoners within their domains.

The conquest of a neighboring domain opened two new options for a paramount seeking to secure his position. First, his own close kinsman could be sent to replace the defeated paramount. Establishing such a kinsman as a ruler in his own right might satisfy the ambitions of at least one of the conquering paramount's noble rivals. Alternatively, the conqueror could incorporate the defeated polity into his own domain.[47] This would increase the number of tribute-paying commoners within the conqueror's domain, increase the size of the royal treasury, and increase the ruler's ability to engage in liberality and display without provoking popular revolt or desertion.

Hence, it is possible to view both the internal and external conflicts of the thirteenth- and fourteenth-century domains as rooted in internal political structure. I think this view is preferable to one citing population growth and population pressure as the causes of conflict because, throughout this epoch of conflict, rulers of the small polities consistently practiced a policy of extending a friendly reception to immigrant populations. For example, the ruler of Culhuacan allotted land to Mexica refugees, despite having played a major role in the attack that drove them from their homes barely two years earlier. The fourteenth-century rulers of Texcoco engaged in expansionary warfare, but they also admitted two waves of immigrants to Texcoco, and they tolerated the settling of two new domains within Texcoco's sphere of influence. Groups of immigrants were accommodated in Cuauhtitlan both before and after Cuauhtitlan became embroiled in a prolonged war with its neighbor, Xaltocan. And even as late as the fifteenth century, rulers seem to have desired to maintain or increase the populations of their domains. In two separate incidents, conquering paramounts sent messengers to defeated peoples fleeing their homes to assure them that they would be treated well and to urge them to return.[48]

If population growth had already reached a point of causing resource shortages and conflicts within and between domains, rulers would not have exacerbated the situation by granting still more people access to their local resources. If, on the other hand, rulers were primarily intent upon surviving elite rivalry and commoner discontent, the open reception of immigrants becomes comprehensible. Like the conquest and incorporation of neighboring polities, it would have increased the number of tribute-paying commoners and the ruler's income without increasing the per capita tribute burden.

Warfare intensified during the thirteenth and fourteenth centuries. Its political benefits were always short-lived, and warfare itself created a situation that engendered more warfare. Over time, the nobles established as rulers in their own right gave rise to local dynasties with their own problems of internal conflict. Under the pressure of warfare, paramounts forged military alliances which decreased the number of domains available for incorporation and increased the number of individuals with whom the fruits of conquest had to be shared. Such alliances were often sealed by marriage between ruling lineages, completely intertwining the genealogies of the different ruling houses. This radically undermined the political stability of the small domains. The threat of usurpation became more serious because local nobles could draw support from their kinsmen who ruled in neighboring domains. And it became increasingly difficult to present a united resistance to attacks by outsiders because neighboring rulers bent on conquest could find allies among their kinsmen in the domains under attack. Wars of usurpation within a domain and wars of expansion between domains became different facets of a single phenomenon. I contend that it was the intensification of civil war, invasion, and shifting alliances that finally produced fundamental structural change in the Valley of Mexico political system.

Aztec State Formation: Step One, Collapse of the Prestate Structure

The late thirteenth through fourteenth centuries were a period of militaristic expansionism.[49] Historical accident and local ecology seem to have favored the paramounts of midlatitude domains within the valley. While the rulers of domains in the more densely settled south (e.g., Culhuacan and Xochimilco) struggled to more or less a military stand-off, the rulers of the closely allied domains of Coatlichan-Huexotla-Texcoco in the east and Azcapotzalco-Tlacopan in the west used their numerical superiority to dominate peoples of the less densely populated north.

Through the conquest and incorporation of the northern polities, the sizes of the midlatitude domains increased to the point where they were able to defeat the larger southern communities. In the last years of the fourteenth century, Azcapotzalco defeated the northern domain of Xaltocan, and the scene was set for a final confrontation between Azcapotzalco and its allies in the west and Coatlichan-Huexotla-Texcoco in the east. The eastern powers were routed in 1418, and Azcapotzalco was established as a dominant power in the Valley of Mexico. Structurally, however, the Valley of Mexico political system remained unchanged. Azcapotzalco's hegemony was founded upon an unstable complex of payoffs and alliances similar to those found in the earlier petty kingdoms, and its power soon disintegrated.

During the final year of Tezozomoc's long and successful reign over Azcapotzalco (1343–1426), a dispute arose among the Azcapotzalcan nobility over the preferential treatment given the rulers of Tenochtitlan and Tlatelolco, two of Tezozomoc's principal allies and both his lineal descendants (daughter's son and son's son, respectively). These rulers had enjoyed a reduction in the quantity of tribute they were required to pay the Azcapotzalcan ruler, and both had been named the recipients of tribute gathered from Texcoco, Huexotla, and Cuitlahuac. When Tezozomoc died, the factions of this dispute threw their support to different contenders for Azcapotzalco's paramount office. Maxtla, leader of the anti–Tenochtitlan-Tlatelolco faction and Tezozomoc's eldest son, managed to seize the paramount office, but the rulers of Tenochtitlan and Tlatelolco conspired with Maxtla's younger brother to usurp the throne. Maxtla discovered the plot and ordered the execution of both rulers. However, the structural basis of conflict remained. In 1427, the conflict between Azcapotzalco and Tenochtitlan erupted into open warfare.

Meanwhile, Maxtla lost control of the eastern side of the valley. Taking advantage of the successional disputes in the west, the rulers of Chalco supported the efforts of Nezahualcoyotl, the deposed heir of Texcoco, to recover his domain. This effort was successful. Nezahualcoyotl managed to dispose of his own half brother and expel Azcapotzalco's administrators from the Coatlichan-Huexotla-Texcoco domains. The following year, Nezahualcoyotl and Itzcoatl (the current ruler of Tenochtitlan and Nezahualcoyotl's mother's brother) launched an offensive against

Maxtla and his allies. Azcapotzalco was defeated in 1428. Itzcoatl quickly established control over the western and southern areas of the valley; Nezahualcoyotl reestablished his control in the east (where many of his nobles had rebelled in protest of the alliance with Tenochtitlan). By 1434, the Valley of Mexico was again dominated by a single ruling clique; the paramounts of Tenochtitlan, Texcoco, and Tlacopan had forged the Triple Alliance.

The civil wars, invasions, and shifting alliances that marked the expansion of Azcapotzalco's power and its final disintegration had eliminated the cliquish nobilities of the local domains in the Valley of Mexico (see Appendix 1).[50] Most high-ranking nobles had been assassinated, killed in warfare, or driven into exile, leaving only the low-ranking nobles of ruling families, all of whom had equally weak claims to the local paramount offices. The surviving nobles could only hope to win out against their rivals for local paramount offices by gaining the backing of the Triple Alliance rulers. Because so many high-ranking nobles had died almost simultaneously, throwing kingdom after kingdom into disputes over succession, no other alliances could be forged. Local resistance to Triple Alliance dominance was undermined as these lesser nobles competed with each other for the patronage of Triple Alliance paramounts. The Triple Alliance paramounts took advantage of this situation to strengthen their administrations in ways that had never been possible before. They initiated organizational reforms of real structural significance; the centralization of power on a regional basis was finally feasible. This was the next step in the formation of the Aztec state.

Aztec State Formation: Step Two, Organizational Reform

The principle of rule by a local ruling lineage member was reaffirmed partly as a public relations gesture (Azcapotzalco's hegemony could then be disparaged as a tyranny that had deprived local paramounts of their rightful patrimonies), and partly as a strategem for balancing the power of the nobility within Tenochtitlan, Texcoco, and Tlacopan. Within the Tenochca sphere of influence, however, newly installed local rulers were forced to pay a price for Triple Alliance patronage: they were required to surrender rights to the produce of some of their patrimonial tribute fields to the ruler of Tenochtitlan.[51] This loss of income to local rulers ensured their continued dependence upon the patronage of Triple Alliance rulers and, at the same time, augmented the ability of Triple Alliance rulers to control their own nobles.

In Tenochtitlan, loyal nobles were rewarded not with administration of entire domains which might serve as a basis for the accumulation of power, but with the receipts of expropriated tribute fields allotted on a field-by-field basis. Tenochtitlan's ruler retained the majority of the fields for the support of the throne, but many others were distributed to individual nobles, specifically, the ruler's dynastic competitors: his sons, brothers, and the descendants of previous rulers.[52] Thus, the ruler acquired wealth in excess of his nobles, and nobles came to share an interest in the perpetuation of Triple Alliance hegemony, which would defend their access to tribute from the newly expropriated fields.

The distribution of tribute fields was determined by criteria of achievement in warfare as well as royal descent. This may have been a useful device for limiting the number of nobles who could put forward a legitimate claim to royal liberality, thus husbanding the paramount's wealth. It may also have created a division of interest among the nobles, preventing them from confronting the ruler as a unified class. At any rate, this distinction between nobles who had demonstrated military prowess and those who had not was formalized shortly after the defeat of Azcapotzalco by the award of honorary titles to distinguished noble warriors.[53]

At this time, too, the threat of usurpation by higher-ranking nobles was reduced by the creation of a four-member royal council.[54] The members of this council were to share in the ruler's executive decision making, and all future rulers of Tenochtitlan were to be selected from among the council incumbents rather than from the nobility at large. In the first council, membership was conferred upon the four men most likely to succeed: two of the paramount's brothers, and two sons of an earlier ruler of Tenochtitlan. Thus, four major collateral lines of the Tenochca nobility were given a voice in high-level decision making and prospects of succeeding to the paramount office. As designated heirs apparent, each of the council members would have jealously guarded against efforts by any of the other three to usurp rule.

Thus, the birth of Triple Alliance hegemony in the Valley of Mexico was accompanied by extensive and significant organizational reform. The reforms allocated administrative and economic power in ways that would ensure continuation of the political status quo. They did little to enhance the efficient flow of information to and the decision-making capability of the state. The administration of Tenochtitlan continued to be provided by a two-level hierarchy. The paramount and his nobles formulated policy; the ward chiefs carried it out. Communication between the paramount and the ward chiefs was effected by nobles who served as messengers of the paramount on an ad hoc basis. Regional administration did involve a three-level hierarchy; the policy decisions of the Triple Alliance paramounts were communicated to subordinate local rulers, and these rulers were expected to mobilize their own populations through communication with their ward chiefs. Still, there was little specialization of administrative personnel by task.[55] True bureaucratic complexity did not emerge until some thirty years after the formation of the Triple Alliance, as the state began to consolidate its power by monitoring a greater range of activities.

Aztec State Formation: Step Three, Consolidation of Power

Almost immediately after establishing control over the Valley of Mexico, the Triple Alliance initiated large-scale public works within the valley and expansionary conquests beyond. The last years of Itzcoatl's reign in Tenochtitlan were marked by the construction of a causeway linking Tenochtitlan with towns on the shore of Lake Xochimilco and by the conquest of towns in Morelos and northern Guerrero, more than one hundred kilometers south of the Valley of Mexico.[56] Itzcoatl's successor, Moctezuma I (1440–69), sponsored a major renovation of Huitzilopochtli's temple in Tenochtitlan and the construction of an extensive royal residence, of a dike spanning Lake Texcoco, of a canal that facilitated access to the market at Tlatelolco, and of an aqueduct that brought fresh water to Tenochtitlan from Chapultepec. Moctezuma's reign was also marked by ceaseless military activity. New conquests were made in Morelos, northern Guerrero, southern Hidalgo, the Valley of Oaxaca, Puebla, and Veracruz.[57]

Much if not all of this activity seems to have been intended to solidify Triple Alliance power within the Valley of Mexico. As Tenochtitlan's population grew, the size of the army it could field against potentially rebellious neighbors increased and its dominance of the valley became more secure. The construction of causeways, canals, and aqueducts facilitated the transport of food and water to Tenochtitlan so that the city's population could grow and its political superiority be maintained. The causeways and aqueducts also served as dikes that defended the city's population from floods, and they enabled the Aztecs to control water levels in the southern lake beds so that the entire area could be reclaimed for agricultural production.[58] Lake-bed agriculture came to supply over half of the food consumed by Tenochtitlan's population, and reclaimed agricultural land was used to satisfy the nobility's demand for individually allocated tribute receipts.[59]

Conquest and tribute extraction from an ever-expanding area were also useful in maintaining Tenochtitlan's demographic preeminence in the Valley of Mexico. Tribute in foodstuffs from nearby provinces supplied another third of the food consumed by the city, and nonfood tribute goods such as cloth and obsidian apparently were circulated through the regional market system, which encouraged food production for market sale by the valley's rural populance.[60]

Moctezuma's conquests also included many towns that paid tribute

primarily in luxury products and raw materials.[61] These conquests seem
to have been made to enable the Triple Alliance paramounts to satisfy the
demand of nobles and subject rulers for high prestige items. Such goods
were acquired directly, through the extraction of tribute in finished
goods, and indirectly, through the extraction of tribute in valuable raw
materials that were converted into finished goods by Aztec craftsmen
working under royal patronage. Luxury goods were also acquired through
state-sponsored, long-distance trade, where goods procured through tribute extraction and the patronage of craftsmen were exchanged for goods
originating in areas beyond the sphere of Triple Alliance conquests.[62]
State involvement in the procurement and distribution of high prestige
goods may well have discouraged Tenochtitlan's nobility and the nobles of
subject city-states from disrupting the existing power structure.[63]

Aztec State Formation: Step Four, Bureaucratic Complexity

The initiation of public works and militaristic expansionism was accompanied by the gradual development of bureaucratic complexity. Although the native histories do not provide a step-by-step account of the
process of bureaucratic elaboration, several sources indicate that significant administrative reforms were made during the reign of Moctezuma
I. For example, Torquemada states that Moctezuma "ordered his house
with great majesty, naming many and diverse officials and . . . increasing the number of priests and instituting some new positions and
ceremonies."[64]

Tezozomoc remarks upon several stages in the growth of administrative complexity in the area of tribute collection.[65] Individuals responsible for the collection and storage of tribute (the *calpixque*) were at first
selected by and responsible to the subordinate rulers of Moctezuma's
domain. But by 1458, Moctezuma had assumed personal responsibility
for naming these officials and had instituted an arrangement of double
staffing where two *calpixque* were appointed for each tribute-paying locale: one stationed at the site of tribute collection, the other stationed in
Tenochtitlan, the site of tribute receipt. By 1462, the office of chief steward (*petlacalcatl*) had been established as a middle-level administrative
post to supervise the performance of all the *calpixque* and to issue orders
to them on Moctezuma's behalf.

Durán credits Moctezuma with having reformed the judicial system.[66] Separate courts were established for nobles and commoners, and a
high court was formed to which lower court decisions could be appealed.
Moctezuma is also said to have instituted a set of sumptuary laws, among
them an ordinance limiting the access of various persons to the different
rooms in Moctezuma's palace. It is clear from Sahagún's description of

Tenochtitlan's royal residence that different rooms housed different segments of the ruler's administrative bureaucracy: the royal council and high court, the lower courts, various grades of military personnel, the constabulary, the heads of the young men's houses of the various wards, the *petlacalcatl*, the *calpixque*, etc.[67] Hence, Moctezuma's sumptuary ordinance may mark the formal inception of discrete, functionally specific branches of administrative bureaucracy.

Ecology, Structure, and State Formation: Some Conclusions

Aztec state formation seems to have occurred in four logically discrete steps:

1. intensification of competition within and between petty kingdoms that broke the power of local rulers and led to Triple Alliance hegemony within the Valley of Mexico;
2. centralization of power through organizational reforms that reduced the economic and political power of subordinate rulers and Tenochtitlan's nobility;
3. consolidation of power through the initiation of public works within the valley and expansionary conquests beyond it;
4. development of bureaucratic complexity characterized by the specialization of administrative personnel by task and by the presence of three or more levels of decision makers in many of the administrative branches.

These steps represent a temporal order of change; each step was made feasible by the transformation that preceded it.

The intensification of competition within and between petty kingdoms was crucial to the entire process of Aztec state formation; it created conditions conducive to political centralization. The flurry of shifting alliances, conquests, and acts of usurpation that accompanied the expansion and final collapse of Azcapotzalco's power virtually eliminated by death or exile the higher-ranking nobility of many petty kingdoms. Political coalitions at the local level were destroyed; networks of kinship alliance between local ruling lineages were disrupted.

Consequently the patronage of Triple Alliance rulers became a critical political resource for the low-ranking nobles seeking access to local offices of rule, and they sought such patronage even though it entailed constraints on their political autonomy and a reduction in their incomes. The decrease in the power of local paramounts was paralleled by an increase in the power of Triple Alliance rulers. In Tenochtitlan, the loyalty of local nobles was secured by increasing the scale of royal generosity.

Through the allocation of tribute fields and other gifts, nobles came to share an interest in the perpetuation of Triple Alliance hegemony, the source of their newly gained wealth.

Access to the labor power of the large majority of commoners residing within the Valley of Mexico helped the Triple Alliance rulers consolidate their power. The construction of public works and expansionary conquests increased the lands and wealth that could be redistributed to local nobles and the compliant rulers of subordinate domains. Moreover, as the Triple Alliance came to dominate the entire valley, commoners could no longer escape the intensification of corvee obligations by moving to some nearby independent kingdom. Expansion of the political domain had finally provided a solution to the structural weakness that had undermined the power of rulers in the earlier autonomous kingdoms.

With greater political leverage, larger tribute receipts, and more labor at their disposal, the Triple Alliance rulers moved to expand the spheres of state concern.[68] Bureaucratic complexity developed in the wake of this expansion.

Without question, ecological variables were implicated in many stages of Aztec state formation. The early importance of Azcapotzalco and Texcoco was probably related to distribution of population within the valley during the twelfth through fourteenth centuries, and this distribution was almost certainly affected by variation in agricultural productivity. The overall agricultural productivity of the Valley of Mexico was also of critical importance. It sustained a great enough aggregate population to enable Triple Alliance rulers to engage in public works and expansionary conquest. Had it not, the consolidation of Triple Alliance power might have been impossible, and the opportunity for state formation brought about by the death and exile of local elites might have been lost. The proximity of the potentially fertile lake bed in the southern valley and the ability to provision Tenochtitlan through waterborne transport supported urban growth, thereby strengthening Tenochtitlan's military capability.

Also without question, Moctezuma's bureaucracy played an active role in the management of numerous ecological variables. It carried out many activities (food storage, flood control, etc.) that protected the population of the Valley of Mexico from life-threatening environmental fluctuations. The development of new agricultural lands, the importation of foodstuffs to the valley in the form of tribute assessments, and the stimulation of rural food production within the valley through the introduction of nonfood tribute into the regional marketing system supported population growth. By the time of Spanish conquest, the population of the Valley of Mexico was roughly four times that of any previous period of the prehistoric epoch.[69] There is little doubt that the Aztec state came to perform many of the ecological functions that those taking the ecological approach would expect of such powerful, bureaucratic political systems. Clearly, then, ecological variables are deeply implicated in the process of statemaking, and an "appropriate" ecological setting constitutes a necessary condition for state formation. This conclusion has been reached by others, and the present analysis confirms their work.[70]

But the evidence at hand does not confirm either of the two existing models of state emergence through gradual improvement in ecological management by prestate political systems. Service, for example, suggests that effective ecological management strengthens the legitimacy of political leaders in the eyes of the governed and so contributes to the centralization of political power.[71] Service envisions a gradual, "bottom-up" development of political authority; the authority of local rulers increases progressively and then gives way to the concentration of authority at the regional level. However, the Aztec data present a rather different picture. First, authority on the local level was weakened as the conflict within and between petty kingdoms intensified (possibly impairing the managerial effectiveness of local rulers); this paved the way for the institution of centralized power on the regional level. Second, the centralization of power on the regional level was brought about by the collusion of local rulers in a centralized system of political patronage; the legitimacy of regional rulers in the eyes of the commoners was largely irrelevant to the process.

Sanders and Price have offered a somewhat different model.[72] They suggest that, among an array of competing local polities, some will possess both greater ecological resources and more statelike (and therefore more effective) structures of political administration. As populations grow and competition over resources increases, the more statelike domains conquer and incorporate the less statelike domains with the eventual emergence of true states on the regional level. However, the Aztec data suggest that the communities responsible for the defeat of Azcapotzalco and the foundation of the Triple Alliance enjoyed no significant advantages in organizational effectiveness at the time of their triumph. On the contrary, real improvement in the organizational effectiveness of the Aztec state dates to Moctezuma's bureaucratic reforms, a generation or two *after* the state had come into being.

In ecological approaches to state formation, there has been a tendency to focus exclusively upon the implications of ecological variables for human populations as whole entities. The structural approach to state formation redirects attention to the implications of ecological variables for prestate political orders specifically. This narrower focus is valuable because political consequences cannot be automatically derived from population status—a point which is sometimes recognized but rarely elaborated upon in ecological analyses of state formation.[73] Ecologically minded anthropologists, taking whole populations as their unit analysis, have not provided a satisfactory answer to the question of how ecological opportunity or necessity is translated into political change. But such an answer is crucial to an adequate understanding of the process of state formation. As Cowgill notes,

> We can never assume that stress . . . will automatically or even typically generate social or cultural development. . . . We always have to ask, *who* is experiencing stress, *who* is in a position to do something about it, and *why* might they see it to be in their interest to do what they do?[74]

Perhaps the conclusion to be drawn from this discussion is not that anthropologists need less ecology in their efforts to understand state formation, but that they need to focus more sharply upon the interplay of ecological variables and political dynamics. Anthropologists need to understand the goals of political actors as generated by different types of prestate political systems, and they need to be able to define how ecological variables present obstacles and opportunities to political actors pursuing their goals. From such studies, it should eventually be possible to derive a general theory of state formation, one that specifies the necessary ecological and political conditions under which state formation occurs.

APPENDIX

Local Dynasties Disrupted by Warfare and Intrigue, 1400–1431

Acolman
1427   Teyolcocoatzin deposed in battle with Nezahualcoyotl.
1431   Succeeded by his son, under mandate of Nezahualcoyotl.

Azcapotzalco
1426   Tezozomoc dies from natural causes. His older son, Maxtla, usurps the rule from the designated heir, his younger brother.
1428   Maxtla deposed in battle with Itzcoatl and Nezahualcoyotl. Azcapotzalco is left without a legitimate local ruler for at least sixteen years.

Coatepec
1418   Totomihua flees his domain after conquest by Tezozomoc.
1427   Totomihua returns to power with Nezahualcoyotl's victory in Texcoco.
1430   Totomihua flees his domain again after an unsuccessful revolt against Nezahualcoyotl. Coatepec is left without a legitimate local ruler.

Coatlichan
1418   Paynitzin flees his domain after conquest by Tezozomoc.

1420   Succeeded by Quetzalmaquitztli, Tezozomoc's grandson.
1427   Quetzalmaquitztli killed in battle with Nezahualcoyotl. Succeeded by Motoliniatzin, a member of Coatlichan's local nobility.
1430   Motoliniatzin flees his domain after an unsuccessful revolt against Nezahualcoyotl.
1431   Motoliniatzin pardoned and returned to rule by Nezahualcoyotl.

Cuauhtitlan
1408   Xaltemoctzin killed by order of Tezozomoc of Azcapotzalco.
1418   Succeeded by Tezozomoc, a noble from Tlatelolco.
1430   Tezozomoc of Cuauhtitlan commits suicide when Cuauhtitlan is razed by Maxtla. Succeeded by Tecocohuatzin, a member of Cuauhtitlan's local nobility and an ally of Itzcoatl.

Culhuacan
1413   Nauhyotzin killed by order of Tezozomoc. Succeeded by Acoltzin.
1429   Acoltzin killed in battle. Succeeded by his son, Xilomantzin.

Huexotla
1418   Tlacotzin (=Itlacauhtzin ?) flees his domain after conquest by Tezozomoc. Huexotla is left without a legitimate local ruler.
1427   Itlacauhtzin brought to power by Nezahualcoyotl's victory in Texcoco.
1430   Itlacauhtzin flees his domain after an unsuccessful revolt against Nezahualcoyotl.
1431   Succeeded by his son, under mandate of Nezahualcoyotl.

Otumba
1418   Quetzalcuixtli sides with Tezozomoc, retains his rule after Tezozomoc's conquest of Texcoco.
1431   Replaced by Quechotecpantzin, under mandate of Nezahualcoyotl.

Tenochtitlan
1426   Chimalpopoca assassinated. Succeeded by Itzcoatl, his father's brother.

Teotihuacan
1418   Quetzalmamatlictzin flees his domain after conquest by Tezozomoc.
1431   Quetzalmamatlictzin returns to power, under mandate of Nezahualcoyotl.

Tepexpan
1426   Incumbent ruler killed in battle.
1431   Successor installed under mandate of Nezahualcoyotl.

Texcoco
1418   Ixtlilxochitl killed in battle with Tezozomoc. Texcoco is left without a legitimate local ruler.
1426   Yancuiltzin, Nezahualcoyotl's half brother, comes to rule under mandate of Maxtla, Yancuiltzin's uncle.

1427 Yancuiltzin flees his domain after Nezahualcoyotl's victory. Succeeded by Nezahualcoyotl.

Tlatelolco
1427 Tlacateotzin assassinated. Succeeded by Cuauhtlatoatzin, his son's son.

Toltitlan
1428 Epcoatl dies in battle. Toltitlan is left without a legitimate local ruler for the next twenty years.

Ecatepec and Ixtapalapa
1428 A dynasty of Aztec lineage is established at Ecatepec.
1430 A dynasty of Aztec lineage is established at Ixtapalapa. The founding of these two dynasties suggests the disruption of local ruling lineages in both these domains.

NOTES

This essay is the outgrowth of questions formulated during a 1972 study group on the Aztecs. I thank the other participants of that group (Charles Gibson, Elinor Melville, Judith Nowack, and Jeffrey Parsons) for creating an atmosphere where half-baked ideas were sent back to the kitchen, not relegated to the garbage heap. I also have benefited from lively discussions on state origins with Gayle Rubin and Henry Wright. Charles Bright and Susan Harding gave constant encouragement while I was writing this essay; they and Lynn Eden offered very acute comments on earlier drafts. I am grateful for their help.

1. Marshall D. Sahlins, *Tribesmen* (Englewood Cliffs, N.J.: Prentice-Hall, 1968), pp. 4–7; Roger M. Keesing, *Cultural Anthropology: A Contemporary Perspective* (New York: Holt, Rinehart and Winston, 1976), p. 348; Norman Yoffee, "The Decline and Rise of Mesopotamian Civilization: An Ethnoarchaeological Perspective on the Evolution of Social Complexity," *American Antiquity* 44 (January, 1979): 5–35; Gregory A. Johnson, *Local Exchange and Early State Development in Southwestern Iran*, Anthropological Papers, No. 51 (Ann Arbor: University of Michigan Museum of Anthropology, 1973), pp. 1–4; Henry T. Wright, "Toward an Explanation of the Origin of the State," in *Origins of the State: The Anthropology of Political Evolution*, ed. Ronald Cohen and Elman R. Service (Philadelphia: Institute for the Study of Human Issues, 1978), pp. 49–68.
2. Julian H. Steward, "Cultural Causality and Law: A Trial Formulation of the Development of Early Civilization," *American Anthropologist* 51 (January–March, 1949): 1–27; Karl Wittfogel, *Oriental Despotism: A Comparative Study of Total Power* (New Haven: Yale University Press, 1957).
3. Richard McC. Adams, "Early Civilizations, Subsistence, and Environment," in *City Invincible*, ed. D. Kraeling and R. Adams (Chicago: Oriental Institute, 1960), pp. 260–95; Robert L. Carneiro, "A Theory of the Origin of the

State," *Science* 169 (August 21, 1970): 733–38; Kwang-chih Chang, *The Archaeology of Ancient China* (New Haven: Yale University Press, 1963), p. 316; René Millon, *Urbanization at Teotihuacan, Mexico: The Teotihuacan Map* (Austin: University of Texas Press, 1973), pp. 47–49.

4. Conrad P. Kottak, "Ecological Variables in the Origin and Evolution of African States: The Buganda Example," *Comparative Studies in Society and History* 14 (July, 1972): 351–80; William T. Sanders, "The Central Mexican Symbiotic Region," in *Prehistoric Settlement Patterns in the New World*, ed. Gordon R. Willey, Viking Fund Publication in Anthropology, No. 23 (New York: Wenner-Gren Foundation for Anthropological Research, 1956), pp. 115–27; William T. Sanders, "Hydraulic Agriculture, Economic Symbiosis, and the Evolution of States in Central Mexico," in *Anthropological Archaeology in the Americas*, ed. Betty J. Meggers (Washington, D.C.: Anthropological Society of Washington, 1968), pp. 88–107.

5. Frank Hole, "Investigating the Origins of Mesopotamian Civilization," *Science* 153 (August 5, 1966): 605–11; William L. Rathje, "The Origin and Development of Lowland Classic Maya Civilization," *American Antiquity* 36 (July, 1971): 275–85.

6. Henry T. Wright, *The Administration of Rural Production in an Early Mesopotamian Town*, Anthropological Papers, No. 38 (Ann Arbor: University of Michigan Museum of Anthropology, 1969).

7. William T. Sanders and Barbara J. Price, *Mesoamerica: The Evolution of a Civilization* (New York: Random House, 1968); Carneiro, "A Theory of the Origin of the State"; David Webster, "Warfare and the Evolution of the State: A Reconsideration," *American Antiquity* 40 (October, 1975): 464–70; Robert S. Santley, "Disembedded Capitals Reconsidered," *American Antiquity* 45 (January, 1980): 132–45.

8. Henry T. Wright and Gregory A. Johnson, "Population, Exchange, and Early State Formation in Southwestern Iran," *American Anthropologist* 77 (June, 1975): 267–89.

9. Stephen J. Athens, "Theory Building and the Study of Evolutionary Process in Complex Societies," in *For Theory Building in Archaeology*, ed. Lewis R. Binford (New York: Academic Press, 1977), pp. 353–84.

10. Robert McC. Adams, *The Evolution of Urban Society: Early Mesopotamia and Prehispanic Mexico* (Chicago: Aldine, 1966); Kent V. Flannery, "The Cultural Evolution of Civilizations," *Annual Review of Ecology and Systematics* 3 (1972): 399–426; Michael H. Logan and William T. Sanders, "The Model," in *The Valley of Mexico: Studies in Pre-Hispanic Ecology and Society*, ed. Eric R. Wolf (Albuquerque: University of New Mexico Press, 1976), pp. 31–58; Wright, "Toward an Explanation of the Origin of the State."

11. Flannery, "The Cultural Evolution of Civilizations."

12. Steward, "Cultural Causality and Law," p. 19; Sanders and Price, *Mesoamerica*, p. 230; Carneiro, "A Theory of the Origin of the State," pp. 735–36; Kottak, "Ecological Variables in the Origin and Evolution of African States," p. 368; Logan and Sanders, "The Model," p. 33; Athens, "Theory Building

and the Study of Evolutionary Process in Complex Societies," p. 366; Santley, "Disembedded Capitals Reconsidered," p. 141.

13. Adams, *The Evolution of Urban Society*, p. 44; Wright and Johnson, "Population, Exchange, and Early State Formation in Southwestern Iran," p. 276; Elizabeth Brumfiel, "Regional Growth in the Eastern Valley of Mexico: A Test of the 'Population Pressure' Hypothesis," in *The Early Mesoamerican Village*, ed. Kent V. Flannery (New York: Academic Press, 1976), pp. 234–49; Conrad P. Kottak, "The Process of State Formation in Madagascar," *American Ethnologist* 4 (February, 1977): 136–55; Stephen A. Kowalewski, "Population-Resource Balances in Period I of Oaxaca, Mexico," *American Antiquity* 45 (January, 1980): 151–65; and possibly David O'Connor, "A Regional Population in Egypt to Circa 600 B.C.," in *Population Growth: Anthropological Implications*, ed. Brian Spooner (Cambridge, Mass.: MIT Press, 1972), pp. 78–100.

14. For example, see accounts of agricultural intensification among the Lowland Maya in Peter D. Harrison and B. L. Turner II, eds., *Pre-Hispanic Maya Agriculture* (Albuquerque: University of New Mexico Press, 1978); Ray T. Matheny, "Maya Lowland Hydraulic Systems," *Science* 193 (August 20, 1976): 639–46; Kent V. Flannery, ed., *Maya Subsistence: Studies in Memory of Dennis E. Puleston* (New York: Academic Press, 1982).

15. Steward, "Cultural Causality and Law," p. 19; Sanders and Price, *Mesoamerica*, pp. 96–97; Carneiro, "A Theory of the Origin of the State," pp. 735–36; Webster, "Warfare and the Evolution of the State," pp. 466–67; Logan and Sanders, "The Model," p. 33; Santley, "Disembedded Capitals Reconsidered," p. 141.

16. Yoffee, "The Decline and Rise of Mesopotamian Civilization," pp. 26–27.

17. Elman R. Service, *Origins of the State and Civilization* (New York: W. W. Norton, 1975), p. 308.

18. J. Friedman and M. J. Rowlands, "Notes Towards an Epigenetic Model of the Evolution of 'Civilisation'," in *The Evolution of Social Systems*, ed. J. Friedman and M. J. Rowlands (Pittsburgh: University of Pittsburgh Press, 1978), pp. 201–76, esp. p. 204.

19. For example, Keesing, *Cultural Anthropology*, p. 223, speculates that the course of cultural change might be partially determined by the "unfolding or progressive development of a particular people's conceptual system." Friedman offers an intriguing model of how nonegalitarian social systems, and eventually the state, might arise from specific cultural definitions of descent, marriage alliance, and ancestor worship (Jonathan Friedman, "Tribes, States, and Transformation," in *Marxist Analyses and Social Anthropology*, ed. Maurice Bloch [New York: John Wiley and Sons, 1975], pp. 161–202). Conrad has attributed the expansion of the Chimu and Inca states to Andean conceptions of ancestor worship and the norm of split inheritance arising from this tradition (Geoffrey W. Conrad, "Cultural Materialism, Split Inheritance, and the Expansion of Ancient Peruvian Empires," *American Antinquity* 46 [January, 1981]: 3–26). Such approaches to state formation seem to grant too

great an autonomy and determinism to socially held conceptual systems, though Sahlins has argued that conceptual systems are endowed with just autonomy and determinism (Marshall Sahlins, *Culture and Practical Reason* [Chicago: University of Chicago Press, 1976]).

20. Frederick Engels, *The Origin of the Family, Private Property, and the State,* ed. E. Reed, trans. R. Vernon (1884; New York: Pathfinder, 1972).

21. I. M. Diakonoff, "The Rise of the Despotic State in Ancient Mesopotamia," in *Ancient Mesopotamia,* ed. I. M. Diakonoff (Moscow: Nauka Press, 1969), pp. 173–203; Morton H. Fried, *The Evolution of Political Society* (New York: Random House, 1967); Morton H. Fried, "The State, the Chicken, and the Egg; or, What Came First?" in *Origins of the State,* ed. Ronald Cohen and Elman R. Service (Philadelphia: Institute for the Study of Human Issues, 1978), pp. 35–47.

22. Service, *Origins of the State and Civilization,* pp. 282–86.

23. Karl Wittfogel, "Developmental Aspects of Hydraulic Societies," in *Irrigation Civilizations: A Comparative Study,* ed. Julian H. Steward et al., Social Science Monographs, No. 1. (Washington, D.C.: Pan American Union, 1955), pp. 43–52; Pedro Carrasco, "Introducción," in *Estratificación Social en la Mesoamérica Prehispánica,* ed. Pedro Carrasco and Johana Broda (México, D.F.: Instituto Nacional de Antropología e Historia, 1976), pp. 7–13; Pedro Carrasco, "La economía del México prehispánico," in *Economía Política e Ideología en el México Prehispánico,* ed. Pedro Carrasco and Johana Broda (México, D.F.: Editorial Nueva Imagen, 1978), pp. 15–76; Eric R. Wolf, "The Mills of Inequality: A Marxian Approach," in *Social Inequality: Comparative and Developmental Approaches,* ed. Gerald D. Berreman (New York: Academic Press, 1981), pp. 41–57; but see Jerome A. Offner, "On the Inapplicability of 'Oriental Despotism' and the 'Asiatic Mode of Production' to the Aztecs of Texcoco," *American Antiquity* 46 (January, 1981): 43–61.

24. Elman R. Service, "Classical and Modern Theories of the Origins of Government," in *Origins of the State,* ed. Ronald Cohen and Elman R. Service (Philadelphia: Institute for the Study of Human Issues, 1978), pp. 21–34.

25. S. N. Eisenstadt, *The Political Systems of Empires* (New York: Free Press, 1963), pp. vii–viii; J. Rounds, "Lineage, Class, and Power in the Aztec State," *American Ethnologist* 6 (February, 1979): 73–86; Herbert S. Lewis, "Warfare and the Origin of the State," in *The Study of the State,* ed. H. J. M. Claessen and P. Skalnik (The Hague: Mouton, 1981), pp. 210–21. Also see Robbins Burling, *The Passage of Power* (New York: Academic Press, 1974), pp. 6–9.

26. M. Fortes and E. E. Evans-Pritchard, *African Political Systems* (London: Oxford University Press, 1940), p. 11; Lloyd A. Fallers, *Bantu Bureaucracy: A Century of Political Evolution Among the Basoga of Uganda* (Chicago: University of Chicago Press, 1956), p. 247; Max Gluckman, *Custom and Conflict in Africa* (New York: Barnes and Noble, 1956), pp. 42–45; Marshall D. Sahlins, *Stone Age Economics* (Chicago: Aldine, 1972), pp. 145–48; Mary W. Helms, *Ancient Panama: Chiefs in Search of Power* (Austin: University of Texas Press, 1979), p. 28.

27. Jack Goody, "Introduction," in *Succession to High Office*, ed. Jack Goody (Cambridge: Cambridge University Press), pp. 1–56.

28. Sahlins, *Tribesmen*, p. 92.

29. See Irving Goldman, *Ancient Polynesian Society* (Chicago: University of Chicago Press, 1970); and Webster, "Warfare and the Evolution of the State."

30. Fallers, *Bantu Bureaucracy*, p. 247.

31. Competition for office is considered to be a primary cause of structural change in prestate political systems in two recent analyses: Burling, *The Passage of Power*, and Friedman and Rowlands, "Notes Towards an Epigenetic Model of the Evolution of 'Civilisation'."

32. Webster, "Warfare and the Evolution of the State"; Lewis, "Warfare and the Origin of the State"; Friedman and Rowlands, "Notes Towards an Epigenetic Model of the Evolution of 'Civilisation',"; Elizabeth M. Brumfiel, "Ecological Theories of the Origin of the State: A Critique and a Possible Alternative" (Paper presented at the Annual Meeting of the American Anthropological Association, Washington, D.C., November, 1976).

33. Timothy Earle, *Economic and Social Organization of a Complex Chiefdom: The Halelea District, Kauai'i Hawaii*, Anthropological Papers, No. 63 (Ann Arbor: University of Michigan Museum of Anthropology, 1978).

34. Ronald Cohen, "Introduction," in *Origins of the State*, ed. Ronald Cohen and Elman R. Service (Philadelphia: Institute for the Study of Human Issues, 1978), pp. 1–20.

35. Friedman and Rowlands, "Notes Towards an Epigenetic Model of the Evolution of 'Civilisation'," p. 203.

36. Friedman, "Tribes, States, and Transformation."

37. Sahlins, *Tribesmen*, p. 93; Earle, *Economic and Social Organization of a Complex Chiefdom*, pp. 172–73.

38. Charles Gibson, "A Survey of Middle American Prose Manuscripts in the Native Historical Tradition," in *Guide to Ethnohistorical Sources, Part Four*, ed. Howard F. Cline, vol. 15 of *Handbook of Middle American Indians*, Robert Wauchope, gen. ed. (Austin: University of Texas Press, 1975), pp. 311–21.

39. William T. Sanders, Jeffrey R. Parsons, and Robert S. Santley, *The Basin of Mexico: Ecological Processes in the Evolution of a Civilization* (New York: Academic Press, 1979), p. 150.

40. This description draws from the following: Pedro Carrasco, "Social Organization of Ancient Mexico," in *Archaeology of Northern Mesoamerica, Part One*, ed. Gordon Ekholm and Ignacio Bernal, vol. 10 of *Handbook of Middle American Indians*, Robert Wauchope, gen. ed. (Austin: University of Texas Press, 1971), pp. 349–75; Carrasco, "La economía del México prehispánico"; J. Rounds "The Role of the Tecuhtli in Ancient Aztec Society," *Ethnohistory* 24 (Fall, 1977): 343–61; "Carta de los caciques e indios naturales de Suchimilco a Su Magestad . . . (2 de Mayo de 1563)," *Colección de Documentos Inéditos . . . de Indias*, vol. 13 (Madrid: José María Perez, 1870), pp. 293–301; Federic Hicks, "Tetzcoco in the Early 16th Century: The State, the City and the *Calpolli*," *American Ethnologist* 9 (May, 1982): 230–49; Jerome A. Off-

ner, "A Reassessment of the Extent and Structuring of the Empire of Techotlalazin, Fourteenth Century Ruler of Texcoco," *Ethnohistory* 26 (Summer, 1979): 231–41; Sanders, "Hydraulic Agriculture, Economic Symbiosis, and the Evolution of States in Central Mexico"; Sanders, Parsons, and Santley, *The Basin of Mexico.*

41. Johnson, *Local Exchange and Early State Development in Southwestern Iran*, pp. 2–3.

42. Goldman, *Ancient Polynesian Society*; Sahlins, *Tribesmen.*

43. "Anales de Cuauhtitlan," in *Códice Chimalpopoca*, trans. Primo Feliciano Velázquez, 1–118 (México, D.F.: Universidad Nacional Autónoma de México, 1945 [1570]), pp. 29, 32; Domingo Francisco de San Antón Muñon Chimalpahin Cuauhtlehuanitzin, *Relaciones Originales de Chalco Amaquemecan*, trans. Silvia Rendón (México, D.F.: Fondo de Cultura Económica, 1965 [ca. 1606–3]), pp. 177–78, 189, 197, 198, 199; Nigel Davies, *The Toltec Heritage: From the Fall of Tula to the Rise of Tenochtitlan* (Norman: University of Oklahoma Press, 1980), p. 19; Eulalia Guzmán, "Un manuscrito de la colección Boturini que trata de los antiguos señores de Teotihuacán," *Ethnos* 3 (July-September, 1938): 89–103, esp. p. 92; Fernando de Alva Ixtlilxochitl, *Obras Históricas*, ed. E. O'Gorman, 2 vols. (México, D.F.: Universidad Nacional Autónoma de México, Instituto de Investigaciones Históricas, 1975–77 [ca. 1600–1640]), 1:309; "Relación de genealogía y linaje de los Señores . . . de la Nueva España," in *Nueva Colección de Documentos Para la Historia de México*, vol. 3, ed. J. Garcia Icazbalceta (México, D.F.: n.p., 1891 [ca. 1532]), pp. 263–81, esp. pp. 271, 274.

44. Ixtlilxochitl, *Obras Históricas*, 1:334, 2:76; "Anales de Cuauhtitlan," p. 35.

45. "Anales de Cuauhtitlan," pp. 30–31; Ixtlilxochitl, *Obras Históricas*, 1:332, 2:35.

46. "Anales de Cuauhtitlan," p. 29; Ixtlilxochitl, *Obras Históricas*, 2:21–22; "Relación de genealogía," p. 274; Hicks, "Tetzcoco in the Early 16th Century," p. 243.

47. Chimalpahin, *Relaciones Originales de Chalco Amaquemecan*, pp. 90–91; Ixtlilxochitl, *Obras Históricas*, 1:313–14, 318, 346–47.

48. "Anales de Cuauhtitlan," pp. 22, 29–30; Ixtlilxochitl, *Obras Históricas*, 1:315–18, 318–19, 323, 379, 2:32, 34, 37; Francisco de Paso y Troncoso, *Papeles de Nueva España*, 9 vols. (México, D.F.: Establecimiento tip. Sucesores de Rivadeneyra, 1905–48), 6:233; Hernando Alvarado Tezozomoc, "Crónica Mexicana," in *Crónica Mexicana-Códice Ramirez*, ed. M. Orozco y Berra (México, D.F.: Editorial Porrua, 1975 [1609]), pp. 223–701, esp. pp. 234, 304.

49. This account is based upon the following sources: "Anales de Cuauhtitlan"; Heinrich Berlin and Robert H. Barlow, eds., *Anales de Tlatelolco*, Fuentes Para la Historia de México, No. 2 (México, D.F.: Jose Porrua e Hijos, 1948 [ca. 1633]); Chimalpahin, *Relaciones Originales de Chalco Amaquemecan, Crónica Mexicáyotl*, trans. Adrian León, Instituto de Historia, Primera Serie, No. 3 (México, D.F.: Universidad Nacional Autónoma de México, 1949 [ca. 1600]); Diego Durán, *Historia de las Indias de Nueva España*, ed. Angel

Garibay K., 3 vols. (México, D.F.: Editorial Porrua, 1967 [1581]); Guzmán, "Un manuscrito de la colección Boturini que trata de los antiguos señores de Teotihuacán"; "Historia de los Mexicanos por sus pinturas," in *Teogonía e Historia de los Mexicanos: Trés Opúsculos del Siglo XVI*, ed. Angel Garibay K., Colección "Sépan Cuantos . . . ," No. 37 (México, D.F.: Editorial Porrua, 1965 [ca. 1530]); Ixtlilxochitl, *Obras Históricas*; Paso y Troncoso, *Papeles de Nueva España*, vol. 6; Tezozomoc, "Crónica Mexicana"; Juan de Torquemada, *Monarquía Indiana*, 2 vols. (México, D.F.: Editorial Porrua, 1969 [ca. 1660]); see Sanders, Parsons, and Santley, *The Basin of Mexico*, pp. 149–53 for a discussion of demographic variation within the Valley of Mexico during the twelfth through fourteenth centuries. For page citations of specific events see Elizabeth M. Brumfiel, "Aztec State Making: Ecology, Structure and the Origin of the State," *American Anthropologist* 85 (June, 1983): 261–84.

50. See Brumfiel, "Aztec State Making" for details.

51. Ixtlilxochitl, *Obras Históricas*, 1:379–80, 2:89; "Anales de Cuauhtitlan," p. 50; Tezozomoc, "Crónica Mexicana," pp. 253, 271, 277.

52. Durán, *Historia de las Indias de Nueva España*, 2:83, 101–2, 114. For a description of the centralization of power within Tenochtitlan see Rounds, "Lineage, Class, and Power in the Aztec State."

53. Tezozomoc, "Crónica Mexicana," pp. 268–69.

54. Durán, *Historia de las Indias de Nueva España*, 2:103–4.

55. Durán, *Historia de las Indias de Nueva España*, 2:112; Tezozomoc, "Crónica Mexicana," pp. 237, 287–89, 291, 335, 348.

56. Tezozomoc, "Crónica Mexicana," p. 277; Isabel Kelly and Angel Palerm, *The Tajin Totonac. Part I: History, Subsistence, Shelter and Technology*, Institute of Social Anthropology Publication, No. 13 (Washington, D.C.: Smithsonian Institution, 1952), pp. 284–90.

57. "Anales de Cuauhtitlan," pp. 53–54; Chimalpahin, *Relaciones Originales de Chalco Amaquemecan*, pp. 99, 199, 201, 206; Torquemada, *Monarquía Indiana*, 1:157–58; Kelly and Palerm, *The Tajin Totonac*, pp. 266–72, 291–95.

58. Angel Palerm, *Obras Hidráulics Prehispánicas en el Sistema Lacustre del Valle de México* (México, D.F.: Instituto Nacional de Antropología e Historia, 1973).

59. Edward E. Calnek, "Organización de los sistemas de abastecimiento urbano de alimentos: El caso de Tenochtitlán," in *Las Ciudades de América Latina y sus Areas de Influencia a Través de la Historia*, ed. J. E. Hardoy and R. P. Schaedel (Buenos Aires: Ediciones A.I.A.P., 1975), pp. 41–60; Jeffrey R. Parsons, "The Role of Chinampa Agriculture in the Food Supply of Aztec Tenochtitlan," in *Cultural Change and Continuity*, ed. Charles Cleland (New York: Academic Press, 1976), pp. 233–57.

60. Calnek, "Organización de los sistemas de abastecimiento urbano de alimentos"; Parsons, "The Role of Chinampa Agriculture in the Food Supply of Aztec Tenochtitlan"; Elizabeth M. Brumfiel, "Specialization, Market Exchange, and the Aztec State: A View from Huexotla," *Current Anthropology* 21 (August, 1980): 459–78.

61. Robert H. Barlow, *The Extent of the Empire of the Culhua Mexica*, Ibero-Americana, No. 28 (Berkeley: University of California Press, 1949); *Información sobre los Tributos que los Indios Pagaban a Moctezuma: Año de 1554*, ed. F. Scholes and E. Adams, Documentos para la Historia del México Colonial, No. 4 (México, D.F.: Jose Porrúa e Hijos, 1957).
62. Frances M. F. Berdan, "Trade, Tribute and Market in the Aztec Empire" (Ph.D. diss., University of Texas, 1975), p. 268.
63. Edward E. Calnek, "The City-State in the Basin of Mexico: Late Pre-Hispanic Period," in *Urbanization in the Americas from Its Beginnings to the Present*, ed. R. P. Schaedel, J. E. Hardoy, and N. S. Kinzer (The Hague: Mouton, 1978), pp. 463–70.
64. Torquemada, *Monarquía Indiana*, 1:169.
65. Tezozomoc, "Crónica Mexicana," pp. 286, 333, 338, 360.
66. Durán, *Historia de las Indias de Nueva España*, 2:213.
67. Bernardino de Sahagún, *Historia General de las Cosas de Nueva España*, ed. Angel Garibay, 4 vols. (México, D.F.: Editorial Porrua, 1956 [1577]), 2:309–14.
68. Donald V. Kurtz, "The Legitimation of the Aztec State," in *The Early State*, ed. H. J. M. Claessen and P. Skalnik (The Hague: Mouton, 1978), pp. 169–89.
69. Sanders, Parsons, and Santley, *The Basin of Mexico*, pp. 183–84.
70. Pedro Armillas, "Northern Mesoamerica," in *Prehistoric Man in the New World*, ed. Jesse D. Jennings and Edward Norbeck (Chicago: University of Chicago Press, 1964), pp. 291–329, esp. pp. 321–22; Angel Palerm and Eric R. Wolf, "Ecological Potential and Cultural Development in Mesoamerica," in *Studies in Human Ecology*, Social Science Monographs, No. 3 (Washington, D.C.: Pan American Union, 1957), pp. 1–27, see also notes 35 through 37.
71. Service, *Origins of the State and Civilization*, pp. 290–308.
72. Sanders and Price, *Mesoamerica*, pp. 132, 187, 209.
73. Sanders and Price, *Mesoamerica*, p. 230; Flannery, "The Cultural Evolution of Civilizations," p. 411; Yoffee, "The Decline and Rise of Mesopotamian Civilization," p. 27.
74. George Cowgill, "On the Causes and Consequences of Ancient and Modern Population Changes," *American Anthropologist* 77 (September, 1975): 505–25.

THE NINETEENTH-CENTURY
EUROPEAN STATE

Raymond Grew

Until quite recently, most writing about the modern state took the nine-teenth century as its touchstone. Accounts of how the state developed since the Middle Ages used that history to explain the differences that remained by the nineteenth century, when each nation was treated as having achieved its characteristic form of the modern state. If the focus was contemporary, the task was to explain how fascism, communism, world wars, welfare societies, and multinational corporations had altered the state as established before 1914. From either perspective the norm was a concept of the state that was shaped by the French Revolution and associated with industrialization, urbanization, and mass literacy; with political mobilization that might include universal suffrage, political par-ties, and representative government; with ideas of nationalism, liber-alism, and Marxism.

Recent writing, however, has emphasized an earlier period and tends to skip from preindustrial society and from politics before the French Revolution to the world today. In fact, the picture of the modern state—particularly when accompanied by a critical view of its centralization, its preoccupation with war, its domestic use of force, its ties to a mode of production, and its service to a dominant class—does seem to be provoca-tively clarified by literally overlooking the nineteenth century. Conclu-sions that depended on such an omission, however, would be suspect. Our intellectual armory remains one largely forged in the nineteenth century; from Hegel to Meinecke, from Bentham to Mill to T. H. Green and Herbert Spencer, from Marx to Lenin and Gramsci the most impor-tant literature about the state reflects the experience of that epoch. Iron-ically, the fact that the nineteenth-century state is mirrored in the theo-ries we still use may have made modern commentators less curious to observe it directly.

Even the fashionable term, *state building*, does a disservice to the political processes of this period. The implication of intent, reinforced by accompanying descriptions covering several centuries, suggests a steady and inevitable development and tends to discount nineteenth-century efforts to restrict and control the state. Yet those efforts were at the center of major conflicts, which is one reason to take them seriously. Because historians of the nineteenth century have traditionally done so, stressing the dismantlement of the absolutist state, much of their work seems irrelevant to "state building," the triumphs of liberalism a digression in history's larger course. But there is a paradox here likely to prove significant: Even when those conflicts appeared to have opposite outcomes— ending with new and formal restrictions on the state's activity or with the defeat of the state's opponents—the results for the state itself were much the same.

Two crucial characteristics of nineteenth-century states are frequently overlooked. First, the growth of the state accompanied astounding changes in European society (as the 188 million people in 1800 became 450 million in 1914, as urbanization increased at a still greater rate, as European power spread around the world and standards of living became higher than ever before). It is not instantly apparent why that should be so. Certainly the regimes that set out in 1815 to repair the effects of twenty-five years of war and revolution fumbled again and again. Most of Europe experienced revolutions, which were both stimulated and stifled by national movements, undermining crowns and constitutions and raising up replacements. Everywhere governments were said to have encountered new barriers and limitations. Yet the states that squeezed society of wealth and blood in World War I appear to have been far stronger, more efficient, and more independent of social or customary constraints than any of their predecessors.

Second—although in the nineteenth century nations may have differed more in prosperity and social structure, states more in their skill at extracting wealth and commanding power, and governments more in their formal constitution than at any time before or since—the republics of France and more briefly of Spain, Italy, and Germany; the parliamentary monarchies of Britain, France, Italy, and Spain; the very different empires of France, Germany, Austria-Hungary, and Russia all undertook activities, relied on institutions, and employed means that were stunningly similar.

> It is a feature of the nineteenth-century state that each operates in its own territory as the sole, exclusive fount of all powers and prerogatives of rule. . . . No individual or corporate body can engage in activities of rule except as an organ, agent, or delegate of the state; and the state alone assigns and determines the extent of those activities according to its own rules, backed by its own sanctions.

The similarities go still deeper. Nearly all states insisted upon the unity of their territory and of their legal system, upon a single currency and fiscal system, and upon a dominant "national" language.

States may be very differently constituted internally—they may or may not, for instance, envisage the citizenry as their ultimate constituency and the seat of sovereignty; they may make the head of state into a chief executive or into a figurehead—but regardless of variations, no nineteenth-century state is constituted and operates "dualistically" . . . [allowing] distinctive, independent powers of rule. . . . In the nineteenth century, all states pursued [these goals] self-consciously and explicitly.[1]

Both points, the tendency of nineteenth-century states to grow and to be similar, need some elaboration. Both realities were masked by the political ideologies and conflicts of the period, and to this day neither the significance nor the reality of these tendencies is universally conceded. Some exploration of them, in part because they are surprising, can provide a useful approach to the larger topic.

Some Measures of Growth

One simple (and deceptively clear) indicator of the growth of the state is total expenditure, and we have some figures for expenditure by central governments.[2] A few rough generalizations can be supported by these statistics. First, after the effort of the Napoleonic wars, there appears to have been a sharp and general drop in expenditures by the central state so that in the 1820s most governments spent less than at any time in the century. Second, expenditures by most governments fluctuate annually, often by quite a bit, suggesting that within a certain range budgets reflected deliberate choices or responses to specific needs. Third, the sharpest sustained increases in central government expenditure occur from the late 1890s to 1913, obviously in large part the result of the arms race preceding World War I.[3] Fourth, for each country earlier dates of sharp increase reflect the costs of wars: 1849–55, 1859, 1866–67 for Austria; 1854–55, 1870 for France; 1848, 1853–56, 1876–77 for Russia; 1855, 1899–1901 for the United Kingdom.

In general, then, the common view that war has been the European state's great stimulus to growth is hardly challenged by these figures. It is also clear that the general trend of expenditure is upward.[4] This trend may be, at least in part, an early version of the displacement effect[5] whereby some of the increased revenues generated to meet military demands are then used in postwar periods for other purposes. We should not leap, however, to the view of the nineteenth century as an extended period of peace in which dominant liberal ideas reinforced a tendency toward limited government and a passive state.

Expenditure is only very indirectly and loosely a measure of the social role of government; and central government expenditures, which omit the role of provincial, local, and municipal governments, are still less an indicator of the influence of the state. Even so, the central governments of Russia and the United Kingdom spent about two-thirds more in the peacetime years of 1880–85 than they had fifty years before in 1830–35; in Belgium and France they spent some three times more. More than military demands caused the central government of Switzerland to double its expenditures of the 1850s in the 1860s, double them again in the 1870s, and by 1912 to budget twenty times the amount spent at midcentury when the Swiss confederation was formed. The Spanish government's expenditures of the 1850s doubled by the 1880s; the new German state annually spent more than twice as much in the 1890s as it had in the 1880s.

Such increased spending generally required more planning and more employees (one measure of larger government). Even as the industrial city changed Europe's social landscape, the largest cities were still likely to be national capitals.[6] If the increases merely paralleled growth in population and wealth, even that would suggest a larger government role in the economy than might be expected of a time when states were not thought to be responsible for economic planning or individual welfare. But at least from the 1860s on (and well before the explosive growth in the decade before World War I), national budgets tended to increase as a percentage of gross national product (GNP).[7]

When, toward the end of the century, the budgets of central governments expanded still more dramatically, that change also occurred relatively easily (preparing the way for the far greater demands of world war itself). An expanding economy undoubtedly lessened the strain of increased spending. Military expenditures and debt payments (largely the result of those expenditures) probably accounted for well over half the national budget of most countries during most of the century; some of that spending was a kind of subsidy for heavy industry, and debt payments obviously went primarily to wealthy investors, increasing their stake in making sure that governments remained reliably and respectably solvent. It was this pattern, whereby many of the bourgeoisie "had a direct interest in state indebtedness" that led Karl Marx to charge that even the July Monarchy "was nothing other than a joint stock company for the exploitation of French national wealth."[8] But that is not enough to explain the state's expansion.[9]

National budgets provide one indicator of the place of the state as a consumer or redistributor of wealth. The number of people employed by the state provides a different, more focused and more concrete measure. Presumably, the larger the number, the higher the proportion of citizens who will encounter the state in their daily lives, the better informed the state will be, and the more likely it is that state officials will come to see their interests and those of the state as distinct from those of society as a whole. Bureaucracy, the hierarchical organization and specialized activities on which it rests, and its tendency to grow, has become a major theme of modern social science since the work of people who, like Max Weber, were close students of the late-nineteenth-century state.

Already a famous model of bureaucratic organization, the Prussian state took its modern form in the reforms that followed Napoleon's victories. Then the number of magistrates (*assessoren*) tripled between 1836 and 1848; and the number of civil servants increased by 10 percent between 1800 and 1850 and tenfold between 1850 and 1911 (when there were 250,000).[10] The new German state, which never had its own field administration, nevertheless had 79 officials and 112 clerks in Reich offices in 1872–73, 749 officials and 1,587 clerks in 1914.[11] In all of Germany there were some 1,200,000 officials by that date and as many more state employees below them. The 63,000 civil servants of the various Italian states in 1860 had become 640,000 civil servants in the Kingdom of Italy by 1900.[12] Russia managed with some 38,000 civil servants around 1800 but needed 113,990 in 1856.[13]

Nor was the phenomenon limited to new or highly centralized states. Victorian reformers found they "had to build an administrative state in an era when few wanted one."[14] By 1854 the decentralized British state had sixteen new departments, and agencies created in the last twenty years included: five independent commissions, six Home Office inspectorates, one commission in the Colonial Office, seven Privy Council departments, and five permanent departments with power to inspect housing, water supplies, and sewers. Some 140 inspectors, and many more subinspectors, observed, prodded, and reported in the interests of the state.[15] By the end of the 1880s there were in Great Britain 150,000 persons in purely civil employment.[16] The number of state officials was thought to have increased sixfold in the course of the nineteenth century (the population increased 32 percent from 1806 to 1901), reaching a total of more than one million by 1908, or one for every eleven voters. Another estimate in 1910 calculated that for every ten thousand inhabitants there were 200 public officials in Belgium, 176 in France, 126 in Germany, and 73 in England.[17]

During the same period the number of municipal employees increased at a still more rapid rate, especially toward the end of the century.[18] Observant contemporaries were amazed at this sort of process. "This executive power," wrote Karl Marx of the French state at midcentury, with its enormous bureaucratic and military organization, with its ingenious state machinery, embracing wide strata, with a host of officials numbering a half-million, besides an army of another half million, this appalling parasitic body, which enmeshes the body of French society like a net and chokes all its pores, sprang up in the days of the absolute monarchy. . . . Napoleon perfected this state machinery. The Legitimist monarchy and the July monarchy added nothing but a greater division of labor, growing in the same measure as the division of labor within bourgeois society created new groups of interests, and, therefore, new material for state administration. Every common interest was straightway severed from society, counterpoised to it as a higher, general interest, snatched from the activity of society's members themselves, and made an object of government activity, from a bridge, a schoolhouse, and the communal property of a village community to the railways, the national wealth, and the national university of France. . . . Only under the second Bonaparte does the state seem to have made itself completely independent.[19]

The Increasing Functions of the State

The expansion of the nineteenth-century state is most easily explained in terms of the enlarged functions it was called upon to perform. In that light even the early Victorian period "is no longer seen as an age of laissez-faire."[20] Capital was increasing enormously, and the state was central to making the system work. The state defended private property; and that required, in addition to game wardens and forest guards, forces of order, new laws, and courts to protect urban shops and factories. Having established its monopoly of the legal currency that facilitated trade, the state was obligated to maintain its worth. In varying ways all states regulated and participated in the banking structure that made capital available at ever greater rates.[21] The state's own debts, an important part of this system, were guaranteed by taxes and supported by the flow of capital across national borders which was both encouraged and supervised by the state. Not only did the state promise to pay its own debts; it made sure that others paid theirs through commercial codes that protected private investors. It established rules of incorporation and of limited liability, regulated their application, and granted patents and copyrights. The state guaranteed contracts, established the rules that governed them, and helped extend those rules to the relations between employers and employees, assuring an available work force that ultimately it would help to discipline.

Having in the nineteenth century completed the elimination of internal trade barriers and created the distinction between domestic and foreign trade, states made tariffs a leading public issue and were thus understood to have a critical part in encouraging economic growth.[22] Less directly but no less critically, the state was everywhere understood to have a responsibility for the encouragement of industrialization through government purchases, state subsidies, the training of engineers, prizes for improved techniques of production, measures to stimulate local markets, and international industrial expositions. Despite differences of pace, skill, competence, and competing interests, everywhere the state accepted as its duty the improvement of roadways and waterways, the encouragement and actual building of railways, which required new bureaucracies, special schools, and enormous expenditures. State ownership or direction of mining and forestry, like the sponsorship of agricultural agents and technical schools, were all intended to stimulate economic growth.[23] Post offices were placed in every hamlet.[24] Thus the state grew in terms of responsibilities, the information and bureaucracy it commanded, and its impact on ordinary civilian life. The critical infrastructure of communication and education essential to a thriving economy were not left to the civic spirit of local elites or the vagaries of profit and private enterprise.

More slowly and unevenly, the state undertook to make urban life more agreeable and the human cost of industrialization more bearable, providing lighting and sewers, housing regulations, measures for public health, intermittent relief to the poor, and eventually accident insurance and pensions. Such programs required the state to collect information and develop new means for dispensing assistance. Formal (and thus disputable) social policies were, in a sense, only an extension of the concept of the state as symbol and guide of the national community, also represented in the greater number of courts applying recently codified laws and the vastly expanded number of schools, more and more of them directly run by the state, which expected to create good citizens, speaking a common tongue and behaving according to common norms. A French law of 1816 required that parents would be eligible for public assistance only if they could show that their children had been vaccinated and sent to school.

Society might rest on religion and custom, but the state was expected to shape it. The hesitant, piecemeal, and well-intentioned reforms that mark the nineteenth century express an earnest concern to make society better. Attempts to "redress admitted evils" even by ad hoc reforms "inevitably expanded England's central administration,"[25] but the quite different reforms sought by Szechenyi and Deak in Hungary or Speransky in Russia had a similarly expansive effect. The very definition of pressing social issues crystallized around the possibility of state action even where state policy worked through indirection, using inspectors with limited powers rather than ministers with administrative authority, public inquiries and reports rather than courts of law or police. The elaborate censuses launched in this period and most other collections of economic and social statistics increasingly depended on state sanctions for the right to probe, compel responses, and publish data. Such information in turn identified needs that argued for new public policies. At the time this effect was less surprising in the autocratic governments of the East than the liberal ones of the West; but everywhere journalists, novelists, and the state were the means by which nineteenth-century society came to know itself.[26] Like public education, the state thrived on belief in the power of knowledge, and new knowledge often stimulated new interventions. Each department of state developed its own procedures and mode of action and became a source of further innovations that led the government into new fields.[27] It may be a modern Marxist claim that in bourgeois ideology "there can be no limit based on law or principle to the activity and encroachment of the state,"[28] but that was also the great fear of Pius IX.

The Universal Standards of the Nineteenth-Century State

As states expanded they tended in important respects to become more similar despite the great differences in the societies that supported them. More alike in the functions they performed than in how (or how well) they performed them, they nevertheless grew more similar in the way they organized to accomplish these ends and in the kind of people who operated the enlarged apparatus of the state. The greatest and most important diversity among Europe's states came to lie rather in their linkages to the larger society, the ties to established social groups, the nature of the political process and the autonomy it was allowed, and the concerns (and weight) of organized interests. But whatever its social basis, there were certain minimum conditions that every state had to meet.

The first was the strength for survival. Not only did the well-established concept of sovereignty and the presence of other states lead to conflict;[29] but, as the geographic spaces of Europe were filled in by larger nation-states, those confrontations and the dangers they implied became more controlling. Weakness, brutally measured by the size and equipment of military force, was the antithesis of the state. In contrast to earlier periods it became difficult for the state to survive major military defeats. Prussia had managed it in 1807 at the price of sweeping reforms; Russia, less severely defeated, instituted less sweeping reforms after the Crimean War and war with Japan; the French state survived in 1815 and 1870 by changing regimes, but still more was required in 1918 of the German, Austro-Hungarian, and Russian empires. Liberals especially were opposed to war; but as Friedrich List was quick to note, even Adam Smith thought the protection of those industries essential to national defense a justification for restrictions on trade.[30] Again and again in the course of the century, economic competition itself seemed to measure the state's efficacy and ultimately even its legitimacy. State action for economic interest could easily appear to be the natural extension of the sovereign right of self-defense.

Important as they were, military demands and the taxes to support them do not seem to have been the driving force, the almost automatic motors of growth, that recent writings on "state building" emphasize for earlier periods. The relative ease and inadvertence of the state's development in the expanding economy of the nineteenth century, during a period relatively free from war, suggests the importance of other factors.

If the state's first obligation wasto prevent defeat in war, its next was to prevent revolution at home, a requirement made unnecessarily explicit at the Congress of Vienna in 1815. Within each nation, standards for the protection of property and of persons became higher and more universal in the course of the century, order an obsession. The highway robbery and personal violence commonplace in earlier eras became a measure of "backwardness" and political failure in the nineteenth century. Not even the most doctrinaire ever claimed that free trade could maintain domestic order;[31] rather they argued for a universal application of rules that became an expression of the state's legitimacy and that required complicated and expanded systems for making rules to be applied by the state through courts and police.

Throughout Europe in the period 1820–50, states created, reformed, and expanded civil police forces. By doing so, they preserved for the military the special duties of warfare and thereby increased their claim to the patriotic support for all citizens. In their stead more ubiquitous and more flexible civil forces with extensive local support could be more attentive to certain individual rights while carrying more deeply into society the requirement for universal standards of behavior. The metropolitan police were established in London in 1829, and by subsequent acts similar organizations were extended to most boroughs and most countries, where they constrained and disciplined (and profited from) prostitution, gambling, cockfighting, public drinking, and "bad" language while also combating theft, violence, and threats of revolution. After the revolution of 1848, the radical police chief, Marc Caussidière, established in Paris a new policy force whose flamboyance frightened many of the bourgeoisie, but his goal too was to create a "neutral" force that would protect property and moral order.[32]

As agents of the state, police were an expression of the state's assumption of increasing social responsibilities. These went well beyond formal coercion and included measures intended to improve the public welfare; for the state, as much as had the upper classes, needed the "affections of the people."[33] The pattern, however, is clear. Attempting to maintain order, the state found it could do so better through explicit rules. Their violation, however, would then be perceived as a public threat to the state. Order so delicate required efficient and effective agencies of investigation and punishment—including police, courts, and prisons—which in turn required further rules whose existence further increased the likelihood of violations. Police and courts were expected to demonstrate the benefits of their presence. With ideological consistency and optimism, middle-class leaders favored legal protections for those beneath them while demanding that the common people should lead their lives with some of that order and regularity characteristic of the middle class itself. A prime agency for that social transformation, with or without compulsion, was the state. Nor did it require pressure from a middle class to persuade governments from Spain to Russia to embrace that function.

Because "through the whole course of development of the modern state legal argument, the appeal to notions of justice and the rightfulness of one's claim, constituted a distinctive and significant (though seldom decisive) component of the political process,"[34] demands made upon the state and the compromises that resulted took legal as well as organizational forms easily translated from polity to polity. Although liberals and Marxists tended to minimize the state's autonomy,[35] they could demand reforms of it in the name of efficiency. Legal systems were the preferred means of resolving conflicts and protecting property everywhere in Europe, and their web of codes and courts and lawyers carried the state into more intimate and complex connections with society as the range of conflicts and the meaning of property broadened.

The European states system experienced a parallel development. Through diplomatic rules and institutions, created by member states, international law (which was modeled on state law) became more formal and detailed, and defined occasional parliaments (meeting as international congresses) and informal contracts (called treaties and alliances). Like the state, the state system could limit itself by declaring its neutrality in certain spheres, extending to the formal neutralization of Switzerland (1815), of Belgium (1839), of merchant shipping (1856), of access to the Danube (1878), and of the Suez canal (1887). States in general sustained these international regulations in part because they recognized that the state itself was built upon Europe's distinctive legal traditions.

The states of Europe also extended their competition from matters military and economic to cultural affairs and domestic well-being, copying each other's policies and institutions. Victor Cousin spurred educational reform in France by reporting on the quality of education in the Netherlands and the states of Germany; Matthew Arnold launched a similar campaign in England by reporting on education in France and other continental nations. Thus laws, forms of organization, systems of training and regulation, moved across national borders like technology, as if states were composed of interchangeable parts. The "normativeness of forms" legitimized by the state, which expressed and shaped the larger culture,[36] also established expectations and standards throughout Europe.

By its very nature bureaucracy contributed to this universalizing of forms and functions, and there is much to the common argument that in the European tradition bureaucracy evolved a kind of intertial energy and that it naturally flourished in a period of rationalism in which specialization and the division of labor spread to every sphere of life. But the state is not the same as bureaucracy. It took no great bureaucracy to award the Legion of Honor or to license doctors and lawyers, but people seemed to prefer to have those things done by the state just as they ultimately chose its administrators over those of the East India Company or private railways. There is more to the growth of the state than rational management; as Weber himself insisted, "no domination is only bureaucratic."[37] To establish that nineteenth-century states tended to expand and to become more similar, to take on more functions and to adopt universal standards as to what the state should do and how it should do it may identify some important characteristics. It does not explain the process by which this occurred nor the energy and enthusiasm devoted to it.

The Popularity of the State

In the nineteenth century there was no lack of nation builders to match the heroes of earlier European statemaking; yet Cavour, Kossuth, Louis Napoleon, Bismarck, Lincoln, and Disraeli had in common a quality that distinguishes them from Henry VII, Richelieu, or Frederick the Great: they were popular and sought to be, and they used their popularity. That was especially true as they defended the state and extended its role. The state kept growing because so many people of influence, and so many more who wished for influence, wanted it to. It is commonplace now to explain this in terms of the self-interest of officials and of those who benefited from services the state performed. Inevitably, officials saw ways in which their duties could be better performed and new needs met if only there were more officials. Officeholders also gained prestige and security with more underlings to direct, and the government official became a social type, dependent upon his office. Much has been written, too, about the hunger with which the newly educated sought a government post and the advantages bureaucrats gained through long tenure over mere politicians.[38] In many ways state services came to seem ever more essential in modern society. Provision of the elaborate infrastructure crucial to industrial development was in fact a remarkable historic achievement.[39] Nor will anyone deny that merchants, investors, farmers, and bankers learned with increased skill and subtlety to use the state's power for their gain, not necessarily through state subsidies, grant, or privilege but by establishing rules of commerce that gave them lasting benefits in the marketplace.

All of these forms of self-interest have been contagiously active; yet as explanation, this risks being too simple. Government jobs are not always the most desirable; specific agencies can be abolished or contracted. The state is not fundamentally different whether or not hygiene or education or transportation are seen as state functions. Which interests have what sort of access to the state can vary significantly over time and in different societies.

If there was something unique and irreversible about the growth of the nineteenth-century state, it may lie rather in matters the state could not undo. Free, at least in principle, to alter policies, no state appears to have been free to reestablish internal, regional trade barriers once they had been abolished. All states, as if by irresistible mandate, encouraged easier nationwide communication and a minimal universal education (whether they actually operated the related agencies or not). No state, having once permitted a formal, written constitution, subsequently managed for long without one (although there proved to be no end of ways in which the declared purposes of the constitution could be subverted). Once citizenship became a formal matter of birth or oaths registered by the state, it remained so even though specific criteria could be altered. Nationwide standards for the right to vote, once defined, could not be easily abandoned; and changes in formal criteria nearly always appeared to increase eligibility rather than withdraw it. Having granted universal male suffrage, the French Second Republic tried to lessen any radical potential by establishing stiffer residency requirements but not by naming a category of citizens who could not vote. Louis Napoleon gained popularity by opposing even that device, then restricted the voters' choices (and their representatives' power) but not the right to vote, a lesson Bismarck quickly learned. These seemingly irreversible arrangements have something in common: they define the political community and do so self-consciously and formally. From the standpoint of the state, this was more fundamental than many matters that affected peoples' lives far more directly—more fundamental even than what the frontiers of the state were (whether they included Alsace-Lorraine, Ireland, or Schleswig), who was liable to military conscription, what was censored, or how taxes fell. Changes on those issues left the concept of the state intact.

It is generally held that liberalism—although associated with economic growth, religious tolerance, legal protection of property and individual rights, parliamentarism, and the interests of the bourgeoisie—had a negative conception of the state. Yet "the creation of the liberal state" can be called "the outstanding achievement of bourgeois liberalism."[40] It may be that the liberal state most effectively combined its own expansion with orderly change, but competing schools of thought—conservative, idealist, Christian, utopian socialist, Marxist, and positivist—all emphasized the state's central social role.[41]

Throughout the century daily politics was very much about the powers of the state and the means for exercising them. If liberal political theorists often seemed to dodge the issue, lawyers and historians, those great representatives of the middle class, wrote about it constantly. Lawyers built to new heights the system that expressed its structure, and historians studied the state more than anything else, making their central themes the building of a European state system (treated as a dynamic form of competition) and the unfolding of the state (treated in romantic vocabulary as the embodiment of the nation). From Alexis de Tocqueville to Otto von Hintze they stressed the continuity in the state's development and the importance of administrative and institutional history. National movements important almost everywhere, and new national states—Greece, Belgium, Italy, Hungary, Germany, Romania, Bulgaria, Norway—made the triumph of such movements seem a natural destiny. The state achieved even more clearly than in the past a status that made it, like the family and the church, inescapable.[42] Its sharpened territorial boundaries, like the legal boundaries of laws and constitutions, divided European society and assigned to the state special spheres within which it could seek to establish that homogeneous unity that was its hallmark. Weber spoke with the voice of the previous century of history in assuming that "the furtherance of the nation-state must take primacy over all other objectives."[43]

Nevertheless, to leaders of the nineteenth-century state, this overarching yet flexible creation seemed easily threatened. Armed with the communitarian ideas of nationalism, they warred against the users of dialects, international Catholicism, regional patriotism, and "outlaws" (whose number was increased to include whole classes labeled as vagabonds, disturbers of the peace, and scofflaws). Excommunication was a more effective weapon for the modern state than it had ever been for the papacy. National anthems, patriotic holidays, and the elaborate ceremonials of investiture, politicking, and justice were the other side of this effort to sustain a definition of the political community. Similarly, changes in the relationship of local to national government, by no means always in the direction of increased centralization, defined that relationship ever more explicitly and circumscribed it so as to sustain a sense of the national state as the formal expression of political community.

From the top to the bottom, from the highest offices of state to the schoolmaster, policeman, postman, and border guard the state proclaimed itself the embodiment of the community it had defined. And this sentiment was as important to democratic as to autocratic service states, for "in democratic communities the imagination is compressed when men consider themselves; it expands indefinitely when they think of the state."[44] Even in the penitentiary, "the anguish of guilt could only be aroused, the reformers realized, in an environment whose self-evident humaneness confirmed the moral authority of the state."[45] No wonder political scientists have found legitimacy and political culture crucial to modern political development.[46]

If the absolutist state had "transformed law from a *framework of* into *an instrument for* rule," from a set of negotiated rights and privileges into general and abstract laws applicable to all,[47] the modern state by a logical reversal also made liability to the law a measure of belonging to the political community, a form of participation, and the system itself ostensibly independent of who held its offices. None of this required a liberal polity, as example after example shows, but it was congenial to liberal concerns about justice (both in the larger sense and as mere legality), the individual as citizen, and political liberty.

To define political community, however, was to declare who was left out—a revelation that created special difficulties for liberalism. Even where they did not directly hold the levers of political power, the middle classes were the principal beneficiaries of the primacy of politics in public life, which brought recognition to (new) men of standing, to the educated and those active in affairs. Professional men—certified by the state, similar to its officials by training and class, and in regular contact with it— were notably prominent in nationalist movements.[48] But just as uniform law and administration established who really had access to the state, so limitations on the legal privileges of Junkers, clergy, or officials exposed the social and economic bases of power. Bourgeois liberals, however, could most effectively promote their interests by presenting them as universal principles. Liberalism, having attacked the power of nonstate institutions, proclaimed that the state could be used to promote individual opportunity combined with social progress, to reconcile freedom and diversity with communal consensus, to institutionalize high principle with the right to challenge it.[49] Out of the tension between promise and reality, reforms were won, which—whether seen as magnificent steps toward progress or niggardly concessions wrung by fear—always proved unsatisfactory. In that process liberalism was fated to advertise values often violated and set standards rarely met, to reveal for all to see which interests were being served even while seeking consensus, and thus to stimulate further expectations of the state.

Expanding the Political Community

Representative politics in the nineteenth century provides the most obvious example of how the formal definition of political community created pressures for its expansion. It is extraordinary that in societies as different as those of the Scandinavian countries, Great Britain, the Netherlands, Belgium, France, Spain, Portugal, Switzerland, and Italy the right to vote in national elections was redefined again and again, each new barrier of wealth or education giving way to another compromise that broadened the suffrage until it was extended to all adult males. As soon as the principle of representation was admitted, governments were likely in sudden moves to catch up quickly to the current European standard of suffrage (as in Germany, Austria, and Russia). Thus formal electoral participation seemed to increase in some rough symmetry with the state's greater penetration and the range of its activities, adding to its authority and stability.

The effect was in part conservative, and the optimistic beliefs of revolutionaries in 1830 and 1848 and of nationalists in Italy and Germany that limited political changes could open the way for a quiet social transformation was harder to sustain once universal suffrage legitimized political systems that rested on the established social order. Constitutions and representative government prescribed predictable behavior and, at least indirectly, resolved important problems[50] by sharply defining the sphere of politics. This process, which made politics appear more autonomous, made it possible to drag ever more questions into the political arena, expanding by implication and eventually by policy the responsibilities of the state. Parliaments, bureaucracies, and political parties jostled each other, adding to the characteristic "open-endedness" of the nineteenth-century state in which the political process is "oriented to abstract, ever-receding targets."[51]

As the suffrage expanded step by step, established elites sought new means to preserve their leadership (and it made a great difference whether they relied primarily on popular appeal, parties, institutions, or local ties).[52] Such techniques, like the state's differential treatment of notables, propertied voters, nonpropertied voters, nonvoters, and those in deepest poverty who most directly felt the force of coercion, helped dramatize class differences.

Voting, of course, is not the only form of participation nor always the most important. To influence legislation and administrative decisions is often a more direct and privileged form of participation. Pushers of interests both old and new soon learned that beyond time-honored techniques of finding friends in power they, too, would gain most by generalizing their aims as larger principles and winning broader support.[53] When influential groups succeeded—like the anti-Corn Law League, urban reformers, the unifiers of Italy and Germany, or ultimately trade unionists—in shaping some policy, they then sought to make the new direction a permanent part of the system. If an independent stock market, public education, or recognition of organized labor could be closely tied to some element of the state itself, new gains were less liable to reversal by mere legislation. In fact, this tactic did not require a parliament at all, and Eastern European landholders, bishops, and generals as well as bankers and ethnic groups learned how to pressure the state to guarantee interests threatened by social change. (If the presence of parliament encouraged the mobilization of interest groups, parliamentary practice, with its shifting majorities and broad-based parties, discouraged their remaining as isolated blocs.) Everywhere, then, the office seeker carrying a dog-eared letter of recommendation joined industrialists and financiers, professional groups and union leaders in expanding the role of the state. The shrewdest leaders learned in turn that as new groups mobilized it was better to accede to their central demands before they became permanently organized. This was most consistently accomplished, of course, in a limited parliamentary system—the effect of the rotation of parties in liberal Spain or *trasformismo* in Italy (raised to a policy by Giolitti); but Szechenyi and Metternich had the same purpose in mind. Increased state activities were thus often the product of preemptive politics.

Underlying this process was the acceptance of politics as an uncomfortable balance. Even bureaucratic rules and laws were often understood as a form of contract binding groups formally outside the state and viewed as contracting parties. When these were in conflict, administrative solutions required a stronger bureaucracy. As the political balance became explicit, challengers learned to allege that the intended balance was out of line, necessitating new laws and regulations to right it. In addition, the expansion of the state, when it maintained an established balance of interests (or seemed to), also served to mask the process of change. When the political community was enlarged, that gave some basis for hope among the powerless that they too might yet make their needs felt. An expanding state thus contributed to stability in a period of change by extending the long European tradition that those who sought justice more even and more consistent than they could get from the local lord should look to the state—the single most important reason for its historic expansion.

But the greatest expansion of the political community came not from voting or influence but from the increased visibility of the state itself. To serve in its army, receive any of its services, or merely be subject to its laws was also recognition of membership in that community. Nationalists used schools, like flags and anthems, to make everyone aware of that.[54] But if nationalism guaranteed the state's legitimacy by mobilizing popular support, it gained strength as an expression (and idealization) of the most common experiences of the state. This expanded political community, which could claim even to include the landless peasants of Eastern Europe, became a hallmark of the nineteenth-century state.

The Similarity and Stability of European States

I have argued that in the nineteenth century the states of Europe expanded and became more similar as they took on more functions, accepted general standards of performance, sought and won greater popularity, and came in effect to define membership in the political community. Although this argument includes no claim that these results were deliberately sought, it raises the question of how such similarities could occur in very different political systems, among populations that were largely literate or illiterate, and among societies industrial or primarily agricultural. It may be, to use another vocabulary, that in order to define the political community (or rather to be seen as the expression of the political community it defined) the state had to strengthen its claim to legitimacy. Certainly the greater penetration of the state into society enlarged the range of social conflicts that were understood to be political, and it broadened the range of interests that found their best protection to come from close ties to the state. But states more closely interconnected with their diverse societies might be expected to have become more different from each other. And increased politicization of public life makes it all the more surprising that the institutions of European states remained relatively stable[55] in a century of unprecedented and rapid change.

In short some common process seems to have cut across social differences and survived the disruptiveness of change. The common goal of domestic order led paradoxically to the increased use of the state to change society but also required states to act as the coordinator and articulator of interests that resided elsewhere in society. Although in practice this occurred everywhere, it was most openly acknowledged and even welcomed in liberal societies because only in liberal thought were conflicting interests viewed as sustaining the state rather than threatening it. The underlying process, then, began with the need for stability, which required that the state be able to balance competing interests, keeping any single interest or group of interests from becoming too strong.

In the nineteenth century, however, new needs and interests kept making themselves felt. The balance among the overlapping circles of interests, established structures, and social groups was constantly shifting, and that was potentially threatening to the system upon which the state rested and which it sought to preserve. Characteristically, two system-maintaining answers were preferred. The state remained in closest touch with those who most favored stability, sought to exclude from an active role in state affairs those opposed, and in effect graded everyone in between. Drawing additional groups or interests into circles that supported the system constituted that Whiggish progress (which incidentally expanded the state's connections with the larger society) contemporaries hailed. As various groups—whether local governments, nationalists, physicians, producers of grain, or entrepreneurs—learned to look to the state, the state learned to offer some stabilizing (or cooptive) response. Second, in the face of a direct challenge, system maintenance required a further assertion of the state, either to defeat the claimants (as in the June Days and the Commune) or to establish an amended balance. The more "artificial" that new balance was (artificial in the sense of bringing together groups or interests that had previously not been in close contact or had proved incompatible, forcing unaccustomed coalitions, or raising new conflicts), the more active and expansive the role of the state was likely to be in establishing and maintaining the new balance.

The state, of course, was not the only active partner in these shifting, interlocking circles. Powerful groups outside the state avoided too close a contact so long as their own interests were secure but turned to the state when faced with new challenges or when so divided among themselves as to require the state to hold them together. The state, too, benefited by loose ties to particular circles of power provided it could mobilize their support when needed. Thus banks, armies, churches, or parties could behave like an arm of the state on some occasions and with dizzying independence on others. Such flexibility was highly sensitive to any social cleavages, and in a time of sweeping social change, the task of building upon and then bridging these divisions (not just of capital and labor, but of merchants and manufacturers, rural and urban regions, clericals and anticlericals, etc.), became a major purpose of politics. Although their societies were different, European states in the nineteenth century expanded in comparable ways to maintain their diverse social systems and to meet the universal standards for the modern state in a period of change.

The Myth of Neutrality

Tied to and dependent upon many centers of power, as states always are, the nineteenth-century state made its increasingly complex juggling of interests legitimate by presenting itself as the neutral balancer of conflicting forces. This claim to the state's neutrality had an ancient European tradition rooted above all in the crown's justice, but propagating the myth of the modern state's neutrality can be seen as a major theme of nineteenth-century history. Every state laid formal claim to being the embodiment of community, to being above interests and separate from them, and to being outside social and ideological conflict; national and liberal states generally did it most convincingly.

It was not just efficiency or increased authority that made nineteenth-century states eschew tax farming, privateers, or systems that automatically assigned to local lords state functions of administration or justice. By freeing itself of such "private" interests, the state asserted its neutrality. Similarly, not the least of bureaucracy's appeal was its claim to an essential neutrality that separated officials from their social origins, assigned them further delimited functions, and required them to operate according to universal, fixed, and written procedures. Behavior normal for public officials in the eighteenth century was denounced as corrupt in the nineteenth, and the standards of probity (measured in terms of direct financial gain, of bribery and peculation) steadily rose across the century. Banks did not lose legitimacy if an employee embezzled, but the Third Republic was rocked by scandals involving shares in the Panama canal.

Such rising standards demark the march of the myth of the neutral state. That state in turn was allowed, within narrow limits, a more independent control of its own functioning in order to restrict the role of "outside" influences and to create an apolitical army, a professional civil service, an autonomous judiciary, and the means for collecting objective information about the condition of society. Many of the century's most famous reforms, in local government, civil service, and police, were among other things efforts to sustain the claim to neutrality by extending formal standards, and therefore the state itself as the agent of neutrality, deeper into the system of rule.

If the state thus advanced, it did so by simultaneously retreating, perfecting the ability to declare certain spheres outside its direct responsibility without relinquishing any of its authority. There were many advantages in doing so. A system of power based on law is endangered by laws it cannot enforce, and gradually most nineteenth-century states abandoned efforts to control wages, consumption, prices, churches, strikes, labor organization, and the press. As a principle of action, the state's withdrawal from certain spheres found its best intellectual support in liberal theory; but the technique, available to all, was used by the monarchies that accepted patrimonial justice on great estates (as in Eastern Europe), by the governments that signed concordats with the Roman Catholic Church (as in Spain in 1851 and Austria in 1855), and by the Tsar when he assigned peasant communes delimited autonomy with the emancipation of the Russian serfs. Unified Germany found in federalism the means to give this technique of withdrawal formal structures, and the state contributed to the development of a particularly segmented society in which institutionalized communities like the military or the universities enjoyed a privileged protection from the state on the understanding they would not mix in public politics. Eventually even subcultures of Catholics and socialists did not prove to be the threat that Bismarck had feared.

By judicious retreat, the nineteenth-century state also sought to avoid the denials of its neutrality that resulted from taking sides in conflicts likely to be forever renewed—between capital and labor, producer and consumer, believer and nonbeliever, lenders and borrowers. As multiple interests became more tied to the state, it benefited more by alienating none than by openly favoring some. Ideologically, the neutral state became a secular state, comfortable with short-term "practical" issues but not philosophic ones.[56] When contentious matters were unavoidable, indirection proved preferable to direct intervention. The reports of inspectors (and their very presence), the publicity of parliamentary inquiries, leaks to the press, the setting of general standards for goods or housing or sanitation, the offer of matching funds[57] were all more appropriate to the neutral stance. Efforts like the attempts to control the press—through stamp acts, the registration of owners, postpublication penalties—in which even indirection proved ineffectual were largely abandoned.[58]

There was a further reason for this emphasis upon the state's claim to neutrality, and that followed from the increased demand for its services discussed earlier. Traditionally the state could respond in three ways: an extension of the system of justice, an extension of the system of administration, or the delegation of someone else to perform the services in question. This last, especially since the French Revolution, had fallen out of fashion. The assignment of tasks and responsibilities to agents outside the state meant the granting of privileges to groups or corporations which, experience had taught, were likely to develop interests of their own that came to impede the state as well as assist it. Such an approach did not meet the universal standards of effectiveness. Thus the systems of justice and of administration were the preferred instruments for meeting the demand for state services, and from Ireland to Russia these systems were reformed again and again in the course of the century. (Their expansion was facilitated and with results most similar in countries that had adopted the Napoleonic model.) Still, there was far more to be done than the state could directly accomplish through its own administrators (after all, operating its own army had for two centuries consumed much of the resources available). And there were in industrializing society far more conflicts than the system of justice could arbitrate.

The Fields of Play

Sometimes the benefits of claiming neutrality could be obtained less expensively and less intrusively by a special application of the technique of withdrawal. Effective justice required the state's neutrality; effective administration required uniform rules, and states could assure that these criteria were met by recognizing spheres of activity, fields of play in which it would neither operate directly nor delegate others to operate in its stead. For these fields of play the neutral state prescribed a general set of rules and then accepted little further responsibility (thereby gaining the advantages of the technique of withdrawal). The state could do this and maintain its claim to neutrality, however, only by doing so explicitly and only so long as (1) activities in these fields of play were in large part organized through established institutions already well integrated into the society, (2) individual behavior was largely shaped by cultural norms thought to be stable, (3) ideologies and activities within these fields did not threaten the system or the state itself, and (4) no forces from outside the society seemed to stimulate or require major social change. These were important limitations. Churches and political parties might ultimately meet these conditions but not Chartists or anarchists, family life but not free love, even radical opposition but not subversion. And few societies since have been so free from outside forces, or able to sustain the illusion of that freedom, as industrializing Europe (and the United States). Nonetheless, politics in the nineteenth century never lost the quality of a private banquet held while some hungry crowd was kept outside, even though political exclusions (of German socialists, trade union leaders, ethnic nationalists, or British atheists and advocates of birth control) generally broke down. Not to have one's needs granted a field of play at all was the telling exclusion.

The accumulation and expenditure of capital was one of these recognized fields. So was production and trade. Although the state was required to facilitate both, it was not responsible for what was produced or traded nor for commercial practice; and external trade barriers were understood merely to define the field of play. There were many other such fields from which the state retreated. Labor relations was one of them, and the legal recognition of trade unions in Belgium, Germany, Austria, the Netherlands, Hungary, and France between 1866 and 1884 is a striking example of how state policies became more alike than economies or political systems. Ultimately religion became such a field of play, while politics became the state's field of play, held not to be properly part of capital relations or religion but a sphere unto itself. Within the field of politics thus quarantined, conflicts could be allowed that would have been dangerous to stability if spread through society as a whole.[59]

Even public spaces, certain halls, squares, parks, and boulevards, were treated as metaphors of fields of play in which demonstrations (of certain types) impermissible elsewhere were allowed, at least at certain times. Out of this emerged the sharp distinction only awkwardly maintained between what was public and what was private. Activities within the fields of play were essentially private: affairs secular and civic were public, matters of state. Definitions of public and private varied, of course, by social class, the conduct of the wealthy in large and isolated homes being far more private than that of the poor in public streets. The respectable, generally free of interference, correctly saw theirs as an unusually free society; the more marginal whose patterns of entertainment and survival led to multiple encounters with the law thought their choices indecently restricted.

Nineteenth-century states nevertheless acknowledged two major responsibilities toward these spheres beyond its direct control. The state was expected to facilitate the play within them, aiding society to function by providing among other things efficient communication, general education and technical training, a solid currency and reliable means for borrowing and paying debts. It also fell to the state to maintain the rules of play. Some of these were explicit and more or less universal: the protection of property and persons, certain civil rights, a ban on violence, the sanctity of contracts. Other rules were particular to each field of play, and interpretations varied as to when or how the state should call the players to order. The more representative a government, the more likely it was that the concept of maintaining the rules would be extended into society. In the interest of fair play the state would be called upon to prevent a private monopoly from controlling a sphere of activity, to assure that established fields allowed some access to newcomers, and to require that each field make its expected contribution to the general welfare. Thus every state at some point set new rules for housing or the organization of labor, restructured education or transportation, or gave special support to some sagging sector of the economy. The state also acted to maintain the boundaries between fields (boundaries that were essential to the system and had been largely defined by the state itself). In the process fields of play came to be narrower, distinct for cities, hospitals, particular industries. In characteristic nineteenth-century language state action within a field of play was described as an intervention and in the liberal vocabulary treated as a momentary intrusion to right some balance in a self-regulating mechanism, a referee's resolution of a dispute that had stopped the play.

In fact, establishing acceptable rules occupied much of political life and extending those rules into factories and private estates and board rooms occupied much of the state's attention, drawing it slowly and reluctantly into regulating the stock market[60] and probing into the family in order to protect children. (Not surprisingly, the great expansion of the state bureaucracy occurred much less in the administrative offices of landrat and prefect than among the agencies that supervised specific fields of play.) In practice these interventions were rarely temporary, and the state's extended involvement with a field of play tended to reveal a lack of neutrality that often led to reforms, creating further regulations and institutionalization. By midcentury most states were as closely tied to financiers as local government had once been to local elites, and elaborate devices including specific regulations, judicial review, and broader suffrage were developed to maintain the principle of the state's neutrality.[61]

The neutral state surpervising multiple fields of play accomplished a remarkable feat. It preserved itself, expanded its activities, and increased its indispensability in radically changing times. The state was in effect insulated from its own failures, from the effects of monopoly here, injustice everywhere, a riot or bankruptcy or strike there. Inspectors and bureaucrats, like customs officials and public health doctors and professional police, distanced the state from its own coercion (so much so that the use of military force against a civilian population became a sign of weakness and of revolution). At the same time a dynamic contradiction began to unfold. Tying itself most closely to those favoring stability, "a state that purports to be the source of all power relations acts in fact as the guarantor of power relations that do not originate from itself and that it does not control."[62]

There was a further problem, less a logical contradiction than a fundamental confusion. Throughout the nineteenth century political battles were fought not just over broad issues and specific policies but on the question of what matters were proper to politics at all. Was a Kulturkampf, pauperism and unemployment, the conduct of business, or excessive drinking appropriate to political dispute or subject to political resolution?[63] Practice constantly shifted. Everyone knew that the various fields of play could by their very nature not be entirely distinct from each other or the state, but some separation was essential to the state's claims to neutrality. Radicals, of course, sought to unmask the myth of the neutral state, and for more than a century their rhetoric and demonstrations were largely shaped by the effort to show how a delimited politics was inherently false because it ignored the ties of capital to the state and of real power to politics. Defenders of the status quo, on the other hand, presented society as composed of fields of play and the state as neutral; but that was to grant the state its own set of independent interests.

Thus the proper limits of state action remained a matter of politics while everywhere the effort was made to remove the mode of that action from the political arena. Whole political careers had rested on the understanding official's, the local notable's, or the parliamentary representative's capacity to use his leverage against the state for the benefit of his clients. Increasingly, however, that form of responsiveness was seen as corrupting. To maintain its claim to neutrality, the state had to establish in advance the rules by which it would operate and the fields of play it would not enter. Even autocratic governments proved remarkably sensitive (and vulnerable) to the charge of serving private interests, and one important function of complex codes of administrative law was to refute such charges. As the state increased its penetration into society, it was ironically required to provide some formal means of redress against its own actions. The arbiter state merely regulating public practices granted the right to sue the state for damages; the citizen state demanding universal male conscription slowly allowed exemptions and later recognized conscientious objectors; the administrative state maintaining its own rules allowed instruments like the French *conseil d'état* to provide citizen redress against administrative actions. Thus, although neither liberal nor labor movements succeeded in winning for individuals the control over their own lives once promised, the narrowed field of matters "private" achieved a kind of sanctity even against custom and public opinion never known before, expanding especially in liberal societies to include consumption patterns, political opinions, religious beliefs, and broadening in our own times to encompass such issues as sexual preference and abortion.

The recognition of fields of play had another profound effect; the players themselves learned to play by the rules, even to depend upon them (and the state). Without ever having to surrender their broader claims, bankers, doctors, and businessmen called upon the state to discipline colleagues and competitors who violated those rules. Even workers "learned what we may call the 'rules of the game' of modern industrial society, and the modern labour movements are the most striking and universal results of their 'education'."[64]

Just as the state, to sustain its claim to neutrality, both became more intrusive and defined new limits to its intrusions, so it could not long admit being accessible only to certain groups. Wider suffrage was followed by reforms to make access to the civil service more open. In Germany, England, and France educational requirements and then examinations were employed, each subsequently amended as they also were proved to be restrictive.[65] Whenever the state succeeded in appearing more truly open, however, its example called into question the contrasting rules in the various fields of play (such as labor relations, marketing or the professions), and pressures built for the state to adjust those rules by its own intervention. The state in the nineteenth century achieved what most socialists thought it could not and most liberals thought it should not, a relative autonomy,[66] using it to maintain the social system by means of its own expansion.

The State, Social Institutions, and National Culture

Fields of play stimulated the growth of institutions organized for limited ends, with rules to regulate their actions, and further constrained by competition with each other. Formally constituted, they appeared responsibly official and public, their general principles well known, their daily functioning a private, administrative matter.

Everywhere organizations proliferated. Symphony orchestras and soccer teams, clubs and lodges; charitable societies and others dedicated to spreading the truth about contraception, vivisection, or alcohol; geographical societies and patriotic ones; professional organizations of doctors, teachers, and lawyers all flourished in a world of political parties, corporate enterprises, financial institutions, and state bureaucracy. Everywhere such organizations were encouraged by the state. Often licensed by it, they gained prestige in proportion to their closeness to it.

These institutions were for the most part expressions of bourgeois culture, their leaders very much like the men who ran the state.[67] When the early nineteenth-century state allowed national suffrage limited to those with property, it tended to make a noteworthy exception: professional people—professors, doctors, and lawyers—holders of the state's degrees. Institutions had a similar status; when a bourgeois died, his obituary would spend most of its space listing the organizations to which he had belonged and the offices he had held. Eager for the advantages of recognition, lawyers, journalists, and scholars cooperated with the institutionalization of the bar, newspapers, and academic disciplines.

The closeness of these institutions to the state is reflected in the fact that within each European society they tended to copy the state's own forms of organization (elective or self-perpetuating, traditional or constitutional, hierarchical with nearly permanent positions of leadership or rotating leaders) and in their own rules for access to the institution. Thus interest groups, political parties, and cultural organizations came to look like the state whose sanction they sought and with whom they increasingly had to deal. Old elites worked comfortably in these similar structures, and new ones learned to, expressing similar values and styles. Groups that eschewed such institutions risked becoming marginal like reactionary aristocrats, benighted peasants, and religious sects.

The Weberian view of bureaucratic rationalization as the essence of the modern state and itself a form of expropriation[68] thus seems both right and too narrow. The "new, sophisticated kind of 'speech about rule'" that evolved through juristic thinking within the state[69] spread through institutions beyond officialdom. Social groups learned to organize both to protect themselves against change or challenge and to influence the state itself. In this way, the widespread political and social mobilization of nineteenth-century society remained associated with (and influenced by) the state even when ostensibly independent of it, and the state itself became less dependent upon any single group or interest. The concept of fields of play represented by reliable institutions provided the state with an indirect linkage to social structure that allowed institutions to serve as shock absorbers.

> The state presupposes and complements a manifold social reality (encompassing, for instance, the social standing, religious affiliations, and economic resources of individuals) that under previous arrangements directly and immediately affected and were affected by the activities of rule; now, however, a set of filters of significance, of standards of mediation, of codings and decodings block off such direct mutual effects.[70]

Steadily, these institutions in effect operated along with the state to erode the independent political position of local notables in France, aristocratic justices of the peace in England, and Junkers in Prussia.[71] State-sponsored institutions (such as professional associations, chambers of commerce, or hospitals and universities) redefined the links between central and local administration, and a wide range of institutions recruited groups previously beyond the prestige and reach of the state for cooperation with it.[72] Just as oaths of office and public investiture permitted bloodless purges of personnel (in unified Germany, Austria-Hungary, or nineteenth-century France) so institutionalization assured reliability and loyalty.

Through institutionalization, finally, the state became a sponsor of high culture, associated with and even a symbol of its great prestige.[73] No achievements of the period—not even the creation of industrial wealth or the spread of European power around the globe—are more impressive than its art, music, writings, and science. To recognize that this high bourgeois culture flourished very largely in institutions and that those institutions were closely tied to the state is to better understand the period. Nineteenth-century institutions encouraged "specifically patriotic (as against parochial or cosmopolitan) loyalties," and the cultural formation that identified an elite was, among other things, essential to the administrative style of the time.[74]

More important, formal, bourgeois culture was a goal and a result of the nationalism that nourished the state, and so the state sponsored and subsidized academies, theaters, opera houses, orchestras, museums, libraries, universities, research institutes, and scholarly publications; and it did so on a scale no royal patron could have matched. Through universal systems of primary education, the state battled the illiteracy, dialects, and local customs that resisted or ignored that culture.[75] National systems of secondary schools in turn selected who would have access to the elite through state-sponsored examinations and certification and membership in associations sanctioned by the state. Rarely did the nineteenth-century state attempt to create culture or to establish its own independent measures of cultural achievement. Rather, it readily adopted the tastes and standards of the cultural elite, and it may well have gained more from wrapping itself in the prestige of culture and the objectivity of science— both seen as neutral—than culture gained from the institutional stability and wealth offered by the state. The point was rather that a flourishing state gained legitimacy in a society with a coherent and admirable culture. An expression of the hegemony of a class, perhaps, this symbiosis not only allowed cultural variety and innovation but had the odd effect of placing the prestige of art and government above that of business.

The Late-Nineteenth-Century Crisis

With all their differences, European states in the nineteenth century had developed comparable techniques for permitting change while preserving remarkable continuity in their particular roles, organization, and personnel. These techniques, which tended to keep change within each sphere from upsetting the whole system, gave the state an increasingly active part in system maintenance, thereby reinforcing pressures from an enlarged political community for more state intervention. And that system, while placing relatively few restraints on the accumulation of capital, had surprisingly avoided many major challenges over the distribution of wealth.[76] By the 1880s, however, the limited compromises of the established equilibrium were threatened. Many historians have stressed the major turning in European social, political, economic, and intellectual history in the last decades of the century, as a series of major political crises occurred in each of the principal nations.[77] When, by 1910, those crises seemed to have been resolved, a significantly altered balance redefined and expanded many of the responsibilities of the state. That new balance in turn brought an expansion of the state less subtle and indirect than earlier in the century, one more easily measured in the classic terms of military demands, bureaucracy, and new social functions.

In part the pressures for this transformation arose from within the state itself. As the state became more complex, it also appeared more artificial,[78] and its multiple (and conflicting) ties to various spheres and interests were more readily exposed. Differing rules of play in different fields, and inconsistent intervention, led to attacks on the state for being not the "natural" reflection of society but a contrived set of regulations and coercions. In both statist and liberal terms there appeared to be a desperate need for a clearer, more consistent, more commanding ideology in order for the state to hold together its elaborate system. Proposed solutions arose from advocates of anti-Semitism, imperialism, and militant nationalism on the right and from proponents of anticlericalism, syndicalism, and socialism on the left.[79] The bitter battles that arose in nation after nation around these issues were in large part conflicts over who should have access to and control over the state. Although redefining the political community was intended to give the state a coherence it lacked, the debates themselves further undermined claims that the state was socially neutral.

In addition, all those institutions the state legitimized tended to develop their own interests and constituencies, cumulatively bringing to bear new pressures from army officers, imperial administrators, and governmental agencies as well as from political parties mobilizing social sectors previously peripheral, and from business groups, professional associations, labor unions, and special interests. Furthermore, the technique of indirect links with the state that had worked so well for elites were neither available nor satisfactory to wage laborers in industry and agriculture, the major new groups becoming effectively mobilized late in the century; and the threat of their mobilization made old elites less confident of merely indirect ties, especially as bureaucrats and politicians developed independent interests of their own. An institutional form of social compromise had also led to the development of a Catholic and a socialist subculture, each with its own political parties, mutual aid societies, social organizations, and newspapers. Initially organized against the state, such institutions brought political strength and an insistence upon a voice within the inner circles of the state.

Current ideas and attitudes developed outside the state amplified these pressures. Social groups in general were increasingly self-conscious, and class consciousness fed by and armed with Marxist analysis more stridently rejected the state's pretense to neutrality. From all sides the autonomy which the state had conceded to certain fields of play was denied legitimacy. At the same time, widespread rejection of traditional bourgeois culture as narrow, overly formal, and excessively rational weakened another source of the state's prestige.

Three additional trends affected all society and eroded the old balance. The second industrial revolution (associated especially with developments in electricity and chemistry, followed shortly by the internal combustion engine) required far more massive amounts of capital controlled by far larger corporations employing a far larger labor force. Such enormous and direct power over both labor and capital was more than could be contained in one field of play without directly challenging most of the others and therefore the balance on which the state itself rested. Heightened industrial competition and a general depression in agriculture everywhere hurt the established economy. Finally, states, too, faced greater competition, marked by imperial clashes and an expanding arms race. An alliance system that began with the sort of limited contracts and assigned spheres of interest that had worked so well in domestic affairs now produced two armed camps, whose competitive thrusts extended throughout Europe and around the world. Those old motors of state building, military expenditure and the resulting need for more taxes, were churning again.

By 1910, however, a new balance was apparent within each state, as crises—symbolized by the fall of Bismarck in Germany, the Dreyfus affair in France, the Spanish-American war in Spain, the Boer war and the Taff Vale decision in Britain, the *fatti di maggio* in Italy, the resignation of the Taafe government in Austria, the economic program of Witte in Russia and by major waves of strikes in every country—led to government by radicals like Lloyd George and Clemenceau and by liberal opportunists like Canalejas and Giolitti, to revolutions in Russia and Portugal, to von Bülow's reconstituted majority and heightened emphasis on foreign policy, to government by decree in Austria, and to the independence of Norway.

Despite fundamental differences, in each country the new balance generally shared certain characteristics. It was marked first of all by broadened political participation, reflected in wider suffrage, efforts at mass political mobilization, gestures toward more open access marked by more reforms of the civil service and of secondary education. In principle at least, the political privileges of established elites were to be reduced. Second, the new balance included a redefinition of fields of play, with the expanded recognition of unions and the right to strike establishing a more consistent neutrality in labor-management relations, with provisions to treat banking and each of the major industries separately, and more formal secularization establishing a safer neutrality toward religious matters (which allowed an increased involvement of Catholic interests in national affairs). Social welfare was made an explicit responsibility of state policies, leading to an impressive array of new measures and social service agencies; and the state reasserted its coercive authority within the limits of these new definitions (for example, by not intervening in ordinary strikes but preventing strikes by public employees).

Third, the state assumed a more direct role in the economy, through high tariffs, aid to agriculture, more supervision of banking policies, programs to encourage and stimulate investment at home and in colonies and allied nations, and explicit measures to aid particular industries and professional groups.[80] All of these conflicts, like the measures to deal with them, tended to be nationwide in scope, coterminous with the sphere of the state. If in general these new accommodations were most easily reached through parliamentary deals, they also occurred where parliamentary traditions were weak. Even while liberalism was under heavy attack, the forms of the liberal state were widely copied. Fourth, the new balance emphasized the arms race (which benefited heavy industry and appealed to militant patriotism) and imperialism (which attracted aristocrats, military men, and church leaders precisely because in colonies they were not constrained to specific fields of play but could enjoy open dominance in an integrated system that need not acknowledge countervailing interests). All of this required the higher taxes (now given a slight redistributive purpose) appropriate to a more activist state.

With major institutions more tightly connected to the state and concessions to specific interests more explicitly negotiated, the system lost some of its flexibility and subtlety. The role of power and the conflict of interests were more directly recognized (something liberals, at least, had always avoided). The states so restructured then plunged into World War I as their citizens cheered, seeking in wartime the social integration the state at peace could not provide.[81] The European state survived world war less damaged than the societies it led, everywhere thereafter collecting and spending far higher percentages of the national product. Yet the altered roles and greater prominence of the European state after 1914 and the more elaborate techniques available to its crisis managers were all, like the ready adaptation to total war, based on the structure of the state quietly established in the previous century.

The state that in the twentieth century defines nationality, modulates or directs the economy, and touches the lives of every citizen would have seemed an unfamiliar behemoth to nineteenth-century nationalists (who thought nations were prior to states), liberals (who believed they had found a formula for limiting the state), and reformers (who had merely argued for efficiency and uniformity). Yet this contemporary state is the result of their efforts more than any purposeful state building. In an era of revolution and industrialization, the European state was notable for continuity. While expanding and becoming more similar, nineteenth-century states gained autonomy, cultural prestige, and deeper ties to their societies. The paradoxes in these statements point to a historical process that has been the subject of this essay. States of every type recognized the need for new and multiple links between state and people and for sharper demarcations between matters public and private.[82] The device of recognizing distinct fields of play, which was so congenial to liberalism, had in practice proved attractive wherever governments faced restrictions to acknowledge or some weakness to hide; and it created a mechanism for maintaining the established social system by expanding the state's activity. Tested by the challenges of the 1880s and 1890s, these nineteenth-century states were instrumental in establishing different equilibriums in which the state had a still more active role.

The European state in the nineteenth century can thus be seen as a historical type,[83] a type shaped by industrialization, national and bourgeois cultures, and the functions all states were required to perform. Such a perspective fits with a strong tendency in current writing to deemphasize the importance of liberal ideals except as useful ideology. But to carry the argument one step farther might well have the opposite effect. Given the expanding authority of these dominating states, the differences liberals so stressed in constitutions, legal rights, political freedom, and responsible government become all the more important. One sees the state more clearly by recognizing that the differences between England and Germany, France and Russia, Italy and Norway did not lie primarily in the nature of their states; that does not make those differences less important. Nor did similarities among expanding states eliminate differences—in wealth, justice, social structure, the content of culture, and the degree of freedom or repression—that were far more important to the quality of life. But it says a great deal that qualities crucial to the social environment had less effect on the form and functions of the modern state. In a period of radical social change, an expanding state was simply the best defense of the status quo even though it too became an instrument of change. As the neutral state of nineteenth-century Europe thereby gained autonomy, it would become one of the most universally adopted inventions of European civilization.

NOTES

The participants in the conference that sponsored this essay made many helpful comments for which I am grateful. In addition, the invaluable criticisms of Charles Bright and Geoff Eley were a gift from friends and experts that the resulting improvements can only begin to acknowledge.

1. Gianfranco Poggi, *The Development of the Modern State* (Stanford: Stanford University Press, 1978), pp. 92–93.
2. B. R. Mitchell, *European Historical Statistics, 1750–1970* (New York: Columbia University Press, 1975), pp. 695–702, gives these figures for France, Russia, and the United Kingdom through the entire century; for Belgium from 1830, and for Austria until 1867, when Austria and Hungary published separate budgets. These figures are not adjusted for fluctuations in prices or currencies, but these were reasonably steady in the major countries prior to World War I.
3. A comparison of central government expenditure in 1909–12 to that of 1872–75 gives the following ratios: Hungary spent 7.5 times as much; Switzerland, 6.5; Romania, 5.4; Russia, 4.7; Norway, 4.5; Greece, 4.5; Austria, 4.3; Germany, 3.0; Belgium, 2.8; Denmark, 2.7; United Kingdom, 2.3; Italy, 2.2; Spain, 2.0; Netherlands, 1.9; France, 1.6. These ratios compare absolute expenditures. Generally, this was a period of deflation, and corrected figures

would give ratios of 3.0 for the United Kingdom and 2.3 for France. Based on Mitchell, *Historical Statistics*, pp. 695–702.

4. The great exception is the United Kingdom. The high of 1814 was not passed, in absolute terms, until 1898! Expenditures dropped sharply in 1815–17, then more slowly (at an annual rate just over 1 percent) to a low in 1833–34. They then began a slow rise, reaching the level of the postwar years in 1847–48, remaining well above that after 1855. From 1875 to 1898 the annual increase averaged over 2.5 percent, swinging up much more sharply after that.

5. Identified, primarily for the periods after the world wars of the twentieth century, by Alan T. Peacock and Jack Wiseman, *The Growth of Public Expenditure in the United Kingdom* (Princeton: Princeton University Press, 1961).

6. In 1850 nineteen European cities had a population over two hundred thousand. Eleven of these were capitals: Amsterdam, Berlin, Brussels, Edinburgh, Lisbon, London, Madrid, Naples, Paris, St. Petersburg, Vienna; four others were administrative centers or regional capitals: Dublin, Edinburgh, Milan, and Moscow. The others were Glasgow, Leeds, Liverpool, and Manchester. In 1900 nineteen European cities had populations of more than five hundred thousand. Of these nine were capitals: Amsterdam, Berlin, Brussels, Budapest, London, Madrid, Paris, St. Petersburg, Vienna; six others were regional or administrative centers: Barcelona, Hamburg, Moscow, Munich, Naples, Warsaw. The others were Birmingham, Glasgow, Liverpool, and Manchester.

7. Central government expenditures as a percentage of GNP:

	1865–74	1875–84	1885–94
France	18.1%		24.4%
Germany		3.5%	7.8
Italy	10.7		12.9
Norway	3.8		6.5
United Kingdom	6.6		6.2

These figures calculated from Mitchell, *Historical Statistics*, pp. 695–702, 779–90, are for the only countries for which all the necessary figures are readily available. The figures for France are based on estimates of Gross Domestic Product in T. J. Markovitch, *L'industrie francaise de 1789 à 1964* (Paris: Presses Universitaires de France, 1966) and conveniently summarized in Mitchell, *Historical Statistics*, p. 797. The difference between GDP and GNP accounts in large part for the higher figure for France, but differences in accounting procedures make it dangerous to attempt any transnational comparisons. Earlier figures can be calculated for France (20 percent, 1815–24; 17 percent, 1825–44; 18 percent, 1845–54; 18.8 percent, 1855–64) and the United Kingdom (showing a general decline from 11.7 percent in 1830–34 to 8 percent in 1865–69; the lower figures after 1870 in part reflect a shift in the method of calculating GNP, and I have raised the figures for GNP in 1865–69 to make them comparable to the later data).

8. Karl Marx, "The Class Struggle in France," in *Selected Writings*, ed. David McLellan (Oxford: Oxford University Press, 1977), pp. 287–88.

9. Patterns of indebtedness, of course, varied greatly (and debts were often held by foreigners). Of the ninety-eight years from 1815 to 1913, the United Kingdom's expenditures exceeded revenue in thirty-four, France's in seventy-one years (income exceeded expenditure in only seven years under the Bourbons, eight under the July Monarchy, twelve under the Third Republic). Based on tables in Mitchell, *Historical Statistics*, pp. 695–702, 706–26.

10. John R. Gillis, *The Prussian Bureaucracy in Crisis, 1840–1860* (Stanford: Stanford University Press, 1971), pp. 34, 194; p. 251 n.11, p. 227 n.25.

11. Herbert Jacob, *German Administration since Bismarck: Central Authority versus Local Autonomy* (New Haven: Yale University Press, 1963), p. 31.

12. The German figure is for 1906–9. Eugene N. Anderson and Pauline R. Anderson, *Political Institutions and Social Change in Continental Europe in the Nineteenth Century* (Berkeley and Los Angeles: University of California Press, 1967), p. 167. Definitions of civil servants, of course, varied greatly by country.

13. Walter McKenzie Pintner and Dan Karl Rowney, eds., *Russian Officialdom: The Bureaucratization of Russian Society from the Seventeenth to the Twentieth Centuries* (Chapel Hill: University of North Carolina Press, 1980), p. 192.

14. David Roberts, *Victorian Origins of the British Welfare State* (New Haven: Yale University Press, 1960), p. 105.

15. Roberts, *Welfare State*, pp. 93–95, 106, 154.

16. Helen Merrell Lynd, *England in the Eighteen-Eighties: Toward a Social Basis of Freedom* (Oxford: Oxford University Press, 1954), p. 174.

17. Anderson and Anderson, *Political Institutions*, p. 167.

18. Anderson and Anderson, *Political Institutions*, p. 410 n.11, gives the following figures for the number of municipal employees (including transport workers) in some German cities: Breslau, 592 (in 1895), 3,703 (1903); Dusseldorf, 775 (1895), 3,035 (1907); Mannheim, 48 (1870), 717 (1905), 1,127 (1906); Leipzig, 1,800 (1890), 3,500 (1908). They also cite Robert Fried's figures for growth in Turin from 30 employees in 1824 to more than 650 in 1859.

19. Karl Marx, "The Eighteenth Brumaire of Louis Bonaparte" in *Selected Writings*, pp. 316–17.

20. William C. Lubenow, *The Politics of Government Growth: Early Victorian Attitudes toward State Intervention, 1833–1848* (Newton Abbot: David and Charles, 1971), p. 9.

21. Rondo Cameron et al., *Banking in the Early Stages of Industrialization: A Study in Comparative Economic History* (New York: Oxford University Press, 1967) is excellent on the range of these activities.

22. On the differing views of protection and the roles of the state in industrialization, see Francesco Caracciolo, *Il processo di industrializzazione* (Rome: Editore Einaudi, 1979).

23. On the critical roles of the state in these matters, see the useful review in Sidney Pollard, *European Economic Integration, 1815–1870* (London: Thames and Hudson, 1974), pp. 44–89; Francois Caron, *An Economic History of Modern France* (New York: Columbia University Press, 1979), pp. 39–47. In the period 1826–50 the self-consciously modernizing little state of Piedmont created new services to inspect mines (1826), build railroads (1847),

construct telegraph lines (1848), and check weights and measures (1850) (Robert C. Fried, *The Italian Prefects: A Study in Administrative Politics* [New Haven: Yale University Press, 1963], p. 50). The range of these activities undertaken by the German state is listed in Geoff Eley, "State-formation, Nationalism, and Political Culture in Nineteenth-Century Germany," in Raphael Samuel and Gareth Stedman-Jones, eds., *Culture, Ideology, and Politics* (London: Routledge and Kegan Paul, 1983), p. 282.

24. There were 1,799 *bureaux de poste* in France in 1829; 2,395 in 1838 (Alfred Rambaud, *Histoire de la civilisation contemporaine* [Paris: Armand Colin, 1906], p. 343). In the United Kingdom some 75 million letters were carried by the reformed postal service in 1840, 329 million in 1849. And note the rapid spread of an innovation such as the postage stamp; adopted in Britain in 1840 and Brazil in 1843, it had spread to most of the West by 1850.

25. Roberts, *Welfare State*, pp. 98–99; Lynd, *England in the Eighteen-Eighties*, pp. 161–74.

26. Brian Chapman, *The Prefects and Provincial France* (London: George Allen and Unwin, 1955), p. 37, notes the importance of the prefects' "monopoly of local information."

27. Roberts, *Welfare State*, pp. 35–95, 103–7. Gillian Sutherland, ed., *Studies in the Growth of Nineteenth-Century Government* (Totowa: Rowman and Littlefield, 1972), pp. 8–10.

28. Nicos Poulantzas, *Political Power and Social Classes* (London: Verso Editions, 1978), p. 219.

29. Poggi, *Modern State*, p. 90.

30. Edmund Silberner, *The Problem of War in Nineteenth Century Economic Thought* (New York: Garland Press, 1972), pp. 144–45; protectionists, however, could imagine war as profitable, pp. 284–87, which free traders would not admit, pp. 284–87.

31. Silberner, *Problem of War*, pp. 283–84.

32. Patricia O'Brien, "The Revolutionary Police of 1848," in Roger Price, ed., *Revolution and Reaction: 1848 and the Second French Republic* (London: Croom Helm, 1975), pp. 136–37. The Municipal Police of Paris had grown from 97 to 480 under the July Monarchy, and the Municipal Guard had 3,900 members in 1848 (p. 145 n.11).

33. The quotation is from a *Times* leader of 1844 cited by Lubenow, *Government Growth*, p. 21.

34. Poggi, *Modern State*, p. 86; also pp. 72–73.

35. Anthony Giddens, *Politics and Sociology in the Thought of Max Weber* (London: Macmillan, 1972), pp. 32–33. Note the complaint that modern political science also ignores the state, in Alexander Passerin d'Entrèves, *The Notion of the State: An Introduction to Political Theory* (Oxford: Oxford University Press, 1967), pp. 59–65. For an assessment of controversy about the state in contemporary Marxism, see Alan Wolfe, "New Directions in the Marxist Theory of Politics," *Politics and Society*, Winter, 1974, pp. 131–59.

36. The phrase is Harry Eckstein's in "On the Science of the State," *Daedalus* (Fall, 1979), pp. 11–12. He adds the important suggestion that this effect is all the greater in a culturally fragmented society that values an integrated policy. Industrialization of course contributed to both conditions.

37. Giddens, *Weber*, p. 51.
38. Anderson and Anderson, *Political Institutions*, pp. 181ff.
39. And a test of the state's efficacy that seems likely to become a universal standard; note Wolfe, "New Directions," p. 143.
40. J. Salwyn Schapiro, *Liberalism and the Challenge of Fascism* (New York: Octagon Books, 1949), p. 397. For the first time, Schapiro argues, the state became "the most efficient instrument of social progress."
41. Harold J. Laski, *The Rise of European Liberalism* (London: George Allen and Unwin, 1962), pp. 154–55, makes a similar point.
42. Albert O. Hirschman, *Exit, Voice, and Loyalty: Responses to the Decline in Firms, Organizations, and States* (Cambridge: Harvard University Press, 1970), p. 33.
43. Giddens, *Weber*, p. 26.
44. Alexis de Tocqueville, *Democracy in America*, trans. Henry Reeve, ed. Phillips Bradley (New York: Vintage Books, 1959), 2:56.
45. Michael Ignatieff, *A Just Measure of Pain: The Penitentiary in the Industrial Revolution, 1750–1850* (New York: Columbia University Press, 1978), p. 213.
46. See the essay, "The Legitimacy Crises," by Lucian W. Pye, in Leonard Binder, et al., *Crises and Sequences in Political Development* (Princeton: Princeton University Press, 1971), pp. 135–58; and Lucian W. Pye and Sidney Verba, eds., *Political Culture and Political Development* (Princeton: Princeton University Press, 1965).
47. Poggi, *Modern State*, pp. 72–73.
48. John Breuilly, *Nationalism and the State* (Manchester: University of Manchester, 1982), pp. 328–29.
49. Breuilly, *Nationalism*, pp. 356–58; Schapiro, *Liberalism*, p. 398.
50. Poggi, *Modern State*, pp. 104–8, 123–24.
51. Poggi, *Modern State*, pp. 110–11.
52. See Giddens, *Weber*, pp. 51–52; André-Jean Tudesq, *Les Grands Notables en France (1840–1849)*, 2 vols. (Paris: Presses Universitaires de France, 1964); Theodore Zeldin, *The Political System of Napoleon III* (Oxford: Oxford University Press, 1958); W. L. Guttsman, *The British Political Elite* (New York: Basic Books, 1963). Robert Justin Goldstein, "Political Repression and Political Development: The 'Human Rights' Issue in Nineteenth Century Europe," *Comparative Social Research* 4 (1981): 161–98, usefully compiles data on suffrage to show that change was not always in the direction of an increase in the percentage of the population permitted to vote. Significant declines, however, only followed a major change of regime (such as a coup d'état); all others were small and usually the result of an increasing population.
53. In Marxist terms, "the contradiction of greatest importance in the capitalist state is that, in order to be primarily responsible for the maintenance of alienated politics, it must simultaneously be a class state and a universal state. . . ," Wolfe, "New Directions," p. 149, where he also comments that "the state is . . . a process."
54. Napoleon's concern to so use the schools is the most famous example, but note the convictions of Fichte and Clausewitz that only the state could make

education possible, Peter Paret, *Clausewitz and the State* (New York: Oxford University Press, 1976), pp. 179–80.

55. Stability is as challenging a historical problem as revolution, notes Charles S. Maier, "The Two Postwar Eras and the Conditions of Stability in Twentieth-Century Europe," *American Historical Review* 86 (April, 1981): 327–28.

56. "The state cannot be teleocratic and remain neutral" (George Kelley, "Who Needs a Theory of Citizenship," *Daedalus*, Fall, 1979, p. 26).

57. A device first used in England, significantly, to encourage the establishment of local police forces (John J. Tobias, *Crime and Police in England, 1700–1900* [Dublin: Gill and Macmillan, 1979], pp. 101–6).

58. Stanely Hoffmann, in his address to the Council for European Studies, October, 1980, noted that the role of the contemporary European state was being redefined by its inability to provide for its own military defense, by the strength of international corporations, and by internal regionalism—conceivably examples of the state's strategic retreat from spheres it cannot control.

59. Marxists have labeled this alienated politics, and Sam Bowles has commented that the restriction of politics to itself is the essence of stateness in bourgeois society. Breuilly, *Nationalism and the State*, p. 355, observes from a very different perspective that "in the public sphere the state exercises sovereignty directly, in the private sphere it does no more than provide ground rules for dealings between individuals and groups."

60. Note the reluctance under the July Monarchy, Bertrand Gille, *Recherche sur la formation de la grande entreprise capitaliste (1815–1848)* (Paris: S.E.V.P.E.N., 1955), pp. 36–38.

61. Thus the problems seem to me broader than Marx's early insight: "From the political point of view the state and any organization of society are not two distinct things. The state is the organization of society. Insofar as the state admits the existence of social abuses, it seeks their origin either in natural laws that no human power can control or in the private sector which is independent of it or in the inadequacy of the administration of the state. . . . In short, all states look for the causes in accidental or intended faults of administration, and therefore seek the remedy for its evils in administrative measures. Why? Simply because the administration is the organizing activity of the state" (Karl Marx, "Critical Remarks on the Article: 'The King of Prussia and Social Reform'," *Selected Writings*, p. 124).

62. Poggi, *Modern State*, p. 95.

63. I owe the point to Michael Geyer.

64. E. J. Hobsbawm, *Primitive Rebels* (New York: Frederick A. Praeger, 1959), p. 108.

65. On the sequence of these reforms, which is especially clear in England, see E. N. Gladden, *Civil Services of the United Kingdom, 1855–1970* (New York: A. M. Kelley, 1967).

66. Poulantzas, *Political Power*, pp. 255–62.

67. S. E. Finer observed that Benthamite ideas spread through these interconnections of intellectuals, reformers, and future administrators ("The Trans-

mission of Benthamite Ideas, 1820–50," in Sutherland, *Nineteenth-Century Government*, pp. 14–19).

68. Giddens, *Weber*, pp. 34–35.
69. Poggi, *Modern State*, pp. 88–89.
70. Poggi, *Modern State*, pp. 96–97.
71. Often rather cautiously, however, see Lysbeth W. Muncy, *The Junker in the Prussian Administration under William II, 1888–1914* (Providence: Brown University Press, 1944).
72. Geoff Eley, *Reshaping the German Right: Radical Nationalism and Political Change after Bismarck* (New Haven: Yale University Press, 1980); Sidney Tarrow, *Between Center and Periphery: Grassroots Politicians in Italy and France* (New Haven: Yale University Press, 1977).
73. Since Gramsci, Marxists have paid particular attention to the importance of this in the nineteenth century. Poulantzas, "Political Power," p. 215; Wolfe, "New Directions," p. 158.
74. Eley, "State Formation," p. 279; John A. Armstrong, *The European Administrative Elite* (Princeton: Princeton University Press, 1973), pp. 135–41.
75. A theme of Eugen Weber, *Peasants into Frenchmen: The Modernization of Rural France, 1870–1914* (Stanford: Stanford University Press, 1976); Fritz K. Ringer, *Education and Society in Modern Europe* (Bloomington: Indiana University Press, 1977).
76. Raymond Grew, ed., *Crises of Political Development in Europe and the United States* (Princeton: Princeton University Press, 1978).
77. Carlton J. H. Hayes, whose *A Generation of Materialism* (New York: Harper and Brothers, 1941) viewed that period with distaste, pointed out its importance as a watershed to his students (see Lynd, *England in the Eighteen-Eighties*, p. vii). More recently a group of historians looking at nine different European countries found the period a critical one in each of them. See Grew, *Crises of Political Development*. Geoff Eley, "Nationalism and Social History," *Social History* 6 (January, 1981): 83–107, offers from a different point of view a chronology that also stresses the increased penetration of the state later in the century.
78. Poggi, *Modern State*, p. 95.
79. The process analyzed here thus strained the state's capacity to maintain its legitimacy, mobilize support, and coordinate these proliferating institutions and fields of play. Interestingly enough, Breuilly sees these as the three functions of nationalism in *Nationalism and the State*.
80. A law of 1905 in France, for example, recognized the desire for state business on the part of lawyers, doctors, architects, and surveyors who only served the state part time, Hervé Detton, *L'Administration regionale et locale de la France* (Paris: Presses Universitaires de France, 1968).
81. Note Meinecke's remarkable faith that the "Prussian-German problem" would be resolved by the war which would create a more integrated German state (Friedrich Meinecke, *Cosmopolitanism and the National State* [Princeton: Princeton University Press, 1970], pp. 31–33, 364–74).

82. Paret, *Clausewitz and the State*, pp. 180–83; Breuilly, *Nationalism and the State*, pp. 352–55.

83. See the discussion, and the argument for 1870 as the moment of change, in Roberto Vivarelli, "1870 in European History and Historiography," *Journal of Modern History* 53 (June, 1981): 167–88.

THE STATE IN THE UNITED STATES DURING THE NINETEENTH CENTURY

Charles C. Bright

Marx saw in nineteenth-century America an advanced form of the bourgeois political order.[1] The characteristic features of universal (male) suffrage, direct legislation, civil liberties, and republican ideology were all well developed. The state, while institutionally innocuous, effectively accommodated a dynamically expanding economy and a vital, mass democracy. With due allowance for such interruptions in success as slavery, civil war, and recurrent economic depression, the United States was a triumph of liberal democratic capitalism.

What accounts for this? Were Americans political geniuses? Were they simply lucky? Did the special conditions of geographical expansion and material abundance during the nineteenth century make the relations between capitalism and democracy uniquely nonproblematic in the United States? Or does the appearance of harmony and success disguise deeper levels of contention and standoff? This essay argues that the peculiar articulation of a full-bodied popular democracy and a rapidly developing capitalist economy was achieved through a stalemated state and that, paradoxically, the paralysis of federal policy, born of political impasse, made possible the successful mediation of capitalism and democracy in the United States under the conditions prevailing in the nineteenth century.

The federal state was institutionally weak throughout the period, and it was getting relatively weaker after 1830. Once the expansion of the activist, Hamiltonian state had been checked in the early decades of the nineteenth century, the federal apparatus ceased to acquire new functions. Under the Jacksonian presidencies, powers accumulated at the national level by federalist statemakers were given up again. "The federal government did very little in 1860 that it had not undertaken before 1830," remarked Leonard White, the historian of federal administration, who added that the fivefold increase in the size of the federal state during the last quarter of the nineteenth century "bespoke an increase in the volume of business coincident with the growth of the country rather than the addition of new functions and activities."[2]

To be sure, what little the federal state did in the nineteenth century was not unimportant to capitalist expansion. It maintained the currency, funded the national debt, collected the customs, registered patents, and—what was most important—assisted in the transfer of public lands and natural resources to private hands and thereby played a key role in the conversion of the vast continental inheritance into commodities for commercial exploitation. Yet because of the extraordinary abundance of the hinterland, this distributional activity involved little ongoing regulation or allocative choices, and thus required little in the way of a national state apparatus to perform. While this does not account for the institutional weakness of the federal state in the nineteenth century, it does suggest that the failure of the political system to sustain the foundations of an activist state did not present serious obstacles to capitalist development. Similarly, the federal state managed, with little administrative effort, to maintain a perimeter of legal defenses around property through the court system and an arena of political combat in Congress where social, economic, and regional conflicts were aired, clarified, and occasionally composed. Indeed, in many respects the federal state conformed to the classic formula of liberal political theory, playing the role of rule maker and referee above the fray of civil society, a seemingly neutral—or neutralized—promoter of the general interest and a democratic arena for the resolution of social and economic conflict.

These promotional activities remained extremely limited and generalized, however, always much less than leading segments of capital wanted. In fact, they represented the lowest common denominator of agreement among politicians who were deeply divided over what role the federal state should play in national development. For the United States was not wholly a capitalist, nor certainly a fully industrialized, society in the nineteenth century. A broad class of petty commodity producers in agriculture, often only partially engaged in market relations and not generally subject to wage relations, as well as a powerful class of slave masters in the South, put up a stiff, albeit fragmented, resistance to the expansion of the industrial sector and the consolidation of capitalist labor relations. Precisely because democratic practices were so well developed, moreover, this resistance was invariably politicized, as forces of opposition entered the political arena to seek redress or, what was more frequent, to block state action in favor of capitalist development. In the 1830s and again in the 1890s, populist forms of agrarian resistance, based on broad democratic mobilizations and often sustaining powerful alternative visions of social and economic development, contested the efforts of leading elements of capital to use the federal apparatus for sectoral interests; in the 1850s and 1860s, opposition from the slave-holding South, drawing upon sectional and cultural loyalties, nearly brought the federal state to ruin.

These broad formulations of opposition to capitalist consolidation comprised "the democracy" in nineteenth-century politics, not only in the literal sense that they were the main constituency of the Democratic party, but also in the more symbolic sense that they raised voices against corporate or monopoly power in what Arthur Schlesinger once called the enduring struggle between the business community and the rest of society. The cry of agrarian insurgents in the 1830s and 1890s, that the federal state was in the clutches of monied monopolies and had to be reclaimed by the people, or the fear, widely cultivated in the antebellum South, that a stronger national state would pose a direct threat to slave property interests, were—like the northern anxieties about "the slave power" in the 1850s—alarms raised by contending forces in the political arena, each seeking to preclude control over the state by its rivals. They bear testimony, not to capitalist domination of the state, but to the fierce struggle over policy being waged among several contending forces whose differential access to the political arena was structured by social and economic struggles in which, at the same time, control of state power was a useful and potentially decisive weapon.

The nineteenth-century American state was, then, in the fullest sense of the term, a contested terrain. Politicians and party managers, competing for offices and influence in the state, reproduced economic, social, and cultural antagonisms as politics and fought each other to a stalemate. A combination of democratic mobilizations and economic struggles for advantage in the political arena produced, by 1830, an impasse in federal statemaking which progressively weakened the federal apparatus and gave rise to a crisis-prone political order. This essay, while only a sketchy outline of the problem, will pursue this argument in four steps: we shall look, first, at the early federalist state and the basis of the first consolidation of power at the national level; secondly, at the sectional and sectoral crises that arose within the federalist state in the early nineteenth century and the competing solutions devised to resolve this crisis in the 1820s, leading, thirdly, to the development of a peculiar state of courts and parties after about 1830 which, finally, survived a sectional crisis in the 1860s only to succumb to a sectoral crisis in the 1890s. An examination of these crises in the nineteenth-century state will, perhaps, suggest the sort of transformational pressures generated in the political arena that gave rise to a new version of the national state in the early decades of the twentieth century.

Statemaking in the Federalist Period

The federal state was built upon an assemblage of local and regional powers. Without feudal antecedents, the United States had no monarch or great lord to act as a catalyst for statemaking; no established landed classes capable of alliances with, or resistance to, statemaking princes; no entrenched bureaucratic or military caste around whom statemakers could build an autonomous administrative capacity at the center.[3] As a settler society, a transatlantic extension of European empires, the United States was composed of communities which, though often isolated and self-sufficient for a time after settlement, fully expected to see the thickening of regional and national bonds promote economic expansion and local opportunity; no large state apparatus had to be deployed, as in Europe, to crack open local cultures or to ensure the political, economic, and legal encorporation of inward-turning, self-sufficient localities. There were some exceptions, of course, some instances of resistance on a European model, as for example, when the federal government incorporated Louisiana and the Spanish Southwest, both previously settled by Europeans, or when it tried to coerce the Mormon settlements in Utah, or most notoriously, when it undertook the reconstruction of Southern society after the Civil War. But the usual pattern was for territories, newly settled and organized, to fall all over themselves to join the federal union. While this was often, paradoxically, a move by local elites to consolidate their power in the territories, it nevertheless lent a voluntaristic, consensual tone to the expansion of the American state and underscored the fundamental originality of the federation: the central government was the creation of its constituent parts.

Like a coral reef, federal power was accumulated from the ground up. This is not to argue, however, that state formation occurred by popular demand, or that the constitutional system was raised up by the voice of the people. Indeed, quite the contrary, the Constitution was drafted by an elite assembly called together by a small group of nationalists from the Middle Atlantic states who were concerned about the weakness of government under the Articles of Confederation. Having resisted to the point of rebellion British attempts to centralize imperial administration and extractive powers, political elites in all the former colonies were extremely jealous of the rights and prerogatives of their respective states, guarding thereby the local foundations of their social position and political power. The governing document they drew up was a hesitant contract, ringed round with reservations and informed by a deep suspicion of central authority and a lively fear of tyranny. Indeed, the fact that a federal state was formed at all bears some examination, for there was little in the patterns of colonial development or revolutionary resistance that made such a consolidation necessary or even very likely, and there was much in the European experience of segmented sovereignties to suggest that a similar regional pattern of state formation might have occurred on the American continent.

What militated against such a fragmentation of sovereignty, at least initially, was weakness. Colonial handicaps of economic marginality and uneven development were not overcome by severing ties with Great Britain.[4] The American economy continued to operate within a very narrow framework of fluctuating prices, unstable markets, and perennial shortages of capital. Northern merchants and financiers were mainly concerned with the impact of heavy debts, inflated currency, and capital shortages upon the fiscal integrity of the various states and their trade links with Europe. Southerners, less burdened by public debts, worried about credit supplies, without which large-scale agriculture was impossible, and even more about the continued presence of the European powers in the continental interior, blocking the paths of territorial expansion wherein lay the future of an agrarian republic.[5] There were serious differences of interest and policy among the political elites of the various states. What brought them together in the 1780s, however, was the fact that a restoration of overseas commerce, the acquisition of foreign credit, and secure control over western territories all depended upon the capacity of the new nation to establish its legitimacy in the world and to conduct successful diplomacy with the European powers. This promoted a certain show of solidarity. The new constitution was meant to establish a permanent mechanism for resolving conflicts among colonial elites so that they might, in de Tocqueville's words, "appear to advantage before foreigners."[6]

A new governing system, however, required a measure of domestic discipline. As Gordon Wood has observed, "all the Federalists' desires to establish a strong and respectable nation in the world, all their plans to create a flourishing commercial economy, in short all of what the Federalists wanted of the new central government seemed in the final analysis dependent upon the prerequisite maintenance of aristocratic politics."[7] The war of independence had involved a broad popular mobilization which had partaken of the long tradition of oppositional rhetoric in British politics running back at least to the seventeenth century and embracing many of the very issues that had provoked migration to the New World in the first place.[8] Once colonial patriotism had triumphed over imperial domination, however, the revolt continued to rumble down through American society, generating new challenges to state government and legitimizing further resistance in western districts to the domination of coastal elites. Popular opposition was especially strong at the state level against efforts to organize public debts. The successful insurgency of debtors in the Rhode Island legislature and the abortive rebellion by Shays in Massachusetts were particularly disquieting.[9] Political elites and creditors, embattled in the several states, reached out to find one another in the hopes that, as Madison observed, "a rage for paper money, for an abolition of debts, for an equal division of property, or for any other improper and wicked project will be less apt to pervade the whole body of the Union than any particular member of it."[10] Centralized government was meant to contain popular forces.

Thus the Constitution represented a successful effort by colonial elites, not only to establish a mechanism for resolving conflicts among themselves, but to check dissident and democratic pressures in American society with a strong governing counterpoise. What made this consolidation of political authority possible was a fragile but crucial working alliance between, on the one hand, commercial and financial interests in the North, centered in New York and Pennsylvania, and, on the other, leading planter interests in the South, especially in Virginia and South Carolina. This mercantile-agrarian alliance of elites, which found its voice in the collaboration of Hamilton and Madison, coauthors of the *Federalist Papers*, reflected a broad agreement among the most cosmopolitan and well-connected of colonial society about the need for a stronger national government and, within limits, about what that government should do.

The working alliance that made possible the Constitution came under increasing strain during the 1790s because of fierce controversies over the policies of Alexander Hamilton, first secretary of the treasury. He developed an ambitious program of state action in support of commerce and finance that extended well beyond the common concern of all elites for economic stabilization and the restoration of trade. Hamilton embraced a grander vision of an activist national state promoting economic development, and he sought to provide the federal government with the capacity to fulfill such a role. He deployed federal power in support of the national economy: a system of currency, postal services, laws of copyright, patent, and bankruptcy, a central clearing bank, and (though his motives on this score remain in dispute) a program for the general promotion of manufactures.[11] Depreciated continental certificates were nationalized for redemption at face value by the federal treasury. The war debts of individual states were taken over and consolidated as a national debt to be funded through customs duties and excise taxes. The entire process of acquiring, surveying, parceling, and disposing of Western territories was taken over by the federal government and tied to the debt settlement. Hamilton's tax structure was deliberately regressive, drawing revenue from the consumers of imported goods and the producers of whiskey into the federal treasury and from there, through the central bank, into the hands of creditors, security holders, and speculators. This was an effective mechanism of accumulation in a capital short economy, as the federal government spent some 80 percent of its annual revenue servicing a debt held by a relatively small number of creditors, mostly residing in port cities north of the Mason-Dixon line. It also secured the public credit, thus providing both merchants and planters with access to European capital resources. In all of this, Hamilton's intention was to tie wealthy citizens from every state to the central regime, creating a national interest dependent upon federal power above the loyalties of state and section. Even by European standards of the day, he constructed an active, capable state structure. But in the process, he steered dangerously close to prevailing definitions of tyranny and shattered the constitutional alliance by driving Southern planters and agrarian dissidents into opposition.

Madison broke with Hamilton over the debt question and the national bank, and together with Jefferson, organized an anti-Hamilton coalition which turned the Federalists out of office in 1800. Yet though the constitutional alliance had broken down, the paradigm of policies remained in place. The Jeffersonians operated within the same framework and were subjected to the same constraints as their Hamiltonian enemies. Despite the fierceness of political dispute, historians have been hard put to discover great differences in policy once the Republicans took control of the federal state.[12] Like Hamilton, Jefferson was an elitist politician, more interested in executive action than popular accountability. While he firmly believed that Hamilton's antiagrarian bias was evil, he recognized "the necessity of yielding to the cries of the creditors . . . for the sake of the Union and to save it from the greatest calamities, the total extinction of our credit in Europe."[13] While Jefferson and his chief economic minister, Gallatin, sought to speed up the retirement of the national debt, they continued to finance the debt with regressive taxation. Jefferson was quite willing to wink at constitutional limitations and stretch presidential powers to suit his policies, as for example in the purchase of the Louisiana territory. If Jefferson's interests in the continental interior reflected his basically agrarian dream of a decentralized republic of yeomen farmers, he and Gallatin developed some very Hamiltonian programs for national development, using federal funds to subsidize education, roads, canals, and other internal improvements.[14] Jeffersonian Republicans were quite prepared, in office, to impose unwanted policies upon minority sections of the country, as when they pushed the commercial embargo against Great Britain to the point of war without regard for the strong opposition of New England states. In the wake of that war, moreover, Republicans embraced the necessity of rechartering the national bank and of employing federal tariffs for the protection of nascent manufactures. Most Federalists were eventually absorbed into Republican ranks, while that party produced many vigorous champions of nationalism and the activist state.

Though the working alliance of merchants and planters that had produced the Constitution had collapsed by 1800, the conditions of weakness and dependency that had fostered that alliance in the first place did not quickly disappear. The broad nationalism of the period reflected less a

slavishness to heady principles than a general recognition by all parties of
the imperatives of survival for a marginal republic perched on the edge of
a vast continent on the fringes of the European commercial system. As
long as the principal focus and preoccupation of the new state was upon
external affairs, the basis for statemaking remained intact. The autonomous political realm created by the Constitution, while generally accountable to the people, was largely concerned with the reconciliation of
elite differences and the coordination of elite interests in the face of
external imperatives. Democracy was limited. The federal government
remained remote from everyday life.[15] It was dominated by small elite
factions that organized themselves around boarding houses and congressional caucuses, nursed the most violent political hatreds, and peri-
odically presented candidates to the people for their selection. Divisions
among politicians were primarily drawn along sectoral lines, as they dis-
puted whether federal action should tilt in favor of agricultural or commercial interests. But since both land and capital were vital elements in
the development of the fledging economy and its commercial ties with
Europe, tacit trade-offs were usually possible. Territorial expansion could
be balanced against measures of trade promotion since both involved
overseas diplomacy. The protracted Napoleonic wars produced a maze of
diplomatic problems and serious disputes among rival politicians, but
ultimately all parties recognized that national security and economic
growth depended upon a vigorous state dealing successfully with foreign
powers. This basic agreement on ends promoted the growth of an activist
state at the federal level. The effectiveness of this state, in turn, created
the context for the tremendous expansion of the American economy after
1815. This plunge into the interior raised new domestic problems and
posed a serious political challenge to the federal state created by Hamilton and his enemies.

The Crisis of the Federalist State

The success of the Federalist state in achieving diplomatic recognition,
access to European capital and markets, and control over the territories of
the interior promoted rapid economic expansion. Broadly speaking, this
growth consisted of two parallel movements, a centrifugal expansion into
new territories and a centripetal concentration of capital, labor, and machinery into factory production. Both movements were well under way by
1820. By the 1850s, settlement had passed the Mississippi River into the
great central plain, and California on the Pacific coast had been annexed.
While a majority of the population still worked in agriculture and the
main sources of power were still animal and human, the factory system
was securely implanted and the development of an internal transportation

network was well under way. By the 1890s, the frontier had been closed and the industrial transformation of the country was nearly complete. Whereas in 1860 there were more slaves in the population than factory workers, by the turn of the century a majority of working people were moving into the manufacturing and commercial sectors of the economy and into the burgeoning urban areas. The value of American manufacturing output surpassed the value of agricultural output for the first time in the 1880s. By the end of the century, it was nearly equal to the value of the industrial output of Britain, Germany, and France combined.[16]

The battles over tariffs in the 1820s marked the emergence of a struggle between agriculture and industry in American politics. Although the tariffs of 1816 and 1820 were, according to Taussig,[17] transitional ones, the industrial sector was already challenging the long-standing agreement between agrarian and merchant interests, dating back to the constitutional convention, that tariffs should be used only for revenue purposes, not for shaping the course of economic development. A rapid shift in orientation ensued during the 1820s, as New England merchant capital moved into industrial investments, carrying its representatives, most prominently Daniel Webster, into the protectionist camp.

Yet while the political strength of the industrial sector grew steadily, it faced an equally fast-growing agrarian sector. Indeed one of the most striking features of nineteenth-century economic development, in contrast with that of Europe, was the continuing expansion and vitality of agriculture in a period of rapid industrialization. This was no backward, traditional sector. As a producer of cash crops for national and international markets, it was intimately involved in the process of transforming continental resources into commodities. It remained a leading edge of national economic growth until at least the 1860s, and it continued to produce over half of American exports until World War I.[18] At several crucial junctures, agricultural expansion provided a decisive spur to the industrial transformation of the United States. And even as manufacturing output surpassed agriculture, the political strength of the agrarian sector in the national arena continued to grow through the 1880s, as settlement across the Great Plains and the Rocky Mountains region added a belt of new farm states to the federal system.

Through much of this period, however, the dynamism of agriculture was based on slave labor. It was cotton that gave energy to the agrarian sector, as the remarkable growth in commercial demand between 1820 and 1860 sucked settlers into and through the Mississippi delta chasing the immense profits to be had from the cultivation of virgin lands. Annual production of cotton rose from half a million to 4.5 million bales in thirty-five years. Cotton made up the bulk of American export earnings in the antebellum period, underwriting the expansion of merchant capital in the

North and the early development of the New England textile industry.[19] Cotton and the structural requirements of plantation slavery bore the South along a peculiar path of development, promoting a social formation distinct from the rest of the country and based upon deference, rigid hierarchy, and forms of hereditary status grounded, ultimately, in racism.[20] The slave society and culture of the South proved increasingly incompatible with the industrializing North and its growing commitment to the free labor market and competitive capitalist values. While the existence of two modes of production within the American economy did not make civil war inevitable, it did produce increasing strains, as the trajectories of development in the two sections, to adapt a phrase from Italian politics, moved along parallel divergences.

The profound sectional split within the agrarian sector between slave and free farming gave an explosive twist to the familiar conflicts between agriculture and industry. Leading spokesmen of agrarian interests were often, also, champions of the sectional interests of slavery. Indeed, agrarian mobilization became a political device for the defense of slavery, and agrarian issues, themselves open to political settlement, often took on sectional overtones that added the animosities of antagonistic social formations to the tensions between economic sectors. The dynamism of Southern agriculture supported an expansionist social order whose elites fully expected to participate in the long-term shaping of the national economy. Southerners were able to exert a degree of influence over the nation's domestic and foreign policies that could match the growing power of the industrial sector and continuously challenge it for control of the federal state.

The implications of this were already clear in 1820, when the controversy over Missouri's admission posed in startling terms the two questions that were to plague national politics for the next forty years: did the slave system have an equal right to expand into the new territories of the hinterland? and, what would ensure the political balance between slave and free states at the federal center when new states were added to the union? The immediate problem was settled by compromise, but not before everyone had clearly seen that the struggle for control of the federal state was, in effect, becoming a struggle to determine whether the federal apparatus would be used to promote or restrict the expansion of slavery.[21]

This in turn colored all other political issues. The conflict between agriculture and industry, typical of all industrializing societies, shifted to constitutional grounds and became a struggle over the nature of the federal state. In opposing protective tariffs, John Calhoun not only denounced them as "an immense tax on one portion of the country to put money in the pockets of another"[22]—the basic agrarian argument—but went on to argue that the use of federal power to promote the interests of the industrial sector upset the original balance of constitutional powers and, through loose interpretation, gave the federal government both the authority and the capacity to act against the vital interests of particular sections. The battle over tariffs shifted to a general argument over the uses of federal power in the promotion of economic development and, not for the last time, Southerners discovered that a defense of agrarian interests quickly became a sectional defense of slavery. Calhoun, never one to ignore the furthest extensions of implacable logic, carried the argument to the point of secession.[23] But well before that point was reached, the framework of elite agreement over the role of the state, which had made national statemaking possible in the previous period, had been shattered, and a political stalemate at the federal center threatened the further consolidation of national power.

Two general strategies emerged in response to this crisis in the federalist state. The first, associated with the Clay-Webster current, sought to promote state-led compromises in the national interest; it failed as national policy but was preserved, albeit in modified form, in the Whig party organization. The second, associated with the Jackson–Van Buren current, resorted to mass mobilizations in the agrarian sector and to national party building; it succeeded by the 1830s in establishing new terms of political combat and then became institutionalized in the Democratic party apparatus.

The nationalist strategy, which grew out of the kind of interest politics practiced in the earlier, federalist period, tried to contain sectional and sectoral tensions at the center, through interelite negotiations and measured doses of federal action to bind elite deals. The Missouri compromise of 1820 provided a model for this sort of nationalist mediation, with congressmen acting as regional ambassadors advocating the cause of their respective sections in solemn debates aimed at clarifying positions and formulating compromise. Clay's "American System," a collection of proposals made during the 1820s for higher tariffs, internal improvements, easier credit, expanded banking facilities, and a general strengthening of federal capacities, also carried with it the larger vision of an active central state promoting a general strengthening of national bonds and arbitrating both sectional and sectoral disputes in the national interest. At its furthest extension, this approach presumably could have embraced the sort of resolutions adopted by the Ohio legislature in 1824 and endorsed by several other Northern states which declared that since "the evil of slavery is a national one," the federal regime should undertake emancipation, compensating slaveholders from federal revenues and resettling freed blacks in colonies outside the boundaries of the United States.[24] Ultimately, whether it involved the federal government attacking the sources of sectional tension or merely riding herd on the incompatibilities of American society through negotiated compromises, the nationalist strategy called upon Hamiltonian traditions of an activist state.

Such views hardly commended themselves to Southerners. Their angry rejection of the Ohio resolutions expressed a broader conviction that a federal state with the capacity to administer intersectional accords was also a state strong enough to meddle with vested Southern property interests. "If Congress possesses the power to do what is proposed in this bill," declared John Randolph in opposing a survey bill for internal improvements, "they may emancipate every slave in the United States."[25] Clay's top-down strategy for containing social conflict, while expressing the supportable belief that economic differences between North and South, as well as between industrial and agrarian interests, were not so great as to be beyond the reach of compromise, foundered upon the political reality that sectional tensions, and the amplification these gave to sectoral strains, destroyed the framework of agreement among national elites about what the federal state should and should not be doing. Had this been a static system, it might have been possible to devise some permanent national solution on a federalist basis which protected sectional interests. But boundaries were not settled, and continuous westward expansion kept reopening the sectional argument over the extension of slavery and the balance of power at the center. Compromise thus had a tendency to hemorrhage on the open frontier.

Part of the difficulty in effecting all-in solutions through federal compromise and promotional activity was the vitality of the competing, Jacksonian strategy. Rather than trying to contain and balance the proliferating differences of an expanding society, mass political mobilization of the kind Jackson and his party managers promoted ran with the patterns of geographic and demographic growth. Thus they were able to tap the enormous expansion of the electorate in the first quarter of the nineteenth century and stimulate a marked increase in the level of popular participation in national politics. They built political alliances along sectoral lines, linking the agricultural regions of the South and West, where sentiment ran against protective tariffs, internal improvements, and the use of federal power for the promotion of banking and manufacturing, with the ethnic outsiders and economic marginals of the Northeast, antagonistic to Yankee commercialism and class domination.[26] This alliance proved especially appealing to Southerners, in that it offered them the possibility of building national majorities within the federal system which could, in turn, contain the threat of federal power to their sectional interests. Mobilization along the agrarian axis crossed and thus tended to obscure the sectional divide. At the same time, it reinforced the hostility of Jacksonians toward an active, centralized federal state, since to deploy the state apparatus in support of agrarian interests risked the danger that the industrial sector, if it gained power, would use the state against the slave system, a sectional interest.[27]

Ideologically, the Jacksonians claimed that large concentrations of wealth, the so-called money power, had latched onto the democratic institutions of the people and were manipulating them for private gain. They argued that an emphatic separation of state and economy would protect government from corruption.[28] Their assumption was that, since economic concentrations were artificial creations of privilege and thus dependent upon access to state power, the removal of the state from economic activity would prove fatal to monopoly. This meant, politically, that the Jacksonians were active in checking and reversing the growth of state power. They conducted a broad assault upon the key components of the state's participation in economic development—lowering taxes, capping tariffs, selling off stocks, reducing contracts and subsidies, dismantling the national road system, and most symbolically, destroying the national bank. At the federal level, the Jacksonian program amounted to "a dismantling operation," and historians have often noted a steady decline in federal activity, especially in economic promotion, after about 1830.[29] At the state level, while the impact of the Jacksonians was less dramatic and less uniform, they were able in many cases to block further participation by state governments in infrastructural projects and, especially after the panic of 1837, to conduct a general withdrawal of state institutions from participation in economic ventures.

Jackson's opponents had to organize an opposition party, the Whigs, to compete for office. Ideologically, the Whigs supported the national bank, internal improvements, protective tariffs, and an active role for the state in economic development, public education, and social reform.[30] During the 1830s, the Jacksonian Democrats and their Whig opponents engaged in a continuous, competitive mobilization of voters. As the two parties took shape, they expressed the interplay of sectional and sectoral tensions at the federal level. On the one hand, their programs offered alternative strategies of economic development, the Whigs seeking to encourage capital growth with state aid and facilities, the Democrats, as champions of laissez-faire doctrines, insisting that capital should go it alone. These reflected the deepening sectoral differences between industry and agriculture in the expanding economy. On the other hand, both parties were, at bottom, sectional organizations, if only because during their formative stages the dynamic core of the agrarian sector lay in the South while the heart of nascent manufacturing was in the North. The Democrats were a Southern party with powerful extensions in the West along the agrarian axis and in the urban machines of the North; the Whigs, later the Republicans, were always dominant in the commercial and industrial Northeast and attracted the more cosmopolitan elements in the South and West, especially those heirs of the Hamiltonian alliance engaged in commerce and banking or interested in state promotion of national economic development. Thus while both parties organized across sectional lines to maintain a national presence and compete for federal offices, both parties, as we shall see, fell back on their respective sectional bases during the two great crises of the nineteenth-century party system, in the late 1850s and the early 1890s.

From the 1830s on, leaders of agrarian and industrial interests, who were also often leading spokesmen of two increasingly hostile sections, organized rival political parties to battle for control of the federal state. Their competitive mobilizations, digging ever deeper into the electoral resources of the country and erecting broad, patchwork coalitions on the basis of local organizations, were really preemptive efforts to prevent the other party from using federal power, however indirectly, in pursuit of its sectional or sectoral interests. While both parties were able to build alliances across sectional lines and thus to bury sectional animosities beneath other differences, neither party could address the root causes of sectional tensions—the two modes of production within the national economy—nor prevent the politics of agrarian and industrial sectors from being inflamed by sectional animosities. As long as there was no agreement on the role of the federal state in economic development, or indeed on the future shape and character of the national economy, even simple sector trade-offs of the kind that had characterized the federalist period were difficult to negotiate, and a Junker-type conservative alliance of agrarian and industrial elites was put out of reach until after the Civil War. Even had the Whigs managed to win control of the federal apparatus with their dream of a stronger central state, it is doubtful whether they could have implemented their activist program without precipitating Southern secession. Federal policy was stalemated, and the federal state, the object of competitive mobilizations, was rendered impotent. Party building and the grassroots mobilization of voters expressed, without solving, the crisis of statemaking at the federal level.

The State of Courts and Parties

The extension of two-party competition undercut the bases of federalist statemaking and institutionalized the paralysis of federal policy in three related ways. In the first place, rival mobilizations by the two parties in every county and precinct in the country had a dramatic impact upon voter participation. In the national elections of 1820, only 9 percent of the eligible population voted; in 1828, the year of Jackson's election, this figure rose to over 55 percent and it topped 80 percent during the next decade, a level of popular participation in politics that was to be maintained with some fluctuations through the remainder of the century.[31] Since the techniques of popular mobilization in the nineteenth century were almost entirely local and direct, involving public meetings, rallies and parades, circuit lecturers, networks of correspondence, the columns of local newspapers, and above all, local party organizations themselves, these new voters were drawn into national politics at the local level. The intensification of political activity in local arenas did not produce the most democratic system imaginable, since local oligarchs were often in control. How these local elites translated social and economic status into political power, and how they retained control over the symbols and ideologies of politics in the local arenas where the electorate was organized, remain areas requiring historical research. But while power and access were not evenly distributed, party organizing did create a mass politics, rooted in popular participation.[32] The consolidation of parties thus shattered the aristocratic foundations of state building in the federalist era and undercut the ability of narrow circles of national elites to control the terms of political competition.

While a vast, decentralized expansion of the political universe took place very rapidly, this did not mean that there was more room in the political arena. For, in the second place, the two parties quickly occupied the extended terrain, competitively covering all possibilities and options in local political discourse. Historians are becoming more sensitive to the bewildering currents of ethnic, religious, cultural, and class animosity that ran through American communities and shaped local political alignments.[33] But they have hardly begun to explain how the two parties, once institutionalized, managed to coopt or absorb challengers and maintain a hegemonic lock on the ideas and symbols of popular political discourse. It is nevertheless clear that successful party building depended upon effective local cadres who could work upon the cultural and economic divisions of communities, organizing people in the localities against each other, encouraging among partisans an unremitting hatred of the enemy, and formulating issues in ways that mattered to people and ensured their vote. To win national office, politicians had to rely on the abilities of local and regional managers to spin together plausible political combinations from these crosscurrents of local affairs. Thus while many of the key issues in national politics in this period turned on economic questions—banking, currency, tariffs, land policy, and internal improvements—they were often framed in the noneconomic language of virtue and justice, evoking cultural visions of the future of the republic and competing assumptions about national purposes which could be translated into the terms of local party combat, capturing thereby the deep religious and cultural cleavages of local communities and forming a common vocabulary that could thread its way through the dense webs of local conflict to organize and hold together "a vast, varie-gated, and decentralized electorate."[34]

Elections were thus highly symbolic and fiercely contested events. Few were disinterested, and the losers rarely abandoned the fight for long. Winners seldom had a decisive mandate and almost never a clear field of action. Since the whole point of mobilization was as much to preclude action by the rival party as to implement a political program, it is hardly surprising that the periods of greatest paralysis in federal policy corresponded with the periods when party mobilization was the fullest and the margins of electoral victory the slimmest, as in the 1830s and 1840s, and again in the 1880s. Conversely, it was in the moments of crisis, as in the 1860s and again in the 1890s, when the Democratic party momentarily collapsed as a national competitor and the Republicans were able to secure unchallenged control over the federal apparatus, that the state gained some capacity for political maneuver and autonomous action. Equally telling, perhaps, is the fact that when a Junker-type alliance among conservative agrarian and industrial elites was finally formulated in the late 1870s, it was in the context of renewed two-party stalemate, following the return of the Democratic party to national politics and its success in the elections of 1874 and 1876, and it was based on the lowest common denominator among divided elites, federal inactivity.

The closer and fiercer the electoral competition, thirdly, the more both parties came to rely on the state apparatus for the patronage and spoils of office necessary to sustain the mobilization effort and to keep their ramshackle national organizations together. Patronage was the currency of politics and the glue of regional and local alliances. From the outset, contemporaries were aware that, in Daniel Webster's words, "a great, a very great change has taken place within a few years, in the practice of executive government. . . . No one can deny that office, of every kind, is now sought with extraordinary avidity."[35] The regular rotation of offices in the state administration, which Jackson inaugurated on the good republican principle of giving every citizen a turn in government, had become by James Polk's time a systematic expropriation of state resources for partisan purposes. By the 1880s, when the party system reached its most extensive elaboration, whole armies of political retainers moved in and out of office in the state apparatus with each change of administration. In federal, state, and local government, political parties fastened onto state administration and squeezed it for sustenance. Most offices in the federal gift were scattered across the country in cities and communities in every state and could thus be distributed to party loyalists in reward for services rendered and in expectation of future political activity in local and regional party organizations. As federal support for economic development and internal improvements declined after

1830, pork barrel compendiums, such as the annual Rivers and Harbors Bill, also became increasingly important to individual congressmen needing to shore up local bases, and the cost of these projects grew accordingly. Federal contracts for provisioning the armed forces, for the naval yards, and for carrying the mail were also systematically turned to partisan ends, as were federal pensions, which after the Civil War were paid out through the veterans organizations of the Union army and used as a means of mobilizing Republican support across the Northern states. The great strength of the party system lay in its techniques for calling down resources from the federal and state apparatus to reward local operatives and to cement local alliances. The link between electoral success and patronage was maintained by the fact that the same organization that mobilized voters and assembled winning coalitions also supervised the distribution of offices and favors.[36]

In this way, political parties penetrated the state at all levels and came to depend upon its resources. Party leaders, occupying the legislative branch at all levels of the state, were able to establish bridgeheads into the executive, controlling appointments to, and the resources of, the administrative apparatus. This close interpenetration of elective and administrative offices enabled party bosses to control city politics, governors' mansions, state legislatures, and through the state legislatures which elected them, U.S. senators, many of whom were political barons themselves or representatives of machine minders back home. Most presidents were products of the party system and beholden to party chieftains. After Jackson, few presidents save Lincoln had the independence of stature to circumvent state party bosses, and while Hayes and Garfield launched symbolic attacks on leading patronage masters in the Senate, a more characteristic picture of nineteenth-century presidents would show Polk or Buchanan assiduously dispensing minor federal offices to the deserving corporals and sergeants of their political armies, or Chester Arthur trying to rise above his origins in Conkling's New York customshouse gang. By imprisoning presidents and coopting state administration, the party system politicized the entire civil service. Although White may overstate the "steady practice prior to 1829,"[37] in order to emphasize how stability, longevity, and efficiency in federal administration were compromised by the party system, it is clear that careers in state service were less secure and more dependent on political connections after 1830, and that those who held appointive offices in the state were expected to render political services and, in most cases, to contribute to party campaign chests in exchange for their jobs. This generally lowered the prestige of the civil service, advanced the careers of opportunists and incompetents, and shattered continuity and professionalism in state administration.

Thus not only was there no agreement about how the state should act, but the competitive mobilizations of rival party machines penetrated the state administration and ransacked it for patronage opportunities, systematically undercutting the state's capacity to act. The general weakening of executive capacities rendered the state incapable of regulatory or supervisory activities. The corresponding strengthening of legislative powers placed the conduct of policy in the hands of politicians whose talents tended to the particular rather than the general and who were inclined to act less in the interest of effective policy or administration than in response to local interests or in pursuit of partisan advantage. Except in the Civil War emergency, Congress rarely took major policy initiatives.[38]

Without the capacity to make policy or to regulate social and economic relations, the state was reduced to gift giving. Aside from the offices and contracts used to cement party organizations, there were many things federal, state, and local government could dispense to its favored citizens: land, access to minerals and raw materials, privileges and immunities, tax concessions, bonds, franchises, rights of eminent domain, powers to dam a stream or collect a toll, tariffs for the protection of manufactures—all useful in doing business and especially helpful in tapping abundant resources and developing new settlements. The state could thus promote generalized growth without having to direct or organize it. The state rarely had to spend money doling out its gifts, and while it occasionally lost revenue through its generosity, it also collected income from its tariff levies and the sale of land.[39] Distributional activities were thus characteristic of the state under party domination.

The corporate charter, for example, was the distributional activity most favored by state legislatures, especially after the panic of 1837 left many with heavy debts and a strong desire to get out of business.[40] A general movement to liberalize the rules of incorporation bore the stamp of Jacksonian democracy, as did the greater access offered to people of modest means by the limited liability of the corporation. At the same time, having granted a charter, there was no need for the legislature to take further responsibility for how the capital thus raised was used. This was ideally suited to a political system that had increasing difficulty marshaling the policy consensus necessary for economic supervision or maintaining the administrative apparatus necessary for effective regulation. It also enabled state governments to follow their Jacksonian inclinations and withdraw from direct participation in economic activity while continuing, through distributional activities, to promote competition and growth. Thus the dispersal of resources, which was all that was left of state activism after 1830, tended to confirm the central tenet of Jacksonianism that insisted upon the strict separation of state and economy. On the one hand, the state under party domination was incapable of effective intervention in economic affairs; on the other hand, few wanted vigorous action, since a state dominated by competitive, opportunistic party professionals could be extremely dangerous to rival business interests if it *did* try to meddle in economic affairs.

It was left to the courts to supervise the activities of business in the economic sphere. Indeed an important corollary to the rise of mass political parties, the cooptation of executive capacity and the retreat of the state from direct participation in the economy, was the important role the courts came to play as policemen of the boundary between state and economy. By providing some supervision and surveillance over economic activity, the courts did what a weakened executive could not do. The courts also ensured what the legislature, dominated by party machines and popular politics, could not ensure: the safety of private property in a mass democracy. The role of the courts was crucial, for it worked both to promote competition and innovation in the market place and to restrict the power of political parties in the legislative branch to intervene in economic affairs.[41]

The drift of judicial opinion in the nineteenth century paralleled the rise of the party system. The nationalism and political activism of the Marshall court dissolved during the 1830s, as the political climate turned against assertions of federal authority and new appointments to the Supreme Court eroded the cohesion of the Marshall court. Under Taney, the court "gave ground before the dynamic forces of Jacksonianism and particularism."[42] Court rulings, at least through the 1870s, proved extremely solicitous of states' rights, avoiding where possible assertions of federal primacy, upholding the competence of state and local government to act in economic matters, and contributing thereby to the decentralized orientation of economic activity. At the same time, the broad movement of judicial opinion in these years ran toward opening up, or democratizing, the marketplace, attacking the exclusive forms of property and anti-developmental protections of traditional corporate law, and substituting the rules of contract for the preclusive privileges and customary relations of common law. Generally, judicial interpretation sought to promote competition, to encourage new entrants into the economic arena, to broaden interpretations of "public use," especially in questions of eminent domain, and to limit the damages incurred by entrepreneurs under traditional common law remedies of trespass and nuisance—all opinions tending toward freeing up productive forces and shifting the defenses of the law from holdings in property to ventures in property.[43] The creation of a commercial jurisprudence and the promotion of economic development reflected both a growing recognition among jurists that the law played a key role in economic affairs and a determination, in the words of one commentator, "that the course of American legal change should, if possible, be developed by courts and not by legislatures."[44]

This suspicion of legislatures grew more pronounced after midcentury, as the courts moved from creating to defending the new commercial jurisprudence, and it reflected a recognition among judges that Jacksonian democracy, as a popular mobilization directed against banks and other forms of economic concentration, posed potential threats to property. The tendency of legislatures to distribute charters and concessions carried, as grants of public power, implicit rights of oversight and regulation. The courts were aware that, while the state rarely possessed the administrative capacity for such supervision, political parties, always sensitive to popular moods and venally opportunistic, were quite capable of exploiting the right. Justice Stephen Field, long notorious as a defender of private property and the rights of capital, has emerged from recent research as a simultaneous defender of the "public right," by which he insisted that state legislatures were limited in their right to devolve public powers of taxation and eminent domain upon the private sector and that businesses in the so-called ordinary trades had no claim upon state concessions.[45] By imposing limits upon what resources the legislature could distribute to the private sector, the courts could also limit the right of the state to regulate or supervise purely private enterprise. Judicial interpretations in the 1880s and 1890s reflected an expanding effort by the Supreme Court to clarify and strengthen the boundary line separating public and private spheres and to construct a defensive perimeter around property based on laissez-faire principles. In assuming responsibility for the legal enforcement of charters and other grants, in restricting the powers of state legislatures to impose compensation, to enforce fairness doctrines, and, with the Wabash decision, to regulate interstate commerce, and in encouraging business to seek legal remedies for economic conflict, the courts were seeking to interpose themselves between politics and economics, party power and business power, and by expanding the sphere of judicial review, to crowd out legislative initiatives in economic affairs.

This system of checkmating legislative power with judicial power, as the courts supervised the economy while political parties minded the machinery of popular democracy, was an ideal instrument for governing the distribution of abundance. As territorial expansion opened up access to new land, minerals, and timber, and new settlements created new arenas for political competition, economic and political resources were continuously renewed. The enormous success of the corporation as an economic organization for the exploitation of abundance helped to sustain high levels of growth without a large state apparatus. Business learned the ways of political corruption, buying favors and concessions, while politicians, preoccupied with questions of self-renewal, allowed the engines of economic growth to carry them along without attempting to coordinate or direct the course of economic development, or to take responsibility for the proliferating consequences of industrial transformation. A political system built upon the distribution of resources tended to shift the terms of combat for control of the state from questions of policy, requiring choices and long-term thinking, to questions of spoils, requiring only continuing abundance. By capitalizing on fluidity and generalized plenty, the state of courts and parties could reinforce diversity and glorify individualism, while absorbing (without resolving) the deeper, structural strains of rapid, unregulated growth.

Crises in the State of Courts and Parties

The nineteenth-century state was a crisis-prone system. Sustained economic expansion, coupled with continuing political stalemate and the systematic crippling of state capacity by a rapacious party system, created strains within the state and in its articulations with the economy and the society which the system of courts and parties could not handle effectively. Two crises will be reviewed here: the first, a sectional crisis in the 1850s, produced civil war; the second, a sectoral struggle in the 1890s, produced a transformation of the state itself. By briefly examining these two crises, we may gain a better grasp of the transformational pressures under which the party state finally began to give way, partially and reluctantly, to an administrative state at the turn of the century.

The economic boom of the 1850s, sustained by the gold finds in California, the influx of foreign investment, and the success of American corporations, especially railroads, in utilizing expanded capital resources, produced new economic links between Northern industry and the free farmers of the West. With the completion of four trunk lines between the Atlantic coast and the Midwest, Eastern manufacturers had their first all-weather access to Western markets. Secure connections and sustained demand encouraged investment in plant expansion and new equipment, making possible the expanded use of unskilled and immigrant labor. With better markets and lower labor costs, Northern industrialists, long advocates of restrictive land policies, could look with greater favor upon the expansion of free-farm agriculture in the West.[46]

This development was paralleled by a second of equal importance. As the huge influx of Irish Catholic immigrants flowed into the Northern cities and the urban machines of the Democratic party during the 1850s, Scots-Irish Protestants and German Lutherans of the middle belt of settlement from Pennsylvania to Illinois, long key Northern elements of the Jacksonian agrarian coalition, abandoned the Democratic party in large numbers, moving first to the Know-Nothings and then into the new Republican party.[47] The agrarian axis began to crack, not because of the slave issue so much as because of economic and political changes in the North. This marked the emergence of a sectional bloc in American politics, based on a North-West, industrial-agrarian alliance that excluded the South.

The effects were dramatic. With no firm footing in the South, political organizers working along the new industrial-agrarian axis in the North had every reason to resort to sectional appeals, both to seal new political alliances and to further separate dissident Northern Democrats from their former loyalties. Southern Democrats, convinced that the future of slave agriculture was menaced by the growing power of the industrial North and its newfound ties with free farming in the West, tried to counter this alliance in Congress by blocking the tariff legislation and homestead act that Northerners wanted. But they found that the bases of Jackson's cross-sectional alliance along the agrarian axis was seriously weakened. A fatal dialectic emerged. Local party managers, seeking to sharpen differences with their opponents, manipulated sectional fears—the Whig-Republicans in the North denouncing the Democrats for their association with the "slave power" while Democrats in the South defeated Whigs by branding them the lesser champions of slavery or, worse, as friends of abolitionism. The minority party in each section, Democrats in the North and Whigs in the South, lost ground and became, not surprisingly, the chief champions of sectional compromise. The national party organizations, however, moved increasingly into outright sectional alignments, thus reinforcing the temptation at the local level to resort to sectional appeals. Without clear issue differences between the parties that could separate some Northerners and Southerners from other Northerners and Southerners, neither party was able to maintain the kind of cross-sectional coalitions that had enabled them, for three decades, to contain sectional animosities.[48] Finally, the Republican party was able to assemble a broad coalition of old Whigs and Democratic defectors across the North and West, based on the widespread fear of the "slaveocracy" and organized around the slogan, "vote yourself a farm—vote yourself a tariff," which neatly captured the terms of the cross-sectoral alliance between Northern industry and Western agriculture. This coalition won the presidency in 1860 and precipitated Southern secession. The economic shifts of the 1850s had made possible a realignment of party combat along sectional lines which, in turn, promoted a sharpening of ideological rhetoric between Northerners and Southerners, as party distinctions were refreshed with sectional hatreds and both sides raised banners in defense of liberty.

In his seminal essay on the causes of the Civil War, Barrington Moore wonders why Northern capitalists and Southern "Junkers" failed to establish the sort of conservative "iron-rye" alliance that appeared in Imperial Germany twenty-five years later and could, in Moore's view, have prevented civil war in the United States. "Were political and economic links missing in the United States that existed in Germany?"[49] Moore places great emphasis upon the divergent economic and social development of the two regions, noting how the dependence of Southern agriculture upon English markets and the growing material ties between Northern industry and Western farming eliminated important reasons not to fight. Without countervailing bonds of interest, there was little to prevent the party system, in its constant maneuvering for partisan position and its congenital need to articulate sharp differences on issues, from gravitating toward the clearer cleavages of sectionalism. Moreover, Moore argues, nothing pushed elites from different sections together. There were no class challengers at the national level—no need to resort to nonmarket mechanisms of labor control in the North; no danger of a political alliance between industrial workers in the North, often women, children, or immigrants, and slave laborers in the South. Nor were there foreign threats to force conservative elites, North and South, to resolve their differences.

Moore's reflections on the Civil War do not pay sufficient attention to the failure of the state. In Imperial Germany, not only was the so-called iron-rye alliance built around the Prussian monarchy and the broad loyalty of elites to the crown, but the state itself played a key role as catalyst and broker of the deals between Junker agrarians and Rhineland industrialists. While recent scholarship has tended to see these alliances as a series of very fragile and tentative trade-offs brokered by a state which was itself badly fragmented and subject to capture by rival factions,[50] it remains clear that without the state's strong interest in maintaining the foundations of conservative power and a political basis for the repression of socialism, the "Junker alliance" and the imperial system it supported could not have been long maintained. In the United States, by contrast, the extreme weakness of the federal state and its inability even to articulate immanent interests of its own, let alone proffer a state-led solution to the sectional crisis, proved fatal. The federal state was the object of dispute, not the means of its settlement. The key question, not resolved until secession, was "whether the machinery of the federal government should be used to support one society or the other."[51] The state of courts and parties was a direct outgrowth of the inability of political elites to settle this question. It could not provide a bridge. Although two-party competition had managed to contain sectional conflict for over a generation, it had also eroded state capacities and enforced the withdrawal of the state from economic activity, so that the state proved incapable of resolving the sectional crisis once it escaped party control. The capacity of the federal government to make policy, let alone to impose it on hostile segments of the society, was too badly paralyzed. In this sense, at least, the Civil War may be regarded as the denouement of Jacksonian democracy.[52]

By eliminating one of the political contenders, the Civil War crisis temporarily ended the stalemate in federal policy. The Republicans, enjoying complete control of the federal apparatus, were able to execute their partisan program unchecked by other arguments. The Morrill Tariff and the Homestead Act consolidated the political alliance between Northern industry and Western agriculture, while the Immigration Act, the creation of a national banking system, and the beginning of federal land grants for railroad construction (the first direct federal support for internal improvements in over a generation) consummated the marriage between the Republican party and industrial capital in the North which was to be the dominant political configuration in the country for the next generation. The hegemony of industrial capital was further consolidated by the wartime inflation, which enabled manufacturers to liquidate debts and break the hold of merchant capital over industry.[53] Most important, the defeat of the Southern power elite and the destruction of the slave labor system upon which it was based transformed the South into an economic colony of Northern capital, marking a large step toward national economic integration. With the resumption of specie payments in the 1870s, guaranteeing the hard currency policies desired by bankers and creditors, the federal state had become, in Moore's words, "a series of ramparts around property, mainly big property."[54] The largest domestic market in the world, protected by high external tariffs and unified by a national railroad and banking system and by an increasingly dominant industrial sector, was poised on the threshold of a rapid industrial transformation.

The Civil War did not significantly alter the structure of the American state, however. The basic distributional characteristics of the state of courts and parties were powerfully reinforced by the proliferation of government war contracts and the steady expansion of the federal bureaucracy. Quadrupling the size of the civil service and adding a score of new agencies to the federal state greatly enriched the funds of spoils, offices, and patronage rewards available to Republican party chieftains, thus strengthening the hold of party barons in Congress over the administrative capacities of the state. If anything, the momentum of wartime disbursements accelerated in the 1870s, with the rapid disposal of public domains to timber, mining, and railroad interests and the multiplication of federal grants and subsidies for the construction of levees, canals, harbors, roads, and railways during the so-called Great Barbecue of the Grant years.[55] The Republican party, as the major beneficiary of this distribution, sought to perpetuate its political hegemony in federal politics with a radical program of social reconstruction in the South, aimed at shattering the old power structure and cultivating a pro-Republican political base in the region.

When this effort failed and the Democrats made a rapid political recovery, first in the South and by the mid-1870s in national politics, the

Republicans were quick to strike a deal. In the so-called Compromise of 1877, wartime gains of hard money, high tariffs, railroad subsidies, and federal promotion of economic expansion were protected by giving Southern Democratic oligarchs access to the flow of spoils created by Republican policy. In effect, the Republicans agreed to do nothing more and the Democrats agreed, for a consideration, not to dismantle anything that had already been done. A key aspect of this accord was that Southern Democrats accepted a subordinate role to Northern capital in exchange for control of federal patronage in their region.[56]

This compromise marked the emergence, for the first time in half a century, of a tenuous conservative agreement in national politics among political elites. But the deal was made necessary by the reemergence of two-party competition in national politics and its common denominator was a passive defense of the status quo. The Democrats established a political monopoly in the South, and Republicans remained dominant in the North. Both parties resorted to Civil War battle lines and sectional loyalties—the so-called bloody shirt appeal—to shore up organizational support in their respective regions, and these ritual incantations proved increasingly important during the 1880s as two-party competition at the national level produced razor-thin margins. Not only had elite agreement institutionalized the practices of party patronage, but the fierce competition for national office, often turning upon the votes of a few swing states, increased the appetite of both parties for spoils and rewards. Federal resources continued to be drawn down to sustain the local bases of party organization. The political compromise of 1877 confirmed this practice, blocking further consolidation of federal powers, without at the same time reversing the wartime expansion of federal powers. Thus the Civil War, while promoting a vast realignment of forces in the national economy, also extended into a period of rapid industrialization a stalemated party state, with its mortgaged administrative capacities and its paralysis of policymaking. This produced growing strains and, during the 1890s, another crisis in the state of courts and parties.

The tremendous growth of railroads during the 1870s, with the proliferation of new lines and cutthroat competition, created a situation of underutilization and falling profits, especially along trunk lines and in the high density commercial areas. Efforts to stabilize rates and maintain revenues through voluntary pools and pricing agreements rarely held up against competitive pressures. By the 1880s, railroad operators were among the chief advocates of expanded state action to regulate and stabilize competition in the free market.[57] They were not alone. For as railroads spread across the continent, penetrating local markets and breaking down regional barriers, they had an enormous, rippling impact upon other elements of the economy. Regional businesses, often with well-established local markets, found themselves confronted with cheaper goods shipped in from afar. In a competitive bid to survive many of them expanded their own productive capacities, forcing price cuts and producing a high rate of failure. Indeed, rising output and falling prices were the main impetus behind the growth of nationwide trade associations, designed to maintain prices by curtailing production.[58] These soon gave way to more complex experiments in business combination, the trust and corporate merger. In addition, businesses seeking to maintain profits in an environment of stiff competition often put strong downward pressure on wages, sparking widespread resistance from labor. The number of strikes, and the number of workers participating in stoppages, grew steadily during the 1880s. In the face of these pressures, American business became increasingly desirous of a more active state, capable not only of distributing resources and promoting enterprise, but also of regulating the economy and repressing the challenge of labor.

The same pressures, however, that created interest among businessmen in a stronger state to contain the chaos of competition stirred equally powerful popular currents in the opposite direction—toward state action to promote competition. Protests against the power of railroads and their manipulation of rates, or against the evils of monopoly combinations, became widespread by the 1880s, especially at the grass roots of politics. This produced action at the state level. While local and regional politicians were not always anxious to respond to popular pressures, and large corporations were often able to thwart legislative action through political pressure and bribery, or through court rulings, many states did produce regulatory laws during the 1880s, often trying to combine promotion with control. State governments thus found themselves administering railroad rates and enforcing competition among corporations which were themselves bent upon price-fixing arrangements.[59] Business leaders turned to the federal government, seeking relief from state-level regulations, legal support for national combinations, and a partner capable, in the words of one, "of affording the protection of the national government against conflicting state legislation and local political enactments and—what is equally important—enforcing well-considered regulations and wholesome restrictions incidental to national institutions."[60] Yet however persuasive these arguments were, congressmen faced strong countervailing pressures, flowing up through the channels of party democracy, to block corporate consolidations and the national organization of prices. Capitalist pressure for federal regulation and legalized price agreements encountered democratic pressure in Congress for action to enforce competition, control railroad rates, and break up giant monopolies.

It was precisely this sort of contradictory pressure that the state of courts and parties was ill equipped to handle. A system designed to distribute favors and rewards found it very difficult to formulate policy based on choices and the reconciliation of conflicting interests. Moreover, regulation, whether for or against competition, required the creation of administrative agencies with the capacity to make independent judgments. This meant a public administration insulated, at least partially, from partisan control, something that went against the grain of the party state. A system designed to milk federal resources for state and local purposes had little incentive to husband those resources or to cultivate independent rivals for power at the center. Not surprisingly, therefore, the response of Congress to the demands for federal action was less than robust. Legislation did appear during the 1880s for the reform of the civil service, the regulation of interstate commerce, and the breakup of monopoly trusts. But these measures were deliberately vague and shapeless, as Congress tried to package up all the conflicting pressures that produced them and trim the whole to the contours of patronage.[61] Such studious imprecision left it to the courts to formulate legal definitions and procedural guidelines. The Supreme Court accommodated by restricting the powers of the Interstate Commerce Commission and limiting the application of the Sherman Antitrust Act to conform to its own concerns for containing legislative intervention in business and for preventing any extension of state administrative powers, dominated by party patronage, to the preserves of property. In sum, the legislature accommodated the conflicting demands of elite and popular interests for action by producing weak laws requiring clarifications which the court provided according to its laissez-faire principles. Thus popular initiatives to curb monopoly and promote competition were defeated, without at the same time providing business with the sort of state regulation and protection that it wanted.

This stalemate expressed the growing difficulties the state of courts and parties had in reconciling, politically, the interests of industrial capital and the imperatives of mass democracy. The federal state could not move against monopoly without destroying business confidence, yet it could not accommodate the needs of business for more active regulatory policies and support of economic rationalization without exacerbating the mounting social strains between farmers and capital which, by the 1890s, were carrying clear class overtones. A lack of agreement on how the state should act confirmed the agreement of party managers not to act. This inclination toward inactivity was strongly reinforced by considerations of patronage and party maintenance. The parties could not let go of the state apparatus, that is, create autonomous administrative capacities for any purpose, without weakening the ability of party managers to organize and control the electorate. As long as political competition remained intense and electoral outcomes were close, neither party was prepared to change its practices voluntarily or unilaterally.

Ultimately, what broke this impasse was the collapse of the Democratic party as a national contender in 1896. This collapse was itself the consequence of the failure of both dominant parties to contain the spreading agrarian revolt against corporate consolidation within the framework of routine two-party politics and of a massive grass roots insurgency at the local levels of politics which undercut the local footings of the Democratic party apparatus.

Both parties showed signs of losing control over political competition at the grass roots level during the 1880s. The number of splinter and third-party movements multiplied, especially in the Western and Plains states. These challengers held the balance of power at least once in most non-Southern states during the 1880s, and in the elections of 1892 they were strong enough to deny either major party a majority in two-thirds of the states.[62] The most serious of these insurgent movements was, of course, populism, the revolt of the tenant farmers and sharecroppers in the South and West who were the principal victims of high tariffs, hard money, and inflated railroad rates and who built a movement during the 1880s based on cooperative principles and a profoundly subversive critique of industrial capitalism.[63] This was a challenge both to the Republican party, in its Civil War alliance with Western farmers and its commitment to industrialism, and to the conservative oligarchy that controlled the Democratic party in the South and had acquiesced in, if they had not always benefited from, the spread of industrial capitalism. Moreover, when the populists crossed the Civil War battle lines during the 1880s, developing farmers' alliances on both sides of the sectional divide, they directly challenged the organization of partisan rhetoric and the alignment of voters by both dominant parties. This not only promised to reorganize the electorate, but it posed for the first time the possibilities of a class alignment in national politics.

The two major parties had long mixed sectional, cultural, religious, and ethnic appeals with those of economic and class interest, partly from expediency, but largely because the problems of constructing national coalitions did not allow either party to rest its appeal, as so often happened in Europe, upon a particular class or cultural stratum. In the 1880s, however, the industrial transformation of the Northeast and the association of both political parties with its progress had produced the possibility of an alignment of agrarian dissidents and industrial workers in opposition. As the populists crossed the Civil War battle lines and organized a national Peoples' party, they made serious, although unsuccessful, efforts to establish links with insurgent labor organizations in the industrial North. Briefly, in the 1890s, there appeared the outlines of that alliance of workers and peasants which, in Europe at least, had often had revolutionary consequences. Not only had the struggle between agrarian and industrial interests escaped the control of dominant parties, but the opponents of corporate consolidation were threatening to reorganize the terms of political combat.

Legitimation—grounding the requirements of capital, to which both Democratic and Republican leaders were committed, in a mass political base for electoral endorsement—proved increasingly problematic. The growing strength of the Peoples' party in 1892–94 and the persistent disloyalty of voters in these years (the incumbent Republicans losing badly in 1890 and 1892, the incumbent Democrats doing even worse in 1894 and 1896) registered the crisis of electoral control under two-party management. Both parties had to scramble for a formulation of programs and popular appeals that could win business confidence as well as national elections. In other words, the political crisis of the party state forced politicians to innovate, either to shore up or to redefine the articulations of capitalism, now national and industrial, with a mass democracy, now fully mobilized and deeply divided.

The Democratic party proved unequal to this task and collapsed among the contradictions. Grover Cleveland, the only Democratic president in the period, was from the conservative "gold bug" wing of the party, deeply committed to hard money and industrial expansion and, for all his conventional laissez-faire beliefs, quite prepared to use federal troops against organized labor. His inept response to the depression crisis of 1893 and the disastrous Democratic defeat in the off year elections of 1894 shattered the unity of the party. The bulk of the party, wounded and in disarray, fell back upon its agrarian bases in the South and West. There, where the populist insurgency had made deep inroads into local party organizations, Democratic politicians trimmed their rhetoric to the radical winds and sought fusion with the Peoples' party wherever possible, trying to overcome a record of depression and antilabor action by embracing free silver, William Jennings Bryan, and the cause of the farmer. For all his electrifying eloquence, however, Bryan failed to understand the central aspirations of populism, and yet, in mouthing the words, he alienated voters in the urban Democratic bastions of the industrial North. Once Cleveland and his conservative allies had split off, the party was in at least three parts, and the Northern urban machines were left isolated and weakened, unable to defend the incumbent president and unattracted by Bryan's agrarian platform.[64]

The Democratic collapse left the industrial regions in Republican hands. They quickly occupied the terrain. With a national organization strengthened by corporate contributions and directed by a national committee under Mark Hanna, the Republicans swept the Northeast and landed William McKinley in the White House with the largest electoral majority in twenty-five years. While the Democratic collapse in the North and McKinley's image as the advance agent of prosperity may explain this initial victory, the continuing success of the Republicans in national elections over the next thirty years testified to their success in reestablishing political links between corporate America and a mass electoral base.

In part, this success was due to the collapse of two-party competition and the general demobilization of voters that followed. With the Republicans in control of the industrial core region and the Democrats cornered in the agrarian fringe, both parties were effectively struck in their regional bastions. The Democrats only gradually rebuilt their urban bases in the North and reestablished their links with labor, while the Republicans developed little support in the agrarian sectors of the South and Southwest. This separation, together with the virtual destruction of the Democratic party in the key swing states of the North and Midwest, reduced the level of two-party competition in national politics. Few states were really contested between 1896 and 1932.[65] Without party competition, the lines of party organization and discipline went slack. In the North, the absence of serious two-party rivalry and the spreading impact of the various municipal reform movements that flourished in the years of Republican hegemony weakened the party machines that had maintained voter mobilization and reduced urban participation by 15 to 20 percent. In the South, where Democratic elites struggled to reestablish their control after the disasters of the populist era, Jim Crow laws enforced a dramatic collapse of voter participation, eliminating blacks altogether and demobilizing large numbers of poor whites who had participated in the agrarian insurgency.[66] Nationwide, turnout fell, in presidential years, from an average of 78 percent of the eligible voters in 1876–96, to 50 percent in 1920–29, and in off year congressional elections, from 63 percent to 35 percent.[67] With the decline of party organization and voter participation went an eclipse of the partisan press and the more dramatic local forms of party combat that had characterized politics in the nineteenth century.

The demobilization of the opposition also enabled the Republicans to build an electoral coalition in the North which gave them virtually hegemonic control over the federal state for a generation. This coalition was based on an ungainly combination of capitalists and workers in the industrial sector, held together by the plausible claim that high tariffs ensured high wages as well as prices and profits, and reinforced by the growing electoral power of new urban middle-class cadres, whose progressive campaigns for city government reform and essentially corporatist values of efficiency and professional management contributed to the weakening of urban party machines and the demobilization of poorer voters, while reinforcing the productivist ideologies of the Republican mainstream.[68] These articulations, coupled with the repression of labor militants and an increasingly strident, jingoistic foreign policy, enabled the Republicans to act decisively in the interests of industrial capital. Safeguarded by rhetorical distinctions between "good" and "bad" corporations and by the total absence of viable political opposition, they were able to promote a major consolidation of corporate power between 1897 and 1904. While the new corporate giants, capitalized on an unprecedented scale and commanding vast productive capacity, greatly reinforced the financial and electoral base of the Republican party, they also placed new demands upon the federal state, especially as the shakedown period which followed the merger movement revealed the precarious and unstable nature of many of the new combinations.[69]

At the federal level, the natural allies of big business were not party or congressional leaders, but the president and the executive offices of state administration. The weakening of party organizations and the confinement of both parties to essentially sectional ghettos greatly enhanced the position of the president as national leader and gave the executive branch expanded room for initiatives in the federal state. Presidents, from McKinley on, took a greater role in policy-making, leading and coordinating congressional action and working with party leaders in the formulation of national policies. Increasingly, presidents became the focus of press attention and were able to assert themselves as spokesmen of a national interest, above the two parties mired in their respective sections. With Theodore Roosevelt and Woodrow Wilson, the presidency achieved enormous popular prominence. At the same time, the erosion of party strength tended to weaken the control of party bosses over the state apparatus, permitting a gradual accumulation of administrative powers in presidential hands and an extension of civil service protection to more federal jobs. Federal offices and resources were less surely drawn down to consolidate party organization at the local base. While most presidents remained party men, they were able to act with increasing autonomy in dispensing patronage and making appointments to federal office.

The slipping grip of party organizations over the administrative apparatus of the state and the increasing ability of presidents to capture some control over federal administration also signaled a shift in the locus of power within the federal state, a movement of power from the legislature, seat of party government, to the executive branch, seat of the administrative state. At the same time, the expansion of the federal bureaucracy and the need to develop a more professional state administration encouraged extensive borrowing of practices and personnel from the business sector. Corporate interests not only found a partner in the executive branch, but were able to penetrate federal administration. Regulatory agencies usually ended up in the hands of the regulated. The easy collaboration between national politicians and corporate leaders, characteristic of the early decades of this century and typified by the collegiality of the

Bureau of Corporations, the use of "businesscrats" in the war mobilization of 1917–18, and the notions of the "associative state" common in Republican circles during the 1920s, reflected not only mutual need and reciprocal assistance, but the growing independence of federal administration from party control.[70] As party managers lost their hold over the administrative apparatus of the state and as federal offices were less easily plundered to sustain local party bases, power could be concentrated at the federal level, and business leaders, themselves emerging onto the broader stage of a national economy, could effectively penetrate the state administration and bend its expanded capacities to their economic requirements. Thus big business and the executive managed to capture elements of state administration from political parties and the legislature, shifting the balance of power within the federal state.

This process was, of course, never complete. The federal state did not detach itself cleanly from party control, nor did business interests capture secure command of federal initiatives or bureaucratic agencies. Administrative capacities remained relatively weak. Congressional leaders continued to resist presidential pretensions, attenuating the growth of executive power. Roosevelt was fought to a standstill in 1907, Taft found Congress impossible to lead, and Wilson came to grief in 1919 in the face of a powerful coalition of congressional opponents. The powers of Congress to investigate, to authorize spending, and to vote appropriations enabled it to keep its fingers in a pie it could no longer divide as it wished. By the same token, while business interests succeeded in gaining assistance from the federal state in their efforts to stabilize their ungainly corporate structures and to defeat organized labor, their domination of federal administration was far from absolute. The state continued to occupy a middle ground between party democracy and the new corporate economy. Indeed, as party power receded and corporate power grew, the presidency gained a certain autonomy as tender of the boundary line and supervisor of the articulations between popular and capital interests. As the only national leader, elected by all the people and now acquiring some administrative capacity for the supervision and regulation of economic activity, the presidency established its claim as a policy-making office.

In fact, of course, twentieth-century presidents have had great difficulty controlling the proliferating administrative apparatus of the federal state, penetrated from opposite sides by business and party power and prone to internal boundary disputes, interagency warfare, and selective alliances with key business and party interests. Still, the center of policy-making and of ideological leadership was now located in the executive branch, where political concerns and economic interests met and competing constraints were, where possible, coordinated in policy and rhetoric.

The struggles within the executive branch for control of policy, and the role that ideology came to play in resolving these disputes—indeed, in securing presidential ascendancy over the entire process—are characteristics of the twentieth-century administrative state.[71]

NOTES

1. "Critique of the Gotha Programme" (1875) in David McLellan, ed., *Karl Marx: Selected Writings* (New York: Oxford University Press, 1977), pp. 564–70.
2. Leonard White, *The Jacksonians: An Administrative History, 1820–1861* (New York: Macmillan, 1954), p. 437; *The Republican Era, 1869–1901* (New York: Macmillan, 1958), p. 2.
3. The European case is well covered in Charles Tilly, ed., *The Formation of National States in Western Europe* (Princeton: Princeton University Press, 1976).
4. The discussion of economic problems is drawn from Merrill Jenson, *The New Nation* (New York: Knopf, 1950); Gordon Bjork, "The Weaning of the American Economy: Independence, Market Changes, and Economic Development," *Journal of Economic History* 24, no. 4 (1964): 541–60; Douglass North and Robert Thomas, eds., *The Growth of the American Economy to 1860* (New York: Harper and Row, 1968), pp. 9–10; and James Henretta, *The Evolution of American Society, 1700–1815* (Lexington: D. C. Heath, 1973).
5. Richard van Alstyne, *The Rising American Empire* (New York: Norton, 1968), esp. chap. 4, and Joseph Davis, *Sectionalism in American Politics, 1774–1789* (Madison: University of Wisconsin Press, 1977).
6. Alexis de Tocqueville, *Democracy in America*, 2 vols. (New York: Vintage, 1954), 1:120.
7. Gordon Wood, *The Creation of the American Republic, 1776–1787* (New York: Norton, 1972), p. 492.
8. On oppositional rhetoric, see Lance Banning, *The Jeffersonian Persuasion: Evolution of a Party Ideology* (Ithaca: Cornell University Press, 1978).
9. See Robert Taylor, *Western Massachusetts in the Revolution* (Providence: Brown University Press, 1954) and David Szatmary, *Shays' Rebellion: The Making of an Agrarian Insurrection* (Amherst: University of Massachusetts Press, 1980).
10. Federalist Paper 10: "Size and Variety of Union as a Check on Faction." John Lewis, ed., *Anti-Federalist vs. Federalist* (San Francisco: Chandler, 1967), p. 274.
11. John Miller, *The Federalist Era, 1789–1801* (New York: Harper and Row, 1960); Leonard White, *The Federalists* (New York: Macmillan, 1948); Carl Prince, *The Federalists and the Origins of the U.S. Civil Service* (New York: New York University Press, 1977); and John Nelson, "Alexander Hamilton and American Manufacturing: A Reexamination," *Journal of American Histo-*

ry 65, no. 4 (1979): 971–95. The discussion of financing is based upon E. James Ferguson, *The Power of the Purse: A History of American Public Finance, 1776–1790* (Chapel Hill: University of North Carolina Press, 1961) and Dall Forsythe, *Taxation and Political Change in the Young Nation, 1781–1833* (New York: Columbia University Press, 1977).

12. Albert Fried, *The Jeffersonian and Hamiltonian Traditions in American Politics* (New York: Doubleday, 1968), pp. 1–21. There is some disagreement about Jefferson's partisan use of patronage. Compare Noble Cunningham, *Jeffersonian Republicans: the Formation of Party Organization, 1789–1801* (Chapel Hill: University of North Carolina Press, 1957), or his *Process of Government under Jefferson* (Princeton: Princeton University Press, 1976), with Carl Prince, "The Passing of the Aristocracy: Jefferson's Removal of the Federalists, 1801–1805," *Journal of American History* 57, no. 3 (1970): 563–75.

13. Reginald McGrane, *Foreign Bondholders and American State Debts* (New York: Macmillan, 1937), p. 1.

14. Carter Goodrich, ed., *The Government and the Economy, 1783–1861* (Indianapolis: Bobbs-Merrill, 1967), pp. 3–42.

15. James S. Young, *The Washington Community, 1800–1823* (New York: Columbia University Press, 1966).

16. On the course of the American economy in the nineteenth century, I rely on Douglass North, *The Economic Growth of the United States, 1790–1861* (New York: Norton, 1966); Stuart Bruchey, *The Roots of American Economic Growth, 1607–1861* (New York: Harper and Row, 1965); Alfred Chandler, *The Visible Hand: the Managerial Revolution in American Business* (Cambridge: Harvard-Belknap, 1977); Harold Vatter, *The Drive to Industrial Maturity: The U.S. Economy, 1860–1914* (Westport, Conn.: Greenwood Press, 1976); and Susan Lee and Peter Passell, *A New Economic View of American History* (New York: Norton, 1979).

17. F. W. Taussig, *The Tariff History of the United States*, 8th ed. (New York: Capricorn, 1962), pp. 19–24, 70–74.

18. Emily Rosenberg, *Spreading the American Dream: American Economic and Cultural Expansion, 1890–1945* (New York: Hill and Wang, 1982), pp. 15–23.

19. Shearer Bowman, "Antebellum Planters and Vormärz Junkers in Comparative Perspective," *American Historical Review* 85, no. 4 (1980): 779–808, and Carville Earle and Ronald Hoffman, "The Foundations of the Modern Economy: Agriculture and the Costs of Labor in the United States and England, 1800–1860," *American Historical Review* 85, no. 5 (1980): 1055–94. Also, Lee and Passell, *New Economic View*, chaps. 7–10.

20. George Frederickson, *White Supremacy: A Comparative Study in America and South Africa* (New York: Oxford University Press, 1981), pp. 150–62.

21. Donald Robinson, *Slavery and the Structure of American Politics, 1765–1820* (New York: Norton, 1979).

22. Quoted in Forsythe, *Taxation*, p. 71.

23. William Freehling, *Prelude to Civil War: The Nullification Controversy in South Carolina, 1816–1836* (New York: Harper and Row, 1966).

24. Kenneth Stampp, *The Imperiled Union: Essays on the Background of the Civil War* (New York: Oxford University Press, 1980), pp. 229–30.

25. Quoted in Forsythe, *Taxation*, p. 93.

26. On the Jacksonian coalition, see Robert Kelley, *The Cultural Pattern in American Politics: The First Century* (New York: Knopf, 1979), and his general essay, "Ideology and Culture from Jefferson to Nixon," *American Historical Review* 82, no. 3 (1977): 531–62. On class issues, Arthur Schlesinger, *The Age of Jackson* (Boston: Little, Brown, 1945) stressed their importance, while Richard Latner has recently reasserted the centrality of Western and agrarian influences on the coalition in *The Presidency of Andrew Jackson: White House Politics, 1829–1837* (Athens, Ga.: University of Georgia Press, 1979).

27. On the interplay of section and sector, see Michael Holt, *The Political Crisis of the 1850s* (New York: John Wiley, 1978).

28. This discussion relies on Marvin Meyers, *The Jacksonian Persuasion: Politics and Belief* (Palo Alto: Stanford University Press, 1957) and Glyndon van Deusen, *The Jacksonian Era, 1828–1848* (New York: Harper and Row, 1963).

29. The term *dismantling operation* is taken from Meyers, *Persuasion*, p. 25. See also Bruchey, *Roots*, pp. 124–28 and White, *Jacksonians*, pp. 479–85. On the bank war, Robert Remini, *Andrew Jackson and the Bank War: A Study in the Growth of Presidential Power* (New York: Norton, 1967) and Bray Hammond, *Banks and Politics in America from the Revolution to the Civil War* (Princeton: Princeton University Press, 1957). On the impact of Jacksonianism on the state level, see Louis Hartz, *Economic Policy and Democratic Thought: Pennsylvania, 1776–1860* (Cambridge: Harvard University Press, 1948); Oscar and Mary Handlin, *Commonwealth: A Study of the Role of Government in the American Economy: Massachusetts, 1774–1861* (Cambridge: Harvard University Press, 1949); and James Sharp, *Jacksonians versus Banks: Politics in the States after the Panic of 1837* (New York: Columbia University Press, 1970).

30. On the saliency of party differences, see Herbert Ershkowitz and William Shade, "Consensus or Conflict: Political Behavior in the State Legislatures during the Jacksonian Era," *Journal of American History* 58, no. 3 (1971): 591–621.

31. William Chamblis and Philip Davis, "Party, Competition, and Mass Participation: The Case of the Democratic Party System, 1824–1852," in *The History of American Electoral Behavior*, ed. Joel Silbey, Alan Bogue, and William Flanigan (Princeton: Princeton University Press, 1978), pp. 174–75.

32. See Ronald Formisano, *The Birth of Mass Political Parties: Michigan, 1827–1861* (Princeton: Princeton University Press, 1971); Donald Ratcliffe, "The Role of Voters and Issues in Party Formation: Ohio, 1824," *Journal of American History* 59, no. 4 (1973): 847–70.

33. Kelley, *Cultural Pattern*, is the most sensitive treatment of this problem. See also Lee Benson, *The Concept of Jacksonian Democracy* (Princeton: Princeton University Press, 1961) and Holt, *Political Crisis*.

34. Ronald Formisano, "Towards a Reorientation of Jacksonian Politics: A Review of the Literature," *Journal of American History* 63, no. 1 (1976): 48.
35. White, *Jacksonians*, p. 303.
36. On party patronage, see White, *Jacksonians*, pp. 170–74, 300–346, 414–15; and Felice Bonadio, *Political Parties in American History*, vol. 3 (New York: Putnam, 1974), especially in that volume David Rothman, "The Structure of State Politics," and Moisei Ostrogorski, "The Politicians and the Machine." Also, Morton Keller, *Affairs of State* (Cambridge: Harvard-Belknap, 1977), pp. 307–12, and John Dobson, *Politics in the Gilded Age: A New Perspective on Reform* (New York: Praeger, 1972).
37. White, *Jacksonians*, p. 300. Cf. Carl Prince, *The Federalists and the Origins of the U.S. Civil Service* (New York: New York University Press, 1977) and Matthew Crenson, *The Federal Machine: Beginnings of Bureaucracy in Jacksonian America* (Baltimore: Johns Hopkins Press, 1975).
38. Loren Beth, *The Development of the American Constitution, 1877–1917* (New York: Harper and Row, 1971) has reckoned that between 1877 and 1901 Congress managed only twenty-one major pieces of legislation, several of these being repeals of earlier efforts (pp. 29–30). See also H. Wayne Morgan, *From Hayes to McKinley: National Party Politics, 1877–1896* (Syracuse: Syracuse University Press, 1969).
39. On distributional politics, see Richard McCormick, "The Party Period and Public Policy: An Exploratory Hypothesis," *Journal of American History* 66, no. 2 (1979): 279–98; and Wallace Farnham, "'The Weakened Spring of Government': A Study in Nineteenth Century American History," *American Historical Review* 68, no. 3 (1963): 662–80. More generally, see David Potter, *People of Plenty* (Chicago: University of Chicago Press, 1959), who stresses "the constant endeavor of government to make the economic abundance of the nation accessible to the public" (p. 123).
40. See Meyers, *Persuasion*, pp. 264–66, and the studies of state-level politics cited in note 29, above.
41. On the courts, I rely upon Morton Horowitz, *The Transformation of American Law, 1780–1860* (Cambridge: Harvard University Press, 1980); James Willard Hurst, *Law and the Conditions of Freedom in Nineteenth Century United States* (Madison: University of Wisconsin Press, 1964); Loren Beth, *Development;* Tony Freyer, *Forms of Order: The Federal Courts and Business in American History*, Industrial Development and Social Fabric, No. 1 (Greenwich, Conn.: JAI Press, 1979); and Harry Scheiber, "Property Law, Expropriation, and Resource Allocation by the Government of the United States, 1780–1910," *Journal of Economic History* 33, no. 1 (1973): 232–51.
42. Don Fehrenbacher, *Slavery, Law, and Politics: the Dred Scott Case in Historical Perspective* (New York: Oxford University Press, 1981), p. 112.
43. Hurst, *Law and Conditions*, p. 24, argues that increasingly, American law in the nineteenth century had "less to do with protecting holdings than it had to do with protecting ventures."
44. Horowitz, *Transformations*, pp. 255–56.
45. Charles McCurdy, "Justice Field and the Jurisprudence of Government-

Business Relations: Some Parameters of Laissez Faire Constitutionalism, 1863–1897," *Journal of American History* 61, no. 4 (1975): 970–1005.

46. On the political realignment, see Barrington Moore, Jr., *Social Origins of Dictatorship and Democracy* (Boston: Beacon, 1966), chap. 3, "The American Civil War: The Last Capitalist Revolution."

47. On the ethnic shift, see Kelley, *Cultural Pattern*, pp. 187–202.

48. Here, I follow the argument of Holt, *Political Crisis*. William Brock, in *Parties and Political Conscience: American Dilemmas, 1840–1850* (Millwood, N.Y.: KTO Press, 1979), makes a similar case, but dates the crisis somewhat earlier. Cross-sectional voting held firm into the 1850s, according to Thomas Alexander in *Sectional Stress and Party Strength: A Study of Roll-Call Voting Behavior in the United States House of Representatives, 1836–1860* (Nashville: Vanderbilt University Press, 1967) and Joel Silbey, *The Shrine of Party: Congressional Voting Behavior, 1841–1852* (Pittsburgh: University of Pittsburgh Press, 1967). Gerald Wolff found sectionalism becoming powerful during the Kansas-Nebraska crisis, in *Beyond the Civil War Synthesis: Political Essays on the Civil War Era*, ed. Robert P. Swierenga (Westport, Conn.: Greenwood Press, 1975), p. 179.

49. Moore, *Origins*, p. 115. See also Stampp, *Imperiled Union*, pp. 191–245, for an excellent review of the literature.

50. See Geoff Eley, *Reshaping the German Right: Radical Nationalism and Political Change after Bismarck* (New Haven: Yale University Press, 1980); Richard Evans, ed., *Society and Politics in Wilhelmine Germany* (London: Croom Helm, 1978); and Isabel V. Hull, *The Entourage of Kaiser Wilhelm II, 1888–1918* (New York: Cambridge University Press, 1982).

51. Moore, *Origins*, p. 136.

52. J. Mills Thornton has made the same point in a different context in his *Politics in a Slave Society* (Baton Rouge: Louisiana State University Press, 1978).

53. Charles Post, "The American Road to Capitalism," *New Left Review* 133 (May–June 1982): 30–51. Also, Charles and Mary Beard, *The Rise of American Civilization*, 2 vols. (New York: Macmillan, 1940), 2:105–15.

54. Moore, *Origins*, p. 150.

55. The term is from C. Vann Woodward, *Reunion and Reaction* (Boston: Little, Brown, 1951).

56. Woodward, *Reunion and Reaction*, is the classic account of the Compromise of 1877. See also Keller, *Affairs of State*, who traces the decline of federal activism in the 1880s.

57. On railroads and competition, see Gabriel Kolko, *Railroads and Regulation* (Princeton: Princeton University Press, 1965), chap. 2. On pooling arrangements, see Chandler, *Visible Hand*, pp. 142–44, and Julius Grodinsky, *The Iowa Pool: A Study of Railroad Competition, 1870–1884* (Chicago: University of Chicago Press, 1950).

58. Chandler, *Visible Hand*, pp. 315–20.

59. On state regulatory efforts, see George Miller, *Railroads and the Granger Laws* (Madison: University of Wisconsin Press, 1971); R. Hal Williams, "'Dry Bones and Dead Language': The Democratic Party," in *The Gilded Age*, ed. H. Wayne Morgan (Syracuse: Syracuse University Press, 1970); R. Hal

Williams, *The Democratic Party and California Politics, 1880–1896* (Palo Alto: Stanford University Press, 1973); and Danney Goble, *Progressive Oklahoma: The Making of a New Kind of State* (Norman: University of Oklahoma Press, 1980).

60. Quoted in Gabriel Kolko, *The Triumph of Conservatism* (New York: Free Press, 1965), p. 69. For a general discussion of business outlook in this period, see James Weinstein, *Corporate Ideal and the Liberal State, 1900–1918* (Boston: Beacon, 1968) and Alan Trachtenberg, *The Incorporation of America: Culture and Society in the Gilded Age* (New York: Hill and Wang, 1982), chap. 3.

61. The process is ably analyzed by Stephen Skowronek, *Building a New American State: The Expansion of National Administrative Capacities, 1877–1920* (New York: Cambridge University Press, 1982), from whom I have also borrowed the term *state of courts and parties.*

62. Peter Argersinger, "A Place on the Ballot: Fusion Politics and Antifusion Laws," *American Historical Review* 85, no. 2 (1980): 287–306.

63. See Lawrence Goodwyn, *The Populist Moment* (New York: Oxford University Press, 1978).

64. V. O. Key, *Politics, Parties, and Pressure Groups* (New York: Crowell, 1952); Walter Dean Burnham, *Critical Elections and the Mainsprings of American Politics* (New York: Norton, 1970); Paul Glad, *McKinley, Bryan, and the People* (New York: Lippincott, 1964).

65. John Broesamle, "The Democrats from Bryan to Wilson," in *The Progressive Era*, ed. Lewis Gould (Syracuse: Syracuse University Press, 1974), p. 84. Walter Dean Burnham has argued that "the functional result of the 'system of 1896' was the conversion of a fairly democratic regime into a rather broadly based oligarchy" ("The Changing Shape of the American Political Universe," *American Political Science Review* 59 [1965]: 23).

66. See C. Vann Woodward, *The Strange Career of Jim Crow* (New York: Oxford University Press, 1955) and J. Morgan Kousser, *The Shaping of Southern Politics: Suffrage Restriction and the Establishment of the One-Party South* (New Haven: Yale University Press, 1974).

67. Gabriel Kolko, *Main Currents of Modern American History* (New York: Harper and Row, 1974), p. 278.

68. Samuel P. Hays, "The Politics of Reform in Municipal Government in the Progressive Era," *Pacific Northwest Quarterly* 55, no. 4 (October 1964): 157–69. David Noble, *America By Design* (New York: Oxford University Press, 1980).

69. On the consolidation of corporations after 1902, see Kolko, *Triumph of Conservatism*, and Richard Edwards, *Contested Terrain* (New York: Basic Books, 1979), esp. chaps. 4 and 5.

70. Kolko, *Triumph*, discusses the Bureau of Corporations. Ellis Hawley, *The Great War and the Search for a Modern Order* (New York: St. Martins, 1979) discusses the "associative state." See also Rosenberg, *Spreading the American Dream*, chaps. 3 and 8.

71. Franz Schurmann, *The Logic of World Power* (New York: Pantheon, 1974), pt. 1.

STATE, PARTY, AND INDUSTRY
From Business Recovery to the Wagner Act in America's New Deal

Kenneth Finegold and Theda Skocpol

As America's productive plant and urban centers age, and as the national economy comes under international economic competitive pressures, calls have been issued for formulation of an industrial policy that would allow the United States to make the "hard choices" necessary for dynamic adjustment and renewed economic growth. Plans for such a policy envisage a great expansion of the role of the federal government in decision making about industry. Lester C. Thurow, for example, suggests the "national equivalent of a corporate investment committee" to promote productivity and economic security; creation of a permanent guaranteed job program; and temporary compensation payments to those who bear the costs of necessary shifts.[1] Ira C. Magaziner and Robert B. Reich advocate a number of specific interventions targeted to the special problems of declining and growing businesses, and the establishment of a governmental body that could coordinate these policies and others, such as defense spending, with important implications for American industrial development. A sound industrial strategy, they note, would require coherence, foresight, accountability, and competence.[2] In recent years, *Business Week* editorials have also advocated "rationalizing" reforms and planned public interventions to achieve reindustrialization.

These proposals have received a great deal of attention as possible answers to the current economic stagnation. They have also received much criticism, both from defenders of the free market and from advocates of a more participatory kind of planning. Yet the history of the most significant peacetime effort at industrial planning in the United States suggests that the possibilities for adoption and implementation of the current proposals will be shaped less by their abstract merits than by the alignments of the party system and the capacities of the national state.[3] Like Reich or Thurow, proponents of the National Recovery Administration (NRA) established in 1933 believed that their program would correct the conditions that had led to economic disaster. With Franklin D. Roosevelt's election in 1932, the party alignment necessary for creation of the NRA had come into place. But what was not present was a national state with the capacity to carry out a complex program of industrial policy, without giving in to capitalists' demands for control over planning for their own sectors. As a result, the NRA failed to bring about economic recovery, and was abandoned by the Roosevelt administration even before the Supreme Court struck it down in the *Schechter* decision of May 1935. One very important unintended consequence of the NRA's collapse was passage of the National Labor Relations Act, better known as the Wagner Act, which greatly facilitated the organization and recognition of American trade unions.

The NRA was set up by the National Industrial Recovery Act (NIRA), signed by Roosevelt on June 16, 1933. According to Roosevelt, the goal of the legislation was "the assurance of a reasonable profit to industry and living wages for labor with the elimination of the piratical methods and practices which have not only harassed honest business but also contributed to the ills of labor."[4] Title I envisaged the pursuit of industrial recovery through the "united action of labor and management under adequate governmental sanctions and supervision." Within each industry, "codes of fair competition" were to be drawn up to regulate production practices. Each code was required to include provisions ensuring workers minimum wages and maximum hours.[5] Section 7(a) required that codes contain guarantees of employees' right to organization.

Within these requirements, the executive branch was given enormous discretion. A new administrative organization was to plan and regulate economic functions formerly shaped by market competition, with the authority to induce cooperation and coerce recalcitrants. Moreover, government officials were allowed plenty of space to initiate plans and regulations to achieve the desired broad goals of recovery, stabilization, and relief. Despite this discretion or rather, as we shall argue, because of what was understandably done with it, the NRA became, over time, increasingly unwieldy, conflict-ridden, and uncertain about its basic goals and preferred means for achieving them.

With the collapse of the NRA, the ideal of overall business coordination gave way to an uneven pattern of government regulation across industries. A few industries achieved special government intervention to help rationalize competition in their own ranks, while most others shied away from further "bureaucratic" entanglements.[6]

In the area of labor policy, the consequences of the NRA's failure were even more striking. The original dream of harmony between corporate management and industrial labor dissolved into ever more bitter conflict, first over the enforcement of NRA-sponsored code provisions protecting labor, and then over the emergence of labor unions independent of direct management control. What is more, labor emerged the victor in this conflict. The Wagner Act, signed into law on July 5, 1935, provided strong guarantees for independent unionism and created an administrative organization capable of enforcing them.

The purpose of this essay is to explore the subtle and multiple linkages between the National Recovery Administration and the Wagner Act. These linkages are not only of historic interest; they suggest patterns likely to characterize other attempts to carry out a program of sustained government intervention in industry in the absence of any preexisting state capacity for the tasks required. More generally, the New Deal provides a case study that shows how state capacity and party alignments can structure the alternatives available to policymakers or popular movements. Our most fundamental point is that the fate of policy choices is shaped by the development of the state and the parties, organizations that have their own historical trajectories and cannot be taken for granted or reduced to manifestations of the current array of social forces. In this respect, our approach differs from pluralist and Marxist theoretical frameworks that have been applied to understand public policy in the United States and other advanced industrial societies.

In the following section, we discuss pluralist and neo-Marxist perspectives along with two other arguments that seem more helpful guides to the New Deal, and to American political development in general. Fred Block's work, we argue, is more concordant with the case of the NRA and the Wagner Act than the alternative neo-Marxisms of Nicos Poulantzas or various "corporate liberal" theorists, while the "postpluralism" of Charles Lindblom is superior to the earlier pluralist formulations of David Truman. But both Block and Lindblom must be made historically specific. This, we suggest, can be done by introducing the concepts of state capacity and party alignment into their rather abstract models of politics. The sections that follow this theoretical discussion attempt to demonstrate the usefulness of our state- and party-centered approach by explaining the origins of the National Recovery Administration, the causes of its failure, and the connections between the breakdown of the NRA and the passage of the Wagner Act. We shall conclude by discussing implications for contemporary industrial policy, the opportunities for which continue to be structured by the policy outcomes of the New Deal.

Pluralism, Marxism, and Beyond

Pluralism and Marxism might not seem to have too much in common. Marxists, both instrumentalists and structuralists, often frame their work with harsh critiques of pluralism, and pluralists have responded in kind. Despite sharp disagreements over the basic source and significance of power in society, however, both of these theoretical approaches seek to explain political outcomes in *socially determinist* ways. Pluralists explain outcomes in terms of the resources of social groups, which compete and cut across one another so as to achieve some, if not perfectly equal, substantive representation for any affected interest. For all their disputes with one another, Marxists would tend to agree on one conclusion: capitalists as a class should benefit most from politics in capitalist society. Neither pluralism nor Marxism gives sufficient recognition to the possibility that states and parties may develop in ways that do not simply mirror the distribution of power in society. For this reason, neither offers much help in explaining the outcome and consequences of the New Deal's attempt to regulate industry.

Pluralist theory focuses on the play of organized interests in society.[7] Theorists of pluralism often place group politics within vague, evolutionist schemes that posit institutional change as an inevitable progression of ever-increasing democracy, governmental effectiveness, and the specialization of political arrangements, all occurring in smooth, adaptive responses to the "modernization" of the economy and society. To the extent that pluralism is concerned with more concrete historical transformations such as those of the New Deal, it suggests that the best organized interest groups in society, and those with access to the greatest political skills and resources, would be the ones to achieve their political goals. Some compromise might have to be reached to satisfy other powerful and interested groups, but the final outcome should be in accord with the distribution of political resources brought to bear on "the governmental process."

"Instrumentalist Marxism" is, perhaps unfairly, most closely identified with Ralph Miliband.[8] Miliband rejects pluralism's "claim (very often its implicit assumption) that the major organised 'interests' in these societies, and notably capital and labour, compete on more or less equal terms, and that none of them is therefore able to achieve a decisive and permanent advantage in the process of competition."[9] On the contrary, Miliband argues, capitalists enjoy decisive and stable political advantages because of their privileged positions both "inside" and "outside" the state. Inside the state, officials tend either to be from capitalist backgrounds or to enjoy close career and personal ties to capitalists. From outside the state, capitalists can exert stronger pressures than any other interest, for they enjoy disproportionate access to organizational resources, can claim that their demands represent "the national interest," and can threaten economic or political disruption if they do not get their way.

The instrumentalist view has been applied to the New Deal by "corporate liberal" theorists such as Ronald Radosh and William Domhoff.[10] The New Deal, it is argued, was a set of clever capitalist strategies to stabilize and revitalize a U.S. economy dominated by large corporations, while providing an appearance of responsiveness to mass pressures that served to forestall more radical changes. Thus, the NRA is seen as the realization of plans put forward by business spokesmen like Gerard Swope, president of General Electric, and Henry Harriman, president of the U.S. Chamber of Commerce. And the Wagner Act is interpreted as a conservative measure that developed out of the ideas of moderates among the corporate elite, and served to channel class protest into trade unions that accepted capitalist class relations.[11]

While instrumentalists emphasize the privileged positions of capitalists inside and outside the state, structural Marxism, exemplified by the early work of Nicos Poulantzas, takes a different view.[12] For Poulantzas, capitalists do not need to staff the state apparatus directly, nor must they put deliberate pressure on government officials. Even without such active interventions, capitalists will benefit from the state's activities, for the state is by definition "the factor of cohesion of a social formation and the factor of reproduction of the conditions of production of a system."[13] The state acts to "disunite" workers, transforming them into privatized individual citizens, competitive in their economic relations and members of a classless "nation" politically. For capitalists, the state acts in reverse; it is "capable of transcending the parochial, individualized interests of specific capitalists and capitalist class fractions."[14] The state can perform these functions, necessary to preserve order in capitalist society and to sustain the conditions for capitalist economic activity, precisely because it is in a position of "relative autonomy" from the capitalists themselves.

Despite their many differences, all these theories would suggest that the political outcomes of the New Deal should have worked disproportionately to the benefit of capitalists. For Poulantzas, this is the structural function of the capitalist state. For Miliband, capitalists could use their privileged position to control policy outcomes. And for Truman, industrial capitalists would stand to win the largest gains because they were the best organized interest at the time. Not only were large firms formidable entities in their own right, there were also effective trade associations in many industries, as well as businesswide bodies such as the Chamber of Commerce and the National Association of Manufacturers.[15] Moreover, from 1931 on, as corporate liberal theorists have stressed, industrialists and their representatives were remarkably unified in pressing upon federal authorities a single major strategy for the recovery of American industry: the relaxation of the antitrust laws and government sponsorship for industry-to-industry cooperation to coordinate prices and regulate production levels and conditions of employment.[16]

Through the National Industrial Recovery Act, capitalists did get pretty much what they had been asking for. And, as it turned out, their control over the implementation of the recovery program was even more complete than their influence in the legislative process that had produced the NIRA. Yet neither pluralism nor neo-Marxism, in either of the varieties so far discussed, would lead one to expect the very unwanted consequences of the NIRA for industrial capitalists: internecine political quarrels, threats of increased government supervision, and the legal recognition of independent labor unions.

Moreover, neither pluralism nor the Marxist theories we have summarized can explain the timing of the two acts discussed in this essay. If the NIRA reflected the dominant resources of business, why could not such a program be enacted earlier, under the administration of Herbert Hoover? Hoover was unquestionably probusiness, yet he "declared that the Swope Plan was 'the most gigantic proposal of monopoly ever made in history,' and he refused point blank to have anything to do with the proposals of the Chamber of Commerce and similar schemes for business rationalization."[17]

The postpluralism of Charles Lindblom, presented in his book, *Politics and Markets*, provides a better handle on the origins of the NIRA.[18] Sounding much like Miliband, Lindblom argues that "[b]usinessmen generally, and corporate executives in particular take on a privileged role in government that is . . . unmatched by any leadership group other than the government officials themselves."[19] Though the achievement of foreign and domestic goals depends on business decisions about investment and allocation, government "cannot command business to perform,"[20] but must try to induce businessmen to perform their economic functions. Thus, businessmen are given protections and benefits, and enjoy tacit or explicit veto power over many areas of policy.

What makes Lindblom's approach superior to many neo-Marxist theories is that in addition to stressing the importance in market societies of capitalist influences upon the choices and actions of politicians, Lindblom also pays attention to electorally mediated democratic influences on policy-making, and to those purely statist influences that are attributable to the ongoing struggles among politicians for authoritative control over governmental organs of administration, coercion, and legislation. For Lindblom, politics is "an untidy process" in which "people who want authority struggle to get it while others try to control those who hold it."[21] In struggling to achieve and maintain control, holders of top authority must rely on "supporting" political organizations, which themselves come to share authority and thus place constraints upon top leaders. In liberal democracies with elements of "polyarchy"—rule by many—social groups will receive varying amounts and kinds of attention from elected politicians, depending not so much on their sheer weight in the voting process as upon their strategic location (or lack of it) in the electoral process. Different forms of party organization, different party systems, and different historical conjunctures of competition for intraparty influence, for governmental office, and for influence within government, will all affect which groups are attended to or ignored as politicians compete among themselves for authority.

Lindblom thus focuses simultaneously on two sets of controls operating on government officials in liberal-democratic capitalist orders: "those of polyarchy and those exercised by businessmen through their privileged position."[22] When these two sets of controls come into conflict, government officials must compromise, choose between, or somehow segregate the spheres of operation of business and popular demands. As we shall see, this is exactly the dilemma Franklin Roosevelt faced in 1933 as he attempted to reconcile popular demands for work sharing with business demands for relaxation of antitrust restrictions. The process by which this conflict produced the NIRA, moreover, can only be understood if we pay attention to the patterns of party organization and electoral competition that Lindblom tells us are so important.

Lindblom's model, then, is far more helpful in understanding the origins of New Deal industrial policy than the other perspectives we have discussed so far. But Lindblom's approach does have its limitations. It does not explain, any more than pluralism or the neo-Marxist theories do, why the NRA could not bring about recovery as planned. And to explain the consequences of the NRA's failure for labor, it is necessary to pay more explicit attention to class relationships in society. Lindblom's "society," like that of Truman, is a collection of more or less organized social groups, differing in their declared interests and immediately available resources, but not understood as systematically related to one another. In the sphere of the economy, however, systematic class relationships, fraught with actual and potential conflicts, tie workers to managers and owners. State intervention in the economy may arouse new class-related issues and generate new political resources for classes to fight their battles with one another and with the government. In this way the NRA, contrary to the intentions of most of its architects, encouraged the organization of labor. At the same time, the failure of the NRA produced a split between Roosevelt and business that helped make possible enactment of the Wagner Act. This legislation, in turn, gave labor further leverage with which to contest the hegemony of capitalists.

Attention to class conflict is, of course, the strong point of classical Marxism. But, as *Politics and Markets* suggests, the autonomous initiatives of politicians must also be taken into account. Neither Poulantzas, for whom the state does whatever is functional for capital, nor the corporate liberal theorists, who see officials as doing whatever big business demands of them, give either the initiatives of politicians *or* class struggle as such sufficient consideration. An alternative neo-Marxist paradigm that connects the class struggle to the role of public officials is presented by Fred Block in his essay, "The Ruling Class Does Not Rule."[23]

Like Lindblom and Miliband, Block argues that state managers normally will not want to do anything that might hurt business confidence, and so will confine themselves to formulating policies that are generally supportive of capital accumulation and not seriously objectionable to any major sector of the capitalist class. But, having explained why governments "are constrained from pursuing anti-capitalist policies," Block asks a further question: "why governments tend to act in the general interests of capital," expanding the state to carry out the rationalization of the economy and society.[24] Block is unwilling to accept the answer given by corporate-liberal instrumentalists, that "a substantial segment of the [capitalist] class that is forward-looking and recognizes the value of extending the state's power" sponsors social reforms.[25] On the contrary, Block holds that capitalists are almost by definition too shortsighted initially to accept, let alone to promote, major reforms or extensions of state power. Such changes come primarily in opposition to capitalist preferences. And they come mostly when, and because, state managers are strongly prodded to institute reforms by the working class. Class struggle, says Block, pushes forward the political development of capitalism, pressuring state managers to institute economic regulations and social reforms.

According to Block, the biggest spurts forward in state activity come during major crises such as wars or depressions. During depressions, the usual constraints on state policy are weakened.

> Low levels of economic activity mean that the threat of declining business confidence loses its power, at the same time that popular demands for economic revival are strong. In such periods, the state managers can pay less attention to business opinion and can concentrate on responding to popular pressure, while acting to expand their own power.[26]

Thus state managers may find it both expedient and possible to grant concessions to the working class. Yet they will do so only in forms that simultaneously increase the power of the state itself. What is more, over the longer run, especially as economic recovery resumes, the state managers will do the best they can to shape the concessions won by the working class in order to make them function smoothly in support of capital accumulation and existing class relations. Thus it can come to pass that reforms and extensions of state power originally won through "pressure from below" can end up being "functional" for capitalism and accepted by many of the very capitalists who at first strongly resisted the changes.

Block's theory is of obvious relevance to the major social welfare and labor reforms of the New Deal. Using Block's theory, there is no need to attribute measures such as the Wagner Act or the Social Security Act either to the farsighted planning of the capitalist class or to the automatic intervention of a capitalist state smoothly functioning to preserve order and promote economic recovery. Instead, according to Block, these measures were made possible by a conjunction of working-class pressures with the willingness of state managers to increase their own institutional power at a time when capitalists' veto power was unusually weak. The reforms provided benefits to many members of the working class, strengthened the state in relation to the working class, and increased the state's capacity to intervene in the capitalist economy. The eventual result was that working-class struggle ended up contributing to the further development of American capitalism.

As a general sketch of the causes of the major social reforms of the New Deal and their eventual consequences, this is impeccable. Still, it must be emphasized that at the very points where Block's class struggle theory of capitalist rationalization becomes most analytically relevant, it also becomes quite vague. What forms does working-class pressure take? What is the relationship between working-class pressures and the activities of state managers? Do the state managers only respond to pressures from below, or are they likely, under certain kinds of circumstances, to *stimulate* pressure from noncapitalists as well? If application of Block's theory to the Wagner Act leaves open many questions, its application to the NIRA presents even more problems. Block suggests that the low level of investment in periods of economic depression reduces the importance of business confidence as a check on state initiatives. Yet as we have said, and are about to show in detail, when the Roosevelt administration sought to restore prosperity, it did so by giving state authority to business. In Block's terms, this seems perverse. Moreover, Block's approach does not provide any more of an answer than those already discussed to what must be considered the most fundamental question about the NRA: why it did not succeed. The National Recovery Administration might be interpreted as an *attempt* at rationalization, but in practice the experiment deepened economic and social conflicts and produced entirely unforeseen political effects.

Because they interpret political outcomes as the product of processes involving the initiatives of state managers as well as capitalists and workers, Block and Lindblom provide more insights into the industrial and labor policies of the New Deal than the socially determinist approaches of Truman, Poulantzas, or the corporate-liberal theorists. But to develop specific causal explanations, it is necessary to go from the abstract "capitalist" and "democratic" dynamics outlined by Block and Lindblom to the concrete political organizations that link officials, businessmen, and workers in different ways in different times and places. In this essay, we shall focus on two types of organizations that seem essential to understanding the path from the NIRA to the Wagner Act: states and parties. In particular, we emphasize the minimal *administrative capacity* of the U.S. national state to intervene in industry and the effects on public policy-making of the internally divided Democratic party.

A focus on state capacity reflects a recognition that decisions made by governments cannot always be carried through; there is no law guaranteeing that governmental authorities will attempt only those interventions that they really can execute.[27] The administrative organization of government is crucial, especially when policies calling for increased government intervention are to be implemented. Successful state economic intervention requires that administrative elites have both the *will to intervene* and an understanding of *what to do* when they carry out interventionist policies.[28] To say that administrative leaders have a will to intervene is to say that they define their roles broadly, to include responsibility for the national economy. John Armstrong has shown how patterns of elite socialization imbue European administrators with this ethos, while Alfred Stepan has demonstrated the development of such an orientation among Latin American militaries during the 1960s.[29]

Knowledge of what to do requires that administrators have the information needed to control a complex industrial economy, and that they have learned from past experience what policies will and will not achieve the desired objectives.[30] Governments that have, or can quickly assemble, their own knowledgeable administrative organizations are better able to carry through interventionist policies than are governments that must rely on extragovernmental experts and organizations. Because of the particular historical course of "state building" in U.S. history, the will to intervene and the knowledge about what to do, and thus the capacity of the national state for autonomous intervention in industry, were quite limited. Given these limits, the grandiose objectives of the NIRA could not be attained.

The study of party alignments and realignments has become a familiar enterprise of American political science. In this essay, we are interested in them for the same reason V. O. Key was: to understand how they relate to policy outcomes.[31] If the autonomous role of public officials is as important as Block and Lindblom suggest, then we must pay attention to the electoral context that shapes their decision making. However, votes do not translate directly into policy outcomes. Different patterns of political party organization, and different alignments of inter- and intraparty competition, not only place different people in power, but subject those in power to contrasting sets of influences. And, because of the fragmented and nonprogrammatic nature of American political parties,[32] fractions of parties can play key roles in policy formulation.

In referring to party alignments, we thus mean not only configurations of party identification among regions, classes, and ethnic groups, but patterns of inter- and intraparty competition among political elites and forms of party organization. In the case of the NIRA, it was important for passage of the act that the Democrats held a majority in Congress, and that Roosevelt, not Hoover, was president. But it was also important that part of the Democratic party was willing to go further than Roosevelt in challenging business controls. Similarly, the increased significance of the urban liberal wing of the Democratic party after the 1934 elections was a major factor in the introduction and enactment of the Wagner Act.

Our approach is posed at a lower level of generality than the theories of Truman, Poulantzas, Block, or Lindblom because we believe that it is only on this level that questions about the origins and consequences of the NIRA, and its relation to the origins and consequences of the Wagner Act, can be answered. Stated most generally, our argument is that state structures and party alignments are important in shaping policy outcomes in advanced capitalist democracies. But just *how* they are important depends on specific historical conjunctures and patterns of prior development.

The tale of the NRA and the Wagner Act that will be told in the following sections of this essay, then, is very much a tale of state and party. The coming to power of the Democratic party made possible a new state initiative in industrial policy; the content of that policy was determined by the conflict of polyarchal and business controls. But the organization that was created by the National Industrial Recovery Act failed to achieve the grandiose goals of its creators because the U.S. national state did not have the historic capacity to intervene successfully in conflicts either within or between industries. The collapse of the NRA helped to bring about gains for labor that far exceeded those business had opposed in 1933, and that contributed further to the legacy of fragmentation that has characterized statemaking in America.

Giving Way to Business: The Origins of the National Industrial Recovery Act

Despite its ambitious intention to regulate production and labor conditions in hundreds of industries, the NIRA was one of the most hastily improvised parts of the early New Deal. As late as April 13, 1933, Roosevelt expressed strong skepticism about any such comprehensive program for industrial regulation and recovery.[33] A month later, however, Roosevelt was willing to endorse the NIRA as a replacement for alternative recovery measures that he—and businessmen—found undesirable. What originally set in motion the scramble to formulate the NIRA was the Senate's insistence in early April on passing the Black Thirty Hours Bill, despite opposition from the administration. And what finally persuaded Roosevelt to sponsor the NIRA was the failure of Labor Secretary Frances Perkins to come up with a substitute for the Black Bill that was acceptable to both Congress and the business elite.

As summarized by Ellis W. Hawley, the Black Bill

> would prohibit the shipment in inter-state commerce of any goods produced by men working more than a six-hour day or a five-day week. The bill reflected the popular notion that available work should be shared; it enjoyed the support of organized labor; and in the atmosphere of the time, it seemed likely to win the approval of the House as well as the Senate.[34]

For in the spring of 1933, Congress was exhibiting more sensitivity than Roosevelt to the distress of the industrial working class, not only in its attention to the Black Bill, but also in its advocacy of public works spending. By the more localized nature of their electoral constituencies, congressional representatives were inherently more likely to respond to pressures from such groups as unemployed workers, bankrupt local governments, and construction groups seeking subsidies. Moreover, urban Democrats had achieved substantial influence in the Congress well before they were to become important in presidential politics. Roosevelt originally came to power within the Democratic party without much urban support, and he mostly took working-class votes for granted in his 1932 campaign against Hoover. Yet from the mid-1920s on, increasing numbers of Democrats from urban backgrounds or constituencies were appearing in Congress. And during Hoover's final years in office, key Northern urban liberals (like Robert Wagner) allied with Progressive Republicans (like George Norris) and with Southern mavericks (like Hugo Black) to propose measures of unemployment relief and public works spending.[35] Thus, well before the national Democratic electoral triumph of 1932, many representatives and senators had become persuaded of the economic usefulness of prolabor legislation. And when the 1932 election brought many new Democrats to office, the effect was only to strengthen congressional willingness to support measures such as public works and the Black Bill. For the newly elected Democrats were especially anxious to consolidate their electoral majorities by enacting popular programs to alleviate unemployment.[36]

To Roosevelt, the Black Bill was an impractical measure, likely to paralyze industry and demoralize businessmen, because of its inflexible standards applying across all industries.[37] Immediate protests from employers confirmed Roosevelt's determination to quash the measure. But the Black Bill was too popular for Roosevelt to turn it away without substituting new legislation that would deal with the same concerns. Frances Perkins, building on her own and Roosevelt's long-standing concern to regulate conditions of employment, proposed an alternative bill raising the maximum hours standard and making it more flexible, instituting minimum wages, and assigning great authority to supervise the new regulations to the secretary of labor. The Perkins substitute, however, also aroused opposition from business leaders.[38]

Industrialists preferred their own vision of government-sponsored "business planning" to popular work-sharing proposals.[39] Aspirations for the relaxation of antitrust laws had been current during the 1920s in competitive industries faced with overproduction. Once the Depression hit, industrial capitalists in most industries found themselves threatened by suddenly declining markets, prices, and profits in competitive environments they could not control. General Electric's Gerard Swope and the U.S. Chamber of Commerce were early proponents of broader plans for industry-by-industry self-regulation of wages, hours, and prices.

During 1931 and 1932, Hoover was pressed to accept programs along these lines, but he rejected on principle the notion of government-sanctioned industrial cartelization. Before April, 1933, Roosevelt too was extremely wary of endorsing an across-the-board relaxation of the antitrust laws. But with the brouhaha over the Black Bill and the Perkins substitute, advocates of business planning got their chance to enter the legislative process. As part of his counterattack against the Black Bill, Roosevelt gave the green light to several groups within the administration who were working on general industrial recovery plans. Each group contained seasoned advocates of business planning.[40] Given Roosevelt's resistance to any programs calling for large amounts of federal spending, the business regulators were able to get their low-cost ideas accepted as the cornerstone of the emerging NIRA by presenting them as the best available route to industrial recovery. No doubt half-convinced themselves, the business planners made extravagant projections of an economic upturn and expanding employment—if only business could eliminate cutthroat competition and put its own industries in order.[41]

The one truly unpalatable compromise that industrial capitalists had to make as the NIRA was formulated and put through Congress was the acceptance of the 7(a) provision that guaranteed labor the right to organize and bargain collectively with employers. Along with the explicit requirement that every industrial code drawn up under the NIRA should stipulate minimum wages, maximum hours, and conditions of employment, this guarantee for labor organization was the result of the persistent determination of Senator Wagner—and ultimately, of congressional liberals in general—that the NIRA would address the needs of industrial labor.[42] Some business associations tried to have Section 7(a) in particular weakened during the passage of the act through Congress. Their efforts failed, but most industrial employers remained optimistic that as the codes were established for each industry, they would be able to control the interpretation and the implementation of the NIRA's labor provisions.

Thus, U.S. industrialists had reason to rejoice when the NIRA was signed into law in June, 1933. Taking advantage of what had seemed a threatening conjuncture, when the Black Bill was on the verge of passage, they had persuaded an otherwise reluctant Roosevelt to sponsor a largely business-generated program as *the* national recovery strategy for the immediate future! Direct business pressure had not been able to achieve government-sponsored business planning. But as Block's general model would lead us to expect, popular pressures put government intervention on the legislative agenda. The policy preferences of capitalists, backed up by Roosevelt's own sense of what was needed for a healthy capitalist economy, prevailed in shaping major features of the resulting legislation. In Lindblom's terms, polyarchal and business pressures came into conflict, and business, largely united in vociferous opposition to a popular measure, seemed to win. Yet politics is a process over time, in which unforeseen and unintended consequences can be quite out of whack with the balance of forces that originally set a sequence of political events in motion. The NIRA had unintended consequences so severe that within two years business leaders were rejecting the program that had embodied their ideas about the way to recovery. But if these consequences were unintended, they were not inexplicable: they can be explained as a legacy of the historic weakness of the American state.

The Failure of the NRA

It is a commonplace observation in the historical literature on the New Deal that important aspects of the National Recovery Administration were influenced by the trade associations established in many industries after World War I. Much less emphasis is placed on the consequences for the NRA experiment of another legacy of pre–New Deal history: the overall administrative weakness of the U.S. national state. Unlike continental European nations, the United States did not inherit a bureaucratic state from preindustrial, monarchical times. During the nineteenth century, therefore, the United States was uniquely "stateless." War and international power, the great spurs to state building in European history, only reaffirmed the pattern of statelessness in the United States: ways were found to meet the challenges of World War I and the 1920s without creating an autonomous administration capable of sustained intervention in industry. Without a knowledgeable, preexisting government administrative organization to draw upon, the NRA was forced to rely on industrialists to regulate industry, and they proved inadequate for the task.

As Stephen Skowronek has put it, the nineteenth-century United States had a government of "courts and parties."[43] A potent judicial system regulated and defended property rights, while locally rooted and highly competitive mass political parties, based on divisible economic benefits, knit together the various levels and branches of government and placed severe limitations on the expansion of any bureaucratic administration or civil service composed of positions outside the electoral-patronage system. After the electoral realignment of 1896, Theodore Roosevelt and successive presidents took the lead in promoting federal administrative growth and bureaucratization. Yet Congress continued to resist efforts at administrative expansion and, at each step, contested the executive branch for control of newly created federal agencies.

Given this history of checked development, existing federal bureaucracies were not prepared to mobilize human resources and coordinate the industrial economy during World War I, so emergency agencies were thrown together for the occasion, mostly staffed by professional experts and "businesscrats" temporarily recruited from the corporate capitalist sector. The major agency for industrial mobilization, the War Industries Board (WIB), was headed by freewheeling financier Bernard Baruch, who used business executives turned government officials to hound corporations into a semblance of cooperation in support of the war effort.[44] Because America's involvement in World War I was brief, and because the task was to orchestrate a profitable overall expansion of production (as opposed to restricting production during depression), the WIB's very tenuous ability to coordinate economic flows, control prices, and manage the interface between the military and industry was never made as glaringly apparent as it might have been. And once the "emergency" of war had passed, Congress quickly dismantled agencies such as the WIB, leaving the U.S. national state as weak in many ways as before the war and leaving corporations on their own to pursue profitable growth, intramural control of their labor forces, and whatever industrywide cooperation they could achieve without violating antitrust laws.

During the Republican administrations of the 1920s, the center of "state building" was the Commerce Department, headed by Herbert Hoover from 1921 to 1928. But Hoover pursued an antibureaucratic strategy based on the concept of an "associative state" that would "function through promotional conferences, expert inquiries, and cooperating committees, not through public enterprise, legal coercion, or arbitrary controls."[45] "Adhocracy" became more significant than bureaucracy, for Hoover used many government officials as facilitators of cooperation within and among powerful private groups, especially business trade associations. While the department as a whole grew during Hoover's tenure as secretary, its supervisory center, the Office of the Secretary of Commerce, actually declined in personnel. The biggest growth came in the Bureau of Foreign and Domestic Commerce, whose work predominantly concerned export trade.[46]

Despite its strategic position during the 1920s, then, the Department of Commerce had relatively little to contribute to the formulation and administration of regulatory codes for domestic industries, and the National Recovery Administration was not placed within the department, but was created as an independent agency, with its head reporting directly to the president. Implementation of the state's new initiative in industrial policy would depend, not on the resources of a preexisting department, but on the individual efforts of the man chosen as administrator of the NRA: General Hugh Johnson, a veteran of the War Industries Board.

The tasks at hand were exhilarating and overwhelming. An entire NRA staff, destined to grow to over three thousand, had to be instantly assembled.[47] With an enormous amount of public hoopla, Johnson consciously modeled the Blue Eagle Campaign on the war bonds drive of World War I in an effort to put NRA "enforcement . . . into the hands of the *whole* people."[48] Meanwhile, Johnson used his formidable powers of personal persuasion to prompt industries to draw up their own individual codes of fair competition. Between June and October, 1933, the major industries were brought under codes of fair competition, and processes were well under way that would result in over five hundred codes covering about 96 percent of American industry.[49]

Business leaders succeeded in formulating the codes so as to allow many loopholes in the required prolabor provisions as well as production cutbacks and noncompetitive, higher prices for most industries. They were able to do so because the early NRA was, in the words of one contemporary observer, "a bargain between business leaders on the one hand and businessmen in the guise of government officials on the other."[50] The key officials of the early NRA, other than Johnson himself, were "deputy administrators drawn almost invariably from the ranks of business," sometimes from the same industries with which they had to negotiate over code provisions.[51] These administrators were strongly sympathetic to the needs of the industrialists for a profitable environment and an end to "cutthroat competition." Industrial executives had a further advantage in that they controlled most of the information about industrial operations on which the

NRA codes and their enforcement would have to be based. "When the recovery program began," Galambos notes, "the government did not have much more information [on the workings of industry] than it had had during the First World War."[52] Nor were there at hand trained government officials experienced in regulating or planning for industry with "the public interest" and some conception of the whole economy in mind. What is more, in the trade associations, industrialists possessed the only organizational means that could be used to implement the codes once approved.[53] Most code authorities established for this purpose were selected and staffed by trade association personnel or industrial executives. Even the "government representatives" serving on code authorities were usually nominated by the Industrial Advisory Board of the NRA, a body made up of elite U.S. capitalists. Labor representatives appeared on less than 10 percent of the initially established code authorities, and representatives of consumers made it onto only 2 percent.[54]

Rapid codification accomplished in this way soon led, however, to increasingly bitter controversies within the NRA. Business executives found that legalized regulation and planning by industries' own efforts, rather than by state initiative, resulted in an incoherent pattern of crosscutting jurisdictions and a proliferation of administrative red tape. And by joining the NRA effort, business executives brought conflicts within and between industries into a political arena. There were "conflicts between large units and small ones, integrated firms and nonintegrated, chain stores and independents, manufacturers and distributors, new industries and declining ones, and so on ad infinitum."[55] The NRA apparatus, itself thoroughly permeated by conflicting business interests, was unable to resolve disputes in an authoritative fashion. And NRA lawyers, responsible for devising a strategy for code enforcement, were split between supporters of business planning and members of the antitrust Felix Frankfurter–Louis Brandeis network, and never able to assert their autonomy against the claims of a Justice Department that doubted the constitutionality of the entire program.[56]

Even the most successful self-regulatory codes, finally, could not ensure market stability and steady profitability. The cotton textile code authority was directly established by the Cotton Textile Institute, and during 1933–34 it was remarkably successful in maintaining its authority against unwanted interference by government officials. Yet the problem of fine-tuning production flows to ensure profitable yields remained, for the code authority, as a representative of firms in the industry, "could react to manifest problems, but could not anticipate difficulties before they impinged directly and decisively upon a large majority of the members." Cotton Textile Institute officials recognized, Galambos notes,

> that prices could not be stabilized so long as the manufacturer's product
> groups had to initiate the decisions to cut production. They needed to

give that responsibility to a person or persons who could keep in touch with the statistical reports and check any overproduction before it became serious. But that idea carried the association leaders onto dangerous ground: the experts who made these decisions might end up being government experts, and to the manufacturers that was an outcome to be avoided at any cost.[57]

By the end of the NRA, expert administrators with their own ideas on how government intervention could induce recovery did emerge. But they were then seen as threatening by capitalists, because they were acting as spokesmen for consumer and labor interests and were advocating social reforms as a concomitant of increased state regulation of certain aspects of business performance.

The idea of a state strong enough to implement a program like the NRA, yet sympathetic to interests of owners and managers, may seem fantastic in view of the history of state development in the United States. Yet the historical development of different parts of the federal government had been uneven, and the kind of state intervention that proved impossible for industry was actually carried out successfully for commercial agriculture. The Agricultural Adjustment Administration (AAA) was set up about the same time as the NRA, with a very similar agenda of producing recovery through raised prices and restricted production.[58] While the Department of Commerce proved of little help to the NRA, however, the AAA was able to draw upon the Department of Agriculture, which enjoyed unusual administrative unity and flexibility. The Department of Agriculture, moreover, was tied to the land grant colleges, in which economists and scientists were trained to plan for entire commodity systems, and even for agriculture as a whole. Whereas the NRA had to rely on businessmen to carry out its tasks, the AAA was largely staffed by these agricultural experts. They proved willing and able to make policy *for*, rather than just *with*, farmers and their organizations. As a result, between 1933 and 1936, the AAA largely achieved its aim of raising farm income. Like the NRA, the AAA was struck down by the Supreme Court. But whereas the failed NRA was, after the *Schechter* decision, given a brief extension "as a temporary, skeletonized agency that could conduct research and approve voluntary business agreements,"[59] the more successful AAA was quickly restored in a form that could withstand constitutional tests.

The very different outcomes of the NRA and AAA had important consequences for class relations in industry and agriculture.[60] A major farm lobby organization, the American Farm Bureau Federation, was able to expand its operations in tandem with the local administration of production control programs under the AAA. In turn, from the mid-1930s on, the Farm Bureau became pivotal in defending its own organizational interests and the class interests of commercial farmers against the claims of sharecroppers, tenants, and farm workers. The collapse of the NRA, in contrast, served to strengthen organized labor and its intragovernmental allies, and to weaken industrial capitalists.

Government Intervention and Class Conflict: The Origins of the Wagner Act

Inevitably, as soon as the federal government launched its intervention into industry, it came face to face with class divisions. Two kinds of consequences followed. Advocates for the rights of labor became active within the National Recovery Administration, and industrial workers were themselves politicized by the turning of government attention to matters formerly left to the private discretion of owners and managers. Labor advocates lost their initial bureaucratic wars within the NRA, but, led by Senator Robert Wagner, continued to fight from niches elsewhere in the government. In 1935, they triumphed with the passage of the National Labor Relations Act. This act, and the independent National Labor Relations Board established to enforce it, facilitated labor organization and recognition, so much so that union membership grew from less than 4 million in 1935 to over 8 million in 1939 and doubled again during World War II.[61]

Why did the New Deal, which began by investing the power to regulate industry in industrialists, end up facilitating and legalizing the enormous expansion of trade unions? Our answer emphasizes the combined effects of state and party. First, in the mid-1930s, urban liberals sympathetic to labor were at an apogee of influence in Congress and the Democratic party. But this alone could not have produced labor's dramatic gains, had not the failure of the NRA—which as we have argued was due to the lack of state capacity in industrial regulation—left industrial capitalists unusually impotent to influence New Deal policy-making. In 1933, both the form and the composition of the leadership of the NRA had seemed to demonstrate the power of business, even in a period of economic depression. But by 1935, the unintended consequences of that program had left industrial capitalists in a position where they were unable even to veto a "one-sided" labor measure—the Wagner Act—to which virtually all of them were adamantly and vociferously opposed.

Section 7(a) of the National Industrial Recovery Act required that NRA codes guarantee employees' rights to organize and to bargain collectively, without employer interference, and prohibit employers from requiring that workers join a company union or refrain from joining or participating in any other labor organization.[62] The effect of these promises was to encourage the trade union movement, which had been devastated by the open shop campaigns of the 1920s and then by the Depression. Using the appealing (if misleading) slogan of "The President wants you to join the union," John L. Lewis's United Mine Workers (UMW) staged an enormously successful membership drive and won agreement with the commercial mine owners by September, 1933. The UMW met more resistance in its attempt to organize the "captive mines" owned by the steel companies, but the National Labor Board ruled that the companies must negotiate with the representatives chosen in its elections, though not necessarily with the union per se. The International Ladies' Garment Workers Union, led by David Dubinsky, joined with New York manufacturers to achieve standardization of the coat and suit industry through an NRA code, then won a closed shop by striking the New York dress manufacturers days before hearings on the dress code were to begin.[63]

Even more important than the revitalization of such previously moribund unions was the organization of workers in the mass production industries. Before 7(a), these industries had remained open shop through a combination of employer resistance to unionism, the reluctance of unions in the American Federation of Labor (AFL) to organize outside the old craft jurisdictions, and the inadequacy of the AFL "federal union" as an intermediate step to craft unionization. Though all these barriers to mass-production unionism remained during the early New Deal, 7(a) encouraged organization in several industries. Despite the complacency of its leadership, the Amalgamated Association of Iron, Steel, and Tin Workers expanded with the formation of locals named "New Deal," "NRA," or "Blue Eagle." In the auto industry, a small organization of tool and die makers became the first union to win company recognition. Section 7(a) inspired an organization drive among Akron rubber workers by the president of the machinists' local and his associates; soon forty to fifty thousand workers had joined up.[64]

Efforts to organize workers might not have produced such bitter conflict under the NIRA had not industrial employers been determined to circumvent or defeat 7(a)'s call for independent labor representation. Some employers responded to the revival of trade unionism by sponsoring company unions, which grew more rapidly than trade unions between 1932 and 1935.[65] Others, as in the rubber industry, resisted unionization in any form. Conflict between workers seeking to organize and employers determined to resist came to a head during the massive strike wave of 1934 when, as Irving Bernstein has concluded, "anybody struck."[66]

Government, of course, could not ignore the conflicts of labor and employers, nor was simple repression of labor a possibility given the 7(a) provision and the political climate of the New Deal. Instead, a succession of administrative bodies attempted to mediate these conflicts through their interpretation and enforcement of 7(a). Initial efforts were to prove so inadequate, however, that administrators of 7(a) were soon led to formulate stronger legislation to enforce labor's rights.

The NIRA itself made no special provision for the administration of 7(a), but in August, 1933, Roosevelt, at the proposal of the NRA's Industrial and Labor Advisory Boards, created the National Labor Board (NLB). The board was composed of three labor members, three industry members, and, as chairman, Senator Wagner, representing the public. The NLB made important contributions to labor policy in its interpretation of 7(a) and its establishment of procedures for adjusting disputes. However, it was unable to enforce its decisions, even after Roosevelt issued executive orders authorizing it to mediate or arbitrate disputes which "tend to impede the purposes of the National Industrial Recovery Act," and empowering the board to conduct representation elections at the request of employees. Supported by the National Association of Manufacturers, several firms refused to appear at hearings or defied NLB rulings. The head of the NRA, Hugh Johnson, and Donald Richberg, NRA General Counsel, repudiated the NLB's policy of "majority rule" (the union endorsed by the majority bargains for all) in favor of separate bargaining rights for minorities and individuals. Finally, in March, 1934, Johnson, with Roosevelt's support, thoroughly undermined the NLB by establishing an Automobile Labor Board independent of its authority. In turn, this new board provided for proportional representation of minority unions and individuals in bargaining with the auto companies.[67]

To provide for stronger administration and to clear up ambiguities such as the representation issue, Senator Wagner introduced the Labor Disputes Bill, drafted by his office with the assistance of the NLB staff, in March, 1934.[68] The bill received support from the existing NLB and from the American Federation of Labor. However, the Roosevelt administration was ambivalent, while most business groups were strongly opposed. A diluted version of the Labor Disputes Bill was reported by Senator David Walsh's Labor Committee. This measure, in turn, was dropped in favor of the still weaker Public Resolution No. 44, drafted by the Roosevelt administration and dictated to congressional leaders by the president. Of this measure, a U.S. Steel vice president wrote privately, "it is not going to bother us very much."[69] In June, 1934, Public Resolution No. 44 passed easily, as both Wagner and Walsh abandoned the earlier bill. The resolution gave the president power to establish a board to investigate disputes. The board would supervise elections, and was empowered to impose penalties for violations of the rules it established. Acting under the resolution, Roosevelt abolished the NLB and created the National Labor Relations Board (NLRB), a body of three public members with semiautonomous status within the Department of Labor.[70]

This first NLRB made some contributions to labor policy, most notably by defining its mission as judicial action against violations of labor rights, rather than the mediation carried out under the NLB.[71] But like its predecessor, the NLRB was unable to enforce its decisions. Enforcement depended upon the Attorney General, who proved rather reluctant to act; "judgements," Irving Bernstein has noted, "were not obtained in any of the thirty-three noncompliance cases referred to the [Justice Department] between July 1, 1934, and March 1, 1935."[72] Though not a member of the NLRB, Senator Wagner remained concerned with its problems. In the fall of 1934, he and his staff, together with the legal staff of the NLRB, drafted a new labor bill. The AFL was consulted about the bill, but—significantly—the Department of Labor, the NRA, and the White House were excluded from the drafting process.[73] The National Labor Relations Bill, introduced in February, 1935, proscribed employer participation or support for company unions; added to employees' right to bargain the requirement that employers participate in good faith; established majority rule; and, perhaps most important of all, created a new, autonomous National Labor Relations Board of three members independent of either industry or labor, endowed with quasi-judicial powers subject only to the review of higher courts.

"One-sided" as it was in favor of labor, the National Labor Relations Bill met with nearly unanimous opposition from business. Henry Harriman, president of the United States Chamber of Commerce and one of the "business planners" whose ideas had helped to shape the NIRA, argued that majority rule was "un-American and unethical."[74] James Emery, general counsel for the National Association of Manufacturers, presented fifty-five pages of testimony to the Senate committee attacking the bill as unconstitutional. (This opinion, and the belief the Supreme Court would strike down the act, was shared by the *New York Times*, by the American Liberty League, and, ironically enough, by many congressmen who ended up voting for the bill to avoid appearing antilabor.) Many trade associations also expressed their opposition.[75] Nevertheless, the bill became law. The Senate committee reported it with only favorable amendments attached; the entire Senate then rejected unfavorable amendments and passed the bill, 63–12. Roosevelt, previously indifferent, endorsed the bill on May 24. In June, the House passed it without a roll call vote. On July 5, 1935, the "Wagner Act" was signed by President Roosevelt.[76]

How can the passage of the Wagner Act be explained? Particularly striking is the turnaround from the 1934 substitution of Public Resolution No. 44 for the Labor Disputes Bill. That earlier sequence fits better with what Block or Lindblom's reasoning would lead us to expect in a democratic capitalist order—a measure strongly opposed by business should be defeated or modified to meet business preferences. Did massive labor unrest perhaps force the federal government to abandon its normal solicitude for business in 1935? This line of explanation has been favored by some social analysts. But the weak Public Resolution No. 44 was passed at the peak of the strike wave discussed earlier, while labor unrest subsequently fell off until *after* the passage of the Wagner Act.[77] To explain the remarkable passage of the Wagner Act, we must instead look to more strictly intragovernmental developments that came together in 1935 to allow advocates of strong legal support for unionization finally to get their way in the legislative arena.

As we have seen, Roosevelt was until the very last minute unwilling to advocate unequivocal federal support for labor unions. He had established proportional representation under the Automobile Labor Board and advanced Public Resolution No. 44 in place of Wagner's Labor Disputes Bill. But Roosevelt's reluctance was not to prove decisive, for Wagner's strategy in 1934–35 was to work through Congress rather than the president. Wagner was able to carry out this plan because, even though he had since the 1920s established a strong reputation for legislative leadership on economic matters, Wagner was not an isolated figure, but the prototype of the urban liberal Democrat in Congress. Part of the explanation for the ultimate passage of the Wagner Act thus lies in Congress's responsiveness to the industrial working class, a responsiveness based on some trends underway before 1934 and intensified by the results of the congressional elections of that year.

Partisan realignment, a gradual process beginning in the 1920s, had transformed the Democrats into a party that mobilized increasing numbers of urban-ethnic voters into national politics,[78] just as the congressional reapportionment of December, 1930, the first since 1910, greatly increased urban representation.[79] Especially after the massive Democratic victory in 1932, Congress was more populated than ever before with urban liberals. Their support, as mentioned earlier, was crucial to the inclusion of Section 7(a) in the NIRA. Still, had events in American politics followed their normal course, the 1934 elections would have brought setbacks for liberal Democrats, because the majority party usually loses seats in off year elections. But instead of losing ground in 1934, the Democrats actually gained nine seats apiece in the House and Senate. The Republican right was practically eliminated, and the proportion of Democratic seats held by Southerners was reduced.[80] Thus Congress in 1935 was even more fertile ground for prolabor arguments than in 1933 or 1934.

These changes in Congress would almost certainly not have proved decisive, however, had it not been for the failure of the National Recovery Administration to maintain business cooperation and further national economic recovery. These failures had important political implications: they led business to break with the New Deal, and business opposition along with the NRA's shortcomings drove Roosevelt to the left. The NRA did not achieve either stability or recovery and, from business's point of view, was by late 1934 becoming overly responsive to labor, consumers, and government planners. As the national economy continued to be mired in depression, the Roosevelt administration responded by purchasing gold and by increasing expenditures for relief and public works programs.

These measures, of course, increased the federal budget deficit and competed with private enterprise, thus arousing still more business opposition. Major corporate figures, including breakaways from the Business Advisory Council assembled in 1933 to support the New Deal, launched the archconservative Liberty League in 1934.[81] And the National Association of Manufacturers, formerly a spokesman for small and medium-sized businesses, was transformed into an anti–New Deal vehicle dominated by big business.[82] The most telling symbol of the business turnaround on the New Deal came at the April, 1935, meeting of the U.S. Chamber of Commerce. The chamber, which had enthusiastically endorsed the NRA at its inception, rejected its extension along with social security, labor legislation, and other pending reforms. Faced with so much business opposition by 1935, Roosevelt moved closer to congressional progressives. His last-minute endorsement of the National Labor Relations Bill was one manifestation of this shift.[83]

Thus, the debacle of the NRA broke up the marriage of business and government embodied in the National Industrial Recovery Act. Indeed, it is arguable that it was the failure of the NRA—rather than, as Block would have it, the Depression itself—that removed the necessity of maintaining business confidence. By demonstrating that businessmen could not deliver economic recovery even when the machinery of government-sanctioned industrial planning was placed in their hands, the NRA discredited businessmen's claims that they knew best what was good for the economy. What is more, the failure of the "business commonwealth" approach to recovery gave added credence to Senator Wagner's arguments that the Depression was caused by underconsumption, that increased consumption required higher wages, and that higher wages could be achieved only by government intervention. In the absence of another viable strategy for economic recovery, these arguments, which were prominent among those used by Wagner in the congressional debates, may have swayed congressmen to ignore business opposition. In this way, it became possible to pass the Wagner Act despite business's nearly unanimous disapproval.[84]

The Supreme Court upheld the constitutionality of the Wagner Act in the 1937 Jones and Laughlin case.[85] By the end of the New Deal, a part of the federal government, the National Labor Relations Board, had a vested interest in promoting unions, as well as the institutional capacity to carry out this aim.[86] Unions in turn were able to translate their new organizational power into an unprecedented (if still modest and limited) degree of political leverage in Congress and the Democratic party.[87]

Along with the gains of commercial farmers and the pattern of regulatory shelters for politically advantaged industries that followed the breakup of the NRA, labor's victory contributed to the establishment of a fragmented broker state: far from becoming a centralized, corporatist order capable of national planning in any meaningful sense, the post–New Deal state became instead an enlarged and more socially intrusive hodgepodge of separate nexuses of power, each a symbiosis of partially autonomous bureaucratic administration, special support in Congress, and the organized representation of a well-bounded socioeconomic interest.[88] For this reason, Otis Graham, Jr., has argued that

> something far worse had happened to Planning by 1940 than simply a failure to get itself realized in the most favorable circumstances history had yet provided in the United States. . . . Planning would be *more* difficult after 1940 than before, for the New Deal era had seen partial planning and broker interventionism built deep into the structure of American public life. Power sectors had been created that would later on resist any nationalizing or rationalizing integration.[89]

Like the Wagner Act itself, this pattern was far from the vision of the business planners who had helped to shape the NIRA.

The passage of the Wagner Act demonstrates that in at least some conjunctures of state and party—perhaps highly unusual ones—the mechanisms pointed out by Block and Lindblom, by which capitalist influence normally constrains government policy making in liberal democracies, can fail to operate. In particular, the most potent weapon of private capitalists, their hegemony with respect to definitions of "what is good for the economy," can be temporarily lost. Our argument has been that by 1935, American business leaders had lost political influence and economic ideological hegemony because of the failure of the National Recovery Administration. When businessmen pushed for the NRA in 1933, they promised more than either they or a U.S. national government without the will or the knowledge needed to regulate industry could deliver. Fatefully, when the NRA failed, the slate was not simply swept clean. Under the terms of the NIRA, bureaucratic efforts had been set in motion that led from 7(a) to the formulation of the Wagner Act. And the NRA's failure created a new balance of political forces, in which business could no longer influence the president, and Congress, already sensitive to labor's interests by reason of its party ties, was willing to override clearly stated business opposition.

The passage of the Wagner Act, then, must be traced back to the failure of the NRA, which in turn can be traced to the lack of state capacity in industry, as well as to the changing party system of the 1930s. Otherwise the act makes little sense. Big business did not support it and the resources of labor were insufficient to guarantee passage in the face of business opposition and presidential reluctance. But once the complex sequences of history are traced, the Wagner Act, and the fragmented broker state it helped to produce, appear as the true offsprings of the originally business-sponsored National Industrial Recovery Act—bastards though they may have been from the standpoint of American capitalists.

Conclusion: Industrial Policy in the New Deal and Today

Advocates of industrial policy like Reich and Thurow are in some ways like supporters of business planning in the 1930s. Certainly their programs for economic recovery are as comprehensive as those of Swope or Harriman. But as in the 1930s, there is a big difference between formulation of programs for industrial recovery and the achievement of it; as Thurow admits, "There is no easy path for getting from here to there."[90] In urging readers to support their proposals, Thurow appeals to a desire for equity, while Reich discusses the need for civic virtue. Both frequently invoke the notion of "choice," with its existential overtones.[91] Yet the experience of the New Deal suggests that the conditions for a great transformation of the American political economy are less moral than structural. Building upon the models presented by Fred Block and Charles Lindblom, we have argued that the origins and outcomes of the National Industrial Recovery Act can be understood in terms of state capacity and party alignments. State intervention in industry requires what Poulantzas termed "relative autonomy." Such autonomy, we suggest, is the product of specific historical circumstances, rather than, as Poulantzas argued, a general condition of advanced capitalism. During the New Deal, the failure of business strategies for recovery and the emergence of urban and labor support for alternative approaches did not entirely remove the constraints imposed by business pressures. But within these constraints, the possibilities for autonomous action by the president and the state became wider.

The same concepts of state capacity and party alignments may help us to understand the possibilities for industrial policy today. As both Reich and Thurow recognize, the party system of today is not conducive to comprehensive policy making. Recent trends in American politics have made it more difficult than ever for parties, or even party factions, to mobilize consent in support of anything but logrolling programs for special interests.[92] To the extent the parties are bound to broader sets of economic principles, it is to neo-laissez-faire and to union-endorsed protectionism, neither of which is compatible with the types of policies advocated by these authors. Still, it is possible that a president or congressman particularly committed to the notion of industrial policy might be able to win enactment of some of the measures suggested by Reich or Thurow.

It is more difficult to see how, once enacted, an industrial policy could be carried out, for the federal government continues to be characterized by the broker state pattern set by the New Deal. Because of this fragmentation, coordination among the different parts of government is even more difficult to achieve than it was during the early 1930s. There is still no government agency with the will and knowledge to make decisions for entire industries, or for industry as a whole. The Department of Agriculture–land grant college nexus trains agricultural experts, as it did before and during the New Deal. But there is still no comparable system to train experts in industry, though the current profusion of public policy schools might someday serve this purpose. In the absence of any state capacity for sustained intervention in industry, a new body charged with this task might well repeat the pattern of the NRA, relying upon businessmen trained only to think in terms of their own firm or division, once again with disastrous results and unintended consequences.

The rapid development of the National Labor Relations Board does suggest that, in the right political conjuncture, state capacity can be created where none existed before.[93] The question is, what would be the right political conjuncture for the development of state capacity to intervene in industrial decision making? The case of the New Deal suggests that patterns of inter- and intraparty competition, the challenge of social movements, and the removal of the normal check of business confidence on state initiatives might all play a part.

Yet the links between the collapse of the National Recovery Administration and the passage of the Wagner Act also suggest that initiatives that fail may be as important to the process of statemaking as those that succeed. Such surprising and ironic twists of state development can only be understood in historically specific ways, taking into account the preexisting or changing organizations of administrative states and political parties. As our case study of one crucial episode in the history of the modern American political economy underlines, grand theoretical schemes fashioned to apply across all political orders or to cover all capitalist social formations are necessarily as limited in their ability to predict the future as they are in their capacity to explain the past.

NOTES

The authors would like to thank Fred Block, Albert Hirschman, Harvey Rishikof, and the participants in the October 1980 Ann Arbor Conference on "Statemaking and Social Movements" for helpful comments during the course of preparing this article.

1. Lester C. Thurow, *The Zero-Sum Society* (New York: Basic Books, 1980), pp. 191–92.
2. Ira C. Magaziner and Robert B. Reich, *Minding America's Business: The Decline and Rise of the American Economy* (New York: Harcourt Brace Jovanovich, 1982), esp. chaps. 17–21 and 27–30. See also Reich, *The Next American Frontier* (New York: Times Books, 1983).
3. Earlier versions of some of the arguments presented in this essay can be found in Theda Skocpol, "Political Response to Capitalist Crisis: Neo-Marxist Theories and the Case of the New Deal," *Politics and Society* 10, no. 2 (1981): 155–201; Theda Skocpol and Kenneth Finegold, "State Capacity and Economic Intervention in the Early New Deal," *Political Science Quarterly* 97, no. 2 (Summer, 1982): 255–78; and Kenneth Finegold and Theda Skocpol, "Capitalists, Farmers, and Workers in the New Deal—The Ironies of Government Intervention," Paper presented to the Conference Group on the Political Economy of Advanced Industrial Societies, American Political Science Association Annual Meeting, Washington, D.C., August 1980.
4. *The Public Papers and Addresses of Franklin D. Roosevelt*, 13 vols., compiled by Samuel I. Rosenman (New York: Random House, 1938), 2:246.
5. Quoted from the text of the act, reproduced in Leverett S. Lyon et al., *The National Recovery Act: An Analysis and Appraisal*, 2 vols. (New York: Da Capo Press, 1972; originally 1935), 2:889. Title II of the act authorized a program of public works spending, to be implemented by the new Public Works Administration.
6. The best general analysis of the NIRA, its failure, and the aftereffects is Ellis W. Hawley, *The New Deal and the Problem of Monopoly* (Princeton, N.J.: Princeton University Press, 1966).
7. The classic statement of the pluralist position is David B. Truman, *The Governmental Process*, 2d ed. (New York: Knopf, 1971).
8. Ralph Miliband, *The State in Capitalist Society* (New York: Basic Books, 1969). The association is somewhat unfair because this book actually includes arguments about politics and the state that have since been crystallized into virtually every major neo-Marxist position on these topics.
9. Ibid., p. 146.
10. Ronald Radosh, "The Myth of the New Deal," in *A New History of Leviathan: Essays on the Rise of the Corporate State*, ed. Radosh and Murray N. Rothbard (New York: Dutton, 1972), pp. 146–87; G. William Domhoff, *The Higher Circles: The Governing Class in America* (New York: Vintage Books, 1971), chap. 6. James Weinstein takes a similar view of the Progressive Era in *The Corporate Ideal in the Liberal State, 1900–1918* (Boston: Beacon Press, 1968).

11. This is the interpretation presented by Domhoff in *The Higher Circles.* Domhoff's views on the Wagner Act have subsequently shifted away from a strictly corporate-liberal position: he notes the opposition of business groups to the Wagner Act in *The Powers That Be* (New York: Random House, 1978), p. 74 n.23, and p. 119 n.105.

12. Nicos Poulantzas, *Political Power and Social Classes,* trans. Timothy O'Hagen (London: New Left Books, 1973); idem, "The Problem of the Capitalist State," in *Ideology in Social Science,* ed. Robin Blackburn (New York: Vintage Books, 1973).

13. Poulantzas, "The Problem of the Capitalist State," p. 246.

14. David A. Gold, Clarence Y. H. Lo, and Erik Olin Wright, "Recent Developments in Marxist Theories of the Capitalist State," *Monthly Review* 27, no. 5 (October 1975): 38.

15. The 1920s was a period when many new trade associations were founded, and when trade association leaders took on increasingly important coordinative functions. On this latter point, see Louis Galambos, *Competition and Cooperation: The Emergence of a National Trade Association* (Baltimore: Johns Hopkins University Press, 1966). For statistics on waves of foundation of associations by U.S. capitalists, see Philippe C. Schmitter and Donald Brand, "Organizing Capitalists in the United States: The Advantages and Disadvantages of Exceptionalism," Paper presented at the Annual Meeting of the American Political Science Association, Washington, D.C., September, 1979.

16. Hawley, *Problem of Monopoly,* chaps. 2 and 3; Robert F. Himmelberg, *The Origins of the National Recovery Administration: Business, Government, and the Trade Association Issue, 1921–1933* (New York: Fordham University Press, 1976).

17. Hawley, *Problem of Monopoly,* p. 42.

18. Charles E. Lindblom, *Politics and Markets: The World's Political-Economic Systems* (New York: Basic Books, 1977).

19. Ibid., p. 172.

20. Ibid., p. 173.

21. Ibid., p. 119.

22. Ibid., p. 189.

23. Fred Block, "The Ruling Class Does Not Rule: Notes on the Marxist Theory of the State," *Socialist Revolution* 33 (May-June, 1977): 6–28. See also idem, "Beyond Corporate Liberalism," *Social Problems* 24 (1976–77): 352–61.

24. Block, "Ruling Class Does Not Rule," p. 20.

25. Ibid.

26. Ibid., p. 25.

27. This point is also central to Jeffrey L. Pressman and Aaron Wildavsky, *Implementation,* 2d ed. (Berkeley: University of California Press, 1979) and the many studies that have followed from it. But their approach sees policy design, not institutional capacities, as the source of the gap between legislative intentions and real-world outcomes.

28. Finegold and Skocpol, "State Capacity and Economic Intervention in the Early New Deal," pp. 275–77.

29. John A. Armstrong, *The European Administrative Elite* (Princeton, N.J.: Princeton University Press, 1973); Alfred Stepan, *The State and Society: Peru in Comparative Perspective* (Princeton, N.J.: Princeton University Press, 1978), chap. 4.

30. The process of political learning is the focus of Hugh Heclo, *Modern Social Politics in Britain and Sweden* (New Haven: Yale University Press, 1973).

31. V. O. Key, Jr., "A Theory of Critical Elections," *Journal of Politics* 17, no. 1 (February, 1955): 3–18. Among the works that have since investigated this linkage are William Nisbet Chambers and Walter Dean Burnham, eds., *The American Party Systems: Stages of Political Development*, 2d ed. (New York: Oxford University Press, 1975); Burnham, *Critical Elections and the Mainsprings of American Politics* (New York: W. W. Norton, 1970); and Benjamin Ginsberg, "Elections and Public Policy," *American Political Science Review* 70, no. 1 (March, 1976): 41–49.

32. Theodore J. Lowi, "Party, Policy and Constitution in America," in *The American Party Systems*, ed. Chambers and Burnham.

33. Frank Freidel, *Franklin D. Roosevelt: Launching the New Deal* (Boston: Little, Brown, 1973), p. 418; Raymond Moley, *After Seven Years* (Lincoln: University of Nebraska Press, 1939), p. 186.

34. Hawley, *Problem of Monopoly*, p. 22.

35. Jordan A. Schwarz, *The Interregnum of Despair: Hoover, Congress, and the Depression* (Urbana: University of Illinois Press, 1970).

36. James T. Patterson, *Congressional Conservatism and the New Deal* (Lexington: University of Kentucky Press, 1967), pp. 4–6.

37. Freidel, *Launching the New Deal*, pp. 419–20; Moley, *After Seven Years*, p. 186.

38. Moley, *After Seven Years*, p. 187; Hawley, *Problem of Monopoly*, pp. 22–23.

39. See Hawley, *Problem of Monopoly*, pp. 22–23, 36–43; Gerard Swope, *The Swope Plan* (New York: Business Bourse, 1931); Galambos, *Competition and Cooperation*, chaps. 7–8; and especially Himmelberg, *Origins of the NRA*.

40. Hawley, *Problem of Monopoly*, pp. 23–26; Himmelberg, *Origins of the NRA*, pp. 201–6; and Galambos, *Competition and Cooperation*, pp. 195–96.

41. Himmelberg, *Origins of the NRA*, p. 201, emphasizes that by mid-April, 1933, business leaders had learned from their earlier failures to convert Roosevelt to antitrust relaxation "the lesson that their objective had to be cloaked more substantially in the rhetoric of recovery planning to attain success."

42. The American Federation of Labor strongly supported 7(a), but given its weakness in 1933 (less than three million members), the Federation's support would have meant little had determined support in Congress been lacking. On Wagner's role, see J. Joseph Huthmacher, *Senator Robert F. Wagner and the Rise of Urban Liberalism* (New York: Atheneum, 1971), pp. 147–48.

43. Stephen Lee Skowronek, *Building a New American State: The Expansion of National Administrative Capacities, 1877–1920* (Cambridge: Cambridge Uni-

versity Press, 1982), chap. 2. This paragraph draws on Skowronek's analysis as a whole.

44. See Robert D. Cuff, *The War Industries Board: Business-Government Relations During World War I* (Baltimore: Johns Hopkins University Press, 1973).

45. Ellis W. Hawley, "Herbert Hoover, the Commerce Secretariat, and the Vision of an 'Associative State,' 1921–1928," *Journal of American History* 61 (June, 1974): 118–19.

46. Hawley, "Associative State," pp. 138–39 n.84; Joan Hoff Wilson, *Herbert Hoover: Forgotten Progressive* (Boston: Little, Brown, 1975), p. 86; and Carroll H. Wooddy, *The Growth of the Federal Government 1915–1932* (New York: McGraw-Hill, 1934), pp. 166–67, 176–77.

47. The figure comes from Hugh S. Johnson, *The Blue Eagle from Egg to Earth* (Garden City, N.Y.: Doubleday, Doran and Co., 1935), p. 286.

48. Ibid., p. 261. Emphasis in original.

49. Lyon et al., *National Recovery Administration*, p. 141; and Johnson, *Blue Eagle*, p. 286.

50. Quoted in Hawley, *Problem of Monopoly*, pp. 56–57.

51. Ibid., p. 56.

52. Galambos, *Competition and Cooperation*, p. 205.

53. Ibid., chaps. 9 and 10 provide an excellent case study of the role of the Cotton Textile Institute in formulating and implementing the NRA code for the cotton textile industry.

54. Hawley, *Problem of Monopoly*, p. 61.

55. Ibid., p. 69.

56. Peter H. Irons, *The New Deal Lawyers* (Princeton, N.J.: Princeton University Press, 1982), pp. 17–107.

57. Galambos, *Competition and Cooperation*, pp. 251–52.

58. The comparison between the administrative capacities of the state in industry and agriculture, and the consequences for the NRA and AAA, is the basis of Skocpol and Finegold, "State Capacity and Economic Intervention in the Early New Deal." Kenneth Finegold, "From Agrarianism to Adjustment: The Political Origins of New Deal Agricultural Policy" (*Politics and Society* 11, no. 1 [1982]: 1–27) discusses the prehistory of the AAA, while Richard S. Kirkendall, "The New Deal and Agriculture," in *The New Deal: The National Level*, ed. John Braeman, Robert H. Bremner, and David Brody (Columbus: Ohio State University Press, 1975), provides a good overview.

59. Hawley, *Problem of Monopoly*, p. 159.

60. See Finegold and Skocpol, "Capitalists, Farmers, and Workers," pp. 74–95.

61. Milton Derber and Edwin Young, *Labor and the New Deal* (New York: Da Capo Press, 1972), pp. 3, 134.

62. Irving Bernstein, *The New Deal Collective Bargaining Policy* (New York: Da Capo Press, 1975; originally 1950), pp. 29–39.

63. Irving Bernstein, *Turbulent Years: A History of the American Worker, 1933–1941* (Boston: Houghton Mifflin, 1970), pp. 37–91.

64. Ibid., pp. 99–125; and David Brody, "The Emergence of Mass Production

Unionism," in *Change and Continuity in Twentieth Century America*, ed. J. Braeman, R. Bremner, and E. Walters (Columbus: Ohio State University Press, 1964), pp. 221–35.

65. Richard C. Wilcock gives figures of 1.25 million workers covered by company unions in 1932 (40 percent of trade union membership) and 2.5 million workers (60 percent of trade union membership) in 1935 ("Industrial Management's Policies Toward Unionism," in *Labor and the New Deal*, ed. Derber and Young, p. 288).

66. Bernstein, *Turbulent Years*, pp. 217–317 (quote at p. 316).

67. Bernstein, *New Deal Collective Bargaining Policy*, pp. 58–62 (quote at p. 59); and Huthmacher, *Wagner*, pp. 160–63.

68. Bernstein, *New Deal Collective Bargaining Policy*, pp. 57–83; Huthmacher, *Wagner*, pp. 164–71.

69. Bernstein, *New Deal Collective Bargaining Policy*, p. 81.

70. The National Labor Relations Board set up under Public Resolution No. 44 consulted Secretary Perkins "on major appointments, but retained control over decisions, hiring, firing, and funds" (Bernstein, *New Deal Collective Bargaining Policy*, p. 84).

71. James A. Gross, *The Making of the National Labor Relations Board*, vol. 1 (Albany: State University of New York Press, 1974), pp. 76–88.

72. Bernstein, *New Deal Collective Bargaining Policy*, pp. 84–87 (quote at p. 87).

73. Irons points out that Wagner's bill, unlike the NIRA or the Agricultural Adjustment Act, was drafted by lawyers, who took care to write the statute in a way that would give the Supreme Court grounds for finding it constitutional (*New Deal Lawyers*, pp. 226–30).

74. United States Congress, Senate, Committee on Education and Labor, *Hearings on S. 1958*. 74th Congress, 1st Session, 1935, 3:465.

75. Gross notes that "throughout March and April 1935, the NLRB tried to find employers who would be willing to testify in favor of the Wagner bill. The regional boards reported 'almost unanimous' employer resistance" (*Making of the NLRB*, p. 138 n.141). This does not provide much support for corporate-liberal interpretations tracing the origins of the Wagner Act to enlightened capitalists. These interpretations are criticized in Howell John Harris, "Responsible Unionism and the Road to Taft-Hartley: The Development of Federal Labor Relations Policy, ca. 1932–1947" (Unpubl. ms., Department of History, University of Durham, England). A revised version of Harris's essay will be published in *Shop Floor Bargaining and the State: Historical and Comparative Perspectives*, ed. Steven Tolliday and Jonathan Zeitlin (New York: Cambridge University Press, forthcoming). See also S. H. Vittoz, "The Economic Foundations of Industrial Politics in the United States and the Emerging Structural Theory of the State in Capitalist Society: The Case of New Deal Labor Policy" (Unpubl. essay, Department of History, Dalhousie University, March, 1980), which shows that two major employers that settled with big labor after the Wagner Act, General Motors and United States Steel, did so out of a desire to avoid the short-term costs of strikes at a time when business seemed to be improving, not out of any farsighted support for "labor's integration into the institutional structures of American capitalism."

76. The legislative history of the act is covered in Bernstein, *New Deal Collective Bargaining Policy*, pp. 88–128; and Huthmacher, *Wagner*, pp. 190–98.

77. Strike statistics can be found in U.S. Bureau of Labor Statistics, *Monthly Labor Review* (Washington, D.C.: Government Printing Office, 1939), 48:1111; they are graphed in Skocpol, "Political Response to Capitalist Crisis," p. 188. Perhaps the most cogent recent advocates of the position that labor unrest forced the government to "concede" the Wagner Act are Frances Fox Piven and Richard Cloward, *Poor People's Movements: Why They Succeed, How They Fail* (New York: Pantheon, 1977), chap. 3. We are indebted to an excellent critique of Piven and Cloward's interpretation of the 1930s: Timothy George Massad, "Disruption, Organization, and Reform: A Critique of Piven and Cloward" (Unpubl. honors thesis, Harvard College, March, 1978), summarized in "Disruption, Organization and Reform: A Critique of *Poor People's Movements*," *Dissent* 27, no. 1 (Winter, 1980): 81–90.

78. Kristi Andersen, *The Creation of a Democratic Majority, 1928–1936* (Chicago: University of Chicago Press, 1979).

79. Congressional Quarterly, Inc., *Congressional Quarterly's Guide to Congress*, 2d ed. (Washington, D.C.: Congressional Quarterly, 1976), pp. 49–50. This point was brought to our attention by Fred H. Cohen, "The Limits of Corporate Power—The Origins of the National Recovery Act: A Case Study" (Unpubl. ms., Princeton University, 1972), p. 21.

80. Arthur M. Schlesinger, *The Politics of Upheaval* (Boston: Houghton Mifflin, 1960), pp. 422–23; and Murray Edelman, "New Deal Sensitivity to Labor Interests," in *Labor and the New Deal*, ed. Derber and Young, pp. 185–89.

81. On the creation and breakup of the Business Advisory Council, see Kim McQuaid, "The Frustration of Business Revival during the Early New Deal," *The Historian* 41 (August, 1979): 682–704.

82. Philip H. Burch, Jr., "The NAM as an Interest Group," *Politics and Society* 4, no. 1 (Fall, 1973): 101–3.

83. General background for this paragraph comes from Schlesinger, *Politics of Upheaval*, pp. 264–67, 270–74; James McGregor Burns, *Roosevelt: The Lion and the Fox* (New York: Harcourt Brace Jovanovich, 1954), pp. 219–20, 224–26; Massad, "Disruption, Organization and Reform," pp. 92–93; and Hawley, *Problem of Monopoly*, pp. 151–58.

84. A version of this argument is made in David Jerome Shyrock, "Business Performance and Public Policy: The Formation of the Revenue Act of 1935 and the National Labor Relations Act" (Unpubl. honors thesis, Harvard College, 1980), pp. 67–69, 88–89.

85. In this essay, we do not explore the reasons why the Supreme Court found the Wagner Act constitutional. The importance of the National Labor Relations Board's litigation strategy, designed to assure that the strongest possible case was the one that reached the Court, is stressed by Irons, *New Deal Lawyers*, chaps. 11–13; and by Gross, *Making of the NLRB*, pp. 173–230.

86. The NLRB's vested interest in labor organization is discussed in Edelman, "New Deal Sensitivity to Labor Interests," in Derber and Young, *Labor and the New Deal*, pp. 170–72. The development of the NLRB's institutional capacities after Jones and Laughlin is discussed in Harris, "Responsible Unionism and the Road to Taft-Hartley" and in vol. 2 of James A. Gross's

study, *The Reshaping of the National Labor Relations Board: National Labor Policy in Transition, 1937–1947* (Albany: State University of New York Press, 1981).

87. J. David Greenstone, *Labor in American Politics* (New York: Knopf, 1969).
88. By-now-classic discussions of patterns of power in the modern U.S. broker state are Theodore J. Lowi, *The End of Liberalism*, 2d ed. (New York: W. W. Norton, 1979); Grant McConnell, *Private Power and American Democracy* (New York: Knopf, 1966); and Morton Grodzins, "American Political Parties and the American System," *Western Political Quarterly* 13, no. 4 (December, 1960): 974–98.
89. Otis L. Graham, Jr., *Toward a Planned Society* (New York: Oxford University Press, 1976), pp. 67–68. Emphasis in original.
90. Thurow, *Zero-Sum Society*, p. 214.
91. Ibid., chap. 8; Reich, *Next American Frontier*, chap. 11.
92. Reich, *Next American Frontier*, p. 268; Magaziner and Reich, *Minding America's Business*, pp. 377–78; Thurow, *Zero-Sum Society*, pp. 212–14.
93. Harris notes that "there was no labor relations profession before the New Deal created it" ("Responsible Unionism and the Road to Taft-Hartley," p. 12 n.32).

THE STATE IN
NATIONAL SOCIALIST GERMANY

Michael Geyer

Observers of the state in the twentieth century are struck by a paradox. State and statelike institutions have grown incessantly. They have penetrated every sphere of public and private life. A more visible, active, and interventionist state has emerged in all advanced industrial countries. The state has become a source of power for whoever captures and controls it or one of its parts. Yet at the same time, the expanding state and its manifold activities are rarely, if ever, contained in a single and coherent arena of politics. Not only has the state apparatus lost much of its cohesion and its monolithic qualities, politics itself has become a very fluid and dispersed affair. It is conducted in a number of arenas. The state is only one center of politics among many. Concurrently, the state apparatus no longer seems to form a coherent site for the implementation of political decisions. The institutions of the state are set loose and follow largely uncharted dynamics. Hence, the continuity of institutions of the state and its appearance as a massive thinglike entity, housed in compact, fortresslike buildings, is misleading. The nature of the state has changed quite fundamentally, while it expanded in leaps and bounds. The state has become a highly dispersed entity whose center and parameters shift continuously in as yet unexplained and poorly understood processes. The state as it was known and interpreted by past political theorists[1] is in jeopardy. In order to understand it we have to reexamine the way in which the state works. For while we do not quite know what it is, we do know that it reshapes public and private life.

It is curious, indeed, that the nineteenth century, which did not know strong states, ultimately may turn out to be the century of the state, if only because the state formed a coherent unit. In the twentieth century we are at great pains to find the proper place of the state and its tasks and to understand the way in which it operates. This is hardly a matter of not having tried hard enough to find appropriate concepts. The difficulties in finding them rather seem to be part and parcel of the development of the state in this century with its shifting parameters of politics and its ambiguous goals. In fact, we may fare better first to unlearn about the (nineteenth-century) state, before we can learn something about this entity in the twentieth century.

The "Crisis" of the State in Theory

The majority of studies on the German state still focus on the classical instruments of that state and their use, that is, domestic and foreign administration, the military, fiscal bureaucracies, and the police. They tend to juxtapose state and society, though they may—in the tradition of Max Weber—postulate a universalization of bureaucratic domination in both state and society.[2] Studies on the Third Reich have taken up this tradition. Hence, it is not surprising that conflicts between the "state" or its parts like the army or the bureaucracy and the National Socialist party or "movement" are seen as one of those elements that constituted and shaped the Third Reich. However, despite such conflicts, the Third Reich was always a state of both highly bureaucratized domination and of a social-ideological movement in power. The nature and the actions of the state in the Third Reich cannot be understood by merely analyzing conflicts between separate spheres of a bureaucratic state—i.e., the military, domestic, or fiscal bureaucracies—on the one hand and the National Socialist party or Hitler on the other.[3] Neither are they as separate as one might think, if one follows a still predominant trend in the historical literature; nor was conflict the only or even the most prominent form of relations between those spheres; nor, finally, do their frictions sufficiently explain the dynamics of the development of the state in the Third Reich. It is, indeed, necessary to reconsider the convenient notion of such separate spheres and entities and their interrelations from scratch.

We could, of course, leave behind these "empiricist" problems of connecting the various elements of the state and society in the Third Reich. Instead, we could use a wider and more dynamic interpretation of "state power" as it has been popular in France and Italy for quite some time now. The political or state system would still be considered as a separate sphere—indeed, the rediscovery of the autonomy of the political is one of the hallmarks of this concept[4]—but it is seen as a much more active "force" with both bureaucratized and nonbureaucratized manifestations that reach from repression to regulation and reconciliation in the process of production and reproduction. The state, in other words, has lost much of its thinglike character and has become altogether more variable and dynamic, even though it is still clearly identifiable as the center of authority and domination. It is formed in social conflicts and changes according to social formations.[5] It is more of a process of organizing authority and domination than a reified structure.

Using this approach we could follow a path which Poulantzas has mapped out; that is, we could analyze the state as participant in the class struggle in the age of imperialism, pointing to its role as the decisive force in reconciling temporarily "the internal contradictions among the classes and fractions of the classes in the power alliance" and in demobilizing the dominated classes either by "sweet" or by "brute" violence.[6] This approach is quite challenging if we want to anchor it in the practice of the state in the Third Reich, but it remains a most promising one that may help us make sense of the dynamics and the directions of the Third Reich.[7] Nevertheless, this approach runs into problems which are not dissimilar from the ones more traditional historians and political scientists encounter.

Focusing on the state, too many on both sides still believe in the dictum that "the Germans have developed to virtuosity the rational, functional (*arbeitsteilig*), and professional organization of all human institutions (*Verbände*) of domination from the factory to the army and the state."[8] Max Weber still stands at the center of the intellectual debate. With his dynamic concept of "universal bureaucratization," that is, the multiplication of producers of domination (literally *Herrschaftsbetriebe*) in every sphere of life, he even seems to have provided a most useful tool for the understanding of the dynamics of the modern state and society. However, already by the interwar years the shortcomings of Weber's approach were criticized. In Germany, the charge came mainly from the intellectual Right. Some of the more prominent state theorists in interwar Germany like Alfred Weber, his more right-radical colleagues in "constitutional law" (especially Carl Schmitt), a few political economists, and some practitioners (like Johannes Popitz) challenged Weber's notion of a clean division between state and society, state and economy as well as between politics, that is, the sum total of human struggles for power, and administration, that is, the domination of everyday life.[9]

On the one hand, these theorists postulated the expansion of the classical institutions of the state, the military and the police, into society, if they wanted to perform their function at all. On the other hand, they felt threatened by what they considered to be an increasing self-organization of society and economy not just as separate entities (as, for example, in monopolies and associations), but within the boundaries of the state. They diagnosed the dissolution of the state in the Weberian sense into an expanding, self-organizing pluralism of partial arenas of powers with statelike qualities, a development they fiercely opposed in order to demand the (re)establishment of the "sovereignty" of the state and in order to reclaim authority through domination as the core of the state's activities. The state in their time, they argued, had become nothing but a shell for disparate activities without an obvious organizing center—that being domination and social control in the "interest of the nation"—and with a myriad of tasks.[10] Their biases were obvious, but, for once, they bypassed the nineteenth-century debate about the "functionalization of the state apparatus" because they had given up the idea of the inherent unity of the state; there was simply nothing coherent to "functionalize" because the state, as the site of the political and politics, as the key organizing element of the administrative "domination of everyday life" was fractured. The conflict among social associations and institutions (*Verbände*) remained, but it took shape in an increasingly disparate and anonymous arena.[11] *Politik* in a Weberian sense was replaced by what a later theorist describes quite poetically as the "genius of incoherence." It is a politics that is reduced to "spasmodic micropolitics which come about by happenstance and are contradictory among themselves." This kind of politics is called "muddling through" (*pilotage à vue*) or "more nobly the absence of a comprehensive vision of society by the state and by its diverse ruling majorities."[12]

Whatever else is said about Poulantzas, this is quite an appropriate starting point; for it begins to destroy the deeply ingrained equation of bureaucracy with rationality, as well as the clean juxtaposition between society and the state. Neither one helps us to understand the modern state and, for that matter, the Third Reich. National Socialist rule did not create a neat division of labor among bureaucracies, but furthered a burgeoning system of bureaucratic domination composed of shapeless and ill-defined institutions. The state in the Third Reich was omnipresent in the sense that almost every organization and association had a statelike quality, that is, gained the quality of bureaucratic domination which is traditionally associated with the state. Some became more statelike than others while a number of institutions quite consciously opposed this tradition. Centralization of power in a contradictory and crisis-prone process on the one hand and extreme dilution of domination into a seemingly endless series of partial statelike organizations on the other hand is the major paradox of the Third Reich. If we want to study the state in the Third Reich, we have to deal with both tendencies.

Focusing on social classes and power in interwar Germany, the concept of a "hegemonic bloc," however, seems rather artificial. If anything, the striking element that urgently needs explanation is the lack of a serious alliance of dominant forces and the lack of cohesion among the subordinated groups in Germany. The virtues of orderliness and organization barely conceal the inability to structure organized political and economic processes beyond the level of "private" associations and to mediate conflicts in the interwar years. That very inability, which can be observed in the labor movement of the interwar years as well, seems to be a more appropriate starting point for the analysis of the Third Reich than the opposite perspective. An interpretation of the Third Reich is well advised *not* to start with assumptions about the cohesion of class forces. On the contrary, the formation of cohesive class forces may turn out to be one of the primary goals of the National Socialist state and the very basis for the National Socialist autonomy of the political. We fare better, in other words, if we consider the interwar years as a period of the unmaking of old class identities and class boundaries and the making of new ones just as it is a period of the remaking of the state.

If we assume that a not so well ordered state and a not so cohesive society must be a weak or even self-destructive one, we just continue to extrapolate from our traditional assumptions about the Third Reich. This argument has certain emotional attractions: it denies the Third Reich the ability to survive on its own or, more fashionably, to reproduce itself, but it underestimates the National Socialist party and the state in the Third Reich. The National Socialists formed a genuine social movement and the Third Reich survived for twelve long years, six of which saw the bloodiest war in the history of the twentieth century so far. The not so well ordered state of the Third Reich must have been quite strong after all, and the not so cohesive German society must have been held together somehow. Hence, the main question of this essay is a simple one: What is it that held this confusion together and gave it focus and direction to take on the rest of the world deliberately and for such a long time?

This is less an essay about the state as such, than a suggestion for an interpretation of the Third Reich that may throw some light on the condition of the state in the twentieth century.[13] In this context we might wonder whether the amorphous character of the state is really something particularly German or whether it is not more a general phenomenon of most states in advanced industrial countries that was given a very specific and barbaric form in the Third Reich, and whether amorphousness is really the best possible approach to explaining the Third Reich.

The "Crisis" of the State in Practice

Ordinarily, studies of the Third Reich distinguish quite sharply between various phases of the rise and fall of the Third Reich and ask different questions for each period. There are quite good reasons for making these periodizations and it sounds somewhat high-handed to emphasize the unity of the interwar years, but the Weimar Republic and the Third Reich together constitute a period of mounting counterrevolution. This counterrevolutionary process never actually came to an end in the Third Reich. As in the case with revolutions, counterrevolutions are only completed when the process of counterrevolutionary change comes to a halt in the establishment of a new social order.[14] This element should be taken extremely seriously: counterrevolutions themselves transform societies like revolutions. They are not simply "conservative" and certainly not status quo oriented. Consequently, we should interpret the Third Reich as an incomplete and open structure. More precisely, it can be characterized as a dynamic and crisis-ridden political system in the pursuit of the establishment of a new society. In this sense, the development of the Third Reich was directional, although fraught with contradictions. The Third Reich aimed at the construction of a society. It was to be a society that was fortified and erected against what the National Socialists and, with them, a good part of German society considered to be the revolutionary and destructive forces of this century. While social scientists and historians may tiptoe around this distinction, the National Socialists were proud of it.

The direction of the Third Reich was toward *war*. War was essential to regain the "autonomy of the political" and to recenter the state by giving politics at least the appearance of purposeful and unified action which it otherwise lacks. In the counterrevolutionary Third Reich war, victorious war, was meant to achieve more than that. War not only happened to be Hitler's main and ultimate goal in the creation of a new German society, it also made the Third Reich an "exceptional state." War permits the "autonomy of the political" to reach its extreme in the age of imperialism. In an "exceptional state" war is neither simply the predatory instinct of special interests, nor the manifestation of atavistic sentiments. Rather, war is fought to create and recreate a society *and* a state which "habitually lives on war."[15] War recenters state and society in combat, domination, and direct exploitation. This is the essence of counterrevolutionary politics.

War, of course, did not automatically follow from the development of the Third Reich; nor did the Third Reich follow Hitler's own martial ambitions blindly. Rather, the conditions for the possibility of counterrevolutionary war were set in a series of struggles that formed the history of the Third Reich. These struggles were less about war and peace as such, than about what constitutes the political site and what focus and priorities politics in the Third Reich should have. As we have already discovered, the parameters of the politics *and* of the state need constant definition and they are open to constant challenges. Thus, the shape of the state, the goals of politics, and the forms of domination in the Third Reich were—from the beginning to the end—outcomes of conflicts and decisions, victories and defeats, however stubbornly individual persons like Hitler or social and professional groups may have clung to a specific set of goals, beliefs, and priorities. The roots of these conflicts and decisions go back to the last years of the Wilhelmine Empire and the formation of the Weimar Republic, specifically to the "red years" between 1917 and 1919–20. The failures of this first republican state in Germany were the mainspring of the system to come. What exactly were the failures of the republic?

Most older histories of the Weimar Republic reduce it to a struggle over parliamentarism, but this was not the key struggle that shaped its fate.[16] The Weimar Republic emerged out of the defeat of revolutionary and counterrevolutionary social movements in the latent and open civil war between 1917 and 1923 that challenged the bureaucratic and authoritarian Wilhelmine state. In this violent period the movements of the Left were defeated, as were Prussian monarchists with their restorative ideals (Kapp-Putsch), and the counterrevolutionary movements of the Right in 1923. It was the state which ultimately dominated and suppressed the social movements on the Left and on the Right. What was this state though? Beyond the core institutions of the state apparatus, such as the military, the congealing state of the Weimar Republic consisted of an uneasy and contradictory alliance of producers of domination and statelike institutions (*Verbände*), that is, entrenched social, political, economic, and cultural institutions which defended their authority to channel interests and their access to resources against the populism of Right and Left. They jointly agreed on very little, except that politics was to be institutionalized as open-ended and routinized struggle for resources among a limited number of entrenched institutions. This instrumental notion of the political arena as a system of procedures, which were meant to structure that struggle, and of the state as the guarantor of that process—rather than as defender of private powers like industry and army against public participation as in Wilhelmine Germany—won out over the revolutionary and counterrevolutionary concept of politics.

The defeated revolutionary and counterrevolutionary politics were quite different indeed. They did not aim at regulating a competition over resources with, perhaps, a different emphasis (the Social Democrats did that on the Left, the Conservatives on the Right). Rather, they aimed at an entirely different kind of politics, a politics that sought to reorganize social relations. For them politics was not instrumental or procedural, but value- or goal-oriented, reflecting notions of a just or appropriate society. It was, in a way, "moral politics" or, more appropriately, "immoral politics." Revolutionaries and counterrevolutionaries differed very radically in their views of society, but they together also differed from the procedural and altogether vacuous politics of the victorious Weimar state.

The victorious state of entrenched institutions was more a bad weather cartel of unwilling members which continued to fight each other in an endless succession of piecemeal power struggles than it was an alliance or "hegemonic bloc." They all had their distinct links to a social base, yet they remained aloof from those bases as they conducted their intramural conflicts.[17] Weakened in the two-front civil war at home against the revolutionary and counterrevolutionary movements which culminated in 1923, a truce was finally reached in the key struggle between organized labor and the industrial bloc, which were the two dominant centers in the cartel of power of the early Weimar Republic. Although the trade unions lost many of their gains of 1918 and although the Social Democrats lost their influence on a national level (which they regained only briefly in 1928–30), they retained their influence over Germany's strongest state, Prussia, where the Social Democratic Party (SPD) continued to control the police and social policy until 1932 in a coalition government. The trade unions retained their power in the organized and state supervised system of "industrial relations." The political arena and the control over the system of domination worked less on the basis of a coalition or alliance which shared power than on the basis of parceling out power and domination in a complex set of allegiances and trade-offs. The Weimar Republic was an industrial, labor, agricultural, laicist, and Christian state, depending on where one looks. Indeed, it was not unlike the advanced capitalist state which more recent theorists describe.

This amalgam of institutions of all kinds was barely able to regulate distribution and to maintain conditions of production, and, in fact, temporarily collapsed in 1923 during the hyperinflation. It might have faced permanent collapse in 1923–24, had one additional element not entered the scene. The uneasy truce of the members of the power cartel in Germany was stabilized by the international economic system through the influx of foreign capital into Germany. It was not the capital as such, but the necessity to maintain the prerequisite for receiving it, political stability, which forced a new truce after a near total collapse. The integration of Germany into the international monetary system became the tie that held the alliance of unwilling members together. The binding element for the quarreling forces in Germany and with it the guarantees for the conditions of reproduction of the Weimer state were externalized. Domestic politics—or, more precisely, the basic compromises that held together the state in the Weimer Republic—were subsumed under international affairs. This was a rather peculiar *Primat der Aussenpolitik* (primacy of foreign politics) and should be distinguished from the more common diplomatic notion of that *Primat* just as well as from simple notions of dependence or interdependence. The international economic system became the underwriter of the cohesion of the political arena and of the legitimacy of the cartel in power in the Weimar Republic. Germany's cartel in power was unable and unwilling to maintain itself. It was this *political* dependence that ultimately counts, not the economic ties as such.

The collapse of the international economic system in the World Economic Crisis removed that cornerstone from German politics. The power cartel fell into pieces between 1929 and 1933. Not only did the system of production fall apart, but the very conditions of maintaining the political arena and of maintaining the relations between entrenched institutions and their social bases—in other and by no means simpler words: the conditions of reproduction of the conditions of production—collapsed as well. This distinguished Germany from all other advanced industrial nations that had their own crises. In Germany the dominant groups were challenged by two sets of issues. On the one hand, the process of production had to be reorganized and, on the other hand, the complete set of social relations had to be negotiated anew. These conditions may explain the extremely high level of politicization of every aspect of German life in this period. The World Economic Crisis tore away the remaining few elements of the truce of 1924. The parameters and the focus of politics, and hence the state, needed to be reconstructed; social relations had to be reshaped. The presidential regimes between 1930 and 1933 failed to solve either problem.[18]

Why under these circumstances was there neither a military dictatorship nor a return to the authoritarianism of a bureaucratic elite? Because both could only redress the balance of classes within an established framework of relations between dominant and dominated classes. Once this framework had collapsed, neither could guarantee the reproduction of the political process. The leading members in the bureaucracy and in the military were forced to realize that, under the prevailing conditions, they simply did not possess the means to end the struggle. They could produce domination, but they were unable to shape and organize a new political arena and new politics.

How did the National Socialist movement fit into all this? Although it had suffered defeats and was far from a powerful movement during the 1920s, the National Socialist agitation and mobilization strategies fit the conditions of the late Weimar Republic in a remarkable way. National Socialist agitation reflected the mentality of a considerable number of Germans and was able to exploit the contradictions of the alliance in power. But the true strength of the National Socialists did not consist in rabble-rousing. The National Socialist movement, by successfully claiming to represent everybody or at least all Aryans, was able to challenge and, thus, bypass the organization of dominance in the Weimar Republic and, more specifically, the ability of the members of the cartel in power to channel access to power and the resources of the state. The National Socialists were never quite as successful as they claimed, but the formation of an omnibus movement—certainly not a "mass" movement, because the National Socialists built their support on a growing wave of association building—was a most innovative act in German politics. The National Socialists did not organize its clusters of members in the classical tradition of German parties, but rather through constant challenges to the power holders. Conflict shaped the actual organization and held the heterogeneous groups together. Organization was not a prerequisite for political struggle, but political struggle became the main, indeed the only prerequisite for organization. In this sense, party cadres were facilitators maintaining contradictions and escalating conflicts, rather than organizers of the movement.[19]

At the same time, however, the National Socialist party counteracted the danger of dilution and fragmentation in its own ranks by the parallel evolution of distinct cadre politics which distinguished them from the rank and file.[20] While the role of facilitators in the grass roots and special interest struggles remained a major one for cadres and while it provided the link between cadre and membership, especially after the party began to grow quickly in 1929–30, the cadres themselves were held together by ideological bonds. Most of their ideological statements appear very vague. They deal, among other things, with rearmament and the greatness of Germany, wholesale attacks on the Weimar and Versailles system, racism and anti-Semitism, and the heroic virtues of German life—issues that had been exploited by other parties and movements on the Right as well. But there was an important difference. In putting forward their themes the National Socialist cadres did not advocate changes in the distribution of power and resources in favor of one or the other interest. They were not tied up with traditional, Weimar-type politics.[21] Ideology as cadre politics remained separate from the interests politics of the rank and file of the movement. It always implied the demand for the creation of an entirely new, and "naturally" better and different, arena of politics. While the party members were pitted against the system of bureaucratic domination, the police, the taxman, the distribution of resources, the party cadre were pitted against the political arena as a whole. It demanded a different state. Ideology in this sense provided a distinct realm of cadre politics and the promise and perspective of a distinct political arena. The main concern of the party cadre was not simply reshuffling the existing power alliance together with the rank and file, but creating a new state which, in turn, was to build a new *Volk*. National Socialist ideology was always more than a means to achieve some partial goal, that false patina of interest politics. (We would underestimate this ideology if we saw in it only an amalgam for conflicting bourgeois interests, just as we would underestimate the nature of the political crisis if we would assume that it could have been resolved by a return of some form of amalgamated interest politics.) It was a series of more or less defined values, goals, and sentiments—in its own inverted and brutal way the notion of a "moral," as opposed to a procedural politics—that were to replace the existing political arrangements. In short, the party cadres were to redefine the state.[22] The success of the National Socialists is largely due to the failure of every other political group to provide more than interest politics.

Ultimately, the National Socialists were able to reshape the state and, to a degree, society, but the overriding reality of their drive to power between 1930 and 1933 was the disintegration of the Weimar power cartel and the concurrent intensification of the struggle of everybody against everybody else both on the streets and in the higher echelons of politics. Politics in this phase reversed to plain intrigue, personalized back room politicking, and gang warfare in the streets. It is impossible to speak of classes or monpoly groups at this specific juncture in any concrete way, so advanced was the decomposition of the political, economic, and social fabric of German life.[23]

The Politics of Domination

This was the exceedingly difficult situation for the coalition government which came into power in February, 1933. It consisted of National Socialists, conservatives with close connections to industry and agriculture, and, above all, the military. While Adolf Hitler was chancellor, this new cabinet was by no means dominated by National Socialists. Within roughly a year the government which was formed in February, 1933, was reshaped in crucial areas and set the pattern for National Socialist domination on the basis of a growing autonomy of the political sphere.[24] A number of processes were responsible for this development.

We immediately have to drop the idea that a new working alliance finally came into existence in the back room meetings that formed the Hitler government in early 1933. The disunity within and between the dominant social and economic groups actually increased throughout 1933. Unity of sorts existed regarding the demolition of labor rights and the establishment of a "strong state" to counteract an expected revolt or strike of the dispossessed members of the truce of 1924.[25] This fear of revolt or revolution—exacerbated by the experience of 1918—formed the basis for the far-reaching emergency laws of March, 1933, and for the initial drive to co-opt social and political associations (*Gleichschaltung*). Beyond that, there was discord and certainly no prearranged agreement about the nature of a future compromise of the dominant forces. We can see the continuation and even intensification of old conflicts—now very often under National Socialist guises.[26]

The state bureaucracies replicated the socioeconomic process of fragmentation, beginning with the special treatment of the armed forces, whose minister, General von Blomberg, even took his oath separately from the rest of the cabinet. The armed forces became what one observer called "sovereign" after February, 1933, that is, independent of the collective decision making of the cabinet and not accountable to the fiscal control of the finance minister and the National Accounting Office. Generally, collective control over the administrations was exercised even less after 1933 than before, partly because the major decisions were made outside of the cabinet, and partly because some administrations emancipated themselves from any political control.[27] At first sight, politics seemed to become rather more disjointed than less.

At the same time, the National Socialist movement began to intensify its own seemingly irrepressible social dynamics. The ideological and the interest-oriented conflicts within the previous power cartel, which it had so carefully nourished before 1933, became the main focus of a vicious and quite popular struggle against the old order in general. This struggle threatened some of the new powerholders—like the military and industry. The National Socialist movement was certainly not a convenient tool in the hands of these groups, as much as these would have liked the National Socialists in this capacity. The main danger for them came from the rank and file, who finally saw their chance to overthrow the existing distribution of power in favor of their own special interests. Not only did the rank and file movement grow—the bandwagon effect was everywhere—but in 1933 the most radical elements grew fastest. SA (storm-troopers) membership jumped from eight hundred thousand in late 1932 to three million in 1933. The SA unleashed a massive wave of terror against the Left and, for that matter, against any sign of political opposition which quickly spilled over into factories, administrations, churches, Jewish businesses, and synagogues. This massive wave of terror was tolerated, even protected and legalized through an auxiliary police force, but it was not guided by the National Socialist cadre, who, along with other power holders, watched it with growing concern.[28]

In sum, the process of political dissolution continued throughout. No hegemonic bloc formed as a new collective political actor or as a new hegemonic alliance; nor was domination and subordination assured by the dynamics of the National Socialist cadres or the rise of Hitler to predominance. Many observers stop at this point and are satisfied by characterizing the emerging system as "chaotic" or amorphous. However, the notion of an amorphous system expresses more exasperation and puzzlement about the growth of the Third Reich than an understanding of it. The task remains to make sense out of the seeming chaotic structure of the state in the Third Reich.

The impact of the rampant and radical interest politics of the National Socialist rank and file was counteracted by another development which increasingly shaped the structure of the Third Reich. This development is quite as exasperating as the rank and file movement because it forces us as well to rethink the nature of the political arena. As the case of the military indicates, producers of domination[29] began entering and occupying the political arena as *autonomous* political actors. This decisively shaped the new politics of the Third Reich. The social-political struggle over power and resources and the bureaucratic-administrative "domination of everyday life," as Max Weber put it, became indissolubly mixed. The two elements which were carefully kept apart in both the liberal and authoritarian traditions of the nineteenth century were now fused. It is not easy to conceptualize this phenomenon because we immediately tend to separate the realm of politics from the bureaucratic-administrative domain, or we create quite meaningless and empty hybrids like "bureaucratic politics." From the point of view of these autonomous actors "domination of everyday life" formed the essence of politics.

We have mentioned the separation of the armed forces from the state apparatus and its development into a de facto autonomous entity within the state which was exempt from the political process. More important, industries very quickly gained extraordinary authority to reinforce their own organizational hierarchies through co-optation. In the process of co-optation they gained quasi-legislative power in their own industrial domain. Industries became "sovereign" like the military. Their power expanded from the associational level into the relations of production through enforced cartels (*Zwangskartellisierung*), price control, wage control, and other means. The transformation of the industrial sphere into authoritarian and autonomous organizations with legal means for maintaining internal discipline and order was one of the major elements of consolidation of 1933. In different ways the same pattern emerged in agriculture with the formation of the Reich Agriculture Estate (*Reichsnährstand*), as well as in the old sphere of working class and social policy with the creation of the German Labor Front (*Deutsche Arbeitsfront*) out of the ruins of the suppressed trade unions.[30]

Something very important was happening. Each of these institutions gained the ability to produce and to enforce control over its own domain autonomously. Indeed, in order to survive in the Third Reich it was vital to build any organization around a nucleus of domination and control. Each of these organizations even gained the ability to mobilize its own resources. In the case of the military the Central Bank signed a blank check for the next eight years; the German Labor Front established its own system of parafiscal extraction which made this particular organization one of the richest in the Third Reich. The ability to impose control and domination defined the boundaries of these centers of power. Thus, the struggle over boundaries and over who controlled what became the essence of politics in the Third Reich. The military, industry, agriculture, and labor are the best cases for this kind of struggle, but they were by no means the only ones.

This struggle redefined the nature of politics. Political power and actual control of resources, not just a procedurally defined guarantee of access, were spread across what traditionally were separate spheres of bureaucracy, economy, and society. The differences between state, society, and economy vanished. They were replaced by pervasive producers of domination. A new and different state was in the making, a state consisting of public actors—some of them were legally "private" like industries, some belonged to the executive like the military, and some were altogether hybrid mixtures like the German Labor Front—which gained their autonomy from their ability to coerce and to gain independent access to resources. (The rationale of this process and its dynamics will be discussed in the section of this essay titled "Toward a Fusion of State and Ideology.") Routinized and institutionalized processes of negotiating access to resources, which are traditionally considered to be the essence of politics, became meaningless in the process of acquiring autonomy. As a consequence, collective decision-making bodies like the cabinet or the Reich's Defense Council rarely met. Nevertheless, the practice of politics in the Third Reich was not shapeless because the interaction between these autonomous power centers was guided by very definite, though unwritten rules. As is to be expected these rules are different from the ones which shape procedural politics. In fact, they seem to point in the opposite direction and to demand contrary behavior. Where sovereignty and independence of public producers of domination counted, *distance,* rather than convergence and cooperation between the power holders needed to be guaranteed, and this precluded the formation of a "hegemonic bloc."

Where distance is more important than cooperation and where domination is fused with the struggle over power, "orderly" political process decays. Nevertheless, a framework for politics has to be established, not to create consensus among dominant groups, but to maintain distance between them. Politics thus became the art of maintaining the potential of growth for each individual autonomous institution without having them clash in open turf struggles. In the Third Reich this was achieved, at least temporarily, by intricate negotiations over priorities, values, and symbols that were to guide and structure the relations between independent power holders.

Negotiation among autonomous institutions did not focus on the actual distribution or redistribution of resources. Instead it argued over the priorities and values which defined status and distance between autonomous centers of power and, thus, indirectly structured access to resources. Hence, we find direct distributive and redistributive conflicts only rarely and in true emergencies—the crises of the Third Reich. Yet, we find a continuous and vicious struggle over the definition of what exactly was important for the Third Reich. The long struggle over autarky and protectionism which led to the Four Year Plan in 1936 has to be seen in this light. At any rate, these priorities tied autonomous institutions together in a hierarchy of priorities and values without forcing them to cooperate in the actual process of the distribution and redistribution of resources. They established their relative importance in relation to each other without foreclosing change. Priorities, however, were only negotiable in political-ideological conflicts. This system was by no means rigid. Those Weberian private and public producers of domination which survived the initial scramble for autonomous status aligned themselves in a new kind of dominating relation around politically negotiated partial and competitive markets of power and domination. This was the emerging new state of the Third Reich.

Equally serious was the impact on the organization of subordination. Recall that the republic granted access through formalized political participation, while the Wilhelmine authoritarian state tried to segregate the private power of industry and the public one of the army from arenas of public participation. In the emerging political system neither was possible. Autonomous state or statelike institutions covered all aspects of private and public life and subordinated them to their "domination of everyday life." This is partly a result of the mushrooming of such autonomous units, but mostly a result of the expansive demands of leading power centers like the military. Thus, the military demanded in addition to general conscription premilitary training, postmilitary exercises, an appropriate air raid system and a host of other such measures. But most of all it demanded that society not organize on its own and spontaneously, for any such association would have counteracted the pervasive "domination of everyday life" in the interest of military preparation for war. The same is true for industry. Industrialists would have preferred that workers not organize at all or only within the confines of their factories, that is, in the interest of optimal production. The National Socialist German Labor Front was considered to be a rather bitter pill to swallow. The expansion of sovereign power centers demanded new social formations. It demanded a classless society of subordinated subjects who are organized or, preferably, organize themselves exclusively in the interest of production and destruction. Here lie the roots for the *Volksgemeinschaft*, at least as far as the autonomous political actors like the *Wehrmacht* and industry are concerned.

One of the most prominent and most consistent priorities was built around armaments. It would be entirely wrong to assume that armaments were pushed by one specific group, for example heavy industry, at the exclusion of others. Indeed, armaments were always a negotiated priority which drew in a variety of groups while, at the same time, allowing change over time and not forcing any particular cooperation. Here Hitler was the "political" facilitator, the armed forces leadership and increasingly the various services were the interested party in the state apparatus. Schacht, as the president of the *Reichsbank*, became the monetary supervisor, while the major armaments firms formed the dominant business side of this constellation. Together they formed a network of interaction which shaped armaments as a negotiated priority. Other such fields could be found in other areas, sometimes in a more nazified, sometimes in a less nazified form. All these networks centered around political priorities rather than around political procedures. Therefore they could be changed by renegotiating priorities. As it was, armament at any price was the first priority that guided German politics after 1934.

Once again: (1) It was distance among power holders that counted and that needed to be maintained, not cooperation and consensus. (2) The setting free of autonomous institutions led to a system of value-oriented— or, as we shall call it, ideological—politics that guaranteed this distance by ascribing status in a competitive field of political values and goals, rather than simply regulating ways and means of "getting something." Hence, the political procedure or process of regulating access to power became meaningless, while statelike spheres sprang up everywhere. (3) Politics melted into permanent conflicts over guiding values and priorities which shaped the parameters of the autonomous units. The "state" as apparatus was omnipresent, yet it only existed in endless variations of more or less powerful autonomous units.

Once the postliberal and postauthoritarian quality of the political realm of the Third Reich becomes transparent, the fortunes of the National Socialist cadres and of Hitler are more easily comprehensible. The National Socialist party underwent most dramatic changes in the remaking of the state after 1933. It cut loose from its social-counterrevolutionary clienteles, culminating in the bloody purge of the SA in summer 1934. This could have been fatal for the party, especially for the middle echelon party functionaries—the "facilitators"—had they not entrenched themselves in state and local administrations and converted the social power of the movement into control over administrations and organizations which were rigorously and brutally nazified. The former clientele-politics were thus carried into the state apparatus, with hair-raising results. The traditional bureaucracies grew larger and larger, new ones were added under the onslaught of National Socialist would-be bureaucrats, and administrative work was parochialized on all levels. The old bureaucracies which had held together the German state on a federal, state, and local level in the past became the targets for predatory politics, losing in this process of co-optation their character of rationally organized producers of state control. These administrations continued, of course, to discharge bureaucratic services, but their main purpose consisted in providing National Socialist patronage. Whole institutions expanded as a means of granting protection and security to party functionaries and of conferring status and paying salaries to individuals, rather than of rationally administering the state. The old authoritarian bureaucratic state was dissolved by the Nazi compradors.[31]

We have to be very careful not to confuse this anarchic struggle for positions—clientele politics—with National Socialist cadre politics. The top cadre of the National Socialist party had to struggle like everybody else,[32] but they set out from the beginning to enforce control in specific domains. They reshaped, partly created, and partly centralized the repressive and ideological state apparatuses. Control of the police, centralization of the ideological apparatuses, and penetration of the military structure, primarily with the help of Himmler's SS, and control over labor through the newly created German Labor Force were rigorously pursued. These domains became the base of National Socialist cadre power in the state.

What did this mean in the emerging Third Reich? We might be inclined to speak of a new division of labor, in which the National Socialists took over the realm of social control much like industry took over the organization of production, or the army the system of war preparations. Indeed, this is the role which some in army and industry envisaged for the National Socialists, but it is not the role which the National Socialists accepted. From the very beginning the National Socialists attempted to control the making of politics. The National Socialists cadre were not ordinary power holders, even though they attempted to control access to power and aspects of domination, much like every other power holder in the Third Reich. The National Socialists distinguished themselves by steadily assuming control over the political directions and values—the priorities that guided the relations among the autonomous institutions. They began to set the rules for ascribing status and rank to the various other power centers and to regulate the relations and the distance between them by defining political values and goals. They controlled the ideological domain whose essence was not the accumulation of power as such, but the guarantee of the political and social distance, which regulated and only made possible accumulation of power. Rather than simply controlling people, they began to control the process of reproduction of the state in the Third Reich. The National Socialist cadres achieved this position only slowly, but they set out to acquire it from the very beginning. The dynamics of this conquest, which ultimately led to a National Socialist monopoly over political directions and values, increasingly shaped the development of the Third Reich after 1934.

In this context, Hitler's role becomes more apparent. Standing beyond the "extreme diffusion and dislocation of authority" and beyond the "highly disordered proliferation of agencies and hierarchies"[33] he was the "leader" (*Führer*) from the very beginning, though not at all in the totalitarian sense of defining the actions of each individual center of power.

We would underestimate Hitler and his powers if we described his role as simple arbiter or mediator in the organizational jungle of the Third Reich. At times, he did exactly that, though more often he failed to mediate, letting conflicts run their disruptive course and bringing upon himself the epithet of being a weak dictator.[34] In fact, however, he eventually occupied the nodal points between the partial fields of power, defining ever more precisely what the conditions for domination were and how they were to be achieved.

The more the National Socialist regime approached war, the more it was anchored in one person alone, Hitler. His unique position neither implies that the dominant groups found a convenient figurehead, nor does it mean that Hitler was there despite them. Hitler occupied an ever more crucial position because the formation of a coherent alliance or a hegemonic power bloc was preempted by the way in which the state in the Third Reich was organized. Hitler increasingly managed to control the conditions that shaped distance and status of autonomous power holders, and he did so by relentlessly driving the Third Reich toward war.

So far we have tried to comprehend a form of politics which runs counter to established (Western) notions of political process and contradicts both an authoritarian and a liberal understanding of the state and politics. Without pursuing the issue further we have hypothesized that this reorganization of politics and of the state may reflect a general tendency which appears in a variety of forms in advanced industrial states. This tendency is characterized by the rise of *Herrschaftsbetriebe* of all kinds, an expansion and transformation of what constitutes political process, and, lastly, a renewed subjugation of society under the imperatives of production and destruction. Rather than systematizing these issues on the plain of political theory we shall continue our historical inquiry; for we have not yet understood National Socialist priorities, their attraction, and their significance as counterrevolutionary ideology. Nor have we shown the dynamics of the struggle over priorities and the reasons why the National Socialists ultimately prevailed. The latter was by no means evident in 1933–34, when the rise of autonomous centers of power, especially of military and industry, redefined the parameters and the working of the state.

State and Ideology

We have mentioned the key role of ideology several times. What was the ideology of the Third Reich and what was its role in National Socialist statemaking? We know that the Third Reich did not work in the way we traditionally assume that states work. It did not routinize access to power, but formed fields of autonomous units whose parameters and whose relations to each other were defined by a few "political" priorities or guidelines such as armaments and war preparedness. The emerging system may look like anarchy to us, and it certainly looked like chaos to all the old civil servants in Germany. In reality the reference to anarchy conceals a number of concurrent historical processes: the rise of new centers of power, their competitive expansion, and the embattled formation of political priorities or, as we call it, ideological politics that regulated the competitive expansion. These developments were closely linked. The National Socialist cadre and Hitler himself concentrated their efforts in the realm of ideological politics, making it the mainspring of National Socialist power. Contrary to virtually all other areas of domestic bureaucracy, ideology and repression were highly centralized, for example, in the Propaganda Ministry, the Gestapo, the German Labor Front, and became after a series of struggles the institutionalized guarantee of the reproduction of the political and economic system of the Third Reich.

What, then, was so distinctive about National Socialist ideology? What was the relation between ideology, the definition of the realm of the political, and social control? We will concentrate in this section on the meaning of ideology and concentrate on the interrelation among ideology, politics, and social control in the subsequent section.

There are considerable difficulties both in analyzing the content of National Socialist ideology and in conceptualizing the notion of ideology. As far as the former is concerned, very few seem to take it seriously, and little wonder; it is very difficult to take it seriously.[35] National Socialist ideology is no more systematic than strong convictions normally are, and its intellectual content has never satisfied academics, even though it has attracted quite a number of them in the past. Academics and the German intelligentsia aside, there seems to be no other aspect of the Third Reich which has as vile an attraction as National Socialist "ideology." Not only adolescents seem to revel in the fake romanticism and brutalism of a Hitler, Himmler, or Rosenberg; even the Holocaust is a major business venture today. National Socialist ideology is very much seen as a perverse and evil, but nonetheless "aesthetic" and fascinating, form of the seduction of the "masses." Alert intellectuals have seen ideology in this way ever since the 1930s.[36] Ideology, in this context, is seen as the substitution of "meaning"; it becomes the fabrication of "plastic" dreams and expectations to cover up for the lack of a "true" understanding and of compassion.[37] The only question that remains is why these dreams and expectations have been accepted by the German people, and—even though this question is hardly ever posed—why German dreams and expectations have to be about politics and war rather than about sex and romance.[38] This is an intriguing, but not altogether satisfactory level of interpretation of ideology. It may help us to describe the interaction between Hitler, National Socialist propaganda, and popular expectations, but it cannot explain the political significance of National Socialist ideology.

Alternately, ideology has been defined as a "process of hegemonic construction (i.e., the enrichment of coercive or repressive state power by conciliation and consent)" and as a way "of holding the allegiance of a mass constituence."[39] This and similar definitions start more or less explicitly from the assumption that ideology grows out of the dynamic and socially disruptive development of capitalism, rearranging and readjusting the constantly threatened legitimacy of the economic and political regime. Ideology readjusts and helps cope with the grievances which are produced by political and economic domination. Where adjustment breaks down a new balance between domination/violence and ideology/consent must be found. Violence follows the breakdown of consent, just as ideology sweetens domination. More generally, ideology is seen as an "objective systematized representation of social relations embodied in real material institutions and practices."[40] Ideology is the sum total of organized popular expressions. In both its specific and general form, ideology has a distinct politicized character, though, given these definitions, it is quite difficult to find a practical way to bridge the gap between the politicized role of ideology and expressions of everyday life. At any rate, rather than emphasizing the seduction of masses, this perspective stresses the relative autonomy and the creative aspects of "ideology" as a process of actively dealing with injustices and inequalities. As such it is very often seen to be an instrument of the "masses" to right wrongs.

Both ideology as politics and ideology as seduction, in fact, played a major role in the National Socialist movement and in the Third Reich. In a few phases they came so close together as to be almost identical. Those were the phases of rapid growth of the National Socialist movement between 1930 and 1933. Seduction through propaganda was readily accepted and transformed into popular myths and into the understanding of social and political reality. Propaganda was vital to the National Socialists' mobilization effort throughout the Weimar Republic. But recent studies have also indicated that ideology was not merely grafted onto the members of the party and sympathizers. Instead, we find the spontaneous and activist creation of collective memories, the formation of a National Socialist popular culture, and of a National Socialist street culture.[41] Indeed, we might even be inclined to deemphasize propaganda before 1933 and stress the very creative—though politically fatal—formation of a National Socialist identity from below which was taken up and reinforced by propaganda from above.[42] It is unpleasant to think of whole groups of people forming and modeling themselves as National Socialists, but this notion is certainly closer to what happened than the notion that a few demagogues imposed their ideas and concepts on the people.

Nevertheless, we must realize that after 1933–34 the situation changed very quickly.

> Disillusionment even among party members, with the party as it was seen in action, especially on a local level, was considerable and growing . . . ; the party became more popular among the sections of society which traditionally formed the social and political elites at the local level. . . . Party functionaries, the "little Hitlers," and especially those social upstarts who had forced their way into office in 1933, were frequently seen to reveal all the faults and vices, sometimes in excessive degree, which they had previously criticized in other politicians. During the first year of the Third Reich the extent of the criticism of the party, . . . the number of complaints of corruption, high-handed behavior, personal scandals, attacks on them as individuals and on the party as an institution, is most striking. It would not be going too far to describe it as a crisis of confidence in the party, certainly on the local and regional level.[43]

The party lost its ability to embody and represent social relations. Participation and interest in party affairs declined. The party became a convenient means of social mobility rather than of social mobilization. The main propagandistic concern became to demobilize, rather than to mobilize people. The participants in major rallies or those who were reborn in Hitler were not to receive or comprehend a political message, but to consume feelings and to learn trust in the state and the Führer. The creation of numbness, rather than political consciousness, was the goal of the Propaganda Ministry.

In other words, political propaganda increased, but it became separate from ideology, that is, from systematic representations of social relations. This turning point was reached very early in the history of the Third Reich, in 1934–35. Ideology and the pursuit of ideological objectives on the one hand and propaganda on the other separated because the National Socialist movement lost its ability to embody social relations when the National Socialist cadres moved into the state. This was the dramatic turning point for the party in 1933–34 and by no means a preconceived one. The National Socialist party ceased to be a movement. Now, the propaganda apparatus under Goebbels indeed became a dream factory because National Socialism in power had forfeited its close link with society. Ideology developed into propaganda by default, however successful that propaganda may have been. Hitler became increasingly popular, but National Socialism lost its popular base. Goebbels's dream factory, of course, manufactured nightmares. Propaganda was intimately linked with terror and repression that were both manifest and physical. Propaganda was backed up by an intricate network of informers to the Propaganda Ministry, the Gestapo, and the Security Service (SD) of Himmler's Reichssicherheitshauptamt (RSHA) which was to report on every aspect of German life. While access to theater, art, movies, and radio were broadened, they were systematically nazified. Alternative sources of information and entertainment were repressed, alternative opinions were persecuted, and nonconforming artists were expelled, their art banned. Thus, National Socialist propaganda orchestrated both the means of persuasion and repression, but it was *not* the source of ideological politics. Indeed, we succumb to a widespread misinterpretation of the crucial elements of National Socialist ideology if we end with this convenient, "propagandistic" interpretation of National Socialist ideology.[44]

National Socialist ideology was neither bad political habits of the "masses" nor bad dreams. The special quality of National Socialist ideology consists in its increasing concreteness. This is what the German intelligentsia disliked about it. It was not words, symbols, and discourses. Ideology was contained in the material practice of politics in the Third Reich.[45] In fact, it increasingly became politics. Its very core, racism and anti-Semitism, was least debated and propagandized, but it was the material practice and the essence of ideological politics in the Third Reich nonetheless. Ideology became massive and brutal reality and was defeated only at the cost of World War II. Goebbels may have reveled in selling propaganda, but Hitler was set to play out National Socialist ideology in real life.[46] The citizens of Germany had a hard time comprehending the unfolding ideological schema, and we should take special pains to comprehend it in retrospect. The National Socialists were not creating some "plastic," right wing "culture" in the tradition of radical nationalism in Europe. They were not changing discourses through propaganda. They were changing people and the world around them. They did not remake *expressions* of social realities; they radically altered social realities. In this respect Hitler was a radical materialist.

The real political muscle of National Socialism came from fusing state and society, as it was often described by German intellectuals in the 1930s.[47] After entering the state they set out to remake the state in order to restructure German society. National Socialist ideology was the set of political values and priorities that both delineated the boundaries of the political and aimed at a restructuring of German society. This was the essence and the special quality of National Socialist policy. Ideology never existed in the abstract—propaganda did—but flourished as political values and ideas which were implemented in a process of massive social, political, and legal engineering. There was no single ideological body (a ministry of enlightenment) or single ideological dogma (the National Socialist ideology) that shaped the restructuring of German society. Those bodies that existed and, like Rosenberg's office, thought they could play a role, never did. Hitler's speeches give a good indication of the changes, but do not show the material practice that is only slowly unearthed. For ideology is the sum total of statist interventions into society for restructuring it. Ideology was not a matter of pictures and symbols, but of the domination of everyday life. In many ways, lawyers who drew up new laws and regulations were better ideologues than journalists, artists, and agitprop specialists. Studying this ideological practice of the Third Reich is a vast undertaking which has barely begun.[48] Of the many examples of this massive and diverse intervention which extended into daily life and into the private sphere—religion, housing, diet, leisure, sexuality, and, of course, work—we can briefly sketch one, which shows the intent and the mechanism of the transformation in a nutshell: the changed role of women.

The status of women was enhanced in some respects, as can be seen in a relatively high level of security and protections, special education, a certain level of welfare and even leisure, or in the cult of young women (*Mädel*). The "honor" of "the woman," the protection and possibly even expansion of her sphere—less innocently in German: her "Lebensraum"[49]—was a major concern of the regime and undoubtedly many women appreciated that. However, the "honor" of "the woman" was tied to the limitation of her role to that of a housewife and childbearer. "The woman" was a link in the chain of domination of men over women over girls—over non-Aryans. The concern of the regime consisted of taking women out of the sphere of production, limiting them to biological reproduction and subjugating their sphere to the domination of men juridically, politically, socially, and sexually as, for example, through the prohibition of abortion and the cruel metaphysics of National Socialist sexuality which freed women from traditional notions of chastity, yet made them objects of male domination.[50]

Ideology in this sense was certainly not a means to mediate and to establish consensus. It was a "process of hegemonic construction"—quite literally—but not the "enrichment of coercive or repressive state power by conciliation and consent."[51] This was Germany, not Italy; it was National Socialism, not the latter-day Catholic Church. The practice of ideological politics broke apart families, alienated young women from older ones, children from parents, and reshaped the relation between men and women—as far as it could. It poisoned the life in villages and houses, broke apart friendships and associations. It is hard to say how successful it was, but a whole array of state policies tried to create a new social structure and new social relations. This new society was to provide stability and harmony, but social stability was not to be obtained anywhere and at any cost. The logic of the diverse interventions in the case of women as well as in others, such as workers, all point to the conclusion that social stability was to be reached outside the realm of production or, at a minimum, by segregating social life from work.

The segregation of social life from the organization of work and the dissolution of the ties between production and social reproduction was, indeed, the key to the ideological reconstruction of German society. The segregation as such is nothing peculiarly National Socialist. It is a common phenomenon of the 1930s in the advanced industrial countries. It is best explained as a response to the social and economic crisis of that period. The same phenomenon can be seen at work in the nascent consumer capitalism and, for that matter, the original British welfare capitalism where consumption or social services provided an antidote or a balance against the organization of work. Like consumer and welfare capitalism, National Socialist ideology left the nineteenth-century fusion of economy and society (production and social organization) behind. In this respect it is thoroughly "modern." Yet it differed from the other two in crucial ways. National Socialist ideology called for the interventionist restructuring of social relations on the basis of a hierarchy of inequality, domination, and subjugation within German society and between Germans and non-Germans. Domination and dependence—the control of "men" over "men" rather than goods or services over "men"—was the logic of the National Socialist society that emerged step by step after 1933. This was the essence of a counterrevolutionary ideology. In rolling back the threat of revolution it had to create its own new society. It was a society that was to be recreated outside the sphere of production. It was to be based on violence.

This form of social counterrevolution—not restoration and not a return to mythical pasts—was so important to the regime that it maintained its stand even when it was economically no longer advantageous. The National Socialist practice of restructuring society was irrational in the sense that it replaced and, at times, openly contradicted a productivist logic, but production as such was never at the center of National Socialist ideology. On the contrary, the recreation of German society outside of the disruptive realm of production was its main goal.

The notion of creating a German society outside the realm of production provides us with the last and most important nexus of ideological politics, the one between domestic and foreign policy or, more precisely, between the creation of a new German society and the obliteration of others. One can argue that Hitler thought of the latter first, and when he thought of annihilation, he thought first and foremost of the annihilation of the Jews. In the practice of the Third Reich the creation of a new German society and the obliteration of others were concurrent processes and must be seen together. The recreation of German society, the sub-jugation of the East European people, and the destruction of European Jewry formed a single, tense unity. It is impossible to isolate one element from the other or to rank them, for they belong together.

The National Socialist distrust of the socially disruptive quality of industry was so great that—according to National Socialists—industry could neither provide the organizational or, for that matter, ecological basis for a future society nor could it provide adequate means for building it. The resources for the reconstruction of German society could only come from violent forms of exploitation and expropriation. Once again: this should not be mistaken as meaning that industry and industrial pro-duction were considered to be unimportant or insignificant. Indeed, there is very little evidence that Hitler or the decisive National Socialist cadres were anti-industrial, as long as the economy did not shape social life. It was good for the production of tools, but was too fickle and too demeaning a basis for social order. Germany, in other words, would always remain an "industrial society"; but it was to be a society in which the imperatives of production could no longer shape the social order of the Germans. The alternative was war and particularly war against the Soviet Union which was to facilitate the most advanced and the most brutal forms of direct exploitation.[52] From its very conception the *Barba-rossa* campaign was not an ordinary military campaign. The war against the Soviet Union was the one war that was to create the material basis for the reconstruction of German society. The concept of Lebensraum, that is, of the physical domination of human and material resources of Eastern Europe completely outside of the productivist logic of industry or, for that matter, the necessities of warfare, was the radical and barbaric answer to the crisis of the legitimacy of the national and international economic system and to the specter of Bolshevik revolution.

War was the essence of ideological politics. National Socialist war was different from the elite tradition of European land warfare. It was a coun-terrevolutionary and ideological war for the sake of social reconstruction, and the Barbarossa campaign shows all the signs of this kind of total, social war. The story has been told many times. It is less obvious that this war was supposed to provide an answer to the problems of modern industrial society without destroying industry. Once Russia was subordinated, the reconstructed German society could "settle" free of the vagaries of the world market—as Hitler explained in 1937[53]—and independent of the unreliable base of industrial capitalism. Direct exploitation—not indus-trial production—was to maintain and guarantee social life and social organization. Industry and private property would flourish as well, but only because the basic task of social reproduction was guaranteed by physical force. Some scholars have seen fit to poke fun at some of the more grandiose plans, mostly of Himmler, and it is true that plans to pastoralize Germans in the East failed ludicrously.[54] However, National Socialist ideology became brutal reality not just in the concentration camps. Many scholars have not considered sufficiently the influx of forced labor into Germany and they have not taken cognizance of the *Herrenmenschentum* of tens of thousands of German bureaucrats in the occupied countries. The combination of these two factors created the conditions for everyday racism which must have had an impact on German life. National Socialist war made possible, even mandatory, the daily routine of domination. The regime made the subjugation of others—German men over women over other "races"—easy and a matter of everyday life. A new German society was in the making in which the Germans were unequal, but other "races" were always the lowliest ones. In fact, by 1942–43 it needed an extraordinary effort and strong convictions to evade the emerging new society; for racism penetrated every aspect of life in occupied Europe. It had ceased to be a matter of individuals embracing racist ideologies. Rather, it was the established practice of social organization which was almost impossible to evade. National Socialism was indeed not just a very material ideology. It was also a very radical one that changed social order at its roots. It is not by chance that industry grew during the war as well as that the modern industrial structure of postwar Germany was established between 1939–41 and 1944. The war years have not been sufficiently studied, but everything points to the fact that National Socialist ideological politics was barbaric and not ludicrous. Everything points to the fact that the segregation between social life and the organization of work was in the making, that the National Socialist counterrevolution was more successful than one might commonly want to acknowledge.

Racism was an eminently rational aspect of National Socialist rule under these conditions. Racism and particularly anti-Semitism were key elements in Hitler's mission to save German society ever since 1919 when Hitler discovered the issue, which henceforth guided his political thinking. They were introduced after 1933 as the central policy of the National Socialist state, in a rising tide of legislation and directives which pushed those who were considered to be non-German to the brink of disaster, long before there was open planning for their mass annihilation. The policies concerning the Jews developed exactly the way ideological politics was made in the Third Reich. The "Jewish problem" and similar "problems" gained reality as a body of laws and regulations that shaped perceptions, were institutionalized in the SS, and merged with a common and vulgar, popular anti-Semitism in Germany and later on in the occupied countries.[55] This racism was not inexplicably attached to all the other seeming irrationalities of the Third Reich, nor did it form the inexplicable core of National Socialist policy and ideology. It was the purest

and most consistent expression of the National Socialist program of rebuilding society on the basis of violence. Racism with its extreme form of
annihilating whole peoples realized and legitimized the extreme form of
subjugation that was necessary to establish a German society outside the
realm of industrial production. It was economically and militarily irrational, but the total subjugation of others which was necessary to rebuild
German society outside the realm of production was only realized in the
readiness and willingness to kill. Only the potential of annihilation established the reality of subjugation and, hence, the very core of National
Socialist ideology in practice.[56] As all ideological politics in the Third
Reich, the holocaust was not a matter of symbols and words, but of
bureaucratic action.

We should not be misdirected by the pseudoscientific and pseudohis-
torical mythology that contemporary intellectuals built around this central aspect of National Socialist policy and that resurfaced among some of
the Nazi cadres. Neither should we be misdirected by comparison with
previous racist and anti-Semitic outbursts which are a common European
heritage. Racism in the Third Reich was not primarily a popular movement, but it became increasingly the central priority of the National
Socialist state as it entered the war. In fact, racism was the essence of the
"autonomy of the political" and became the basis for the ideological definition of the state and its autonomous units which were to facilitate the
reconstruction of German society.

Toward a Fusion of State and Ideology

The Third Reich was not an authoritarian regime, content with securing
the autonomy of a hegemonic bloc, but it became a counterrevolutionary
regime, ready to establish the primacy of ideological politics in order to
change people. The predominance of ideological politics did not come
easily and at once in 1933 or 1934. It only came after protracted struggles
over the priorities of the regime. While conservative and authoritarian
politicians like Hugenberg and Papen were outflanked in a matter of
months in 1933, the new centers of power and domination in industry and
the military were difficult to move. Indeed, during the first years of the
Third Reich they moved the National Socialists.

The strength of the National Socialists initially consisted in their
ability to rally broad support from a variety of classes and regions and to
forge them into a popular national movement. This ability and the
ruthless destruction of the remnants of the 1918 revolution gave the
National Socialists their extremely strong position in the first months of
1933 which allowed them to outmaneuver conservative and nationalist
politicians and parties. However, this period ended quickly because the

rank and file of the National Socialist movement was hard to control. Three of the key mobilizing agents of the party, the Sturmabteilung (SA), the representatives of middle-class protectionism, and the German Labor Front clashed frontally with the newly established centers of power. The formation of a National Socialist middle-class movement and a National Socialist labor movement and the self-organization of industry proved to be mutually exclusive. The SA began to compete with the military or—to be more precise—the military began to compete with the SA for mass support. The SA threatened to create an alternative "Lumpen" army, small business and artisans demanded "excessive" protection and rights, and the German Labor Front openly interfered with the self-organization of industry. Industry and the military neither tolerated the formation of class organizations nor competition in their own realm. They expressed the classical authoritarian calamity of wanting to mobilize support for production and military preparedness and armaments but being unable and unwilling to honor this support. Within a year the National Socialists were forced to discard, restructure, or severely curtail the operations of these associations. In this process they cut the most important links to the "people" and forfeited the ability of social mobilization. Within a year the National Socialists had lost their main basis of power because the social dynamics of their popular support were irreconcilable with the imperatives of the regime. For the time being these were defined by the dominant centers of power.[57]

In the years 1934–38 the parameters of the unfolding competition over priorities were set by the strongest and most coherent centers of power, the military and industry. The reduction of the social costs of production as a prerequisite for economic recovery was one of these parameters. It was guaranteed through the repression of working-class organizations, control of the factor markets, control of prices and output through enforced cartelization, and other such measures. They were demanded by a majority of industrialists who did not necessarily care for the National Socialists, but who preferred organized industrial activities— that is, the formation of an autonomous industrial domain of control and domination—over unorganized market conditions and preferred the subordination of workers and the destruction of their organs over the "bolshevik threat."[58] Rearmament as a means of war preparation rather than as an economic stimulant was the other one of the parameters. The military were guaranteed the unhindered formation of a large army that was able to conduct offensive warfare and began to build it according to their own designs.[59]

The National Socialist cadres survived as independent actors despite the dramatic shifts in their power base during the first year of the Third Reich. First of all, one cannot emphasize enough that they were needed because the conditions of dominance under the Weimar Republic had not yet changed. The military and industry remained hard-pressed for support and legitimacy and were unable to generate it on their own. This was the golden moment for the propaganda apparatus, which now came into its own, and for the opening up of bureaucracies for patronage. The Riefenstahls and Goebbels set to work on what has been called the "falsification of conscience" by creating "plastic" symbols of the unity of the *Volk*.[60] Others created upward mobility through patronage. This aspect of National Socialist rule is well known and has been described above. It is also easily overemphasized because the National Socialist cadres did not stabilize their position in this way. They successfully shifted the basis of their power. The very special aptitude of the National Socialist power holders, and particularly of Hitler, consisted in creating space for the rapid growth of each one of the centers of power and domination and in preventing major clashes. The competition within and between these autonomous institutions was fierce. Agreement on priorities—including rearmament—was difficult to achieve. Hitler mediated and increasingly controlled the competitive struggles over boundaries between the various centers of power and domination. In particular he took on the role of shaping the key area in which industry and military overlapped, but did not necessarily agree: armament. More than that, he shielded armament against the much feared outside intervention. Hitler and other Nazi cadres like Goering thus moved from the position of "providers" of mass support into the position of organizers of the politics of the Third Reich.[61] The National Socialist cadres overcame the crisis of 1934 by moving from social mobilization to statemaking, that is, they became the guarantors of the distances between the autonomous centers of power.

Had there been unanimity on rearmament between the military and industry, and had rearmament been without tremendous social costs and far-reaching political-economic choices, it would not have needed an Adolf Hitler. However, armaments were possible only at a very high price and only at the basis of large-scale rearrangements in the productive apparatus. Armaments were not a matter of pushing through special interests, but a matter of reconciling them and of carrying the burden of redistribution. Thus, National Socialist cadres, industry, and the military were engaged in very tense relations. While each one formed autonomous domains, they were nonetheless tied to each other and remained dependent on each other to the very end.

Two kinds of dynamics shaped the regime after 1934 up to a crucial turning point in 1938 when ideological politics became predominant. On the one hand there were the directives and decisions of the large centers of power and domination, which unfolded in a dramatic and unprecedented way in the rearmament boom. Altogether different is the other dynamic, the one which was to reforge the links between the National Socialist cadres and society. This linkage was to be formed by the complete transformation of society. It is the dynamics of what we have called ideological politics.

The armaments boom caused its own dynamics and crisis. The definite external and internal limits to growth became evident after 1936. The Third Reich still participated in a slumping international economy and was caught in it, despite attempts to escape the international market by barter arrangements. Domestically, the scarcity of resources became serious after 1936–37. When the capacity of creating space for the various rival centers of power and the ability of mediating between them declined, the nature of the basic directions of the regime was at stake. Was growth to continue in the same direction and in the same extensive way as before, or was it to be based on a more intensive use of resources, even a complete reallocation of resources? A crisis of the regime generally and of the autonomy of its members was in the making. The overheating economic boom, expectations of an arms race in Europe, serious clashes between the ideological realm and military-industrial demands, and a quickly deepening currency crisis forced redistributive issues to the forefront for the first time in the Third Reich.

The Four Year Plan of 1936 was a first answer to this situation.[62] The martial and aggressive language of this plan and the formation of a massive new bureaucracy can be taken as a sign of the growing organization, or subjugation, of industry by National Socialist cadres and of a concomitant loss of military power in the military-economic planning. However, the Four Year Plan did not turn into what it was supposed to be: the center for the government's redistributive decisions. Instead, it developed into just one more of the independent power centers that acted quite like the others once the dust of the original conflicts had settled. The Four Year Plan affected the balances within the centers of power—it favored the chemical industry and the air force—but it was distinctly not the much propagandized bureaucratic center that organized political-economic relations for which radicals in the military, economic, and ideological domain had pleaded since 1934. The autonomous units continued to insist on distance rather than on cooperation and coordination.

The armaments boom continued after 1936–37 and with it the crises which it produced. Turmoil and tensions grew both within and between the power centers and culminated in the coup d'état of the National Socialist cadre against the military in 1938.[63] As important and consequential as these events were for the rise of ideological politics, they first of all demobilized a threatening conflict between the economic and the military sphere. While Schacht fought for an open monetary dictatorship and for the primacy of a monetarily guided industry, the orthodox military like Beck and Fritsch fought for an ever more relentless course of rearmament after 1935–36 and particularly in 1938. By replacing them, the mounting antagonism between the two centers of power which had previously shaped much of the Third Reich could once more be deflected into the various centers of power and domination. The events of 1938 were multifaceted, but part of the story is that an impending major directional conflict between industry and the military was staved off.[64]

This was done at very high cost for both industry and especially the military. While the working principles of the military and of industry remained largely unaltered after 1938, both lost their ability to transfer internal demands directly into political imperatives of the regime under the umbrella of the priorities of rearmament and industrial profitability which had guided the regime up to this point. Profitable production and military preparedness—as defined by the military professionals and the industrialists—no longer shaped the key directions of the regime sufficiently or primarily. They were reinterpreted by Hitler, whose intervention now increasingly overruled the directional struggles between the autonomous centers and set the imperatives of the regime. This is the point when ideological politics had a chance of becoming the prevailing force in the Third Reich. Hitler grasped this chance eagerly and ruthlessly. Ideological politics could come into its own. It could become, in a manner of speaking, the center of the state.

In 1938 industry and military had reached a serious impasse. They had come to a point at which the maintenance of the twin priorities of profitable production and military preparedness was no longer possible without shifting the internal arrangements within each domain (as, for example, altering the balance between the services and the various industries which were allied with them or between heavy industry and capital goods industries) and between them. Every further acceleration of armaments could lead to financial collapse, as Schacht warned in early 1939, to serious disruptions in production, and to rising costs of production. In other words, the distance between the centers of power collapsed. Since a formal political process did not exist which possibly could have served as a means of channeling negotiations, a mad scramble for control began which threatened to get out of hand and end in virtual chaos. However, rearmament remained the top priority for both industry and the military. The military had not yet completed its ambitious plans and industry, especially heavy industry, was scared by the prospect of collapsing foreign markets after the short world economic recovery in 1936–37. This contradictory situation allowed Hitler to come to the fore. Much has been made of the gallant protest against this "seizure of power," but, more importantly, the majority of the military and of industry were willing to relinquish some autonomy in order to save rearmament and profitability rather than reconsidering their priorities. This impasse made it possible to reestablish an "autonomy of the political." However, this autonomy did not come as reconstruction of an (authoritarian) political process, but as ideological politics.

At this point we almost automatically fall into the arms of a school of thought that identifies the rise of ideological politics with a trivialized notion of a relentless unfolding of certain dogmatically held goals.[65] But there is no reason to assume that ideological politics could either just unfold or suffer fewer contradictions than industrial and military politics. The opposite is the case. Not only had the National Socialists lost their ties to society, but their policies of interfering and changing social life had met resistance. By 1938 the very credibility of the National Socialist cadre—though not of Hitler—and with it the role of National Socialist politics in the state system was endangered. Domestically German society proved to be exceedingly resistant to any form of social engineering that threatened to change its established beliefs and social relations. (German society also proved to be frighteningly "disinterested" in anything that did not affect the basic social networks, and terrifyingly brutal, if it could gain from National Socialist repression. Somebody, after all, took over the Jewish businesses, and that somebody was mostly not a Krupp or Flick, but a local dentist, artisan, or retailer.) Political opposition was destroyed by 1936, but basic social solidarities remained hard to change. The party had long lost its credibility. The more ambitious schemes of reeducation in the struggle against the churches had failed. Regional differences were as strong as ever, and class differences were barely muffled by various attempts to create a *Volksgemeinschaft*.[66] As far as we know, some of the attempts in this direction, like "Strength through Joy" and the large party rallies, were great successes, but they were welcomed as temporary festivities and entertainments by those who had the time for them, not as true changes in the construction of reality.[67]

National Socialism did make inroads in reconstructing social reality; very few Germans, moreover, actively opposed the Third Reich. But the solidarity of basic social groups and basic beliefs and behaviors remained largely unchanged until deep into World War II. In addition, German society rapidly changed in ways contrary to the expectations and the intent of National Socialist ideology. The ever more rapid pace of rearmament drove farmers into factories and women into work. It destroyed an independent, artisanal middle class. Worse than that, work conditions deteriorated rapidly after 1938–39. Exhaustion, lack of discipline, widespread illness, and growing alcoholism were reported for all industrial centers. The rearmament boom took a heavy toll.[68] Most of all, it made the organization of work into the center of social life. In effect, the National Socialist reason for being in power was profoundly challenged by the unfolding social realities of Germany in the late 1930s. It is quite typical that the question arose again and again whether women should be drafted or otherwise encouraged to work after all.

Internationally the situation did not look much better. If the nation was to become ready for war, it had to rearm ever faster because the military and Hitler anticipated a major arms race in Europe, which the Third Reich did not expect to win.[69] Without war, though, and without the expansion of *Lebensraum* the National Socialists considered the reconstruction of German society to be impossible. If one waited too long, war might turn out to be unfeasible. The neurotic nervousness of Hitler in these years is not at all amazing. The whole state of the Third Reich and its ideological goals were at stake. Of course, there was no automatism that led to war. But if Hitler and the National Socialist cadre wanted to pursue their goal of transforming German society, they had to start war as soon as possible, even if war was premature from a professional point of view. There can be little doubt: National Socialist timing was not arbitrary and it was certainly not determined by economic necessity or by the military readiness of the German people and the military. It was neither the degree of military and paramilitary preparation nor the economic "crisis" per se, but the degree of perceived decomposition of German and international society that moved them.

Thus, the contradictions of ideological politics began to move the state in the Third Reich after 1938. These were contradictions of politics, not some "objective" crisis. They were measured against the National Socialist goal of creating a new society. The National Socialist leadership and particularly Hitler were indeed dogmatic. They were fanatics insofar as they stuck to the conditions that formed their raison d'être and that brought them to power even against adverse circumstances. In this sense they were clearly not opportunistic, nor were they bound by any special interests as some of the more simplistic notions of fascism would like it. But neither were their ideological politics arbitrary and inexplicable— some kind of atavistic craziness that overcame Germany out of the blue. Not only were there ominous traditions of right radicalism. It should be also very evident that the reorganization of politics and the restructuring of social relations were necessary due to the collapse of German politics in World War I and due to the decomposition of social relations throughout the interwar years—the latter process being most closely linked to the long inflation between 1916 and 1924. The National Socialists, in other words, did not simply invent an issue that otherwise did not exist, but they responded to the serious political and social dislocations in Germany during the interwar years. They found a most barbaric answer to the pressing problems of the time. This was certainly not the only answer possible, but it was the one that succeeded due to the power of its supporters and due to the lack of alternatives. The inordinate blindness of a military that made rearmament into an idée fixe and into a solution of all its problems, but also the lack of vision of the republican parties and a completely disoriented Left, their unwillingness to even concede that there were serious political and social problems to be solved which went beyond instrumental politics—all this contributed to the rise and the success of National Socialist ideological politics.

Ideological politics itself did not simply unfold, as if all the answers were found in 1921–22 and only needed to be put into practice. It was formed under the tremendous pressures of the revolutionary years between 1916 and 1923. It succeeded in mobilizing masses in the early 1930s because National Socialism was the only movement that did not rely on instrumentalist politics. It was finally pressured into the open as a result of the increasing discrepancies between the counterrevolutionary goals of the National Socialist cadre and the realities of social life in Germany on the one hand, and as a result of the growing resistance to the aggressive National Socialist course on the other. It could become predominant due to the impasse of the military and industry. Even after ideological politics became predominant in 1938, it did not simply *lead* to war. It still needed decisions which were made for ideological reasons under highly contradictory domestic and international circumstances. It was a long way from 1938 to 1941–42, but the decisive turn to war was taken.

War was the cornerstone for the creation of a future German society and the trigger for the destruction of whole societies. It was chosen under mounting pressures, but it was chosen deliberately. In this respect Hitler remained true to an old German predicament that society can only be rebuilt from the outside. The war against the Soviet Union and the concomitant annihilation of the Jewish population in occupied Europe was to make the impossible possible, the reconstruction of German society and its transformation into a new and harmonious society that had overcome and defeated national and international revolution and reestablished itself on the basis of racist domination. This vision was not destroyed from within. The resistance of the British, the struggle of the Soviet and other Eastern European nations, and the production of the American war machine defeated both the vision and the internal practice of the Third Reich at the cost of many million men and women dead, missing, and mutilated.

NOTES

Without the help and encouragement of Charles Bright, Susan Harding, Isabel Hull, MacGregor Knox, and Tessie Liu this essay could not have been written. I would also like to thank the Woodrow Wilson International Center for Scholars, Washington, D.C., for its kind support.

1. Michael Stolleis, *Staatsdenker im 17. und 18. Jahrhundert* (Frankfurt: A. Metzner, 1977); Shlomo Avineri, *Hegel's Theory of the Modern State* (London: Cambridge University Press, 1972); Kenneth Dyson, *The State Tradition in Western Europe* (New York: Oxford University Press, 1980).

2. See Edgar Loening, "Der Staat (allgemeine Staatslehre)," *Handwörterbuch der Staatswissenschaften*, 2d ed., 8 vols. (Jena: Gustav Fischer, 1906), 6:907–40; Adolf Wagner, "Der Staat in nationalökonomischer Sicht," ibid., 6:940–51; Richard Thoma, "Staat (allgemeine Staatslehre)," ibid., 4th ed., 8 vols. (Jena: Gustav Fischer, 1926), 7:724–56; Adolf Wagner and Franz Oppenheimer, "Staat in nationalökonomischer Sicht," ibid., 7:757–79; Peter Koslowski, *Gesellschaft und Staat. Ein unvermeidlicher Dualismus* (Stuttgart: Klett-Cotta, 1981).

3. In one or the other form this remains one of the basic assumptions even in recent work that has shown the fragility of boundaries between state and society and the fluctuations within the sphere of the state. Compare the contributions in Gerhard Hirschfeld and Lothar Kettenacker, eds., *The "Führer-State": Myth and Reality; Studies on the Structure and Politics of the Third Reich* (Stuttgart: Klett-Cotta, 1981).

4. Nicos Poulantzas, *Fascism and Dictatorship* (New York: Schocken, 1974) has made this notion very popular again. See also Timothy Mason, "Der Primat der Politik—Politik und Wirtschaft im Nationalsozialismus," *Das Argument* 8 (December, 1966): 473–94; also in Stewart J. Wolfe, ed., *The Nature of Fascism*, 2d ed. (London: Methuen, 1981). The godfather of this notion is Franz Neuman, *Behemoth: The Structure and Practice of National Socialism* (New York: Oxford University Press, 1942).

5. Most clearly outlined and without the prevalent mechanistic ring in Alain Touraine, *La voix et le regard* (Paris: Edition du seuil, 1978), pp. 133–77.

6. Nicos Poulantzas, *Les classes sociales dans le capitalisme aujourd'hui* (Paris: Edition du seuil, 1976), pp. 85–86; Pierre Bourdieu, "Les modes de domination," *Actes de la Recherches en Science Sociale*, 1976, pp. 122–32.

7. Jane Caplan, "Theories of Fascism: Nicos Poulantzas as Historian," *History Workshop* 3 (Spring, 1977): 83–100.

8. Max Weber, *Staatssoziologie: Soziologie der rationalen Staatsanstalt und der modernen politischen Parteien und Politik*, ed. Johannes Winckelmann, 2d ed. (Berlin: Duncker and Humblot), p. 45.

9. Max Weber was very careful in emphasizing again and again that *Verwaltung*, which is normally translated as "bureaucracy," does not just "organize" the world "rationally," but literally *produces domination* (i.e., *Herrschafts-Betrieb*) in a routinized fashion. This understanding was not part of the Max Weber revival in the United States.

10. See Alfred Weber, *Die Krise des modernen Staatsgedankens in Europa* (Stuttgart: Deutsche Verlagsanstalt, 1925), pp. 69–90, but also the staunchly liberal Moritz J. Bonn, *Die Auflösung des modernen Staates* (Berlin: Verlag für Wissenschaft und Politik, 1921); Carl Schmitt, *Staatsgefüge und Zusam-*

menbruch des zweiten Reiches; der Sieg des Bürgers über die Soldaten (Hamburg: Hanseatische Verlagsanstalt, 1934); Hans Freyer, *Der Staat,* 2d ed. (Leipzig: E. Wiegand, 1926).

11. See the alternative interpretation of the same phenomenon by Leon Duguit, *Le droit social, le droit individuel et la transformation de l'état* (Paris: Alcan, 1911) and his *Law in the Modern State,* trans. Frida and Harold Laski (New York: B. W. Huebsch, 1919).

12. Nicos Poulantzas, "Les transformations actuelles de l'État, la crise politique et la crise de l'Etat," in *La crise d'État,* ed. Nicos Poulantzas (Paris: Presses Universitaires de France, 1976), pp. 19–58, quoted at p. 57.

13. This is also to suggest that the discussion on comparative "fascism" may not be the most useful approach to understanding the Third Reich. Unquestionably, the common European tradition, aspects of political culture and of social background of fascists need to be explored. However, the social, economic, and political conditions in Germany and other fascist countries differ so widely that the comparative analysis of fascism is only of limited heuristic value particularly after the National Socialists came to power. It would be rather more stimulating in the current situation to engage in a thorough and systematic study of the paths out of the world crisis of capitalism in the interwar years among the advanced industrial nations.

14. William Rosenberg and Marilyn Young, *Transforming Russia and China* (New York: Oxford University Press, 1982).

15. Goetz Briefs, "Kriegswirtschaftslehre und Kriegswirtschaftspolitik," *Handwörterbuch für Sozialwissenschaften,* 4th ed., 10 vols. (Jena: Gustav Fischer, 1923), 5:984–1022.

16. Michael Stürmer, ed., *Weimarer Republik: Belagerte Civitas* (Kronberg/Ts.: Athenäum, 1980); on the limits of parliamentarism Charles Maier, *Reshaping Bourgeois Europe* (Princeton: Princeton University Press, 1975).

17. Gerhard A. Ritter, "Kontinuität und Umformung des deutschen Parteiensystems 1918–1920," in *Arbeiterbewegung, Parteien und Parlamentarismus,* ed. Gerhard A. Ritter (Göttingen: Vandenoeck and Ruprecht, 1976), pp. 116–57; see also the excellent summary by Gian Enrico Rusconi, *La crisi di Weimar. Crisi di sistema e sconfitta operaia* (Torino: Einaudi, 1977), pp. 5–36, 75–94.

18. This is clearly evident in the massive compilation by Ilse Maurer and Udo Wengst, eds., *Politik und Wirtschaft in der Krise 1930–1932; Quellen zur Ära Brüning,* 2 vols. (Düsseldorf: Droste, 1980), less so in David Abraham, *The Collapse of the Weimar Republic* (Princeton: Princeton University Press, 1981).

19. Among others Joseph Nyomarkai, *Charisma and Factionalism in the Nazi Party* (Minneapolis: University of Minnesota Press, 1967); Martin Broszat, "Soziale Motivation und Führerbindung des Nationalsozialismus," *Vierteljahrshefte für Zeitgeschichte* 18 (1970): 392–409.

20. In recent years the importance of the party structure has been rather downplayed. Without it, though, the "charismatic" success of Hitler as leader

would have been quite impossible, as shown by Udo Kissenkoeter, *Georg Strasser und die NSDAP* (Stuttgart: Deutsche Verlagsanstalt, 1978).

21. This seems to be the decisive point in Henry A. Turner, "Grossunternehmen und Nationalsozialismus," *Historische Zeitschrift* 221 (1975): 18–68.

22. Wolfgang Horn, *Führerideologie und Parteiorganisation in der NSDAP 1919–1933* (Düsseldorf: Droste, 1972); U. Wörtz, "Programmatik und Führerprinzip. Das Problem des Strasser-Kreises in der NSDAP. Eine historisch-politische Studie zum Verhältnis von sachlichem Programm und persönlicher Führung in einer totalitären Bewegung" (Ph.D. diss., Erlangen/Nürnberg, 1966).

23. With somewhat different conclusions this theme is most impressively explored by Eve Rosenhaft, "Working-Class Life and Working-Class Politics: Communists, Nazis, and the State in the Battle for the Streets of Berlin 1928–1932," in *Social Change and Political Development in Weimar Germany*, ed. Richard Bessel and E. J. Feuchtwanger (London: Croom Helm; Totowa, N.J.: Barnes and Noble, 1981), pp. 207–40.

24. As general overview Karl Dietrich Bracher, *The German Dictatorship* (New York: Praeger, 1970).

25. A detailed analysis of the events leading to the so-called Röhm Putsch is still missing. The most comprehensive account is Karl Dietrich Bracher, Wolfgang Sauer, and Gerhard Schulz, *Die nationalsozialistische Machtergreifung. Studien zur Errichtung des totalitären Herrschaftssystems in Deutschland 1933/34*, 2d ed. (Opladen: Westdeutsche Verlagsgesellschaft, 1962).

26. A most interesting reminder of this issue is Peter Hüttenberger, "Interessenvertretung und Lobbyismus im Dritten Reich," in *The "Führer-State"*, ed. Hirschfeld and Kettenacker, pp. 429–55 (with English summary).

27. Bracher, Sauer, and Schulz, *Nationalsozialistische Machtergreifung*, with details. On the Reichswehr becoming "sovereign," see M. Oshima, "[Reichswehr and National Accounting Office. The Importance of the Cabinet Order of April 4, 1933]," *Mita Gakkai Zasshi* 69 (1976): 298–318 (original in Japanese).

28. Mathilde Jamin, "Zur Rolle der SA im nationalsozialistischen Herrschaftssystem," in *The "Führer-State"*, ed. Hirschfeld and Kettenacker, pp. 329–57 (with English summary).

29. See above, in the discussion of *Herrschaftsbetriebe*.

30. Arthur Schweitzer, *Big Business in the Third Reich* (Bloomington: Indiana University Press, 1964); Timothy W. Mason, *Sozialpolitik im Dritten Reich* (Opladen: Westdeutscher Verlag, 1977); J. E. Farquharson, *The Plough and the Swastika. The NSDAP and Agriculture in Germany 1928–1945* (London and Beverly Hills: Sage, 1976).

31. This process has been described by Hans Mommsen, *Beamtentum in Dritten Reich* (Stuttgart: Deutsche Verlagsanstalt, 1966); Martin Broszat, *The Hitler State: The Foundation and Development of the Internal Structure of the Third Reich* (London: Longman, 1981); Jane Caplan, "Civil Service Support for National Socialism: An Evaluation," in *The "Führer-State"*, ed. Hirschfeld and Kettenacker, pp. 167–90.

32. Peter Hüttenberger, *Die Gauleiter: Studien zum Wandel des Machtgefüges in der NSDAP* (Stuttgart: Deutsche Verlagsanstalt, 1969); Shlomo Aronson, "Heydrich und die Anfänge der SD und der Gestapo" (Ph.D. diss., Berlin, 1967).

33. Caplan, "Theories," p. 90.

34. Hans Mommsen, "Hitlers Stellung im nationalsozialistischen Herrschaftssystem," in *The "Führer-State"*, ed. Hirschfeld and Kettenacker, pp. 23–40, and his "Die innere Struktur des nationalsozialistischen Herrschaftssystems," *Politische Bildung* 5 (1972): 37–52.

35. Those historians who take National Socialist ideology seriously mostly concentrate on foreign policy and, more recently, on anti-Semitism; see Andreas Hillgruber, *Hitlers Strategie: Politik und Kriegführung 1940–1941* (Frankfurt: Bernard and Graefe, 1965). If one considers the powerful analyses of Arendt, Nolte, and others, this casts a rather peculiar light on the historians' understanding of ideology.

36. Walter Benjamin, "Das Kunstwerk im Zeitalter seiner technischen Reproduzierbarkeit," in Walter Benjamin, *Gesammelte Schriften*, 12 vols. (Frankfurt: Suhrkamp, 1980), vol. 1, pt. 2, pp. 471–508; Ernst Bloch, "Erbschaft dieser Zeit," in *Gesamtausgabe*, ed. Ernst Bloch, 16 vols. (Frankfurt: Suhrkamp, 1977), 4:35–36, 70–75.

37. To take an innocent example, Karl Jaspers, *Man in the Modern Age* (New York: H. Holt and Co., 1933).

38. See the intriguing interpretation of Rudolph Binion, *Hitler among the Germans* (New York: Elsevier, 1976).

39. Geoff Eley, *Reshaping the German Right: Radical Nationalism and Political Change after Bismarck* (New Haven: Yale University Press, 1980), p. 165.

40. Ibid., p. 166.

41. Rosenhaft, "Working-Class Life and Working-Class Politics," and Rudy Koshar, "Away from the Center: Two Recent Studies of Nazism from the Federal Republic," *Social History* 8 (1983): 77–86.

42. Ian Kershaw, *Der Hitler-Mythos: Volksmeinung und Propaganda im Dritten Reich* (Stuttgart: Deutsche Verlagsanstalt, 1980).

43. Ian Kershaw, "The Führer Image and Political Integration: The Popular Conception of Hitler in Bavaria during the Third Reich," in *The "Führer-State,"* ed. Hirschfeld and Kettenacker, pp. 133–61, quoted at p. 141.

44. This is one of the more popular American beliefs about the Third Reich. It identifies National Socialist ideology with, as the saying among students goes, "a kind of P.R." See, for example, E. Hertzstein, *The War that Hitler Won: The Most Infamous Propaganda Campaign in History* (New York: Putnam, 1978); Ernest K. Bramstedt, *Goebbels and National Socialist Propaganda* (East Lansing: Michigan State University Press, 1965).

45. It seems that intellectuals have tended to idolize ideology as soon as it became material practice. See, for example, Project Ideologie-Theorie, *Faschismus und Ideologie* (Berlin: Argument Verlag, 1980). Ideology as material practice is explored by Mary Douglas and Baron Isherwood, *The World of Goods* (New York: Basic Books, 1979).

46. The otherwise fascinating interpretation of Broszat, *The Hitler State*, falls short in this respect.

47. Carl Schmitt, *Staat, Bewegung, Volk. Die Dreigliederung der politischen Einheit* (Hamburg: Hanseatische Verlagsanstalt, 1933).
48. Some of the best examples of this kind of study are Timothy W. Mason, *Arbeiterklasse und Volksgemeinschaft. Dokumente und Materialen zur deutschen Arbeiterpolitik, 1936–1939* (Opladen: Westdeutscher Verlag, 1975); Martin Broszat, et al., eds., *Bayern in der NS-Zeit*, 4 vols. (Munich: Oldenbourg, 1978–81).
49. Claudia Koonz, "Lebensraum for Women inside the Third Reich." (Paper presented at the Colloquium "The Rise of Nazism 1929–1936," Center for European Studies, Harvard University, March 1983).
50. Jill Stephenson, *Women in Nazi Society* (London: Croom Helm, 1975); Doerte Winkler, *Frauenarbeit im Dritten Reich* (Hamburg: Hoffmann und Campe, 1977); *Der alltägliche Faschismus. Frauen im Dritten Reich* (Berlin: J. W. Dietz Nachf., 1981); Timothy Mason, "Women in Germany, 1925–1940: Family, Welfare, and Work," *History Workshop* 1 (1976): 74–113 and 2 (1976): 5–32. See also the reproduction of paintings in Georg Bussmann, ed., *Betrifft Reaktionen. Anlass Kunst im Dritten Reich. Dokumente der Unterwerfung* (Frankfurt: Frankfurter Kunstverein, 1974).
51. See note 39.
52. Most clearly stated in the essay of Andreas Hillgruber, "Die Endlösung und das deutsche Ostmoerium als Kernstück des rassenideologischen Programms des Nationalsozialismus," in *Hitler, Deutschland und die Mächte*, ed. Manfred Funke (Düsseldorf: Droste, 1976), pp. 94–116.
53. Michael Geyer, *Aufrüstung oder Sichererheit. Die Reichswehr in der Krise der Machtpolitik* (Weisbaden: Steiner, 1980), pp. 436–38.
54. Heinrich August Winkler, "Der entbehrliche Stand. Zur Mittelstandspolitik im Dritten Reich," *Archiv für Sozialgeschichte* 17 (1977): 1–40. See, however, Adelheid von Saldern, *Mittelstand im Dritten Reich: Handwerker, Einzelhändler, Bauern* (Frankfurt and New York: Campus, 1979).
55. Uwe Adam, *Judenpolitik im Dritten Reich* (Düsseldorf: Droste, 1972); George L. Mosse, *Toward a Final Solution: A History of European Racism* (New York: Howard Fertig, 1978); Fred Weinstein, *The Dynamics of Nazism: Leadership, Ideology, and the Holocaust* (New York: Academic Press, 1980).
56. This point has first been advanced by Hannah Arendt, *The Origins of Totalitarianism* (New York: Harcourt, Brace, and World, 1968).
57. See Wilhelm Deist, et. al., *Ursachen und Voraussetzungen der deutschen Kriegspolitik* (Stuttgart: Deutsche Verlagsanstalt, 1979).
58. Arthur Schweitzer, *Big Business in the Third Reich*, pp. 110–238.
59. Wilhelm Deist, *The Wehrmacht and German Rearmament* (London: MacMillan, 1981).
60. John W. Baird, *The Mythical World of Nazi Propaganda 1939 to 1945* (Minneapolis: University of Minnesota Press, 1974); Fritz Sänger, *Politik der Täuschungen* (Wien: Molden, 1975).
61. Bernice Carroll, *Design for Total War: Arms and Economics in the Third Reich* (Den Haag: Mouton, 1968); Fritz Blaich, "Wirtschaftspolitik und Wirtschaftsverfassung im Dritten Reich," *Aus Politik und Zeitgeschichte*, February 20, 1971, pp. 3–18.
62. Dietmar Petzina, *Autarkiepolitik im Dritten Reich. Der Nationalsozial-*

istische Vierjahresplan (Stuttgart: Deutsche Verlagsanstalt, 1968). The following interpretation differs considerably from the standard one that there was a major shift to "full fascism" in 1936.

63. Klaus-Jürgen Müller, *Armee, Politik und Gesellschaft in Deutschland 1933– 1945* (Paderborn: Schöningh, 1979), pp. 11–50; Michael Geyer, "Rüstungsbeschleunigung und Inflation; Zur Inflationsdenkschrift des Oberkommandos der Wehrmacht vom November 1938," *Militärgeschichtliche Mitteilungen* 2 (1981): 121–86.

64. The best analysis of the military is Klaus-Jürgen Müller, *General Ludwig Beck; Studien und Dokumente zur politisch-militärischen Vostellungswelt und Tätigkeit des Generalstabschefs des deutschen Heeres 1933–1938* (Boppard: Boldt, 1980). Studies on industry and banking are missing.

65. Klaus Hildebrand, "Innenpolitsche Antriebskräfte der nationalsozialistischen Aussenpolitik," in *Nationalsozialistische Aussenpolitik*, ed. Wolfgang Michalka (Darmstadt: Wissenschaftliche Buchgesellschaft, 1978).

66. Ian Kershaw, *Popular Opinion and Political Dissent in the Third Reich; Bavaria 1933–1945* (Oxford: Clarendon Press, 1983).

67. W. Buchholtz, "Die nationalsozialistische Gemeinschaft 'Kraft durch Freude'; Freizeitgestaltung und Arbeiterschaft im Dritten Reich" (Ph.D. diss., Munich, 1976); Timothy W. Mason, "The Workers' Opposition in Nazi Germany," *History Workshop* 11 (1981): 120–37.

68. Mason, *Arbeiterklasse*, provides a host of documents.

69. Gerhard Weinberg, "The German Generals and the Outbreak of War," in *General Staffs and Diplomacy before the Second World War*, ed. Adrian Preston (London: Croom Helm, 1978).

CAPITALIST CONFLICT
AND THE STATE
The Making of United States
Military Policy in 1948

Lynn Eden

In the early post–World War II period, the United States made a series of fateful decisions on military policy which greatly limited its ability to raise troops and which, at the same time, laid the foundations of American reliance on nuclear weapons. This essay will examine one critical turning point in this process, the spring of 1948, when the Congress of the United States took action on several important military measures.

In its most important action, Congress defeated the centerpiece of the Truman administration's plan to provide manpower for the military;[1] this measure was known as universal military training, and it would have provided military training for virtually all young men. Its proponents thought universal military training would produce a pool of trained men, which, by being capable of relatively quick and very large-scale mobilization, would act as a deterrent to internal upheaval in Western Europe as well as a deterrent to Soviet political or military moves there. Given presidential determination in the postwar period to build American military power, the massive trained manpower furnished by universal military training provided the single best alternative to the large-scale development of nuclear weapons. Universal military training and nuclear weapons were not mutually exclusive. But the very lack of substantial military manpower was to be an important incentive in developing more, and more powerful, nuclear weapons. With universal military training, the nuclear arms race might have occurred anyway; without it, the nuclear arms race was virtually inevitable.

In examining the defeat of universal military training, two other congressional actions in the spring of 1948 must be examined as well. First, over the objections of the Truman administration, Congress voted for a substantial increase in spending for the procurement of military aircraft. This was a mandate for reliance on nuclear weapons, and provided for an expansion of the basic structure of the air force, whose most important, and most publicized, mission was the ability to deliver the atomic bomb. Importantly, this measure was the legislative device used to defeat universal military training.

Second, Congress cut back from five to two years a proposed authorization for the conscription of selected young men into military service. This measure was a selective service, or draft, measure, and it differed from universal military training. Selective service required conscription into military service, but only a selected portion of the eligible male population was affected by the measure. Universal military training required training for the entire male population of a particular age group, but it was not a conscription measure; one was not obliged to serve in the armed forces. There were advantages and disadvantages to each. Briefly, selective service provided a ready combat force, a force-in-being, to use military parlance. Naturally, this was attractive to the army, but because traditionally selective service was approved only in times of war and only for limited periods, army planners believed that American public opinion probably would not support a continuing peacetime draft. In contrast, they thought that not only was Congress more likely to pass universal military training but that, once passed, the measure would not require as frequent reauthorization. The disadvantage was that universal military training provided only a pool of trained men, not a force-in-being.[2]

Selective service had been proposed by the Truman administration in early 1948 as a stopgap program to raise men for the army until universal military training took full effect. However, once Congress defeated universal military training, the draft became the only source of military manpower, and its importance increased greatly. But Congress authorized the draft for only two years, and its renewal was to be debated in the spring of 1950, shortly before congressional elections. Because election year politics are notoriously partisan and volatile, the measure did not provide a secure source of manpower for the military.

Taken together, the defeat of universal military training, the expanded air force, and the restricted draft greatly limited the ability of the United States to deploy conventional, or nonnuclear, force and in so doing helped lay the foundation for American reliance on nuclear weapons.

On the face of it, these congressional actions are puzzling. They occurred in the heyday of "bipartisanship," when a Republican-led Congress overwhelmingly approved major foreign policy initiatives sought by the Democratic Truman administration. Indeed, it was in this same period that Congress approved the Marshall Plan, a program of massive economic aid to Western Europe, and also approved what was known as the Vandenberg Resolution, which provided the basis for American adherence to the North Atlantic Treaty in 1949. The Marshall Plan and the American military and political commitment to Europe embodied in the evolving North Atlantic Treaty were integral to the administration's overall diplomatic strategy toward Europe. And underpinning this strategy was American military might. According to the Truman administration, the most effective military force in the situation was conventional force, heavily dependent on manpower. Yet it was precisely programs to provide this manpower to the military that Congress defeated in this period.

Thus we must ask: why was the administration able to gain congressional approval for the Marshall Plan and the Vandenberg Resolution, but not for either of its programs to support those measures, universal military training and a five-year authorization for selective service? How did the United States develop a self-contradictory foreign policy in which the diplomatic ends were not fully supported by the military means? To answer this we must understand the goals of key political actors and understand the relationships of power within the executive branch, within Congress, and between those two institutions.

Stated slightly differently, the problem is one of understanding decision making within the state. In non-Marxist analyses, class backgrounds and class interests of political actors are generally ignored. In the analysis that follows, however, I will examine conflict between the leading elements of American capital—those whose priority was international, whom I will call corporate internationalists, and those whose priority was domestic, often with a regional or local focus, whom I will call business nationalists.[3] These two groups represented the parameters of intracapitalist conflict in the period immediately following World War II. These two groups were represented in varying strengths in different parts of the state. In the period under discussion, those oriented toward a system of international capitalism were preponderantly represented within the Truman administration in high-level appointive positions. They largely shaped the administration's priorities and programs. The strength of those whose economic orientation was more domestic than international in scope and who represented more regionally focused sectors of the economy was lodged in the isolationist wing of the Republican party in Congress. The actions of both groups were shaped by considerations of labor, but the working class was not often directly involved in their struggle. Rather, the conflict was over how to ensure best the survival and flourishing of American capitalism. In particular, there was disagreement about what role Europe was expected to play in America's economic future. And, just as these two groups had conflicting notions about the basic requirements of American capitalism, so too they had conflicting conceptions of appropriate American military force. For each, the two were logically related.

Although I will emphasize conflicting class visions in this essay, I will also take into account the political structure of the post–World War II American state and the political maneuvering that occurred within that structure. In contrast to much Marxist literature on the state, I will attempt to follow Theda Skocpol's injunction to give "sufficient weight to state and party organizations as independent determinants of political conflict and outcomes . . . organizations with their own structures, their own histories."[4]

Indeed, it was precisely two such organizations which, along with corporate internationalists and business nationalists, determined United States military policy in the spring of 1948. The military services based their actions on conceptions of interest that developed out of long-standing and separate service traditions. These interests, forged in the heat of intense bureaucratic competition, were relatively insulated from class considerations. And Senator Arthur Vandenberg led the internationalist wing of the Republican party, not on the basis of a consistent class vision, but on the basis of the purely political goal of promoting party unity by bridging competing intraclass interests within the party.

Only by understanding conflicting class visions of major political actors and political structure and process can we comprehend the strange disjuncture that developed by the spring of 1948 between United States economic and political commitments to Europe and United States military capabilities.

Corporate Internationalists

Within the Truman administration, the major voices shaping policy were those oriented toward a system of international capitalism.[5] By 1947, New Dealers from the Roosevelt administration were gone from government, but a number of more conservative Roosevelt appointees remained. These men came predominantly from Wall Street banking firms or from major New York or Washington law firms. Many of them had professional ties with each other, and many were friends. This group included Dean Acheson, David K. E. Bruce, William Clayton, Lewis Douglas, William Draper, Jr., James Forrestal, W. Averell Harriman, Robert Lovett, John J. McCloy, Paul Nitze, and Robert Patterson.

All these men had entered the government within about a six-month period following the fall of France in June, 1940—well before the United States officially entered the war in December 1941—in order to prepare the country for war on the side of the Allies.[6] Of those publicly affiliated with the Democratic party—Acheson, Bruce, Douglas, Forrestal, and Harriman—only Harriman had participated in the New Deal.[7]

It was not a coincidence that Wall Street bankers were heavily represented in appointed positions. As major mobilizers of capital, they were in a strategic location to take a long-range view of the requirements of American capitalism. And, like lawyers, their work involved solving a wide range of complex problems in areas in which they might have little previous knowledge. The ability to think strategically about the economy, as well as the ability to solve large problems on short notice, were extremely useful assets for working in government.[8] Forrestal, Nitze, and Draper came from the aggressive investment banking firm of Dillon, Read. Forrestal had been president; Nitze and Draper vice-presidents under him. Forrestal was secretary of the navy and secretary of defense under Truman; Nitze and Draper both played important roles in the formulation of postwar foreign economic policy. Lovett and Harriman were also Wall Street bankers, partners in the private banking firm of Brown Brothers Harriman. From its inception, Brown Brothers had been heavily involved in merchant banking, especially in financing foreign trade with Europe. Harriman's own background was in investment banking. Lovett was under secretary of state from mid–1947 to 1949; Harriman secretary of commerce and then the top-ranking United States representative to Europe under the Marshall Plan. Bruce came from a background in industry and banking; at one time, he was associated with Harriman's investment banking firm. Bruce was assistant secretary of commerce under Harriman, chief of the Marshall Plan mission in France, and in 1949, United States ambassador to France.[9]

Corporate and international lawyers were also well represented. Patterson and McCloy had been partners in prestigious Wall Street law firms, and Acheson had been partner in a prominent Washington law firm. Patterson was secretary of war from 1945 to 1947, and McCloy was president of the World Bank from 1947 until he became high commissioner for Germany in 1949. Acheson was under secretary of state from 1945 to mid–1947, and then secretary of state from 1949.[10]

Clayton and Douglas had somewhat different backgrounds from the others. Clayton had been the head of Anderson-Clayton, the world's largest cotton factoring firm, with vast international operations. Under Truman, he was under secretary of state for economic affairs. Douglas had been involved in mining and insurance. In 1946 he declined nomination as president of the World Bank after being criticized for his Wall Street connections. In early 1947, Douglas became United States ambassador to Great Britain.[11]

These men came from the very sectors of the economy that historically had close ties with Europe, and especially with Great Britain. As private commercial bankers, they were involved in myriad financial transactions with Europe; as investment bankers, they had profited in selling United States securities abroad, in marketing foreign securities in the United States, and in underwriting securities issued by large domestic corporations, a number of which invested in and exported to Europe. As corporate and international lawyers, they represented large firms with investments and markets in Europe, major commercial and investment banks, and, not infrequently, European governments and clients.

These men saw Europe as the historical linchpin of a system of international capitalism in which the Europeans were important trade partners and provided crucial expertise and financial resources. The Europeans paid for large quantities of United States goods through their sales of goods and services to nations in Latin America and the Far East; these nations in turn supplied the United States, as well as Europe, with raw materials.[12]

Historically, Europe had been the most important market for United States exports, and it continued to be a major market in the postwar period.[13] Closely related was American direct investment in Europe, that is, investment in which United States companies participated in the management of European companies; this investment was undertaken to facilitate access to markets abroad. In many cases, investment in foreign plants facilitated American exports of parts, goods assembled abroad, and capital goods—machinery and products used in the manufacturing process itself. Those companies that participated in the great twentieth-century expansion in direct investment tended to be big, and typically to be large exporters.[14]

The involvement of corporate internationalists in Europe was more than strictly economic; bankers, lawyers, and executives did not simply "do business" with their European counterprts. Business was embedded in dense cultural, institutional, and personal networks. Those doing business with Europeans often went abroad, some from the time they were children, or lived abroad for extended periods of time. They had European friends, and in general had an exposure to the economic and political outlooks of their European counterparts, especially the British. Thus, they took European interests and the changing economic and political situation in Europe very seriously in calculating their own interests and in forming their perceptions of United States interests.

In the view of these men, the fundamental problem confronting the United States in the postwar period was how to maintain war-induced prosperity without the stimulus of war. The immediate problem was how to reconvert the economy to peacetime production, and, in particular, how to minimize the effects of reconversion in war-bloated industries, among them shipbuilding, aircraft production, and machine tool manufacture. The curtailing of large numbers of war-related jobs was inevitable. Only high levels of peacetime production throughout the economy could cushion inevitable dislocation.

Providing jobs for those displaced by the curtailing of war industries was part of a larger problem of postwar employment and economic growth. The employment problem was formidable. It was estimated that after the war seven to ten million more jobs would have to be provided than were available in 1940, the year of highest prewar employment.[15] There was general consensus among businessmen from all sectors of the economy that high levels of peacetime employment should be achieved and maintained by private economic expansion. Provision of jobs by government was to be kept to a minimum, as was government planning and regulation which cut into the profits and prerogatives of private capital.[16]

Although it was understood that the predominant market for American businessmen would be the domestic one, it is not surprising that internationally oriented bankers, lawyers, and corporate executives thought foreign markets, particularly the revival of European markets, and unfettered foreign investment opportunities crucial to a prosperous American economy.[17] It was not that these men thought the United States could not survive without foreign markets; rather, they wished to avoid the radical domestic readjustments that would be necessary without them. In a discussion bordering on understatement, Averell Harriman said,

> I am not suggesting that the United States could not endure the loss of European markets. However, production of many industrial and agricultural products in this country and in many other countries has developed based on the participation of Europe in international multilateral trade. The decline of Europe would require far-reaching readjustments of agricultural and industrial production and distribution in this country. It might well affect our ability to obtain needed imports and particularly essential raw materials.[18]

For corporate internationalists, foreign trade offered essential alleviation of postwar problems of reconversion and employment, and it provided a basis for sustained growth as well. The argument for foreign trade was sometimes phrased in terms of the aggregate effects of exports on the American economy. In the aggregate, 1947 merchandise exports stood at an all-time high, $14.3 billion, and represented approximately 7 percent of the nation's gross national product. This roughly translated into five million jobs,[19] no small number to those concerned with providing seven to ten million new peacetime jobs after the war.

Some argued that export markets were essential to alleviate excess capacity in specific industries. Stacy May, of the National Planning Association, claimed:

> What the United States will be able to produce most advantageously after the war happens to be what the larger part of the war-riddled and ill-equipped world will wish to buy: machines and equipment to rebuild

destroyed or deteriorated factories and to provide more fruitful employment for the world's manpower. Exports can thus provide not only employment, but a period of 5, 10, or 20 years in which the presently distorted industrial structure can be corrected in an orderly and far less painful manner.[20]

Others argued that foreign markets were essential to long-term growth. H. J. Heinz II, president of the food-processing firm, said:

> A businessman has the responsibility of looking ahead and protecting the long-term interest of his business. At present domestic demand is generally in excess of domestic supply; but we must look forward to, and provide for, the time when foreign markets and foreign trade will be the key to that marginal production and employment which means the difference between good and bad times in our own country.[21]

Despite the corporate internationalists' belief in the desirability of foreign markets, by 1947 it became clear that these markets could not be sustained; the Europeans simply were not producing enough to pay for high levels of United States exports on a continuing basis. The European inability to pay for these exports would not only directly threaten major sectors of the American economy, but would also threaten the viability of the entire international capitalist system, in which Europe was a vital link.

The corporate internationalists envisaged two lines of solution, one economic and the other military. Both were designed to promote a politically and economically stable capitalist Europe. The crux of the economic solution was that Europe had to increase its exports of goods and services to the United States and other countries. This was the basis of the Marshall Plan, a program of massive American economic aid designed to increase European productivity, first formulated in the early spring of 1947. As Harriman put it forthrightly in his testimony supporting the Marshall Plan: "We seek the recovery of Europe's industrial productivity so that she may be able to sell abroad in payment for what she needs to buy abroad. To be sure, there will be more competition for certain of our products. There will, however, be bigger and sounder markets in Europe and elsewhere."[22]

There was a political dimension to this economic assistance. In the words of Lewis Douglas, United States ambassador to Great Britain, "capital, private capital, does not seek investment when political conditions are unstable."[23] The political instability that corporate internationalists feared was, in large part, the result of the political and economic strength of the organized Left, especially in France and Italy. In order to staunch the flight of capital from European countries, particularly from

France, as well as to encourage new private investment from European and foreign sources, demands for wages and social programs would have to be contained, and the danger of Left coalitions of communists and socialists gaining national power foreclosed. The vast infusion of funds furnished by the Marshall Plan, as well as the American political commitment to European capitalists implicit in the plan, provided a basis for containing the Left and hence for encouraging private investment and capitalist recovery. Lewis Douglas put it this way:

> Now, one of the great purposes as I understand it of the European recovery program [the Marshall Plan] is to provide the sinews, the financial sinews, with which political stability can be restored in Western Europe, and with the restoration of political stability progressing parallel with economic stability, the creation of the environment which capital seeks will follows.[24]

But by itself economic aid was not sufficient to stabilize the political and economic situation in Europe. A second element of the internationalists' solution was military commitment. This meant, first, stating American willingness to intervene if necessary in Europe, as expressed in the Vandenberg Resolution of 1948 and the North Atlantic Treaty of 1949, and second, enhancing American military capabilities to intervene. In a speech before the National Foreign Trade Convention, John J. McCloy explained in broad terms the relationship between the economic and political situation in Europe and the American military commitment to Europe.

> The prevailing lack of confidence in European currencies is perhaps most dramatically reflected in the flight of capital now going on. The causes, of course, are both political and economic. There can be no financial stability in the absence of sound financial policies, but there can also be no financial stability without confidence on the part of the people in the political future of their country. This explains why the problem of military guarantees, now so widely discussed, has such direct and vital economic implications.[25]

Let us look more closely at the assumptions embedded in this statement. Those committed to rebuilding an internationally oriented capitalist Europe perceived three major problems undermining the confidence of European elites in the political futures of their countries. First, both the French and Italians were concerned about the strength of the Left and internal political instability. Second, corporate internationalists believed the capitalist reconstruction of at least the western zones of Germany imperative to the general resurrection of capitalism in Europe.

But to go ahead with this, French fears about potential German political and military power would have to be calmed. And third, Europeans voiced some fear of the possibility of a Russian invasion, particularly in the event of massive political upheaval in Western Europe.

In general, corporate internationalists believed that the American military capabilities that would best meet European fears were an occupation troop presence in Germany for the near future, and a long-term program of universal military training, which would provide large numbers of trained men who, in the event of emergency, could be drafted and quickly sent to Europe. There was some division among corporate internationalists as to whether universal military training or selective service was the more effective foundation for conventional force. However, because the highly respected army chief of staff during World War II and secretary of state in 1947 and 1948, George Marshall, championed universal military training, and because there was strong organizational support as well for such a measure, universal military training was put forward as the administration's major proposal and generally received the support of corporate internationalists.[26]

Men such as Forrestal and McCloy also wanted an American atomic weapons capability to deter any possibility of a Soviet invasion of Western Europe, or to respond should it occur, but they understood that such weapons could not guarantee internal political stability in Western Europe, nor could they guarantee French safety against Germany, both more pressing problems than the hypothetical possibility of a Soviet invasion. In the event of a communist electoral victory followed by civil war or massive strikes or uprisings in Western Europe, was the United States to drop atomic weapons on the capitals of Western Europe? Nuke Moscow? Only conventional force could be used, and only the threat of using such force was fully credible. When, in the spring of 1948, the choice had to be made between supporting universal military training or expanding the air force, Secretary of Defense Forrestal, and others oriented toward a system of international capitalism, spoke resolutely for universal military training. They also supported the Truman administration's proposal for a five-year authorization for selective service to provide military manpower until universal military training took full effect.

Business Nationalists

Those oriented toward a more domestically focused capitalism had their greatest strength in the isolationist wing of the Republican party in Congress. Isolationists were important in both the House and Senate, but because the most important party leaders were in the Senate, I will only discuss the Senate. The isolationist Republicans comprised a bloc of approximately twenty senators, mainly from the midwest and mountain states, who opposed the Truman administration on both its economic and military programs. These men included, among others, Brooks of Illinois, Butler of Nebraska, Dworshak of Idaho, Ecton of Montana, Kem of Missouri, McCarthy of Wisconsin, Malone of Nevada, Moore of Oklahoma, Revercomb of West Virginia, Taft of Ohio, Watkins of Utah, Wherry of Nebraska, Williams of Delaware, and Wilson of Iowa.

These men came from areas that looked mainly to the home market for prosperity, saw United States agricultural and industrial exports exacerbating shortages at home, and in some cases, the wool industry being the most notable example, saw themselves threatened by foreign imports.[27] A number of these senators came from the same backgrounds as those for whom they spoke—they were engaged in relatively small, if prosperous, business enterprises which sold to local or regional markets. Kenneth Wherry from Nebraska, for example, the voluble Republican party whip, was known as "Lightning Ken" for his dazzling salesmanship; his family business included an automobile agency, a furniture store, and a funeral parlor. In addition, Wherry practiced law. Hugh Butler, also from Nebraska, was co-owner of a grain mill and was active in the national trade association of grain and feed dealers. Homer Capehart from Indiana made his fortune selling jukeboxes (and attributed his technique to a book called *The Salesology of the Butter-kist Popcorn and Peanut Machines*).[28]

In the United States Senate, Robert Taft, from Ohio, was the Republican party spokesman on domestic policy. He was not the party spokesman on foreign policy, but as the most influential member of the isolationist bloc, his voice could not be ignored. The son of a United States president, Taft's background was considerably more cosmopolitan than those of other isolationists, and on matters of foreign policy he was among the most moderate of them.[29] Despite differences in tone and focus of argument, Taft articulated more fully and carefully than any of the other isolationists the views to which they all generally subscribed, and it is through him that we may best understand the logic of isolationist thought.

Taft's approach to the economic problems facing the country in the postwar era was not a macroeconomic one. He did not worry about the specific number of jobs to be provided in the postwar era, nor concern himself with the sectoral economic adjustments that would be necessary in the face of reconversion. Rather, Taft wanted a return to the qualities that had provided the foundation of American invention and entrepreneurship. For him, these qualities were embodied in the concept of liberty: "At home, liberty is the basis of the success which we have achieved. Our standard of living was brought about by the initiative, the genius, the daring, and the inspired hard work of our people. These qualities could only have come into existence through liberty of thought and liberty of action."[30] Liberty also meant local self-reliance, the ability of "states and localities to rule themselves without orders from Washington." And it meant restraining the increasing concentration of power at the federal level: "We must draft our measures without delegating unrestrained authority to Federal bureaucrats so that the liberty which men have may be protected."[31]

For Taft, the major postwar problem was to unshackle the citizenry and economy from the pernicious effects of the New Deal. He wanted to free the creative forces of the American people by encouraging small business initiative, lessening the power of organized labor, reducing government regulation and spending, and lowering taxes.[32] Although it is fair to characterize Taft as fiscally conservative when it came to government spending, this does not wholly characterize his position. He *was* fiscally conservative, but then, so was President Truman. However, unlike Truman, Taft was less willing to support social welfare programs. While Truman wanted to cap federal spending and maintain current tax levels to control inflation, Taft wanted to slash federal spending and cut taxes to free up capital.

Taft's vision was one in which the American economy was largely self-contained. Given the right domestic conditions, economic growth would be achieved primarily within the home market; foreign trade was not the key to American prosperity. In arguing against the American loan to Britain in 1946, Taft said, "Foreign trade by this country . . . can never be the key to our prosperity. The home market must be our reliance to that end. It is now our reliance, and it must continue to be."[33] Whereas corporate internationalists thought it important to raise imports into the United States in order to maintain current and future levels of United States exports, Taft favored limiting imports into the United States and argued that the postwar volume of American exports was "dangerous" and "abnormal."[34]

Not surprisingly, Taft did not believe in the efficacy of foreign lending. Further, he was concerned that the high levels of government spending required for such lending would necessitate continued high levels of taxation,[35] which, of course, he opposed. Taft did not oppose all foreign loans, but he consistently tried to scale down the amounts involved. Taft voted against the loan to Britain in 1946 and for weakening amendments to the Marshall Plan. He did ultimately vote for the Marshall Plan on the grounds that restoring the economic strength of Europe would help Europe resist communism, but this was a limited commitment on his part. Taft did not see European capitalism as necessary to the viability of American capitalism, and he frequently saw negative effects to the American economy in allowing too high levels of imports, exports, and foreign aid.

Taft's views on military policy fit like a glove on the hand of his political and economic assumptions. He strongly and consistently opposed all postwar plans for universal military training. First, Taft saw "universal military training [as] contrary to the whole concept of American liberty." He argued, "It is hard to think of any more drastic limitation of personal freedom than to permit the state to take boys from their homes, their education, or their chosen occupations and subject them for a year to the arbitrary direction of some military officer, and indoctrination courses prepared by some ideological bureau in the War Department."[36] Second, Taft believed that American military force was not to be used to aid American diplomatic goals abroad but only for continental defense: "Above all, I believe we must insist constantly that the problem we have to meet is a problem of defense. The American people do not want to become imperialists. They do not want a force prepared at any moment to attack every other nation in the world. . . . We cannot yearn for any military force . . . prepared at the drop of a hat to march around the world."[37] And finally, Taft argued that universal military training was of no military value for defense. Against the only enemy he contemplated, Russia, he argued that ground forces had never been successfully used in the past, nor, given geography, could they be in the future.[38]

Instead, Taft favored building up the air force, which he saw as less onerous to the population and tailored for defending the United States rather than for meddling in European or world politics. Taft believed that the next war would be won by the country that controlled the air: "Only by means of the air may modern weapons be carried into final effect against political enemies. . . . If we do retain control of the air it is difficult to see how anyone can possibly attack the United States."[39]

Taft consistently spoke out against universal military training in the early postwar years. Throughout the spring of 1948, he explicitly linked his opposition to universal military training with his advocacy for a buildup of the air force.[40] It was a tactic that was to prove effective. Although Taft did not like a peacetime draft, he found a highly limited one less objectionable than universal military training. In 1948 he voted for the two-year authorization for selective service.

The American State: Structure and Process

The making of military policy in the spring of 1948 involved more than corporate internationalists and Taft Republicans. More broadly, it involved the president and his representatives from the executive branch, collectively known as the administration, who proposed legislation regarding military policy and who were also responsible for the execution of approved legislation, and it involved Congress, which authorized legislation and appropriated funds. Neither the administration nor Congress were monolithic organizations in their dealings with one another. It is only by understanding the fault lines of conflict within the administration and Congress, and the alliances formed among factions of both, that we can understand the inconsistencies in American foreign policy that developed in the spring of 1948.

Executive Branch

Presidential power had never been greater than when Harry S. Truman inherited the office of the president in 1945. Not only had the years of domestic crisis and world war under Roosevelt expanded enormously the domestic scope of presidential power, consolidating fifty years of gradual growth,[41] but the world war, in rendering the United States the most powerful nation on earth, further enhanced the power of the president, whose constitutional mandate in the realm of foreign affairs was very far-reaching.[42]

Despite the power of his office, Truman's tenure in it was precarious, especially after the 1946 congressional elections gave the Republicans control of both houses of Congress for the first time since 1928. Facing a presidential election he was expected to lose in November, 1948, Truman was considered, if not quite a lame duck, a very weak one. This mitigated the unprecedented power he held, particularly since presidential power is, as Richard Neustadt has observed, largely persuasive.[43]

Nonetheless, Truman was not without persuasive power. Among other things, he could make speeches to the nation, urging the public to influence Congress, he could frequently rely on supporters within Congress to present his case, and he could seek to persuade Congress with the testimony of experts. The most important experts Truman used in persuading Congress on issues of military policy, were, not surprisingly, his own military spokesmen: the Joint Chiefs of Staff; the civilian secretaries of the army, navy, and air force; and the civilian secretary of defense. To advance the president's position, these men had to agree with him publicly and to speak with one voice.

It was division among the military that proved critical to the administration's undoing in the spring of 1948. In the early postwar years, the military was riven with internal conflict. Interservice conflict frequently focused on who got what share of the military budget. Decisions about the budget defined the ability of each service to determine the capabilities it would have in the event of war. Each service arrived at this determination on the basis of its own strategic worldview, and strategic understandings differed by service and were core to the identity of each. Thus, conflicts among the military, although often fought on the terrain of the military budget, were really about service prerogative, service strategy, and even service identity; interservice conflict was not so much about the present allocation of funds as about the future relationship of the services to each other. The enormity of the stakes explains the ferocity of the struggle.

Conflict over the budget inevitably entailed conflict over the making of war plans to fight World War III. In these plans, it was envisaged that the Russians would invade Western Europe and that the United States would respond first with a strategic atomic bombing attack on the military and industrial infrastructure of the Soviet Union, and then follow up with a massive conventional attack by naval and ground forces to retake Western Europe. This, very broadly, was the basic plan that had been developed by the spring of 1948, and which bore the apposite code name BROILER.[44] Although all the services agreed that a strategic bombing attack on the Soviet Union was to be the first order of business in the event of World War III, they disagreed about how efficacious strategic bombing would be, and about how much of the military budget should be accorded this mission. The air force believed that nothing else would be necessary to force a Soviet surrender and lobbied hard for seventy air groups, a goal first formulated by air force planners in August, 1945, and considered by them essential to carry out an effective strategic air attack.[45] In January, 1948, the air force received a boost in the report of the President's Air Policy Commission, known as the Finletter Commission, which advocated a seventy-group air force as essential to national security. Truman ignored the recommendations. Congress, however, did not. In the spring of 1948, the air force had fifty-five air groups, many of them at less than full strength. Although the army did not dispute the priority of the strategic bombing attack, it was certain that a war to retake Europe would, in former army chief of staff George Marshall's words, "end in the mud and on the ground"[46] and would require massive manpower. The navy had the least faith in air force plans for strategic bombing and, not surprisingly, placed highest priority on naval missions.

Although lines of conflict generally broke down with the army and air force on one side and the navy on the other, in the spring of 1948 the major conflict was between the army and the air force—the army advocating universal military training and selective service, and the air force, though paying lip service to these proposals, pressing for increases in aircraft procurement that would provide the basis for a seventy-group force. The navy stood to gain some increase in the strength of its fighter plane force from increased aircraft procurement, but it did not stand to gain all that much, particularly in comparison to the air force. The navy had no reason to get deeply involved in this fight, and did not.

There was no easy way to resolve these conflicts among the military. The institution of the Joint Chiefs of Staff was relatively new, without established procedures for resolving internal conflicts, and the secretary of defense, James Forrestal, generally refused to resolve the chiefs' disagreements for them. In addition, because so little precedent had been established, decisions taken in the early postwar period would become the basis of future procedure, making the stakes all the higher, and agreement all the more difficult to reach. In such an undefined situation, daring tactics could be risked and used to great effect. In particular, the air force went beyond the usual channels of communication with the secretary of defense and the president and, breaking dramatically with the administration, forged an alliance with the isolationists in Congress that would have far-reaching consequences for the administration's military program.

Congress

Congress was the other branch of the state crucial to the making of military policy. The House of Representatives and the Senate of the United States are publicly elected, extremely busy, large, collegial bodies. Election to Congress, and mobilization within Congress, is organized through political parties. Party leaders in Congress mobilize congressional votes by articulating positions that appear to be consonant with overall party philosophy, exhorting members to be loyal to the party, and mixing implicit or explicit promises—including perquisites of various sorts and resources that facilitate reelection—with implicit or explicit threats. In 1947 and 1948, both houses of Congress were controlled by the Republicans, and for this reason the structure of Republican party leadership is more important to understand than that of the Democrats. For Truman to be successful, he had to work closely with the leadership of the Republican party. Indeed, to have any chance of success he required nothing less than the imprimatur of Republican sponsorship. On the face of it, this would not appear to be easy to obtain. Ironically, Truman could generally count on the loyalties of Democrats when he had strong Republican support. When he did not securely command Republican votes, however, his own party could act in unpredictable ways.

In this period there was an unusual concentration of power in the Senate. Indeed, the reins of Republican party power were held by just two men: Senator Robert Taft, the acknowledged spokesman for the party on domestic policy and the most articulate Republican opponent of Truman's foreign policy; and Senator Arthur Vandenberg, from Michigan, chairman of the Senate Committee on Foreign Relations, who, in the postwar period, became a proponent of a cautious but committed internationalism, working closely with the Truman administration on a variety of foreign policy programs in what was called "bipartisan" cooperation. These men controlled opposing blocs within the Republican party, and their relationship to each other was decisive in determining the outcomes of legislative proposals.

Why was power so concentrated in the Senate? Vandenberg, who first came to the Senate in 1928, and Taft, elected in 1938, both had great seniority in a party that had been decimated by Franklin Roosevelt's popularity and was just beginning to rebuild substantially with the 1946 elections. Also, both men were potential contenders for the presidency in 1948, and the only contenders from Congress. Taft was an announced candidate; Vandenberg was not, but the possibility of his candidacy could not be dismissed. In a year in which it was expected that the Republicans would win the White House, the possible candidacy of Taft or Vandenberg was taken very seriously by the two men in governing their relationship to each other.[47]

We have seen the beliefs of Robert Taft and the bloc he led; it is more difficult to characterize the internationalist wing of the Republican party led by Arthur Vandenberg. Vandenberg, and the votes he commanded, seemed more dominated by pragmatism than conviction. His bipartisan support seemed to rest, in historian John Morton Blum's phrase, "on the blandness, the soft consensus of senatorial internationalism."[48]

This soft consensus can be understood as the result of the precarious coalition Vandenberg held together. On the one hand, he spoke for powerful Republican corporate international interests, the most influential spokesman of whom was John Foster Dulles, senior partner at Sullivan and Cromwell, one of Wall Street's leading law firms. Dulles and Vandenberg worked closely together. That the Republicans were expected to win the presidential election in November, 1948, could only have reinforced the seriousness with which these interests were regarded in the Senate. Vandenberg supported a variety of internationally oriented legislation, the most important of which were the Marshall Plan, which Vandenberg brilliantly ushered through the Senate, and the Vandenberg Resolution.

On the other hand, Vandenberg was confronted with building Republican support for programs opposed by the powerful Taft wing of the party. Although Vandenberg prevailed on the final votes on legislation that he sponsored, often with handsome majorities, the Taft wing frequently commanded almost half of Republican party votes on amendments modifying Vandenberg's legislation.

Thus, the power of the Taft wing was a heavy constraint on Vandenberg. If Vandenberg pushed too hard, he could provoke an open break with Taft himself and the resulting party disarray would be a severe liability in the upcoming elections. Instead, in the words of Vandenberg's son, "a tacit and informal understanding between Vandenberg and Senator Taft developed. . . . There were differences between the two leaders at this time, such as the scope of the Marshall Plan aid, but both men sought to minimize them and avoid direct conflict."[49] Although Taft frequently challenged Vandenberg on foreign policy issues, through speeches, pressure during committee hearings, and by sponsoring or supporting weakening amendments once legislation reached the floor, he did not try to obstruct legislation once passage was inevitable. Taft sometimes went along with Vandenberg on final votes and, against later onslaughts by the House, even supported legislation he had previously tried to weaken.

The price Vandenberg paid for Taft's cooperation was threefold. First, he did not challenge Taft's leadership on domestic issues. Second, he trimmed foreign policy legislation to make it more palatable to the Taft wing, a complicated and intricate process which required much political skill, especially since Vandenberg often kept the heart of the legislation intact. Third, Vandenberg very carefully picked his foreign policy issues. In late March, 1948, Vandenberg still had not secured full congressional approval of the Marshall Plan; the House had yet to authorize it, and neither house had yet voted on appropriations for it. Further, Vandenberg would soon begin working on the legislation that became known as the Vandenberg Resolution. These pieces of legislation were his main concern. In order not to jeopardize their chances of passage, Vandenberg was silent on universal military training, a measure deeply opposed by Taft, although Vandenberg's support for it would have been consistent with his other foreign policy positions. Nor did Vandenberg challenge Taft's arguments for expanding the air force.

In sum, on foreign policy issues, Taft could force modification of legislation that Vandenberg sponsored, and he limited the number of issues Vandenberg would speak out on. This dynamic within the Republican party explains the strong Republican counterpoint led by Taft to the Truman administration's military programs. It was this opposition, in conjunction with the actions of the air force, that accounts for the failure of the administration's proposals.

Political Process

On March 17, 1948, President Truman urged Congress to pass the Marshall Plan, universal military training, and a temporary selective service measure. The request for selective service was added at the end of the speech-drafting process, after study by the Joint Chiefs of Staff indicated that the training program could not quickly enough bring troop strength up to that required to implement the recently approved emergency war plan, BROILER, and that a temporary, or "stopgap" selective service measure would be necessary until universal military training had been in effect long enough to produce sufficient volunteers.[50] In the previous two years, the administration had avoided campaigning concurrently for selective service and universal military training, thinking that requesting the draft measure would weaken chances for passage of the training legislation. Truman's request at this time for both measures did not enhance the chances for passage of universal military training, but neither was it the decisive factor that killed it; it seems probable that even if selective service had not been proposed by the administration at this time, Congress, for reasons to be discussed below, would have defeated the training measure anyway.

In his speech, the president did not request additional aircraft procurement, nor did he envisage an air force larger than the current fifty-five groups. Given the desire on the parts of both the president and Congress to keep a tight lid on federal spending, a substantial increase in spending for aircraft procurement would, in all likelihood, mean a weakening of congressional support for universal military training, a program admittedly expensive.

The question was whether the Taft Republicans, guided by a philosophy of business nationalism, could build sufficient support for expanding the air force to seventy groups, with a concomitant increase in aircraft procurement, to crowd universal military training off the congressional agenda and weaken support for selective service.

On the face of it, the Taft Republicans had some reason to believe they could be successful. First, the committee that would guide the manpower legislation through the Senate was not the Committee on Foreign Relations, headed by Senator Arthur Vandenberg, but the Committee on Armed Services, headed by the much less influential Republican from South Dakota, Senator Chan Gurney. Unlike Vandenberg, Gurney could not garner votes on the strength of his endorsement, nor did he have Vandenberg's ability to develop compromises that preserved the essence of legislation. Second, because Vandenberg was not directly involved in preparing the manpower legislation, and because Vandenberg was deeply involved in shaping other legislation, he remained silent on the issue of universal military training, thus enhancing Taft's ability to rally support for a buildup of the air force and, at the same time, rally opposition to universal military training. Third, business nationalists were influential in the House as well as in the Senate. Indeed, as was the case with the Marshall Plan, opposition to the administration's military programs was stronger in the House than in the Senate. The Republican chairman of the House Committee on Rules had kept the universal military training legislation bottled up in committee since July, 1947, and there was no indication he would change his mind. He also opposed passage of selective service.[51]

Yet, at first, the Truman administration also had reason to believe it could win the congressional battle. The administration had been successful in all its other foreign policy legislation, and its military requests certainly were consistent with its overall plans to stabilize Europe. Although Senator Chan Gurney did not have the stature of Senator Arthur Vandenberg, Gurney was an internationalist and a supporter of universal military training. "Personally, I am for it—as strong as horse radish" he had said on one occasion.[52] Further, the Senate Committee on Armed Services was considered generally "friendly" to the administration's military manpower proposals. The committee was an important one, and it would not have been unreasonable for the administration to expect that the committee's strong endorsement would be capable of overcoming opposition from other congressional quarters. After all, the Taft wing had vociferously opposed other foreign policy legislation, such as the Marshall Plan, to little ultimate effect, and the administration need not have supposed that its opposition in this case would be fatal. And, with sufficient pressure from Senate Republican leadership, House leadership could be forced to give way, which would have greatly increased the chances that the House would pass the administration's military manpower proposals.

However, if the Truman administration could have predicted opposition from business nationalists in the Senate and House to its military manpower programs, it could not have anticipated the undeniably audacious actions of the air force, without which Taft's opposition would likely not have been fatal.

Beginning in late March, the air force publicly defected from the administration's plan by advocating a seventy-group air force, and later went so far as to state that seventy groups should have priority over universal military training.[53] Without the defection of the air force, it is possible that Gurney could have rallied internationalist forces to pass universal military training over Taft's opposition. But as the support for the air force began to build in Congress, Gurney became unable to control the agenda of his committee. On April 6, the committee was reported to "feel the question of the size of the air force must be decided before going ahead with the draft and UMT."[54] The next day the secretary of the air force, Stuart Symington, and two air force generals spoke in closed session before the committee; it was reported that "when this meeting ended it appeared that sudden changes of mind had occurred within the Senate group."[55] With the administration unable to sway the Senate Committee on Armed Services, it lost not only Republican support it had commanded in other foreign policy legislation, but, given that it was an election year, Democratic votes it otherwise would have commanded as well. Additional appropriations for the air force were voted by both houses by vast bipartisan margins. Some sentiment remained in the Senate Committee on Armed Services for universal military training and for a five-year authorization for selective service, and the committee continued to consider both manpower measures. But the Senate did not have the strong leadership that could have turned the tide in the Senate and then pressured House leadership to bend to the Senate's will. Indeed, the intransigence of House leadership was so strong that the Senate committee finally dropped any provision for universal military training. Finally, following the lead of the House, the Senate reduced authorization of the selective service measure from five to two years.[56]

This situation stands in marked contrast to the situation with the Marshall Plan when, first, Vandenberg, not Gurney, led the fight for the administration; second, Taft ultimately deferred to Vandenberg and even joined him in successfully pressuring the House to acquiesce to the will of the Senate; and third, there was no defection among administration spokesmen from the president's proposals.

The result was a lopsided foreign policy in which Congress, under Vandenberg's leadership, passed the Marshall Plan and the Vandenberg Resolution, both linchpins of the corporate internationalists' program for Europe, and at the same time, under Taft's leadership in alliance with the air force, defeated the administration's military manpower programs meant to underpin American foreign policy in Europe.

The defeat of universal military training, the weakening of selective service, and the decision to fund additional aircraft procurement contributed to a larger and extraordinarily secret process of building the United States military establishment on a foundation dependent on nuclear weapons. By blocking the option of universal military training and providing only a weak selective service measure, Congress gave notice to the Truman administration that it could not rely on the implicit threat of intervention with massive conventional force to enforce its foreign policy in Europe. This left the administration in a dilemma: either it could develop nuclear weapons, which, because of their very destructiveness, were far less credible than conventional force as a threat to help maintain political order in Western Europe, or it could support its policies in Europe with virtually no military force at all. On the assumption that too big a stick was better than none at all, the administration, not surprisingly, opted for the development of nuclear force.

In the late 1940s and in early 1950, decisions were made regarding military strategy, air force capabilities, and the numbers and kinds of bombs in the nuclear arsenal that deemphasized conventional military capabilities and laid stress on nuclear ones. The single most important decision of this period was the decision in early 1950 to develop the hydrogen bomb. With the overall increases in military spending that accompanied the Korean War, the development of nuclear weapons continued apace, and then accelerated under succeeding presidential administrations. Unfortunately, such development continues today.

Conclusion

Military policy, like virtually all state policy, must be understood in the context of conflicting interests between classes and within classes. Military policy is always a means to some end; an explanation of it cannot simply describe conflicting military strategies but must show how those strategies relate to larger class-based visions of the world. In 1948, the relevant visions to which military strategy must be related were those of corporate internationalists and business nationalists.

However, the state is not a neutral scale that weighs class interest and awards victory to the class, or portion of a class, represented in greater measure. First, the structure of the state itself gives rise to interests that articulate with, but are independent of, class. In the making of military policy in 1948, the interests of two organizations within the state stand out. The military's interest lay in developing the capabilities and prerogatives it thought necessary to prepare to fight in a future war. But conceptions of the military's interest divided along service lines. All three services ostensibly supported the Truman administration's recommendations for universal military training and for a five-year authorization for selective service. However, in a bold and risky move, the air force bolted from the administration's program, giving priority to the building of a seventy-group air force over universal military training. The air force's interests were congruent with the broader class vision of those Republicans in Congress oriented toward business nationalism, for whom a strong air force and weak conventional force meant strong continental defense, internal liberty, and no undue meddling in the affairs of other nations.

Yet, this alliance between the air force and Republican business nationalists cannot by itself explain the defeat of the Truman administration's military programs. We must also understand the interests of the Republican party during this period. Despite deeply felt intraparty conflict, the leaders of the two major factions, Vandenberg and Taft, had an informal understanding that prevented such conflict from destroying the party unity essential for legislative effectiveness and for strength in forthcoming elections. On those issues that Vandenberg chose to take a strong position on, he prevailed, sometimes even gaining Taft's support in the final stages of voting. In exchange, Vandenberg not only framed foreign policy legislation to make it more appealing to Taft and Taft's supporters, but he very carefully chose his issues and allowed Taft to take the lead on other legislation, both domestic and foreign. It was Taft's leadership on military issues in the spring of 1948, in conjunction with the air force's defection from administration policy, that explains the defeat of the administration's military programs in this period.

Besides creating interests distinct from class, there is a second way in which the state plays an independent role in the shaping of historical outcomes and is not a neutral mediator of class interest. State structure—that is, the highly regularized procedures of the state, frequently the legacy of generations of precedent—shapes the possibilities for political action. These procedures are not necessarily neutral with regard to class interests. To mention just two examples, President Truman was required to gain congressional authorization and appropriation for his conventional military manpower requests; this enhanced the role of business nationalists in the making of conventional military policy since their strength in the state was lodged in Congress. And, Congress voted on an issue-by-issue basis, a procedure that allowed for the development of shifting coalitions and inconsistent congressional policy.

Third, state structure shapes not only political action, but political discourse as well. In particular, the frequent requirement that actors from more than one part of the state act together in order to get most things done (neither the military, nor the president, nor Congress could solely determine the military policy issues of 1948) means that diverse class and political interests must be appealed to. In situations in which diverse interests must be pulled together, rhetoric which obscures class differences is far more effective than rhetoric which makes class issues obvious. Class interest is represented within the state, as we have seen, but it is generally obscured by political discourse.

State structure shapes interests that are independent of class and shapes the form and language of political action, but *specific* political outcomes are determined by the political calculations of key actors in concert with those who follow their lead. Two things follow from this. At high levels of policy-making, the understandings and actions of individuals really do matter, not simply because such people represent class or other interests—though we must understand them in that light—but also because such people actively invent the courses of action that make history.

And, political process is not entirely predictable. A highly knowledgeable observer will likely be able to figure out the range of relevant interests and the possibilities for political action in any given situation. But what calculations all relevant political actors will make can only be guessed. If political actors are consistent in striving for political advantage; they are by no means intellectually consistent from issue to issue. One might have supposed that if the Republican party voted to support the diplomatic and foreign economic programs of the corporate internationalists that they would also have supported the corporate internationalists' military programs. Such, obviously, was not the case. President Truman, working closely with Senator Arthur Vandenberg, was able to win congressional support for the diplomatic and economic programs of the corporate internationalists, but when Truman was met by a silent Vandenberg and an obstreperous Taft, whose position was greatly bolstered by the defection of the air force from the administration's program, Truman was unable to gain support for the corporate internationalists' military programs.

In sum, to explain specific historical outcomes, we must examine class interest, political structure, and essentially unpredictable political process.

NOTES

1. Universal military training did not come up for a vote before the full House or Senate. Because of widespread congressional opposition, the measure never made it past committee.

2. Proponents of universal military training favored the measure for other reasons as well. Because it was universal, it spread the burden of military obligation far more widely in the population and was inherently more democratic than selective service. And, it was thought that wide exposure through training would provide enough volunteers to staff a small standing army. Such an army ran with the grain of American political tradition. For an interesting discussion of force-in-being versus training, see James M. Gerhardt, *The Draft and Public Policy, Issues in Military Manpower Procurement 1945–1950* (Columbus: Ohio State University Press, 1971), chaps. 1 and 2. Hanson Baldwin, the influential *New York Times* military correspondent, was among those who were sympathetic to the need for greater conventional force but who opposed universal military training on grounds of ineffectiveness. Baldwin frequently voiced his opposition to universal military training in his newspaper articles. For his relatively early belief in force-in-being, see Council on Foreign Relations, *Conference on Proposals for Postwar Universal Military Training*, March 16–17, 1945, Records of Conferences, vol. 4, Archives of Council on Foreign Relations, New York.

3. These categories roughly correspond with those engaged in large-scale enterprise, and with medium and small businessmen, respectively, mentioned by Ralph Miliband, *The State in Capitalist Society: An Analysis of the Western System of Power* (New York: Basic Books, 1969), p. 157.

4. Theda Skocpol, "Political Response to Capitalist Crisis: Neo-Marxist Theories of the State and the Case of the New Deal," *Politics and Society* 10, no. 3 (1980): 199.

5. The term *corporate internationalists* denotes the same people referred to by Fred Block as *business internationalists*. See Fred L. Block, *The Origins of International Economic Disorder, A Study of United States International*

Monetary Policy from World War II to the Present (Berkeley: University of California Press, 1977), chap. 3.

6. Strictly speaking, David K. E. Bruce was the only exception. However, he was certainly involved in preparing the country for war on the side of the Allies. In 1940 and 1941, he was a delegate to Great Britain for the Red Cross, and in 1941 he helped organize the Office of Strategic Services (OSS), the forerunner to the Central Intelligence Agency (CIA). On recruitment into the government see Henry L. Stimson and McGeorge Bundy, *On Active Service in Peace and War* (New York: Harper and Brothers, 1948), pp. 323–44. Also see John Morton Blum, *V Was for Victory, Politics and American Culture during World War II* (New York: Harvest/HBJ Book, 1970), pp. 119–20.

7. Both Acheson and Douglas had served briefly under Roosevelt, but neither could be considered New Dealers. Harriman had been an administrator of the highly controversial National Recovery Act.

8. I would like to thank William Burr for pointing out the strategic location of Wall Street bankers, and for his generous help with the entire section on corporate internationalists. For the training of Wall Street investment bankers, see my interview with Paul Nitze, January 15, 1980 and William Burr's interview with Paul Nitze, March 5, 1981, both in possession of the author.

9. *Forrestal:* Robert Greenhalgh Albion and Robert Howe Connery, *Forrestal and the Navy* (New York: Columbia University Press, 1962), pp. 2–3; when Forrestal was brought into the government in 1940, he was described in a memo to the president as "the acknowledged leader of your crowd in Wall Street." *Lovett:* see particularly Margaret Case Harriman and John Bainbridge, "Profiles: The Thirteenth Labor of Hercules," pts. 1 and 2, *New Yorker*, November 6, 1943, pp. 30–39; *New Yorker*, November 13, 1943, pp. 29–34. *Harriman:* E. J. Kahn, Jr., "Profiles: Plenipotentiary," pts. 1 and 2, *New Yorker*, May 3, 1952, pp. 41–67; *New Yorker*, May 10, 1952, pp. 36–57. *Brown Brothers Harriman:* John A. Kouwenhoven, *Partners in Banking, An Historical Portrait of a Great Private Bank, Brown Brothers Harriman & Co., 1818–1968* (Garden City: Doubleday and Company, 1968). *Bruce: Current Biography*, 1949 (New York: The H. W. Wilson Co., 1950); also *Current Biography*, 1961.

10. *Patterson: Current Biography*, 1941. *McCloy: Current Biography*, 1947, and Paul Hoffman, *Lions in the Street, the Inside Story of the Great Wall Street Law Firms* (New York: Saturday Review Press, 1973), pp. 10, 81. *Acheson: Current Biography*, 1941, 1947, and Joseph Goulden, *The Superlawyers: The Small and Powerful World of the Great Washington Law Firms* (New York: Weybright and Talley, 1972), pp. 24–29, 44–49.

11. *Clayton: Current Biography*, 1944. *Douglas: Current Biography*, 1947.

12. See testimony by Averell Harriman, U.S. Congress, Senate Committee on Foreign Relations, *Hearings, European Recovery Program*, January 12, 1948, p. 249.

13. For figures see U.S. Bureau of the Census, *Historical Statistics of the United States, Colonial Times to 1957* (Washington, D.C.: U.S. Government Printing Office, 1960), p. 550.

14. Mira Wilkins, *The Maturing of Multinational Enterprise: American Business Abroad from 1914 to 1970* (Cambridge: Harvard University Press, 1974), pp. x, 60–91.

15. *Seven to ten million more jobs:* Council for Economic Development figures given in testimony by Paul Hoffman, U.S. Congress, House Special Committee on Post-War Economic Policy and Planning, *Hearings, Post-War Economic Policy and Planning,* April 19, 1944, p. 194. For other estimates in same range, see same hearings, pp. 196–97.

16. See for example, statement by Council for Economic Development, House Special Committee, *Hearings, Post-War,* p. 194.

17. They were also concerned that Europe be revived as an industrial supplier to nations in Latin America and the Far East, both of which supplied the United States with raw materials. See Harriman, Senate Foreign Relations, *Hearings, European Recovery,* p. 249.

18. Harriman presumably meant the decline of Europe would affect the supply of raw materials because Europe would not supply essential capital goods to producers of raw materials and/or trade would be restricted through bilateral state trading agreements (Harriman, Senate Foreign Relations, *Hearings, European Recovery,* p. 249). Arguing in the same vein, others made more extreme statements than Harriman. In an often quoted passage, Acheson argued that nothing less than a complete reorganization of domestic politics would occur if foreign trade were eliminated: "If you wish to control the entire trade and income of the United States, which means the life of the people, you could probably fix it so that everything produced here would be consumed here, but that would completely change our constitution, our relations to property, human liberty, our very conceptions of law. And nobody contemplates that. Therefore, you find you must look to other markets and those markets are abroad" (House Special Committee, *Hearings, Post-War,* p. 1082).

Also, James Forrestal saved several reprints of an essay by Russell C. Leffingwell, a partner at J. P. Morgan, on managing the postwar American economy. Leffingwell said: "This is an essay about managing *our* economy and so concerned chiefly with domestic politics. But our economy cannot be managed in isolation. We must find outlets abroad, foreign markets, for our surplus production. We are geared to produce far more of many things than we can consume among ourselves. To do so we must buy, as well as sell, goods and services abroad; and make foreign loans and investments" ("Managing our Economy," *Yale Review* 34 [Summer, 1945]: 15, in Forrestal Papers, Leffingwell folder, box 21, Seeley G. Mudd Manuscript Library, Princeton University, Princeton, New Jersey).

19. *All-time high: Historical Statistics,* p. 544; *7 percent:* Harriman testimony in Senate Foreign Relations, *Hearings, European Recovery,* p. 255; *five million jobs:* H. J. Heinz II testimony in Senate Foreign Relations, *Hearings, European Recovery,* January 26, 1948, p. 908.

20. House Special Committee, *Hearings, Post-War,* November 29, 1944, p. 1041. Machinery was the single largest item of export after the war; in 1947,

out of total U.S. merchandise exports of $14.3 billion, machinery accounted for $2.4 billion, or almost 17 percent of exports. See *Historical Statistics*, pp. 544, 546.

21. Senate Foreign Relations, *Hearings, European Recovery*, January 26, 1948, p. 908. Also see foreign markets as sustaining influence: Paul Hoffman, House Special Committee, *Hearings, Post-War*, p. 210.

22. Senate Foreign Relations, *Hearings, European Recovery*, p. 249. Because Europe was so central to world trade, the Marshall Plan would not only facilitate European capitalist recovery, but world trade recovery. One example of the importance of the recovery of world trade from the point of view of the United States is that the Europeans did not have to sell only to the United States to pay for American exports. Sales to their traditional customers in the underdeveloped world, who in turn sold raw materials to the United States, would also help the Europeans earn American currency with which to buy American goods. For the implementation of the Marshall Plan drawing on previously classified material, see Michael J. Hogan, "Paths of Plenty: American Recovery Planning and the Conference on European Economic Cooperation," *Pacific Historical Review* 53 (August, 1984), and William Burr, "American Stabilization Policy in Western Europe" (Ph.D. diss., Northern Illinois University, forthcoming).

23. Senate Foreign Relations, *Hearings, European Recovery*, January 8, 1948, p. 32.

24. Senate Foreign Relations, *Hearings, European Recovery*, p. 32.

25. McCloy was speaking of the not yet signed North Atlantic Treaty, but his statement applies as well to United States military capabilities. John J. Mc-Cloy, "The International Bank and World Trade," in *Report of the Thirty-fifth National Foreign Trade Convention*, November 8, 9, 10, 1948 (New York: National Foreign Council, 1949), p. 59.

26. For example, see the generally sympathetic discussion at Council on Foreign Relations, note 2.

27. For a discussion on isolationists one generation before those under discussion, but perfectly applicable here, see Justus Doenecke, *Not to the Swift, The Old Isolationists and the Cold War Era* (Lewisburg, Pa.: Bucknell University Press, 1979). Also see Malcolm E. Jewell, *Senatorial Politics and Foreign Policy* (Lexington: University of Kentucky Press, 1962), pp. 51–52, 180.

28. *Wherry:* Marvin Stromer, *The Making of a Political Leader, Kenneth S. Wherry and the United States Senate* (Lincoln, Nebraska: University of Nebraska Press, 1969), p. 3; William S. White, "Portrait of a 'Fundamentalist,'" *New York Times Magazine*, January 15, 1950, p. 20. *Butler:* Justus F. Paul, "Butler, Griswold, Wherry: The Struggle for Dominance of Nebraska Republicanism, 1941–1946," *North Dakota Quarterly* 43 (Autumn, 1975): 52. *Capehart:* see annotated bibliography in William Pickett, "Homer E. Capehart: The Making of a Hoosier Senator" (Ph.D. diss., Indiana University, 1974).

29. For details on other isolationists, see my dissertation, "The Diplomacy of

Force: The American State and the Formation of American Military Policy toward Europe in 1948" (University of Michigan, 1984). The best biography of Taft is James T. Patterson, *Mr. Republican, A Biography of Robert A. Taft* (Boston: Houghton Mifflin Co., 1972).

30. "Return to Liberty," delivered in Kansas City, Missouri, February 12, 1946, before the Missouri Republican Club, reprinted in *Congressional Record*, Extension of Remarks of Robert Taft, March 1, 1946, in Robert A. Taft Papers, Speeches and Articles, Addresses, Republicans of Texas, February 14, 1946 folder, Manuscript Division, Library of Congress, Washington, D.C.

31. "Return to Liberty."

32. See "Return to Liberty"; "A Republican Program," delivered January 3, 1947, over NBC radio, reprinted in *Congressional Record*, Extension of Remarks of Robert Taft, January 6, 1947, in Robert A. Taft Papers, Speeches and Articles, Broadcast—A Republican Program, January 3, 1947 folder; and Address of Robert A. Taft to the Ohio Society of New York, delivered in New York City, November 10, 1947, Robert A. Taft Papers, Speeches and Articles, Address—Ohio Society of New York, November 19, 1947 folder.

33. "The British Loan," speech of Robert A. Taft, in Senate, April 24, 1946, Robert A. Taft Papers, Speeches and Articles, Address—U.S. Senate (British Loan), April 24, 1946 folder.

34. *Limiting imports:* "A Republican Program." *Exports:* Address to Ohio Society, p. 14.

35. Address to Ohio Society, pp. 11, 12.

36. "National Defense," an address of Senator Robert A. Taft before the Lincoln Club of Denver, Colorado, February 14, 1948, p. 5, Robert A. Taft Papers, Speeches and Articles, Address—National Defense, February 14, 1948 folder. This is Taft's fullest statement on military policy.

37. "National Defense," p. 2.

38. "National Defense," pp. 4–5.

39. "National Defense," p. 4.

40. See Taft quoted in *New York Times:* January 9, 1948; January 16, 1948; February 15, 1948; March 17, 1948; March 20, 1948; April 8, 1948.

41. See William M. Goldsmith, *The Growth of Presidential Power, A Documented History*, vol. 3, *Triumph and Reappraisal* (New York: Chelsea House Publishers, 1974), pp. 1478ff.; Barry Dean Karl, *Executive Reorganization and Reform in the New Deal, The Genesis of Administrative Management, 1900–1939* (Cambridge, Mass.: Harvard University Press, 1963), especially chap. 5, "The Presidency," for an elegant historical overview of presidential power; for reorganization under Truman, see William E. Pemberton, *Bureaucratic Politics, Executive Reorganization During the Truman Administration* (Columbia: University of Missouri Press, 1979).

42. Nelson W. Polsby, *Congress and the Presidency*, 2d ed. (Englewood Cliffs, N.J.: Prentice-Hall, 1971), p. 14.

43. Richard E. Neustadt, *Presidential Power, The Politics of Leadership* (New York: John Wiley and Sons, 1960), p. 10.

44. Kenneth W. Condit, *The History of the Joint Chiefs of Staff*, vol. 2, 1947–1949, *The Joint Chiefs of Staff and National Policy* (Washington, D.C.: Historical Division, Joint Secretariat, Joint Chiefs of Staff, 1976, declassified 1978), p. 285. During the spring of 1948, FROLIC, a revision of BROILER, was discussed but not approved, and another revision, HALFMOON, was approved (Condit, pp. 285–88). For authoritative discussion of American postwar military strategy, see David Alan Rosenberg, "American Atomic Strategy and the Hydrogen Bomb Decision," *Journal of American History* 66 (June, 1979): 62–87 and Rosenberg, "Toward Armageddon: The Foundations of United States Nuclear Strategy, 1945–1961" (Ph.D. diss., University of Chicago, 1983).

45. Perry McCoy Smith, *The Air Force Plans for Peace, 1943–1945* (Baltimore: Johns Hopkins Press, 1970), p. 73.

46. U.S. Congress, Senate Committee on Armed Services, *Hearings, Universal Military Training*, March 17, 1948, p. 21.

47. On the impact of the possible nomination of Vandenberg on the Taft-Vandenberg relationship, see H. Bradford Westerfield, *Foreign Policy and Party Politics, Pearl Harbor to Korea* (New Haven: Yale University Press, 1955), p. 271, and Jewell, *Senatorial Politics*, p. 69. The other leading candidates were Dewey and Stassen (Westerfield, *Foreign Policy*, p. 297).

48. Blum, *V Was for Victory*, p. 315, referring to the United Nations vote but applicable here.

49. Arthur H. Vandenberg, Jr., ed., *The Private Papers of Senator Vandenberg* (Boston: Houghton Mifflin Co., 1952), pp. 318, 319.

50. Walter Millis, ed., *The Forrestal Diaries* (New York: Viking Press, 1951), p. 393.

51. *New York Times*, March 18, 1948, p. 2; Clyde E. Jacobs and John F. Gallagher, *The Selective Service Act: A Case Study of the Governmental Process* (New York: Dodd, Mead and Co., 1967), p. 69.

52. *New York Times*, June 5, 1947, p. 1.

53. See Senate Armed Services, *Hearings, Universal*, March 25, 1948, pp. 360, 390–95, and *Washington Post*, April 8, 1948, p. 13.

54. *Washington Post*, April 7, 1948, p. 1.

55. *Washington Post*, April 8, 1948, p. 1. *New York Times*, April 8, 1948, p. 1.

56. The congressional process was more fraught with complication and surprise than I have conveyed here. For a more detailed discussion, see my dissertation, "The Diplomacy of Force."

States and Social Movements

SWORDPLAY AND STATEMAKING
Aspects of the Campaign against the Duel in Early Modern France

Robert A. Schneider

On October 30, 1632, Henri II de Montmorency, duke and governor of Languedoc, mounted a scaffold specially constructed in the courtyard of the Hôtel de Ville at Toulouse and placed his head on the executioner's block. Only a select audience was in attendance to witness the last moments of the duke's life, for Cardinal Richelieu, who along with Louis XIII and the royal family had journeyed to Toulouse to supervise Montmorency's trial, feared that a more public execution might provoke a popular disturbance. Montmorency's crime was treason. For months he had plotted with the king's brother, the Duc d'Orléans, to put an end to the cardinal's imperious rule and to block his plans for the imposition of a new fiscal regime on the province, and that September he had committed his troops to the battlefield with the design to spark a general rebellion. Defeated and wounded in battle, Montmorency was summarily tried by the magistrates of the Parlement of Toulouse, many of whom were his friends and clients. And though the evidence was incontrovertible and the penalty a foregone conclusion, they reportedly wept as they pronounced a sentence of death. In the days before the execution the king was besieged by a procession of appeals for clemency on Montmorency's behalf from the queen, the Princess de Condé, the Duc d'Angoulême and even an emissary from the pope. Louis XIII, however, remained inflexible, for he was intent on making an example of Montmorency, and when the axe fell that day in Toulouse it ended not only the life of one of France's most illustrious noblemen and warriors, but also his family's century-long monopoly of the governorship of Languedoc. Never again would that position be entrusted to an independent and powerful noble household. Thus concluded another episode in Richelieu's campaign "to humble the great."[1]

But 1632 was not the first time the executioner's axe had struck the Montmorency family. Five years earlier the duke's younger cousin, the Comte de Montmorency-Bouteville, was beheaded along with his kinsman, the Comte de Rosmadec des Chapelles. The two had been found guilty of participating in a duel, in defiance of a royal ban, in which another nobleman had been fatally wounded. It was not merely an isolated incident, however, which led to their arrest. Montmorency-Bou-teville was the most notorious duelist in France; he was known to have participated in twenty-two duels, and this last transgression followed by only a few months another encounter which had forced him to flee the realm. Angered at the king for refusing to pardon him of this crime, Montmorency-Bouteville boasted that upon his return he would "fight in Paris and in the Place Royale!" Having made good his promise, he and his comrade-in-arms were promptly arrested, tried by the Parlement of Paris and condemned to death. Then also there were supplications for clemen-cy from the highest ranks of the nobility, including a tearful appeal from a delegation of princesses, duchesses, and Bouteville's pregnant wife be-fore the queen in her private chambers.[2] And then too the royal resolve, seconded by Richelieu's support, remained unbroken. Montmorency-Bouteville and Des Chapelles paid with their lives for their dueling ardor; but with their deaths, observed Richelieu, "one saw serving the extinc-tion of duels those who had had no other care than to foment them."[3] The cardinal's observation, however, proved to be premature. "There have in the past been so many edicts issued with the unfilled hope of preventing duels that it is difficult to know just what to do to put an end to the continuation of this plague," he confessed in his *Political Testament.*

> Frenchmen hold their lives in such contempt, as we know from experi-ence, that the extreme penalty has not always been the best one with which to curb their frenzy. They have often fancied that it was even more glorious to violate such edicts, demonstrating by so extravagant a gesture that they valued honor above life itself.[4]

The fate of the two Montmorencys—one a rebel, the other an inveterate duelist—illustrates well Louis XIII's and Richelieu's policy of uncompromising severity toward noble "disobedience." But do these two episodes really belong to the same story? The problem of noble conspir-acy and revolt against the crown is a complex one involving a range of factors, from court politics, religious factionalism, and Spanish diplomacy to fiscal reform, provincial privileges, and popular discontent. Where does the duel fit into this series of issues? Indeed, one way to think about the duel is to consider it as merely an epiphenomenon, as a symptom or outgrowth of the more fundamental and serious problem of noble opposi-tion and organized violence against the crown's authority, and to view its elimination as an example of the larger process of the monarchy's eventual pacification of the nobility. This is undoubtedly why royal officials viewed the duel with such disfavor, for in it they recognized all that was trou-blesome in a nobility that was headstrong, above the law, and armed.

Nevertheless, in this essay I will examine the duel as a distinct and separate problem—to be sure, as an instance of noble disobedience, but one distinguished by a strange combination of respectability and dead-liness. Surely the specificity of the duel was appreciated by contempo-raries, especially as they contemplated its unpredictability and danger—its potential for turning polite intercourse between noblemen into mur-derous encounters. There is something sacrificial in the duel, noted crit-ics such as Jean Savaron, who likened the custom to the bloody sacrifices of the ancient Gauls or the gladiator games of the Romans.[5] A threat to public order, duelists most directly threatened other noblemen, and this is why so many of them campaigned against it. It is this concern for the reform of the duel and the point of honor on the part of the nobility that I want to emphasize in what follows. In addition, I want to stress the unique nature of the crime, and in particular its ritual and ideology, which set it apart from other forms of noble violence and which must be central to any discussion of the duel.

Even the crown recognized that the duel grew out of a highly indi-vidualistic mindset; witness the symbolic punishment Montmorency-Bouteville received for one of his earlier dueling escapades. The walls of his house were razed—a common enough treatment for the property of major offenders—but also the trees surrounding it were cut down to size by exactly half.[6] There could be no better exemplar of the personal aspect of the offense, of its brazenness and perverted heroism, than this particu-lar effort to degrade and shame the offender. The point is that by the late sixteenth century the custom of the duel was embedded in a highly developed code of conduct, one which vaunted individualism, heroism, and honor. In order to appreciate the campaign against the duel we will have to take note of the weight of these sentiments. I want to suggest also that attempts to reform the nobility—the larger issue surrounding the problem of the duel—entailed a transformation in mind and behavior running contrary to the reigning noble ethos of individualism, a transfor-mation designed to reorient the elite in the direction of public accountab-ility and responsibility. To follow the campaign against the duel is thus to observe some of the problems and paradoxes confronting the proponents of public authority; it is to appreciate that the struggle between the crown and nobility was complex and prolonged, making its outcome, the early modern French state, an edifice of remarkable size and intrusiveness.

To begin, we need to remind ourselves that the duel was indeed a prob-lem of major proportions in early modern Europe. No mere medieval vestige, the practice of private combat in the duel attained its greatest popularity in the sixteenth and seventeenth centuries, and nowhere was the "plague" of dueling more virulent than in France. There is ample testimony confirming the extent of noble bloodletting in duels, especially during the reign of Henri IV. It was the judgment of François de la Noue, a military man, that more noblemen were killed in private combat than had perished on the battlefield in the recent Wars of Religion.[7] Writing in 1609, the Parisian diarist Pierre de l'Estoile estimated that the duel claimed the lives of between seven and eight thousand noblemen in the previous twenty years.[8] Tavannes calculated a figure of six thousand cut down.[9] The observations of the Venetian ambassadors echo these estimates. Two of them reported that duels were a daily occurrence in Paris; another, writing in 1608, placed the death toll at eight thousand since 1598; still another cited the figure of twenty-five hundred slain noblemen for a period of just three years.[10] In the wake of the Montmorency-Bouteville episode, the *Mercure François* of 1626 reported laconically that "duels had become so common among the French nobility that the streets of Paris usually served as the field of combat."[11] And in 1610 Jean Savaron claimed, perhaps with some exaggeration, that there were "few or no noble houses exempted from this carnage."[12]

All of these estimates and observations come from the period following the Wars of Religion, and it may be argued that they are thus misleading, that they reflect merely a heightened concern with noble violence and lawlessness after several generations of warfare and near-anarchy. Indeed, the pacification of the nobility was the order of the day for the French crown in this period, and, next to banditry or outright rebellion, nothing epitomized noble resistance and a propensity to disrupt the public peace more than the practice of dueling. Observers were undoubtedly sensitive to the issue of noble conduct under the law, and their sensitivity led perhaps to some exaggerated estimates of the duel's death toll. But it cannot be doubted that for the overall period of the Wars of Religion and their aftermath, the mania of dueling, and dueling to the death, reached unprecedented proportions in France. In the late sixteenth and early seventeenth centuries the practice of the duel far surpassed in incidence and severity what it had been in previous times, when it was recognized as a legitimate form of judicial combat, a sanctioned means of settling quarrels between noblemen.[13] Moreover, as Montaigne lamented in his essay, "Cowardice, Mother of Cruelty," a sixteenth-century innovation in dueling customs was the added participation of seconds, and even thirds and fourths, frequently leading to the degeneration of the ritual combat into a mass brawl.[14]

What explains the increase in dueling and its heightened ferocity in the late sixteenth century? Several factors must be considered, one being quite simple. Sometime in the mid-sixteenth century the sword underwent a technological advance leading to the widespread adoption of the needlepoint rapier, which increased greatly the deadliness of the duel. Previously duelists would hack away at each other for hours with cumbersome broadswords before either inflicting incapacitating wounds or ending the combat in mutual exhaustion; now a quick single thrust could prove fatal.[15] The rapier was Italy's contribution to the art of dueling. So too was the full development of the code of honor, another contributing factor to the increase in dueling.[16] Honor aggrieved was grounds for the duel, and a great sense of personal honor had always been a part of the noble mind-set. But moralists of the Italian Renaissance had lately transformed the notion of honor into a sophisticated code, dissected its meaning, specified degrees of insult, and elaborated an entire etiquette of social relations between gentlemen. Thanks to the newly articulated code of honor, the nobleman was now well informed of those myriad occasions when he was compelled to feel aggrieved. He was now forced to seek the satisfaction of honor in the drawing of his sword.

While important, these sixteenth-century developments—the adoption of the rapier and an elaboration of the code of honor—were not solely responsible for the deadly dueling mania. They relate to the "superstructure" of the phenomenon, not its causes. We shall return to these factors in due course, but for the moment it is important to explain some of the social conditions which increasingly set noblemen in competition with one another, sometimes fueling the fires of civil strife, but other times leading to combat of an individual sort.

First, it should come as no surprise that the confessional conflict itself provoked and aggravated rivalries among noblemen. Once the French Wars of Religion began in 1562, various noblemen—from princes of the realm and governors to petty squires and backwoods *hobereaux*—joined in the fray, taking the lead in mobilizing their followers into fighting brigades, raising the level of conflict to that of a general conflagration which consumed the entire nation for nearly half a century. The vocation of warrior, however, was not new to most noblemen, for these internal wars merely enlarged the opportunities for a military career that had been available since the Italian campaign of Charles VIII. What was new was that after 1562 French noblemen were fighting each other, and their contests on the battlefield frequently spilled over into personal quarrels, breeding long-standing feuds and vendettas where questions of honor and reputation, rather than religion, were at stake. In this way, the stage was set for the duel.

But recent work has shown that the religious wars themselves were in part a by-product of a breakdown in the Renaissance system of patronage, an arrangement that had ensured a measure of internal harmony to the nobility and cemented its loyalty to the crown as well. Until the mid-sixteenth century royal largesse had been free-flowing: money, pensions, offices, and other favors poured forth from the crown into the laps of princes and magnates who in turn dispensed this bounty to their noble followers. As long as the distribution of patronage continued, and as long as opportunities for foreign adventure remained available, the nobility remained more or less content and internecine strife was contained. In the 1550s, however, the largesse was halted: a fiscal crisis of the state turned off the spigot of patronage, and what ensued was a scramble for power and honors within the nobility. Now bereft of handouts and favors, noblemen attempted to galvanize followers on the basis of religious partisanship, family loyalty, and local ties. No longer a broker at court, a magnate looked to his region and sought a constituency there among the lesser nobility and urban oligarchs whom he organized in confessionally based parties. And denied the normal channels of advancement, young nobles in particular turned to brigandage or the duel as a means of building a reputation, accumulating honors, and attracting followers. "In this way," concludes Robert Harding, whose excellent work on the provincial governors, *Anatomy of a Power Elite*, I am following here, "the extraordinary receptivity of the French lesser nobility to the code of the duel after 1560 was directly related to the crisis of the old system of clientage that hitherto had given them a means of advancing themselves."[17]

A second pathway to the duel originated in changes in the social structure, changes that increasingly challenged the traditional nobility's identity and values. Whether these changes were also undermining the wealth of the nobility is presently a question of some debate among historians.[18] But apart from the material vicissitudes of its fortune in the sixteenth century, one development haunted the nobility more than any other: the devaluation of its status. And devalued it was, primarily from the crown's policy of creating titles and selling offices, but also through a steady turnover of noble lands to *roturiers*. Not even the upper reaches of the nobility were immune from this inflationary trend. Between 1515 and 1600 the crown created twenty-eight new peerages, and Henri III alone was responsible for the establishment of fifty-five additional counties, marquisates, duchies, and principalities.[19] When we examine the lower ranks of the nobility this trend turns into a boom. To take but one example, in 1576, as a fiscal expedient, the crown offered for sale a block of one thousand letters of ennoblement.[20] Clearly, a nobleman of the late sixteenth century found himself in a greatly augmented company of peers and rivals, a situation, I would suggest, which could only aggravate those conditions leading to the duel. So thought Louys de Chabans, a noble delegate to the Estates General in 1614, who laid the blame for the increase in dueling on the crown's distribution of honors regardless of birth or merit.[21] A glance at England tends to confirm Chabans's argument. It was under James I, in fact, that one saw both a dramatic inflation of honors, after the long depression of Elizabeth's reign, and a near simultaneous outbreak of the dueling mania.[22] So severe was this outbreak that James himself was moved to pen "A treatise against duelling."

Perhaps even more troubling to the traditional nobility than the distribution of titles was the growth of the *noblesse de robe*, that class of civil
servants whose offices, usually venal, ennobled the purchaser and his
descendants. The most dramatic illustration of the enlargement of the
Robe is found in the Parlements, which experienced nearly a doubling of
their members in the course of the sixteenth century.[23] The growth of the
noblesse de robe not only swelled the ranks of the nobility, it also challenged the Sword with a competing view of the gentleman. Men of law,
who served the state by virtue of their education and wit, *robins* asserted
their claims to all noble privileges and honors, and implicit in their pretentions was a critique of the excess and violence for which the traditional
nobility had lately become notorious.[24] The duel in particular presented
the Robe with an occasion to redefine the image of nobility, to break with
the "point of honor" and its violence-provoking imperatives. "Is there
anything stranger than to kill each other daily without knowing what
constitutes a sufficient cause for fighting?" asked one *robin* in 1594.[25]
Champions of civility and enemies of the duel, the Robe nevertheless
contributed to the dueling mania, if only as a source of anxiety to the
traditional nobility, as a rising social group which challenged its primacy
and therefore its honor. The jurist Charles Loyseau, a spokesman for the
Robe, even had the temerity to suggest that magistrates were superior in
rank to the military nobility.[26] But *robins* too were capable of resorting to
the sword in disputes of honor. In fact, duels between younger members
of the Robe and military men became so commonplace that Louis XIV
was forced to issue a special edict banning such encounters.[27] And Pierre
de l'Estoile describes how the son of one Robe official slew a gentleman
who dared to question his noble rank.[28]

The sale of offices, the inflation of honors, the rising presumptions of
the *noblesse de robe* were all contributing factors to what was universally
decried as the "confusion of ranks" in sixteenth- and seventeenth-century
French society. Not surprisingly, such confusion prompted attempts, if
only symbolic ones, to impose or create order, as if social change could be
defied by the magic of ceremony or in the exaltation of tradition. We see,
for example, the promulgation of sumptuary laws governing dress, the
insistence on an exact etiquette and a precise ordering by rank in every
public procession, the elaboration of a code of honor—attempts aimed at
better defining the privileged, hereditary elite, but which, in provoking
endless *disputes de préséance*, conflicts over honor, and even duels, usually bred the disorder they were designed to overcome.[29] An extreme
response to be sure, the duel was one way in which noblemen "adjusted"
to a social situation characterized by an increasingly crowded field of
elites in which the grounds for advancement, the criteria of rank, indeed,
the very nature of the hierarchy were open to question. Restraints against

violence were few in the old regime, even within the officialdom: a solemn religious procession could easily break out into fisticuffs, as various *corps* jostled for rank. Among members of the traditional nobility, with swords at hand and a taste for blood gained on the battlefield, this quickness to violence over essentially trivial matters simply took a more deadly turn.

A third explanation for the rising fashion of the duel lies in changes that had recently transformed the nobility's traditional role in society, that of "those who fight." By the mid-sixteenth century the art of warfare had undergone a revolution in techniques and organization amounting to the eclipse of the cavalry and the ascendancy of the infantry. The Swiss phalanx of pikemen, a massive fighting unit easily capable of overrunning and destroying any mounted force, was primarily responsible for this transformation. Soon the battlefields of Europe were entirely given over to mercenary armies of pikemen, and the day of the armored knight, the noble warrior who led his troops into combat, had passed. Other changes were to follow, those amounting to what Michael Roberts has called "The Military Revolution," which introduced large-scale, disciplined armies and the widespread use of artillery and gunshot to the battlefields of Europe. Though cavalry regained some of its former importance, it was, as Roberts notes, "now open to all who could sit a horse and fire a pistol."[30] No wonder the nobility lost its sense of military duty, and, as was demonstrated on numerous occasions, no longer responded to royal summons of the feudal levy, the *ban* and *arrière-ban*.[31] Other men stepped into the breach, and what we find in the latter part of the sixteenth century is nonnobles increasingly assuming a leadership role in the military. With combat came honor, and in such a fashion the traditional nobility was again challenged by the pretentions of "outsiders." Even Brantôme, a warrior nobleman par excellence (and an apologist for the duel) was forced to acknowledge the noble qualities of fighting commoners: "From the nothings they were they rise to be captains equal to gentlemen having as much honor and reputation as the most noble, and performing acts as virtuous and noble as the greatest of gentlemen."[32]

What was the connection between the nobility's declining role in the military and its increasing fascination with the duel? I would suggest that the connection was a psychological one, that noblemen found in the duel a way of recapturing the sense of individual combat that the military revolution had rendered *depassé*. It must be pointed out that the rapier was a weapon suited only to single combat of a ceremonial sort and was totally inappropriate to the new style of mass warfare.[33] Thus, as Montaigne argued, duelists were not sharpening their martial skills;[34] on the contrary, they were indulging in a deadly sport which preserved and celebrated the qualities of chivalry and individualism even as these were becoming obsolete in the realm of actual warfare. Once again, the duel can be seen as a sort of adjustment on the part of the nobility to a changing world in which traditional roles and values were called into question. Here, however, dueling represented a tradition rarefied, a ritual both ludic and agonic which allowed noblemen to affirm their autonomy and purposefulness, even if that affirmation took a suicidal form.

It is not my primary purpose in this essay to present an explanation for the rise in the popularity of the duel in the latter part of the sixteenth century. Rather, my main concern is to explore some of the problems inherent in efforts to effect its eradication, although any appreciation of these efforts presupposes some awareness of the forces behind the dueling fashion. Here I want merely to point out two aspects of the duel's evolution in this period. First, despite appearances, its degeneration into a major form of mutual bloodletting among French noblemen did not result from atavism, nor from outmoded, medieval sentiments which somehow possessed them in a moment of stress. The blame for the increase in the incidence of dueling must be ascribed to social, fiscal, administrative, and military changes, all eventually connected to the growing needs of the state. Second, what we are witnessing in the dueling mania is not merely an increase in an isolated practice, but the evolution of a mind-set or an ideology, of a code of behavior and an image of the self which came to define the nobleman not only on the battlefield or in private combat, but in all facets of his life.

Now it might be argued that the duel was simply a crime, albeit a highly ritualized one, and that it should thus be considered alongside other forms of noble criminality which especially blighted French society in the sixteenth and early seventeenth centuries. Indeed, the case for summarily condemning the nobility for outlawry is convincing. Many noblemen, especially those of the provinces, were nothing short of petty tyrants or gangsters who embraced violence as a way of life. Not only did they take up arms against royal magistrates and tax officials—this, after all, could be justified by high-minded principles—they also waged war against the peasantry and frequently fought to the death among themselves as a matter of sport.[35] In his *Mémoirs* Claude Haton summarized the indictment against the nobility in no uncertain terms: "The noblemen who once were gentlemen of virtue are now plunderers and murderers, heretics, infidels, irreverent, idolaters, insane, cruel, proud, arrogant, pillagers of other people's property, sacrilegious, oppressors of the people."[36] Molière, of course, has given us an enduring image of this petty tyrant in the character of Don Juan, a blasphemer, womanizer, duelist, thief, and murderer who recognizes no law, either earthly or divine, except that of his own sadistic will. But it appears as though Don Juan was not purely a figment of the dramatist's imagination, for there is evidence that he was modeled after a real person, one Chevalier de Roquelaure, a notorious delinquent of high birth who narrowly escaped the block only because he was protected by his friends at court.[37]

Many duelists were criminals of this sort. By all accounts, Montmorency-Bouteville was a seventeenth-century version of the gangster, a bully with a sword. Dueling had been a crime in France since the mid-sixteenth century. But I would suggest that in order to understand the fashion of dueling, as well as the campaign against it, we must make a distinction between the duel and other forms of criminal violence. For there were important distinctions which lead one to believe, in fact, that the duel represented a higher stage of conflict, a more refined, though no less deadly form of combat than the wanton, primitive violence to which so many noblemen had become addicted. Murderous though it could be, the duel presupposed a level of civility which recognized an etiquette of conflict, acknowledged the essential honorability of combatants, and respected definite limits on violence. Tallement de Réaux supplies us with an incident which illustrates well the rule of civility between duelists: The Duc de Montmorency and the Duc de Retz once dueled over an insult the former had leveled at the latter, and after honor had been satisfied the two dukes proceeded first to lunch together at the hôtel de Montmorency and then to dine at the hôtel de Retz.[38] We must remember that even the private duel was a trial of sorts and, like all forms of justice, relied upon a strict observance of rules and ceremony for its legitimacy. It was also a sport, a form of play in Huizinga's use of the term, in which contestants entered a separate realm distinguished by its own ritual, a sense of seriousness and the suspension of quotidian concerns.[39] To be sure, such considerations are relevant only to the ideal form of the duel, not the sneak attacks and mass brawls into which drawn swords frequently degenerated.[40] But my point is that we must take very seriously precisely this "ideal" aspect of the duel; we must consider its ideology, its "superstructure," for herein lies not only an explanation for the duel's persistent popularity, but also a key to the nature of the campaign against it.

Let us turn to the "point of honor" and its importance in the ideology of the duel. Honor had been at the center of the noble identity from time immemorial. Since Aristotle the philosophical dissection of the notion of honor had been a staple of the European intellectual discourse, and late medieval chivalry had certainly raised the contemplation of love and honor to the level of art. But during the Renaissance moralists and literati began to ponder the notion of honor with greater interest and acumen in keeping with both the new learning and the new sources of power and patronage available at court.[41] To simplify greatly, there emerged out of the Renaissance two interpretations of honor. The first, best epitomized by Castiglione's *The Courtier,* framed honor in terms of service to the prince, and also stressed the pursuit of virtue as the honorable gentleman's true vocation. In love, in battle, and at court he was to temper his quest for glory with moderation and reason, and he was to fix the interests of his lady and prince in center view. Castiglione's courtier, though a full-blooded nobleman endowed with a healthy drive for personal honor, was no headstrong individualist. For here we have one of the most successful depictions of the marriage of the nobility and the state, an ideal in which the latter preserves its noble character and the former sacrifices its private ambitions to princely service. In *The Courtier* the love of honor is perfectly commensurate with the rule of reason, with the interests of state, and with the pursuit of virtue.[42]

This entirely humanistic view of noble honor, however, did not prevail over all others. Since the marriage between the nobility and the state in early modern Europe was rarely a happy one, it should come as no surprise that there emerged a line of thinking which more accurately reflected the nobility's pretensions to independence and its fidelity to more traditional and private notions of honor. What characterized this second view of honor was its celebration of the passionate, willful quest for honor and glory, the coupling of honor with violent impulses—those of wrath, revenge, and even lust. While the courtly gentleman of the Renaissance would accept the limits of duty on his desire for personal honor, the Renaissance nobleman recognized in such bonds only a challenge and asserted instead his right to pursue personal honor come what may. Such sentiments found a voice in a line of writers in the sixteenth and seventeenth centuries. In the libertine world of Rabelais, Gargantua's Abbey of Thélème was ruled by the motto, "Do what thou wilt." There, "men that are free, well-born, well-bred, and conversant in honest companies, have naturally an instinct and spur that prompteth them into virtuous actions, and withdraws them from vice, which is called honor."[43] The relevant message of Rabelais's tale, as Hiram Haydn points out, is that "instinct usurps the function of natural reason," an example of the intellectual trend Haydn calls the "Counter-Renaissance," in which "the last and most basic prerogative of reason is taken from it, and handed to honor."[44] In Elizabethan England this sentiment found a more violent expression in a series of plays endorsing the principle of revenge.[45] And out of France's Wars of Religion there emerged warrior-writers, such as Blaise de Monluc and Pierre de Brantôme, who took up their pens to champion the life of noble adventurism. Of course, it was in the seventeenth century that the noble ideal of individualism, glory, and honor found its greatest expositor in Corneille, whose most famous play, *Le Cid*, presented a world in which the true warrior's striving for honor, his furious struggle to defend name and family, not only ensures his personal triumph but rescues the state from peril as well.[46]

All of these literary representations were influenced by the Italian "point of honor," in which the notion of personal honor was systematized and enshrined as the paramount concern of the noble temperament. And it is in the Italian literature where the issue of honor and the duel were most clearly joined.[47] The point of honor was designed to regulate behavior among gentlemen and to sensitize them to the pitfalls and niceties of exacting social intercourse. But the true regulating principle seems to have been the threat of the duel: the sword hung Damocles-like over the social relations of the nobility, for central to the point of honor was a trip-wire sensitivity to insult.

Now, it is hardly uncommon for people to respond violently to injury, insult, slander, and the like, and the nobility traditionally displayed a great sensitivity to personal imprecations. But in several respects the prescriptive literature coming out of sixteenth-century Italy managed to raise this sensitivity to new levels. For it insisted that, while others might let an insult pass, it was the mark of a gentleman to leap to the defense of his honor. At the very least he was bound to "give the lie" to a slanderous affront. If nothing else, the point of honor underscored the nobleman's superiority over ordinary men, a superiority demonstrated by a pose of great self-consciousness among them. Such a pose was not without purpose, for a nobleman was forever on trial before the public, his peers, rivals, and followers—a trial in which his reputation, his credit in society, was being put to the test. Without honor, a nobleman could not hope to command the loyalty of his peers or the obedience of his followers, and without these he was not only powerless but also experienced a sort of social death.[48] Thus it should be of no surprise that the point of honor conveyed the sense that for a true gentleman to receive an insult to his name or reputation was tantamount to a bodily assault. As G. N. Clark notes, for noblemen "to draw the sword for this cause was equivalent to self-defense."[49] Georg Simmel wrote about "the ideal sphere placed around man by his 'honor,'" and this identification of one's self with one's reputation is what he meant.[50]

Treatises on the point of honor also outlined a variety of scenarios for the proper response to an insult. A typical scenario would go as follows: A nobleman would receive an insult. (And here there was no lack of specification as to what qualified as an insult—the slander of one's wife; an expression of doubt about one's virtue, courage, or legitimacy; the lack of proper address; a snub, slap, or blow; the epithet of cuckold or traitor; and so on.) The injured nobleman would have a choice of responses. He could reply, "You depart from the truth," "That is a lie," "You lie in your throat."[51] Or if he were truly artful he could simultaneously "give the lie" and deliver a challenge in the manner of Brantôme.

> Monsieur, you are such an insignificant thing that, were it not for the insolence of your words, I should never be able to remember you. The

bearer of this will tell you the place where I am waiting, with two swords the choice of which will be yours. If you have sufficient assurance to reach the spot by your own strength, I shall relieve you of the necessity of remembering the way back.[52]

The lie "given," both parties stood with honor impugned, the assailant for having been called a liar, the insulted for having his reputation publicly calumniated. The impasse called for a resolution, and theoretically, barring a polite retraction, an apology, friendly mediation, or a loss of nerve, a duel would ensue. At this point the proceedings would be guided by another aspect of the literature on the point of honor, that which addressed the etiquette of the duel itself—the exchange of cartels, the inclusion of seconds, the choice of weapons, the selection of a field of combat, and the like.

Perhaps what is most striking about the point of honor is that this code of conduct, ostensibly designed to regulate or mitigate conflict between armed gentlemen, should in fact have frequently provoked disputes even in the absence of any real acrimony or injury. It was not unheard of, for example, for two duelists, having just fatally wounded each other, to exchange expressions of respect and love with their dying words. "The greatest bond between them is that of the duel," observed the Venetian ambassador to France, and his observation testifies to the importance of the ideology of honor among the nobility.[53] "The rules of the point of honor," wrote Cheffontaines, a critic of the duel, "are so widespread among nobles today that there is not a boy of worthy parentage, no intelligent man, who cannot recite them by heart."[54] The solidarity of any class or other social group depends to some degree on the expression of shared beliefs or ideals. Here, however, we have a code of conduct, a set of common ideals which celebrated precisely those values of individualism, competition, and pride which constantly sabotaged the nobility's unity. Paradoxically, the shared values of the French nobility were never so apparent as in the duel, something illustrated in an incident related by the eighteenth-century writer and administrator, Sénac de Meilhan. The great Condé had once challenged to a duel a nobleman of an inferior rank after an exchange of insults. Because duels were fought only between equals, the man could only respond with gratefulness for the honor being displayed to him, and "immediately threw down his sword at the Prince's feet and embraced his knees."[55]

One of the greatest obstacles facing the crown in its campaign against the duel was its own lack of resolve. In the duel it confronted, as I have tried to argue, not merely an isolated practice but a code of conduct central to the self-image of the nobility; thus, to challenge the nobility on these grounds was to challenge the ideology of the class upon which the power of the monarch ultimately depended. Nevertheless, attempts were made to face the problem with sternness and to exact the greatest penalty from transgressors. In 1566 unauthorized dueling was declared a capital offense and in 1576 it was deemed a matter of *lèse majesté*.[56] In 1599 the Parlement of Paris issued an *arrêt* against duelists and "all those gentlemen and others who call and favor said combats or attend the assemblies held on the occasion of said quarrels."[57] Similar royal and parlementary interdictions were promulgated throughout the seventeenth century. The royal edict of 1609 was particularly severe, affirming dueling as a capital offense and also declaring that those who failed to separate combatants would suffer the suspension of their charges, offices, or pensions for a period of six years.[58] Richelieu used the occasion of Montmorency-Bouteville's arrest to reissue past decrees, and, more importantly, his determination to see the notorious duelist executed was convincing testimony of the royal resolve to follow the letter of the law even in the case of a highborn offender.[59] One of Louis XIV's first actions upon attaining his majority was to ban the duel and to swear an oath that violators would never again benefit from the much abused *lettres de grace*.[60] The sternness of these measures was tempered with a ruse: in order to entice gentlemen to forsake the point of honor, the crown in 1626 and again in 1643 offered compensation to anyone who refused to accept a challenge to duel.[61]

In practice the crown frequently contradicted its professed policy of opposition to the duel. Both Henri III and Henri IV had issued challenges before their accession; Henri IV in particular seems to have shared in the duelist's mentality and on several occasions expressed frustration that he could not join in the fray.[62] During his reign, in fact, the tendency was to pardon duelists more than to pursue them: Pierre de l'Estoile reports that between 1598 and 1608, seven thousand *lettres de grace* were issued to combatants, a practice which convinced L'Estoile that the crown hardly took its own hard-line policy seriously.[63] Even the royal edict of 1609, a milestone in the legislation against the duel, contained a proviso stipulating that in certain cases the king, the constable and marshals of France, or other high officials, could grant permission for the staging of a duel.[64]

The crown's ambivalence toward the duel stemmed from several sources. For one, there was the realization of many statesmen, Sully and Richelieu among them, that draconian measures were unenforceable and impractical.[65] It was thus thought wiser to pursue a policy of selective prosecution, such as in the case of flagrant duelists like Montmorency-Bouteville or against small-fry offenders, rather than risk having the law appear a dead letter, but the result was to leave considerable room for intrepid noblemen who saw in the crown's tergiversation only an invitation to danger. For another, successive monarchs were genuinely of two minds when it came to the duel and the point of honor, for the crown could hardly castigate as criminal the duelist's courage and prowess without also impugning those same qualities so valued elsewhere, especially in war. There were intellectual arguments against prosecuting duelists as well. Bodin, the philosopher of absolutism, reasoned that dueling should be tolerated as a safety valve, a guarantee against more serious breaches such as feuds or rebellions.[66] Indeed, it is not unlikely that his words were recalled in the first half of the seventeenth century, when the threat from noble conspirators and *frondeurs* loomed greater than swordsmen's sport. The Jesuits too offered their casuistry in support of the duel, arguing that because a gentleman's honor is as valuable to him as his property, it could be defended with the same degree of justice. Here we see that the church, like the state, was divided over the combat of honor, for the official position of the Tridentine Church was to condemn the duel uncompromisingly.[67]

Indeed, there was no one official view of the duel, and this alone should warn us against thinking of the various parties in the campaign as monolithic "blocks." For just as some statesmen proved weak-willed or ambivalent in dealing with a crime they knew to be pernicious, so too did many members of the nobility express a desire to see the suppression of a custom which, after all, was depleting their ranks. In other words, the problem of the duel did not simply pit the state against the nobility as two opposing camps. In all societies, the state and the privileged elite function as interlocking social formations whose interests, if not identical, overlap at crucial points, and in early modern France one of those points was the quelling of intramural noble conflict. Thus, far from resisting the campaign against the duel, many noblemen actually participated in and even initiated reforms aimed to transform their class into a law-abiding, pacific group. At the Estates General of 1588, in fact, it was the delegation of the nobility which called for the death penalty for duelists.[68] In the balance of this essay I would like to turn to two examples of noble participation in the campaign against the duel. The first was a special court, the Tribunal of the Marshals of France, which settled disputes between noblemen which threatened to lead to duels; the second was the secret society of devout noblemen, the *Compagnie du Saint-Sacrement,* which in the 1640s took up the cause of eliminating the duel. In each we will note not only elite opposition to the custom, but also the particular nature of that opposition, and how it encouraged noblemen to assume a greater public function in society, a more responsible position commensurate with their role as members of a governing elite.

Since medieval times, a select number of noblemen, whose rank placed them above the dukes and peers and whom the king addressed as "cousins," were granted the titles of the constable and marshals of France. Collectively they were known as the Tribunal of the Marshals of France, a court with jurisdiction in disputes between noblemen over questions of honor, hence its other name, the *Tribunal du Point d'honneur*.[69] Traditionally the tribunal adjudicated in all instances when noble rights and privileges were at issue. This could involve hunting and fishing rights, as well as other honorific claims, such as those pertaining to rank in procession, precedence in church, the taking of oaths, rules of deference and the like—cases where a settlement depended upon the examination of titles and a decision regarding degrees of nobility. Increasingly in the sixteenth century the authority of the marshals was invoked in relationship to the duel. As early as 1566, at the Estates of Orléans, the crown issued an edict calling upon all those who received insults to take their grievances before the "Messieurs les connétable et maréchaux de France."[70] The tribunal did not deal with cases of actual duels—this was left to other royal judges—but rather attempted to prevent such altercations by intervening at the moment when injury to honor occurred. To aid in its task the tribunal had the assistance of the lieutenants of the marshals of France, the provincial governors and their lieutenants, as well as the constable's archer-guards and the *prévôté*.

It is difficult to assess how effective the Tribunal of the Marshals was in the campaign against the duel, but clearly it was seen as essential from the crown's perspective, for it figured prominently in nearly every edict issued in the course of the seventeenth century. The edict of 1602 called upon offended gentlemen to bring their grievances directly to the tribunal, which was charged to order the surrender of all parties to the dispute upon pain of imprisonment, fine, or banishment, and also to place those noblemen who complied with the marshals' order under the protection of the king.[71] The 1609 edict added that only in rare instances, when "it was necessary for their honor," might the marshals authorize gentlemen to duel; it also stipulated that a gentleman who failed to appear before the tribunal would "have his honor suspended, be rendered ineligible to carry arms and sent before the Parlement . . . to be punished."[72] The edict of 1617 again stressed the role of the tribunal and again warned that once there was a "challenge, duel or combat" the case would be placed before the parlement.[73] The most thorough piece of legislation against dueling issued in the old regime, the royal edict of 1651, contained thirteen articles (out of twenty-four) relating to the Tribunal of the Marshals of France. Claiming that "there is nothing more honest, nor more worthy of public and individual affection than stopping quarrels at their source," the edict granted the marshals the right to select "one or several gentlemen" in the provinces to aid other high noble officials in preventing slights of honor from escalating into duels. The edict also added that henceforth any offense to honor or reputation delivered unjustly would not only be considered an injury to the accused but to the king as well.[74]

How the Tribunal of the Marshals carried out its task can be seen in an incident from the beginning of the seventeenth century. In 1608 a difference arose between the valets of the Duc de Ventadour and the Duc d'Aumont. The masters soon took up the quarrel. Word of their dispute reached the marshals, who quickly dispatched two lieutenants to serve as guards for the noblemen in order to prevent them from coming to blows. Ventadour, however, refused his guard, claiming that as a *Duc-et-Pair* he was not under the tribunal's jurisdiction, and to make his point he had the lieutenant thrown out of his *hôtel*. More gracious, d'Aumont kept his guard waiting at the door. Upon learning of the dukes' refusal to accept their guards, the king ordered them to appear, accompanied by the lieutenants, before the tribunal. Ventadour complied, but d'Aumont remained adamant in his refusal, and apparently fought off the guard as he tried to mount his carriage. Although the dukes were now prepared to present themselves before the tribunal, neither the marshals nor the king were satisfied, for the point was to have them appear in the company of their assigned guards—a tacit admission that they had submitted to royal surveillance. Finally this condition was met. The episode ended as the two dukes, flanked by their guards, stood before the tribunal's doyen, who pronounced their dispute of no consequence, forbade them to resort to arms, and ordered them to embrace.[75]

The essential lesson from this incident is that Ventadour and d'Aumont had not drawn swords, and yet the authority of the crown had intervened. Moreover, the intervention had taken the form of a swift imposition of royal guards into the very households of the two noblemen. The tribunal was not a court established to try duelists, but to prevent duels from occurring, and it did this primarily by recognizing the legitimacy of the point of honor and entertaining complaints of wounded honor. An arm of the crown, the tribunal was composed of men of unquestionable nobility.[76] An instrument of state in an age of absolutism, it nevertheless respected noble values and the special qualities which led noblemen to duel.[77] Royal edicts, while deploring the "monstrous" custom of dueling and the "demon" of false honor, always acknowledged the nobility's sensitivity in matters of honor, and in this way these edicts went well beyond the problem of the duel. In fact, they strove to regulate noble behavior. After 1651, sanctions became much more severe for insults of any kind: if one gentleman called another a fool, a coward, or a traitor, he risked a month's imprisonment; in 1679 the punishment was increased to two months. In 1651 an accusation of lying or the delivering of threats carried a punishment of two months in prison; in 1679 such infractions were judged worthy of four months' incarceration. In 1651 the striking of a gentleman would result in the imprisonment of the offender for six months, and in addition the injured nobleman had the right to retaliate with a slap. The 1679 edict increased the punishment greatly.[78] All of these infractions of word and deed—those short of the duel, that is—were adjudicated by the Tribunal of the Marshals or its official representatives. In such a fashion the state intervened, not only in actions of a life-threatening nature, not only in violent crimes such as the duel, but in relatively minor breaches of conduct, like verbal affronts or physical slights of a symbolic sort.

It should come as no surprise that the seventeenth-century French state was concerned with the conduct of elites. This was, after all, the century of the *honnête homme* and the gentleman courtier. The question is not whether the manners and morals of the nobility were transformed but rather, what were the social and psychological forces behind this transformation. For it is not entirely clear why the crown had to get into the business of regulating behavior. One view has it that new standards of *politesse* were a result of the crown's insistence, especially under Richelieu, that it and its delegates were to be met with proper, even punctilious, displays of respect, deference, and the like.[79] In such a way, a more refined behavior among elites evolved as a by-product of their submission to royal authority.

But this view addresses only relations between crown and subject. What of social interactions of a horizontal sort, those between equals? Here too the crown played a central role, as can be seen in the case of the duel, although its role was not a simple one. The duel's very popularity, as well as its ideological baggage, meant that any serious attempt to extirpate it would have to confront it at its source, which was none other than the nobility's habits of social intercourse. These habits in themselves were not a problem; it was only as provocations to the duel which made them such. True, the state was led to meddle in private disputes primarily because of the presence or possibility of violence. In the case of the duel, however, the dynamics of public intervention in private affairs entailed a rather complex process, one in which a psychological and cultural predisposition to quarreling and competition, aggravated by the point of honor, not only created the pretext for such intervention, but also ensured that once the state intervened it would have to do so at the level of social interactions, that the conventions of private conduct would have to become a public concern. This was the obligation assumed by the Tribunal of the Marshals of France, which created a public arena in which issues of personal honor were made matters of state.

In order to act effectively against the duel, the crown had not only to enter the realm of private dispute; it also had to overcome a well-devel-

oped code of ethics which vaunted personal glory and inculcated noblemen with the expectation that insult would be met with drawn sword.
Ultimately, this code capitulated to another, that of the *honnête homme*—
the worldly gentleman who relied upon wit, grace, and dissimulation to
move with ease in society, pleasing all and offending no one. How seventeenth-century Frenchmen were transformed from Cornelian heros into
students of La Rochefoucauld's *Maximes* in the course of the seventeenth
century is not entirely clear, although it is certain that along the way they
at least had to learn to curb their instincts, especially when tempted by
the immediate gratification found in vengeance. They had to think in
terms of their interests, and eventually in the cause of public justice,
rather than indulge their passions. On an intellectual plane the question
of how a moral social order was to be fashioned out of the greed and self-
love which characterized human nature was one which exercised several
generations of French moralists, from Corneille, Guez de Balzac, and La
Rochefoucauld to Pascal and Pierre Nicole.[80] And for some, the duel
epitomized the problem. Jean Silhon, Richelieu's secretary and a disciple
of Descartes, argued that in denying men the "natural right" to exact
vengeance through the duel, the state not only assumes the role of arbiter
in disputes but also acts to enforce the rule of reason over men's passions.[81] On a more down-to-earth level, this was precisely the design of
the Tribunal of the Marshals of France, whose importance was recognized
by at least one literary architect of the culture of *honnêteté*. In *Le Misanthrope*, Molière has the marshals acting swiftly—acting, in fact, even
without having been summoned—to settle the dispute between Alceste
and Oronte over the quality of the latter's verses. Says Philinte:

> Oronte and he have fallen out
> Over some verse he spoke his mind about;
> The Marshals wish to arbitrate the matter[82]

One of the decrees to emerge from the Council of Trent was a firm
condemnation of the duel and the point of honor.[83] For several reasons,
however, the French clergy was slow to enact the church's ban. For one,
the French church had relied upon the military support of the nobility
during the Wars of Religion, and it thus would have been awkward for
bishops to turn against their erstwhile protectors over the duel. For
another, the Tridentine decrees were not formally registered by the
French parlements until the second and third decades of the seventeenth
century, and even then acceptance was difficult for many followers of the
Gallican Church. Finally, as noted before, the most influential order in
France, the Society of Jesus, took a rather indulgent view of the duel,
regarding it as a pardonable infraction rather than a serious crime. For all

of these reasons, when religious opposition to the duel emerged, its source was a lay group and not the ecclesiastical hierarchy.

That lay group was the Company of the Holy Sacrament, a secret network of brotherhoods in Paris and throughout the realm which was in the forefront of many of the accomplishments of the French Counter-Reformation, from poor relief and the policing of morals to the persecution of Protestants and the reform of the clergy. Founded in 1629 by a group of nobles, high officers, and clergymen, the *Messieurs* of the company worked tirelessly for their vision of Catholic reform and, by lobbying at court and in the parlements, managed to exercise an influence far beyond their numbers until the group's suppression in the mid-1660s.[84] The duel belonged on the company's list of "evils" to exorcize because it was one source of "disorder" that, the *Messieurs* claimed, blighted an unregenerated society. But in addition, their condemnation of the duel and, more precisely, their contempt for the point of honor, stemmed from Jansenist thinking, which held that such an inflated sense of personal worth, such an obsession with one's name and reputation, was the height of vanity and worldliness, hence, an execrable custom which smacked of idolatry and blasphemy.[85]

Accordingly, the company set out to break the French nobility's support for the duel and its fidelity to the point of honor. The campaign began in 1646 and, like all of the *Messieurs'* projects, was carried out with the company remaining *sub rosa*. In that year J. J. Olier, a priest of the Seminary of Saint-Sulpice in Paris, and a leading *Monsieur*, founded a confraternity, the Company of the Passion, dedicated to "abolishing duels, blasphemies and oaths." Among its first *confrères* were Baron de Renty, Duc de Liancourt, Marquis de Saint Mesmes, Comte d'Alban, Vicomte de Montbac, and other noblemen of impeccable lineage, all of whom had experience on the field of honor.[86] Perhaps the most illustrious member of this devout coterie was the Marquis de la Motte-Fénelon. A more unlikely candidate for an antidueling league could hardly have been found in all of France, for Fénelon was well known for his heroic exploits on the battlefield as well as for a chivalric attachment to the duel. But, largely through the influence of Olier, Fénelon had recently been converted to the pious life, and one of his first actions as a *dévot* was to spearhead the campaign against the duel.[87]

On Pentecost day in 1651 Fénelon led the *confrères* of the Company of the Passion to the chapel of Saint-Sulpice, where they publicly signed a declaration vowing never again to accept a challenge, nor to fight a duel, nor to recognize the "false point of honor."[88] With this, the campaign against the duel began in earnest and the *Messieurs'* lobbying efforts proceeded on several fronts. On the first of July, the Marshals of France issued a decree endorsing the declaration of Fénelon and his *confrères* and calling upon other gentlemen to follow suit.[89] On August 10, fifty doctors of the Sorbonne expressed their opinion that all those who failed to sign the antidueling declaration were "incapable of receiving the benefits of absolution and all the sacraments of the Church."[90] On August 28, a group of twenty bishops of France added their support to the antidueling movement.[91] In all of these actions the influence of the Company of the Holy Sacrament can be detected. In addition, the *Messieurs* induced their allies, the Queen Mother and Vincent de Paul, to convince the king to allow Fénelon to gather signatures for his declaration at court.[92] And in September the young king issued his edict against the duel, the most uncompromising measure to date, in which was announced his resolve never to pardon offenders, as had been the practice of his predecessors.[93] It is more than likely that this edict was drafted in consultation with the *Messieurs* of the Company of the Holy Sacrament.

The company soon had an opportunity to confront the dueling "monster" in reality. In 1652 two great noblemen, Comte d'Aubijoux and Comte de Brissac, dueled in the Place Royale. One of D'Aubijoux's friends was killed in the fray. Pursued by the authorities, the two duelists found refuge in the protection of the king's brother, Duc d'Orléans—precisely the way the law was circumvented time and again, especially in the case of high noblemen with important friends. But it was not the company's habit to be inhibited by the power of the great. Led by Fénelon, the *Messieurs* proceeded to stir up public opinion against the duelists and, in an effort to recruit judges against them, went from door to door in the Robe quarter announcing, "We are seeking an example for the glory of God."[94] Whether D'Aubijoux and Brissac were successfully prosecuted is not known.

The company's campaign extended to the provinces as well. The *Messieurs* ensured that the royal edict of 1651 against the duel was swiftly registered by the provincial parlements.[95] In 1655, Guillaume de Lamoignon, a member of the company, presented a set of ordinances against dueling before the estates of Brittany; and he also recruited three hundred noble signatures of the antidueling declaration.[96] In 1656, the Bishop of Cahors, Alain de Solminihac, and another *dévot* collected signatures from the nobility of Quercy for the declaration. And in 1661 the governor of Languedoc, the Prince de Conti, an associate of the Company of the Holy Sacrament, also introduced measures against "the false point of honor" in his province.[97] Such a concerted, nationwide campaign was possible only because the *Messieurs*, whose chapters stretched across the realm, were practiced in coordinated action aimed at pious ends and the public good.

Perhaps the most effective measure taken against the custom of dueling in the old regime, the Company of the Holy Sacrament's campaign is persuasive proof that the nobility participated in its own reform, at least as far as the duel was concerned. The *Messieurs* were not a handful of cranks; they were solid members of the nobility, true "insiders," and many had had military experience. Nor were they merely instruments of the crown. On the contrary, the company harbored many Jansenists and several *frondeurs,* and Mazarin considered its very existence a standing threat to the regime. In short, the company's autonomy cannot be doubted. Its preoccupation with the duel stemmed from religious and social concerns ultimately connected to a desire to regenerate society according to high Christian standards of purity and austerity. The *Messieurs* saw themselves as forming the vanguard of a movement toward this regeneration, in which the nobility would constitute a truly pious and moral elite. Critics of the regime, they were nevertheless guardians of the prevailing social order, which granted privilege, power, and esteem to the nobility. Their major concern in this respect, borne out in the campaign against the duel, was that the nobility should prove worthy of such advantages, that it should purge itself of prideful individualism and violent contentiousness, and that it should appear before the public as the embodiment of high moral purpose and pious fraternity.

Herein lies an important aspect of the larger transformation which, it seems to me, the campaign against the duel entailed. Though rooted in the ideology of a class, the duel's most fertile soil was the highly individualistic temperament of a nobility willing to come to swords' point over issues of personal honor. Thus, the undoing of the duel could only result from the dismantling of this individualistic mind-set and its replacement with a set of values and a standard of conduct more commensurate with public-mindedness and responsibility. Put differently, the abandonment of the duel called for an enlargement of the nobleman's concerns, a widening of his interests beyond the narrow domestic sphere of self, family, and friends, and a commitment to a greater collectivity, that of class, community, religious group, state, and the like.[98] The Company of the Holy Sacrament, a brotherhood of pious servants to the public weal, represented one such collectivity. So too did the hundreds of confraternities which proliferated during the Counter-Reformation, lay groups whose statutes, incidentally, nearly always stressed both public charity and peaceful relations among *confrères.*[99] And in a different fashion, the Tribunal of the Marshals also functioned as an advocate for greater public consciousness among the nobility by bringing essentially private quarrels into a formal judicial arena, by making them matters of state.

But while the Tribunal of the Marshals fostered patterns of obedience to the crown, the Company of the Holy Sacrament, in many respects a source of opposition to the court, projected an attitude of defiance rather than servility. The *Messieurs* were part of the *dévot* party, a segment of the elite which opposed the crown on religious and moral grounds, and especially for its anti-Habsburg foreign policy. Central to its position was the belief that affairs of state should be guided by religious principles, not so-called Machiavellian tenets; that a concern for the confessional unity of Europe, for example, should prevail over short-term gains from an alliance with Protestant forces against Spain; and that domestic tranquillity should not be sacrificed for the sake of an expansionist war policy.[100] Accordingly, the *dévots'* stance had a somewhat antimartial character, both in its particular opposition to France's involvement in the Thirty Years' War, and in its more general critique of the heroic ideal as embodied in the warrior type. In the context of the campaign against the duel this attitude proved serviceable to the state in its quest to pacify the nobility. In a larger sense, however, such sentiments only fueled the embers of moral discontent with the crown's overall policy on the grounds that therein lay the responsibility for much of the disorder in society, for the cynical manipulation of religious sympathies and for the abasement of the nobility. A pressure group of a highly ideological character, the *dévots* attacked the duel for different reasons (and with more success) than the crown did, primarily as one aspect of a larger campaign to reform both the regime and society according to the principles of the Counter-Reformation. In securing the crown's support for their war on the duel, they thus elicited official though tacit endorsement of their moral vision, a vision that was, of course, generally unflattering to the regime's conduct and orientation.

The role of the Tribunal of the Marshals in the campaign against the duel shows us that in order to achieve its purpose of quelling internecine violence the state had to enter the realm of social relations and monitor noble conduct. In the case of the Company of the Holy Sacrament's attack on noble violence and the "idolatry" of the point of honor, an alternative set of values was implied, one critical of "reason of state." In both cases, we see that the realization of a goal of the state could have unintended and even unwelcome consequences.

The campaign against the duel is but an example of the larger process of the pacification of the nobility, itself only one phase in the history of early modern state formation. I have suggested that the ideology and etiquette of the duel should distinguish it in our minds from other forms of noble criminality, and indeed, the special efforts undertaken to eradicate it confirm this suggestion. Special though it might have been, what does the campaign against the duel tell us about the larger process of early modern state formation?

One thing should be clear: the campaign against the duel shows us an example of the nobility cooperating with the crown in an effort to extend instruments of public justice. Insofar as these instruments were aspects of monarchical power, the example also depicts the nobility aiding in the creation of the early modern state. We are accustomed to seeing the monarchy and the nobility playing a zero-sum game, a view which has led some to conclude that the early modern regime was antinoble or even bourgeois.[101] Certainly the relationship between the two was characterized by great conflict, but this should not blind us to the myriad ways the crown promoted and defended noble interests, nor to the ways the monarchy remained fundamentally aristocratic in outlook. It was clearly of great concern to leading noblemen that their class was plagued by a code of conduct which bred such violence and vicious competition. How were they to shake off this pernicious custom without appealing to a greater authority? To play a part in the regime implied the establishment of a social truce: "Let us not be so unnatural as to arm ourselves against ourselves, to defeat ourselves by our own devices," pleaded Savaron.[102] More than anything else, the early modern state was a means of promoting that social truce; in this respect it was also instrumental in creating the conditions whereby the nobility could constitute a true class and not a factious assortment of parties, clans, and individuals.

The process of class formation is usually explained with reference to economic factors, and no doubt these are fundamental to the rise or decline of a given class, as well as to its relationship to other classes. But material factors cannot solely explain the internal coherency of a class, or rather its constitution as a class in any meaningful sense of the concept. For this we must turn to politics, law, culture, religion, and the like. I have suggested that the interests of the early modern French state and the nobility converged over the duel, and that in attempting to rid itself of its violent habits the nobility was not only promoting public order, but also transforming itself. This transformation was ultimately cultural and psychological in nature, as reflected in the emerging code of civility, and it was realized in a variety of ways—in salons, academies, and *collèges*, or at court, for example, as well as in the two institutions I have discussed in this essay. What bears repeating, it seems to me, is that this transformation entailed not only a change in noble behavior but also a change in the very boundaries of the aristocracy as it perceived itself. On the one hand, noblemen in the seventeenth century grew increasingly jealous of their privileges and resentful of attempts on the part of *roturiers* to enter their ranks. On the other, they were enlarging their horizontal sense of community, in large part by discarding old notions of rivalry, honor, and the legitimacy of private justice. Both sentiments were aspects of class self-consciousness, and both were indicative of the nobility's claim to play a leading role in the regime and in society.

All of this is not to say that the nobility remained indifferent or docile to the demands of the state. In fact, we might view the duel as symptomatic of the more serious difficulties which the nobility presented to the centralizing monarchy. This is not the place to begin a discussion of French absolutism, but central to its development was surely the fact that in nearly all its endeavors the state encountered such a formidable obstacle in the nobility. The nobility challenged the crown not because it was composed of backward-looking, "feudal" lords, whose minds and interests could not bend to the demands of a modernizing state. On the contrary, though threatened by new social forces, the nobility that emerged from the turmoil of the sixteenth century exhibited signs of strength and maturity. It had profited from the collapse of monarchical authority during the Wars of Religion and it had gained a degree of sophistication and self-confidence from the culture of the Renaissance.[103] This not only explains why the subsequent period in French history was so chaotic and violent, but also why the edifice of state that emerged was so imposing: the greater the obstacle, the greater the effort to overcome it.

This leads me to a final point. An outgrowth of the Renaissance, the code of honor reflected noblemen's self-image and sensitivities in a world in which they had grown to expect much. A civilized form of combat, the duel was a custom between men who took each other seriously, who perhaps saw themselves as Cornelian heros, and who in any case haughtily assumed as a matter of right that their quarrels of honor were private affairs, beyond the reach of public justice. These are the assumptions of men with great pretensions, but also with a heightened sense of self-consciousness. This, I would suggest, is what the crown and other reformers confronted in the duel: not an inchoate, primitive form of violence, but a thoroughly articulated code of behavior. This is what made the campaign against the duel so difficult, and this is also what made serious attempts to eliminate dueling go well beyond the crime itself and take up matters relating to individual conduct, moral consistency, and public duty. It is one example of how the early modern state was led into the private realm, a process that has continued to this day.

NOTES

1. On Montmorency and the revolt of 1632, see Paul Gachon, *Les Etats de Languedoc et l'Edit de Béziers* (1632), (Paris, 1887) and C. Devic and J. Vaisette, *Histoire générale de Languedoc*, 15 vols. (Toulouse, 1872–93), 11:1042–58. Richelieu commented on Montmorency's execution in his *Testament Politique*, ed. Louis Andre (Paris, 1947), pp. 124–25.

2. On this incident see Richard Herr, "Honor versus Absolutism: Richelieu's fight against Duelling," *Journal of Modern History*, 1955, pp. 281–85, and

Victor-L. Tapié, *France in the Age of Louis XIII and Richelieu*, trans. D. M. Lockie (New York, 1975), pp. 163–65.

3. *Mémoires du Cardinal de Richelieu, sur le Regne de Louis XIII, depuis 1610 jusqu'a 1638*, ed. M. Petitot, 10 vols. (Paris, 1823), 3:305.

4. *The Political Testament of Cardinal Richelieu*, trans. H. B. Hill (Madison, 1961), p. 22.

5. Jean Savaron, *Traicté contre les duels* (Paris, 1610), pp. 76–77.

6. "Arrest de la cour de Parlement contre les Sieurs de Bouteville, Comte de Pongibault, Le Baron de Chantail, et des Salles, pour s'être battus en duel le jour de Paques, donné le 24 avril 1624," in C. De Chatauvillard, *Essai sur le duel* (Paris, 1836), pp. 287–90. Hereafter cited as Chatauvillard.

7. François de la Noue, *Discours Politiques et Militaires* (Geneva, 1967), p. 281.

8. *Mémoires-journaux de Pierre de l'Estoile*, 12 vols. (Paris, 1875–1896), 9:277.

9. G. and J. de Saulx-Tavannes, *Mémoires*, ed. Michaud and Poujoulat (Paris, 1881), p. 154; cited by Robert R. Harding, *Anatomy of a Power Elite* (New Haven, 1978), p. 77.

10. Edmund H. Dickerman, "Henri IV of France, the Duel and the Battle Within," *Societas* 3, no. 3 (Summer, 1973): 207.

11. Cited by Herr, "Honor versus Absolutism," p. 282.

12. Savaron, *Traicté contre les duels*, p. 49.

13. Henri Morel, "La Fin du Duel Judiciaire en France et Naissance du Point d'honneur," *Revue historique du droit francais et étranger*, 1964, pp. 574–639; Jean-Marie Carbasse, "Le Duel Judiciaire dans les coûtumes meridionales," *Annales du Midi* 87 (1975): 385–403.

14. Montaigne, "Cowardice, Mother of Cruelty," in *The Complete Essays*, trans. D. Frame (Stanford, 1958), p. 525.

15. On the introduction of the rapier, see Lawrence Stone, *The Crisis of the English Aristocracy, 1558–1641* (Oxford, 1965), pp. 244–45.

16. Frederick Robertson Bryson, *The Point of Honor in Sixteenth-Century Italy: An Aspect of the Life of the Gentleman* (New York, 1935).

17. Harding, *Anatomy of a Power Elite*, p. 80.

18. The argument that the nobility in the sixteenth century experienced an economic decline is put forth by Gaston Roupnel, *La ville et le compagne au XVIIe siècle: Etude sur les populations du pays dijonnais* (reprint; Paris, 1955), p. 234 and *passim*, and Pierre Goubert, *Beauvais et le Beauvaisis de 1600 à 1730*, p. 213 and *passim*. The opposing view is suggested by J. Russell Major, "The Crown and the Aristocracy in the Renaissance," *American Historical Review* 69 (April, 1963): 631–45, and "Noble Income, Inflation and the Wars of Religion in France," *American Historical Review* 86 (February, 1981): 21–28; and by John Wood, *The Nobility of the Election of Bayeux, 1463–1666* (Princeton, 1980), and "The Decline of the Nobility in Sixteenth and Early Seventeenth Century France: Myth or Reality?" *Journal of Modern History* 48, Supp. (1976): 1–29.

19. Major, "The Crown and the Aristocracy," p. 631; Jean-Pierre Labatut, *Les Ducs et Pairs de France au XVIIe Siècle* (Paris, 1972), pp. 57–61.

20. Davis Bitton, *The French Nobility in Crisis, 1560–1640* (Stanford, 1969), p. 95.

21. Louys de Chabans, *Advis et Moyens pour Empescher le désordre des duels, proposez au Roy en l'Assemblée des Estats Généraux* (Paris, 1615), pp. 17–18.

22. C. R. Mayes, "Sale of Peerages in Early Stuart England," *Journal of Modern History* 29 (1957): 21–37; J. P. Kenyon, *Stuart England* (New York, 1978), pp. 77–78.

23. Roland Mousnier, *La Vénalité des Offices sous Henri IV et Louis XIII* (reprint; Paris, 1971), p. 43.

24. On the educational background of office holders, see Richard Bonney, *Political Change in France under Richelieu and Mazarin, 1624–1661* (Oxford, 1978), pp. 90–92. On the tensions between Robe and Sword, see R. Mousnier, J.-P. Labatut and Y. Durand, *Deux cahiers de la noblesse pour les Etats Généraux de 1649–51* (Paris, 1965), pp. 31–36.

25. Anon., *Discours des querelles et l'honneur* (Paris, 1594); cited by George Huppert, *Les Bourgeois Gentilhommes* (Chicago, 1977), p. 100.

26. Charles Loyseau, *Traicté des ordres et simples dignitez* (Paris, 1610), foreword and chap. 1; Roland Mousnier, *The Institutions of France under the Absolute Monarchy, 1598–1789*, trans. Brian Pearce (Chicago, 1979), pp. 13–15.

27. Franklin Ford, *Robe and Sword: The Regrouping of the French Aristocracy after Louis XIV* (New York, 1965), pp. 69, 75.

28. Huppert, *Les Bourgeois Gentilhommes*, p. 99.

29. Bitton, *The French Nobility in Crisis*, p. 100; M. E. Vaisse-Cibiel, "Les Arrêts Somptuaires du Parlement de Toulouse," *Mémoires de l'Académie des Sciences, Inscriptions et Belles-Lettres*, 7th series, 2 (1870): 248–66; Hubert Pierquin, *La Juridiction du Point d'Honneur sous l'Ancien Régime et le Tribunal des Maréchaux de France* (Paris, 1904).

30. Michael Roberts, "The Military Revolution, 1560–1660," in his *Essays in Swedish History* (London, 1967), p. 209. For an overview of the evolution of military techniques and its relationship to social and political developments in Western Europe, see Samuel E. Finer, "State- and Nation-Building in Europe: The Role of the Military," in *The Formation of National States in Western Europe*, ed. Charles Tilly (Princeton, 1975), pp. 84–163. For a critique of Roberts, see Geoffrey Parker, "The 'Military Revolution,' 1560–1660—a Myth?" *Journal of Modern History* 48 (June, 1976): 195–214.

31. Robert Mandrou, *Introduction to Modern France, 1500–1640*, trans. R. C. Hallmark (New York, 1977), p. 105; Bitton, *The French Nobility in Crisis*, pp. 28–30; Pierre Deyon, "A propos des rapports entre la noblesse française et la monarchie absolue pendant la première moitié du XVIIe siècle," *Revue Historique* 88 (1964): 341–56.

32. Pierre de Bourdeilles, Seigneur de Brantôme, *Oeuvres Complètes*, ed. Lalanne (Paris, 1864–82), 5:367–68; cited by Bitton, *The French Nobility in Crisis*, p. 36.

33. On this point see the brilliant essay by S. P. Zitner, "Hamlet, Duellist," *University of Toronto Quarterly* 39 (October, 1969): 5. I am grateful to Natalie Zemon Davis for this reference.

34. Montaigne, "Cowardice, Mother of Cruelty," p. 527.

35. On the topic of noble criminality and violence, see George d'Avenal, *La*

noblesse francaise sous Richelieu (Paris, 1901); C. J. Burckhardt, *Richelieu and His Age*, trans. B. Hoy, 3 vols. (New York, 1970), 2: *passim;* Yves-Marie Bercé, *Histoire des Croquants*, 2 vols. (Paris and Geneva, 1974), 1:135–37, and "De la criminalité aux troubles sociaux: La noblesse rural du Sud-Ouest de la France sous Louis XIII," *Annales du Midi* 76 (1964): 41–59; C. Barrière-Flavy, *La chonique criminelle d'une grande province sous Louis XIV* (Toulouse, 1926).

36. Claude Haton, *Mémoires*, ed. F. Bourgquelet (Paris, 1857), 2:854–55; cited in Mandrou, *Introduction to Modern France*, p. 104.

37. René Pintard, "Les adventures et le procès du Chevalier Roquelaure," *Revue d'Histoire de la Philosophie et d'Histoire Général de la Civilisation*, January, 1937, pp. 1–24.

38. Tallement de Reaux, *Histoirettes*, ed. A. Adam, 2 vols. (Paris, 1960), 1:1033–34; J. H. M. Salmon, *Cardinal de Retz: The Anatomy of a Conspirator* (New York, 1969), p. 15.

39. Johan Huizinga, *Homo Ludens, A Study of the Play Element in Culture* (Boston, 1955), and *The Waning of the Middle Ages* (Garden City, 1954), p. 80.

40. Montaigne, "Cowardice, Mother of Cruelty," p. 526.

41. The continuity between medieval chivalry and the Renaissance notion of honor is emphasized by Paul Benichou, *Morales du Grand Siècle* (Paris, 1948), pp. 20–23, and Huizinga, *Waning of the Middle Ages*, pp. 40, 69. Jacob Burkhardt argued that in this and in other respects the Renaissance marked a clear departure from medieval aristocratic ideals. See his *The Civilization of the Renaissance in Italy*, trans. S. G. C. Middlemore, 2 vols. (New York, 1958), 2:428–29.

42. Baldassare Castiglione, *The Book of the Courtier*, trans. T. Hoby (London and New York, 1928). A major exponent of Castiglione's views in France was Nicolas Faret, whose *Honnête homme ou l'art de plaire à la cour* (1630), was a standard source on aristocratic *politesse*. On this topic see Maurice Magendie, *La Politesse mondaine et les théories de l'honnêteté en France de 1600 à 1660* (reprint; Geneva, 1970).

43. Francois Rabelais, *Gargantua*, Book 1 (New York, n.d.), p. 44.

44. Hiram Haydn, *The Counter-Renaissance* (New York, 1950), p. 573.

45. Fredson Thayer Bowers, *Elizabethan Revenge Tragedy, 1587–1647* (Princeton, 1940).

46. On the relationship of Corneille's work to the changing values of aristocratic society, see Benichou, *Morales du Grand Siècle*, pp. 13–76; Antony Levi, *French Moralists* (Oxford, 1964); and Orest Ranum, *Paris in the Age of Absolutism* (Bloomington and London, 1979), pp. 132–66. The topic of the reemergence of aristocratic notions of heroism in the seventeenth century is also discussed by Paul Hazard in his *The European Mind, 1680–1715*, trans. J. Lewis (Cleveland, 1963), pp. 321–23.

47. Bryson, *The Point of Honor in Sixteenth-Century Italy*.

48. The relationship of noblemen to their *fidèles* in the early modern period is stressed by Roland Mousnier in his various works. See, for example, his

Peasant Uprisings, trans. B. Pierce (New York, 1970). The importance of the code of honor for a Southern gentleman is treated by B. Wyatt-Brown, *Southern Honor* (Oxford, 1982).

49. G. N. Clarke, *War and Society in the Seventeenth Century* (Cambridge, 1958). See also Bryson, *The Point of Honor in Sixteenth-Century Italy*, p. 39.

50. Kurt Wolff, ed., *The Sociology of Georg Simmel* (Glencoe, 1958), p. 321.

51. Bryson, *The Point of Honor in Sixteenth-Century Italy*, pp. 55–72.

52. Cited in W. L. Wiley, *The Gentleman of Renaissance France* (Cambridge, Mass., 1954), p. 182.

53. Cited in Dickerman, "Henri IV and the Duel," p. 208.

54. C. Cheffontaines, *Chrestienne confutation du point d'honneur sur lequel la noblesse fond aujourd'hui ses querelles et monomachies* (Paris, 1568), p. 51; cited by Harding, *Anatomy of a Power Elite*, p. 77.

55. Sénac de Meilhan, *Considérations sur les Richesses et le Luxe* (Paris, 1787), p. 89; cited by C. B. A. Behrens, *The Ancien Regime* (London, 1967), p. 74. The Bishop of Nantes, writing to Richelieu in support of Des Chapelles, sounded the theme that the French nobility was wedded to the point of honor almost despite itself: "our ancestors, perhaps without reason, became so attached to honor that even the oldest and wisest could not rid themselves of this notion" (*Les Papiers de Richelieu*, ed. Pierre Grillon, vol. 2 [Paris, 1977], p. 195).

56. Pierre Chaignon, *Le Duel sous l'Ancien Régime* (Paris, 1936), p. 8.

57. "Arrest de la Cour de Parlement contre les Duels, du 26 juin 1599," in Chatauvillard, pp. 219–21.

58. "Edit du Roy sur la prohibition des querelles et duels, donné à Fontaine Bleau au mois de juin 1609," in Chatauvillard, pp. 230–44.

59. "Arrest de la Cour de Parlement contre Bouteville et Des Chapelles, du 21 juin 1627," in Chatauvillard, pp. 321–24.

60. "Edit du Roy contre les Duels et Rencontres, donné à Paris au mois de septembre, 1651," in Chatauvillard, pp. 423–54.

61. Chaignon, *Le Duel sous l'Ancien Régime*, p. 23.

62. Dickerman, "Henri IV and the Duel," p. 212.

63. *Mémoires-journaux de Pierre de l'Estoile*, 9:277.

64. "Edit du Roy sur la prohibition des querelles et duels, donné à Fontaine Bleau au mois de juin 1609," (article V), in Chatauvillard, p. 235.

65. Chaignon, *Le Duel sous l'Ancien Régime*, pp. 42, 50.

66. Jean Bodin, *The Six Books of a Commonweale*, ed. R. McRae (Cambridge, Mass., 1972), pp. 494–96.

67. *Canons and Decrees of the Council of Trent*, ed. and trans. H. J. Schroeder (St. Louis and London, 1941 and 1960), p. 251.

68. J. Russell Major, "The Crown and the Aristocracy in France," p. 645 n.57.

69. On the Tribunal of the Marshals, see M. de Beaufort, *Recueil concernant le Tribunal de Nosseigneurs les Maréchaux de France*, 2 vols. (Paris, 1784); Hubert Pierquin, *La Juridiction du Point d'Honneur sous l'Ancien Régime et le Tribunal des Maréchaux de France* (Paris, 1904); Chaignon, *Le Duel sous*

l'Ancien Régime, pp. 15–22; Roland Mousnier, *The Institutions of France under the Absolute Monarchy, 1598–1789*, trans. B. Pierce (Chicago and London, 1979), pp. 141–46.

70. Chaignon, *Le Duel sous l'Ancien Régime*, p. 7.

71. "Edit du Roi pour la defense des duels, donné à Blois au mois d'avril, 1602," in Chatauvillard, p. 227.

72. "Edit du Roi sur la prohibition des querelles et duels, donné à Fontaine Bleau au mois de juin 1609," in Chatauvillard, pp. 325, 237.

73. "Lettres patentes du Roi sur l'observation des édits, ordonnances et declarations faites sur la défense des duels, avec amplification (1617)," in Chatauvillard, p. 273.

74. "Edit du Roi contre les duels, donné à Paris au mois de septembre 1651," in Chatauvillard, pp. 426–27, 431.

75. Beaufort, *Recueil concernant le Tribunal de Nosseigneurs les Maréchaux de France*, 1:46–56.

76. Beaufort lists the members of the tribunal during the old regime; all are of the highest ranks of the nobility (*Recueil concernant le Tribunal de Nosseigneurs les Maréchaux de France*, 1:93–136).

77. That Richelieu, in particular, cherished aristocratic values and the destiny of the aristocracy is stressed by Orest Ranum, "Richelieu and the Great Nobility: Some Aspects of Early Modern Political Motives," *French Historical Studies* 3, no. 2 (Fall, 1963): 184–204.

78. Beaufort, *Recueil concernant le Tribunal de Nosseigneurs les Maréchaux de France*, 1:254–60; Pierquin, *La Juridiction du Point d'Honneur sous l'Ancien Régime*, pp. 63–64; Mousnier, *The Institutions of France under the Absolute Monarchy*, p. 144.

79. Orest Ranum, "Courtesy, Absolutism and the Rise of the French State," *Journal of Modern History* 52 (September, 1980): 426–51.

80. On this topic, see Benichou, *Morales du Grand Siècle*; Levi, *French Moralists;* A. J. Krailsheimer, *Studies in Self-Interest, From Descartes to La Bruyere* (Oxford, 1962); Nannerl O. Keohane, *Philosophy and the State in France, The Renaissance to the Enlightenment* (Princeton, 1980); Albert O. Hirschman, *The Passions and the Interests* (Princeton, 1977).

81. For a discussion of Silhon, see Lionel Rothkrug, *Opposition to Louis XIV* (Princeton, 1965), pp. 56–58, and Keohane, *Philosophy and the State in France*, pp. 287–89.

82. *The Misanthrope*, trans. Richard Wilbur (New York, 1954), p. 73 (act 2, scene 7).

83. *Canons and Decrees of the Council of Trent*, p. 251.

84. The main source on the company is H. Beauchet-Filleau, ed., *Annales de la Compagnie du St.-Sacrement par le Comte René de Voyer d'Argenson* (Marseille, 1900). Also crucial are Raoul Allier, *La Compagnie du Saint-Sacrement de l'Autel: La Cabale des Dévots* (Paris, 1902), and Emmanuel Chill, "The Company of the Holy Sacrament: Social Aspects of the French Counter Reformation" (Ph.D. diss. Columbia University, 1960).

85. Chill, "The Company of the Holy Sacrament," p. 231. See also the sixth of Pascal's *Lettres Provinciales.*

86. Allier, *La Cabale des Dévots,* pp. 324–25; Chill, "The Company of the Holy Sacrament," p. 224.

87. Allier, *La Cabale des Dévots,* p. 325; Chill, "The Company of the Holy Sacrament," p. 226.

88. Allier, *La Cabale des Dévots,* p. 326.

89. "Jugement de Messieurs les Maréchaux de France sur la declaration faite par plusieurs Gentilshommes de refuser toutes sortes d'appels," in Chatauvillard, pp. 470–72.

90. "Avis des Docteurs de la Faculté de Paris sur le même sujet," in Chatauvillard, pp. 479–80.

91. "Résolution de Messieurs les Prélats sur cette matière," in Chatauvillard, pp. 473–78.

92. Allier, *La Cabale des Dévots,* p. 328; Chill, "The Company of the Holy Sacrament," p. 225.

93. "Edit du Roi contre les duels, donné à Paris au mois de septembre 1651," (article XXIV), in Chatauvillard, pp. 452–53.

94. Allier, *La Cabale des Dévots,* pp. 329–30.

95. Allier, *La Cabale des Dévots,* p. 332.

96. Barthélemy Pocquet, "La Compagnie du Saint-Sacrement à Rennes," *Revue de Bretagne* 32 (July, 1904): 221–25.

97. Allier, *La Cabale des Dévots,* p. 333; Chill, "The Company of the Holy Sacrament," p. 229.

98. For an interesting interpretation of the Reformation in France along these same lines, see Donald R. Kelley, *The Beginning of Ideology* (Cambridge, 1981).

99. This aspect of the Counter-Reformation is emphasized by John Bossy, "The Counter-Reformation and the People of Europe," *Past and Present* 47 (May, 1970): 51–70. Bossy, however, downplays the role of lay confraternities in quelling feuds and establishing social peace, something I point out in a paper delivered at the annual meeting of the American Historical Association in Washington, D.C., on December 30, 1982, "The Catholic Community of Seventeenth-Century Toulouse."

100. Georges Pagès, "Autour de grand orage. Richelieu et Marillac: deux politiques," *Revue Historique* 79 (1937): 63–97.

101. This was one conclusion of the article by Roland Mousnier and Fritz Hartung, "Quelques problèmes concernant la monarchie absolue," in *Relazioni del X Congreso Internazionale di Scienze Storiche,* vol 4, *Storia moderna* (Firenze, 1955), pp. 1–55. Mousnier subsequently modified his views in "Recherches sur les soulèvements populaires en France avant la Fronde," *Revue d'histoire moderne et contemporaine* 5 (1958): 81–113. For a Marxist view of the absolute state as representing the interests of the bourgeoisie, see A. D. Lublinskaya, *French Absolutism: The Crucial Phase, 1620–1629* (London and New York, 1968), pp. 330 and *passim.*

102. Savaron, *Traicté contre les duels*, p. 81.
103. Major, "The Crown and the Aristocracy in the Renaissance," and "Noble Income, Inflation and the Wars of Religion in France." The aristocracy's interest in education during the Renaissance has been underscored by J. H. Hexter, "The Education of the Aristocracy in the Renaissance," in *Reappraisals in History*, 2d ed. (Chicago, 1979). For figures demonstrating the relatively high proportion of sons of aristocrats enrolled in Jesuit *collèges*, see F. de Dainville, "Collèges et fréquentation scolaire au XVIIe siècle," *Population* 3 (1957): 470, and Frijhoff and Julia, *Ecole et Société dans la France de L'Ancien Régime* (Paris, 1975), pp. 12–13. For a discussion of the ways in which the French nobility was forced to adapt and change in accordance to the challenges of the late sixteenth century, see Ellery Schalk, "The Appearance and Reality of the Nobility in France during the Wars of Religion: An Example of How Collective Attitudes Can Change," *Journal of Modern History* 48 (1976): 17–31.

SOCIAL MOVEMENTS AND NATIONAL POLITICS

Charles Tilly

Languedoc: 1682

Imagine yourself strolling in sunny Narbonne, France, during a summer almost three centuries ago. On the first of August, 1682, according to the report the Intendant of Languedoc sent to Paris,

> there was a little movement in Narbonne on the occasion of the collection of the *cosse* tax, which had been ordered by an act of the royal council. Many women gathered with the common people, and threw stones at the tax collectors, but the Consuls and the leading citizens hurried over and put a stop to the disorder.[1]

A *cosse* was a local grain measure which held something like five liters. More important, it held one-fortieth of a *sétier* of grain; to collect one *cosse* per *sétier*, which was the aim of those tax collectors, was to tax grain at 2.5 percent. The royal domain had long held the legal right to collect the *cosse* on all grain sold by outsiders at Narbonne, but the sixteenth-century Wars of Religion had interrupted the collection of the tax. In 1682, the royal council (guided by Colbert in its incessant search for revenue to pay for royal wars and regal display) had authorized the royal property agent to begin anew the collection of the *cosse*. The agent ordered the construction of toll booths at the city's gates, and directed his clerks to collect the tax on all grain brought in by nonresidents.

The city's consuls did what they dared to oppose the *cosse*—and, especially, its collection at the gates rather than at the market—on the ground that it would discourage trade and raise the price of food in the city. But their daring did not go very far. While the consuls filed ineffectual protests, the city's women gathered and stoned the tax collectors. Their "little movement" failed to halt the collection of the tax. Yet after years of conflict and negotiation, in 1691 the intendant finally arranged the conversion of the *cosse* into a general cash payment from the Estates to the royal property agent.[2] For all their disapproval of protest in the streets, the authorities recognized that the reinstated tax was inconvenient, and perhaps unjust.[3]

Let us neglect the complexities of seventeenth-century finances, and focus on that "little movement" of Narbonne's women. It resembled many other local French conflicts of the seventeenth century in that it involved direct action against the royal attempt to levy new taxes. It resembled many other troubles following the midcentury Fronde (but differed from many before and during the Fronde) in that the authorities, despite their opposition to the royal measure, immediately stepped in to repress the popular resistance. It resembled many other struggles of the time in which women played an especially prominent role in that the immediate issues concerned food, marketing, and the cost of living. In these regards, the August confrontation of Narbonne stands for thousands of other seventeenth-century conflicts.[3]

What should we call it? The local authorities called it not only a *petit mouvement,* but also an *émotion populaire* and a *désordre.* All these terms belonged to the period's standard vocabulary; they designated a localized collective action by ordinary people which the authorities considered necessary and proper to end by force. But what should *we* call it? That is a conceptual question. Using the terminology of the time is one possible answer to the question; perhaps we should settle for *émotion* or *désordre,* much as we usually insist on calling the royal officers of the time by their rightful titles instead of substituting the closest twentieth-century equivalent. Yet the terminology of the time brings along its own ambiguities, variations, and overtones, and makes it the more difficult to undertake the sort of comparison we might want to try between the fighting women of Narbonne in 1692 and the fighting women of, say, Los Angeles in the twentieth century.

Since the authorities of Narbonne themselves used the word *mouvement,* would it be legitimate to apply the venerable label *social movement?* That would probably cause more confusion than insight. Somehow a social movement should be more durable than that fleeting encounter between Narbonne's women and the tax collectors; it should pursue broader aims than the blocking of a particular toll. If, on the other hand, we were convinced that the little affair of 1682 was only one incident in a long series, that the women of Narbonne were aware of their common interests and distinct identity, and that they were self-consciously seeking a set of changes considerably larger than the suspension of one tax or another, then we might comfortably begin to think in terms of a social movement.

The Camisards

In the Languedoc of that time there was at least one set of people who came close to those demanding standards. They were not the women of Narbonne, but the Protestants—women, men, and children alike—of the mountains. For about four decades, beginning the the 1670s, the same correspondence of the intendant which reported the Narbonne affair was packed with discussions of the "fanatics." During the 1670s, the intendant followed royal policy by squeezing out of public office those Protestants who refused to abjure their faith. The measures against the RPR (Religion Prétendue Réformée, "So-Called Reformed Religion") broadened and intensified during the early 1680s.

The Protestants prepared to defend themselves. "The Huguenots of the Vivarais," reported the intendant in August 1683,

> continue not only to preach in forbidden places, but also to prepare for war. It is true that they have no chiefs, not even halfway-qualified gentry, in their party; we took care of that by seizing all the leaders that appeared, or that we suspected, right at the start. All the same, they have managed to set up a sort of military base. They have organized companies under specific commanders. They have captured some castles. They are digging in, they have ammunition and arms. In a word, whipped up by ministers who preach nothing but sedition and rebellion, they give every appearance of planning to resist the king's troops.[4]

The most serious was yet to come. In 1685, with the revocation of the Edict of Nantes, began the major drive to convert, or at least to suppress, the many Protestants of the Cévennes, the Vivarais, and other regions of Languedoc. From that time on, relations between the province's royal officials and its Protestants swung between open war and troubled peace.

Immediately after the revocation, a new intendant of Languedoc, Nicolas de Lamoignon de Basville, declared his hope of mastering the enemy by means of severe and ostentatious repression; an early effort was his hanging seven and decapitating one of the illegal assembly of "new converts which had killed two of the soldiers sent to break it up." ("New converts" were people who had nominally subscribed to Catholicism, but had actually retained their Protestant ties.) "There are no ministers preaching," he wrote contemptuously, "there are nothing but miserable preaching carders and peasants who lack even common sense; I hope to arrest two or three of them that I haven't been able to find yet."[5] Vain hope. The "assemblies in the desert" multiplied, Protestant military forces sprang up in the backlands, and the royal troops found themselves beginning a guerrilla operation that lasted intermittently for twenty-five years.

By the end of the 1680s, inspired prophets—men, women, boys, and, especially, girls—were preaching in the Vivarais. By the end of the century, poor men and women possessed by ecstatic trances and the gift of prophecy were communicating divine instructions to the people of the Cévennes. There in the Cévennes the Protestant rebels took on the name of Camisards. In 1703, the same intendant who had hoped, seventeen years earlier, to break Protestant resistance through spectacular but limited punishment resorted to ordering the entire Protestant countryside of the Diocese of Mende evacuated, and dozens of villages burned to the ground. The strategy of scorched earth did not begin in the twentieth century.

Even with that ferocious treatment, it took another year to check the major Camisard rebellion, another six years to smash the last Camisard military force, another ten or twenty years to fragment and tame the region's Protestants to the point that they no longer posed a serious challenge to royal authority. As late as 1710, a royal patrol fell upon "an assembly in the parish of Saumane, of five armed men and twenty women," killing two men and four women in the process.[6]

Who were these zealots? The question is a nettle, difficult to grasp without being stung; the answer varies according to our choice of time point, region, and (most importantly) criterion of membership. At one extreme, we might be thinking of all the Protestants in Languedoc: 202,794 of the province's 1,561,541 inhabitants, according to the ludicrously precise statistics reported by the intendant in 1698.[7] At the other extreme, we might take only the few thousand who at one time or another actually engaged in armed combat with royal troops. Somewhere in the middle, we might place the many thousands who at least one time joined one of those illegal "assemblies in the desert" to hear a sermon, a prophecy, a reading of the Bible, and an exhortation to resist the Antichrist.

One might justify the first definition—the entire Protestant population—by pointing out the important moral, political, and material support the activists drew from the general population of the Protestant regions; then the Camisards would appear to be a movement drawn disproportionately from the prosperous and commercial milieux of Languedoc. But the more stringent the criterion of membership, the more plebeian the Camisards become: wool carders, weavers, carpenters, bakers, agricultural laborers, and other ordinary rural workers seem to have provided the bulk of the day-to-day activists, female and male. By the standard of open rebellion, it was clearly a popular *mouvement*.

And what did they want? Again the answer varies with the precise phrasing of the question. At times Camisard leaders bid for the abolition of taxes. They often declared against the ecclesiastical tithe. They consistently sought—and acted out—the freedom to assemble in the name of their faith. From time to time they dreamed and prophesied the return of their exiled pastors. Emmanuel Le Roy Ladurie writes of "an explosive mixture of prophetic neurosis and fiscal agitation," while Philippe Joutard emphasizes the Camisard "refusal to submit blindly to the central power, and affirmation of the superiority of the conscience."[8] All these, and more, are possible definitions of the interests, grievances, beliefs, and demands around which the Camisards built their movement.

A Social Movement?

But, once again, is the word *movement* appropriate? The query is not a finicky doubt about English usage, since a precisely parallel concept appears in other European languages: *Bewegung, dvizhenie, movimento, rörelse*. So far as common English is concerned, for that matter, we unquestionably have the right to call the actions of the Camisards a movement of some kind; all the dictionary requires is a "series of actions and endeavors of a body of persons for a special object." Yet consider one of the more careful efforts to turn the catchphrase *social movement* into a workable tool of analysis:

> A social movement is a deliberate collective endeavor to promote change in any direction and by any means, not excluding violence, illegality, revolution or withdrawal into "utopian" community. . . . A social movement's commitment to change and the *raison d'être* of its organization are founded upon the conscious volition, normative commitment to the movement's aims or beliefs, and active participation on the part of the followers or members.[9]

Well! If *that* is a social movement, it is debatable whether the Camisards qualify. The commitment to change is debatable, the minimal organization is debatable, even the normative commitment to a presumably unitary set of aims raises a shadow of doubt. If the coherent Camisards do not qualify as a social movement, on the other hand, who does? In fact, a number of groups which have formed and acted in Languedoc over the last century do seem to meet Wilkinson's tests for a social movement: deliberate collective endeavor to promote change, and so on. One dramatic case in point is the winegrowers of the Midi, who responded to the overproduction crisis which began in the 1890s by organizing unions, staging strikes and demonstrations, and, in 1907, mounting a great "revolt" which featured vast meetings, huge demonstrations, attacks on prefectures, and temporary takeovers of major cities.

The phylloxera blight had wiped out a large part of Languedoc's vines in the 1880s, but the replanting and expansion of the 1890s soon made up the deficit. At the same time, the growing importation of cheap Algerian wine and the employment of beet sugar in the manufacture of potable wine from inferior grapes flooded the market and provided the Midi's winegrowers with unprecedented competition. Their markets contracted and their prices fell. From shortly after 1900, various leaders of the region's winegrowers began to agitate for the prohibition of the new sugar wines, for the right to distill part of their vintage and, sometimes, for the suspension of taxes. The day laborers of the wine fields began to organize unions and to demand better wages.

After a roving parliamentary commission had come to hear the complaints of the producers in March 1907, a great campaign of organizing, meeting, and federating took place throughout the vineyard areas. By the fifth of May, some sixty to eighty thousand people were meeting in Narbonne, and being addressed by the socialist mayor Ferroul. In succeeding weeks, to take the minimum estimates, there were 120 thousand at Béziers, 170 thousand at Perpignan, 220 thousand at Carcassonne, 250 thousand at Nîmes, 600 thousand at Montpellier. Soon a taxpayers' strike and a series of ostentatious resignations by municipal officers were under way. By mid-June, the government was sending troops into the region, demonstrators were fighting gendarmes and, back in Narbonne, militants were attacking the subprefecture.

From June through September, the government replied with a few concessions and a good deal of repression. There were hundreds of arrests, and a half-dozen deaths. The formation of the General Confederation of Winegrowers, at another meeting in Narbonne the twenty-second of September, marked the end of the year's turbulence. Then began the negotiations, the trials, the acquittals, the amnesties, and the demobilization of the Midi's winegrowers.

Was that a social movement? It is interesting to scan the text of the speech that Ernest Ferroul, physician, socialist, and mayor of Narbonne gave at Perpignan on the sixteenth of June. At that point, Ferroul faced an acute political problem: The most visible organizer of the agitation was the innkeeper Marcellin Albert, head of the winegrower's committee in the village of Argelliers; but it was time, thought Ferroul, to shift the agitation from its village base and loose organization to an urban base and a larger scale—led, perhaps, by the socialist mayors of crucial cities. If the Argelliers committee, said Ferroul,

> has prepared magnificent, unprecedented marches, without historical parallel; if it has organized the great winegrowers' demonstrations you know, which are characterized by a marvelous calmness, solidarity and agreement, it is now impossible for the committee to direct from its own home such a grand movement, spread across four departments.[10]

And later he declared:

> This movement is not political. It is deep and human. It is not the agitation of a party, but the uprising of men who want to live, and who are protesting against their hunger.[11]

The word *movement* recurs in a different context and with a different tone from the *petit mouvement* of 1682. Narbonne's mayor wants to stress the winegrowers' numbers, commitment, and internal discipline, their orientation to deeply serious matters, the fact that they stand above and beyond routine party politics. Somehow that series of actions at the beginning of our century exemplifies what Wilkinson and other scholars have in mind when they discuss and define social movements. So do a number of other phenomena—labor movements, political movements, even Protestant religious movements—which Languedoc has produced since the later nineteenth century. The comparison of the twentieth-century winegrowers with the seventeenth-century Protestants raises the suspicion that the notion of the social movement is more closely tied to the social organization of our own time than the abstract phrasing and universal sweep of the usual definitions suggest.

The suspicion is well founded. Both the concept and the phenomenon it represents are largely nineteenth-century creations. The concept of "movement," in the sense of sustained collective action, drew some of its initial appeal from its mechanical analogy. Then there was *the* Social Movement—die soziale Bewegung—the historical trend which most observers identified with the rise of the working classes. That idea of a dominant historical trend tied to the changing position of a particular class of people was one of the chief tools of social analysis bequeathed by the nineteenth century to the twentieth. The idea of many such movements, not all of them beneficent or even connected with one another, is a simple adaptation of the basic concept in the face of a stubbornly diverse reality.

The Rise of Social Movements

The reality itself was largely a nineteenth-century creation. People have, to be sure, banded together more or less self-consciously for the pursuit of common ends since the beginning of history. The nineteenth century, however, saw the rise of the social movement in the sense of a set of people who voluntarily and deliberately commit themselves to a shared identity, a unifying belief, a common program, and a collective struggle to realize that program. The great bulk of the earlier uprisings and popular fervors to which we are tempted to apply the term were fundamentally defensive actions by groups which had long existed. During the aggressive seventeenth-century expansion of states, for example, the standard case was the concerted resistance by the people of long-established communities to the imposition of new forms of taxation which infringed their rights and jeopardized their survival. Although plenty of nineteenth-century movements had defensive origins, the remarkable feature of that century was the shift to the deliberate constitution of new groups for the offensive pursuit of new rights and advantages.

Here we need a distinction. The general phenomenon we are examining is the organized, sustained, self-conscious challenge to existing authorities. A wide variety of authorities receive such challenges: not only rulers of states, but also bishops, bosses, landlords, and college presidents. Let us retain the name *social movement* for that general sort of challenge to existing authorities. A special, crucial class of social movements pits challengers against the people who run national states. Let us call them *national* social movements. These are my claims:

- that the national social movement took shape and spread as a way of doing political business in western countries during the nineteenth century
- that the development of national electoral politics and the proliferation of created associations as vehicles for collective action promoted the rise of the national social movement
- that the availability of a model of action at the national level facilitated the formation of social movements at other levels, in the form of challenges to other authorities than the managers of national states
- that the characteristic structures and histories of social movements vary significantly as a function of the kinds of authorities to which they are oriented, and that national social movements therefore differ importantly from other kinds
- that analysts of social movements have ordinarily taken national social movements as their starting points, and have therefore confused a crucial but historically specific form of action with the whole phenomenon

Two things happened in the nineteenth century, then: National social movements crystallized and multiplied, and other social movements became much more common.

The rise of the national social movement belongs to the same complex of changes which included two other profound transformations in the character of popular collective action—the growth of national electoral politics, and the proliferation of created associations as the vehicles of action. Notice the difficulty faced by Rudolf Heberle, in a standard American textbook on social movements, when he seeks to dissociate the movement from the political party. After adopting Schumpeter's description of a political party as a group of people who "propose to act in concert in the competitive struggle for political power," Heberle goes on to say,

A genuine social movement, on the other hand, is always integrated by a set of constitutive ideas, or an ideology, although bonds of other nature may not be absent. Furthermore, a party is by definition related to a larger group, within which it operates against at least one partial group of similar character. Parties can appear in all kinds of corporate groups, but a political party by definition can occur only within a body politic, that is, only within a state. A social movement, on the other hand, need not be restricted to a particular state or to a national society. In fact, all major social movements have extended over the entire sphere of Western civilization and even beyond.[12]

The net result of all this maneuvering is not, ironically, to clarify the differences between social movements and political parties, but to stress their resemblance. They are *frères ennemis*, each taking part of its identity from the contrast with the other. A social movement is essentially a party with broad aspirations and a unifying belief system. A political party is a tamed, nationalized social movement. That is why Heberle can step easily into the analysis of nazism and communism, and why we sense a vague unease when attempting to treat the seventeenth-century Camisards as a social movement.

Let me spare you a review of the various, ambiguous, and sometimes sloppy uses to which the concept *social movement* has been put. My aim here is neither to castigate other conceptualizers, nor to plead for more precise, adequate, and comprehensive definitions, nor yet to argue that "social movement" is a poor concept because it is historically specific. Far from it. I want to argue that the recognition of the historical specificity of the forms of collective action is the beginning of wisdom. I hope to situate the concept of social movement in its historical setting, and to suggest how its strengths and weaknesses reflect the realities of that historical setting.

To be specific, I want to argue the following points: It is a mistake to conceive of a social movement as a group somehow parallel to (but also opposed to) a party. Indeed, it is a mistake to think of a social movement as a group of any kind. Instead, the term *social movement* applies most usefully to a sustained *interaction* between a specific set of authorities and various spokespersons for a given challenge to those authorities. The interaction is a coherent, bounded unit in roughly the same sense that a war or a political campaign is a unit. Such interactions have occurred from time to time ever since there were authorities of any kind. The broadest sense of the term *social movement* includes all such challenges. In a narrower sense, however, the national social movement draws its form and meaning from an interaction with the authorities who staff a national state. To improve on Wilkinson, Heberle, and other group-oriented theorists, we need a definition on this order:

A social movement is a sustained series of interactions between power holders and persons successfully claiming to speak on behalf of a constituency lacking formal representation, in the course of which those persons make publicly visible demands for changes in the distribution or exercise of power, and back those demands with public demonstrations of support.

A *national* social movement, then, pits such challengers against the people who run a national state. Like all such definitions, this one poses practical choices: setting some minimum number of interactions, arriving at tests of the "success" of claims to speak for à constituency, deciding how little formal representation is a lack of it, defining thresholds for the visibility of demands and the demonstrations of support for them, and so on. But the definition excludes a variety of phenomena—religious innovations, crusades, local rebellions, and others—to which the term *social movement* has often been loosely applied. In this narrower sense, both the concept of social movement and the sort of interaction the concept fits best are products of the nineteenth-century growth of popular electoral politics on a national scale. In any case, the definition does not single out groups, but interactions.

No groups? Let me be clear on that point. Groups are crucial to social movements, as armies are crucial to wars and parties to electoral campaigns. At one point or another in the history of every social movement, the organizers of the challenge in question claim to speak for at least one important group which has an interest in the challenge's outcome. (In the French winegrowers' movement of 1907, one of the points at issue between Marcellin Albert and Ernest Ferroul was who had the right to speak for the winegrowers as a whole.) The organizers may well recruit participants and supporters from the group whose interest they claim to represent. (Albert's genius was his ability to draw local communities of winegrowers into the common regional effort.) The activists with respect to any particular challenge commonly originate in well-defined groups, and often form new groups in the process of making the challenge. (The creation of the General Federation of Winegrowers marked a major transition in the movement of 1907: the start of sustained negotiations between group and government.) At the very center of the nineteenth-century transformation which made the social movement a standard way of doing political business came a great broadening of the conditions under which new groups could form and mount challenges to the authorities, and old groups could bring challenges into the public arena.

In order to see the nineteenth-century transition more clearly, we should reflect on the specific means that ordinary people use to act together on their interests, and on how those means changed in the nineteenth century. Over the last few hundred years, ordinary people have used a remarkable variety of means to act together. If we run forward in time from the era of the Camisards to our own day, we encounter inter-village fights, mocking, and retaliatory ceremonies such as Riding the Stang and Katzenmusik, attacks on tax collectors, petitions, mutinies, solemn assemblies, and many other forms of action, most of them now long abandoned, in the early period. As we approach our own time we notice electoral rallies, demonstrations, strikes, attempted revolutions, mass meetings, and a great variety of other means, most of them unknown in the time of the Camisards.

Now, there are two important things to notice about these forms of action. First, they *are* forms: learned, understood, sometimes planned and rehearsed by the participants. They are not the "outbursts" and "riots" dear to authorities and crowd psychologists. Second, at a given point in time a particular group of people who shared an interest had only a few of these means at their disposal. At their disposal? The group knew, more or less, how to execute them, and was capable of identifying some conditions in which it would be both possible and legitimate to use those means. The women of seventeenth-century Narbonne knew how to attack the tax collector, but they also knew how to assemble and deliberate, how to seize the goods of a baker who overcharged for bread, how to conduct a *charivari*. They did not, however, have at their disposal the creation of an association, the launching of a strike, the organization of a demonstration, or any number of other means which are commonplace in our own time.

Let us think of the set of means which is effectively available to a given set of people as their repertoire of collective action.[13] The analogy with the repertoire of theater and music is helpful because it emphasizes the learned character of the performance and the limits to that learning, yet allows for variation and even continuous change from one perfor-mance to the next. The repertoire of collective action typically leaves plenty of room for improvisation, innovation, and unexpected endings. Change in our repertoires occurs through three main processes.

1. the invention or adoption of new means, e.g., the deliberate creation of the "sit-in" by American civil rights workers of the 1950s
2. the evolution and adaptation of means which are already available, e.g., the way London radicals expanded the long-established custom of sending a delegation to accompany a petition into mass marches with thousands of supporters for a petition to Parliament
3. the abandonment of means which have proved inappropriate, ineffec-tive, impractical, or dangerous, e.g., the Parisian crowd's abandon-ment of ritual execution, with the display of traitors' heads on pikes, after the initial years of the Revolution

This last example identifies one of the difficulties in the serious study of repertoires: how to distinguish a form of action which is in some sense known and available, but is in fact never used because a likely opportunity for its effective use never comes along. The answer must again draw on the analogy with music and theater. If the performer never performs the piece in public or in private we eventually conclude that the performer has forgotten it, or never knew it. The commonsense rule of thumb has the advantage of confining the study of repertoires to forms of action which real actors have performed, rehearsed, or at least discussed.

Why Study Repertoires?

The study of repertoires provides a splendid opportunity for joining the general analysis of collective action to the concrete realities of day-to-day contention. For any particular set of people who share an interest, we may undertake to describe the means of action realistically available to them. In the context of their time, what forms of action did the Protestants of the seventeenth-century Cévennes have at their disposal? What forms did they know, and what forms were feasible? What were the likely costs and consequences of the alternatives open to them? Assembling in village councils to petition the intendant, for example, was a standard procedure of the time, but it was a dangerous and ineffectual way to resist a royal policy as vigorously pursued as the drive against Protestantism. The collective appeal to a powerful patron had worked well in an earlier age, but became less and less feasible as the seventeenth-century French state expanded its range and power. And so on.

The inventory of available means of collective action draws us at once into a specification of opportunities, threats, repression, facilitation, power, and—most important—the relative costs and likely benefits of the array of choices actually confronting the group in question. It is not necessary to assume that the Camisards, or any other set of collective actors that concerns us, were cool calculators in their own right. In fact, the Camisards had an extraordinary capacity for hysteria, rage, delusion, and blind devotion. All that is necessary is a logic of the situation which limits the options, entails some likely costs and consequences for each option, and provides us with enough information to begin the reconstruction of the decision rules the participants followed.

If the prevailing repertoire of collective action changes significantly at some point in time, the change is prima facie evidence of a substantial alteration in the structure of power. In France, to take the case I know best, the largest repertoire changes of the last four centuries appear to have occurred around the middle of the seventeenth century and again around the middle of the nineteenth century. The Fronde and the Revolution of 1848 are convenient markers for the shifts in repertoire. At the earlier point, the most visible change was the rapid decline of the classic form of rebellion of some constituted body (a village, a military unit, a trade, or something else) which consisted of assembling, deliberating, stating grievances, formally suspending allegiance to the governing authority, choosing a temporary alternate leader, then setting conditions for a return to obedience. In contemporary English, only the word *mutiny* comes close to capturing the character of that old form of rebellion.

During the Wars of Religion and the many rebellions of the early seventeenth century, groups of peasants and artisans who rebelled had frequently elected a local noble as their *capitaine.* That is one reason why, at the end of the seventeenth century, the intendant of Languedoc scanned the Camisards anxiously to see if they had access to Protestant nobles; a link between Protestant countrymen and the regional nobility was much to be feared. By then, however, that link and that form of rebellion had almost disappeared. The defeat of the Fronde and the seventeenth-century co-optation of the nobility, I believe, played a major part in destroying it. The seventeenth-century rise of royal power and expansion of the state was one of the two or three most important alterations in the structure of power over the last four centuries. A major alteration in the repertoire of popular collective action accompanied it.

The nineteenth-century change in the prevailing repertoire of collective action is better documented, and no less dramatic. Around the time of the Revolution of 1848 the tax rebellion consisting of an attack on the collector or his premises went into rapid decline. Although protests of high prices and food shortages continued in other forms, the standard bread riot practically disappeared. So did the *charivari* and a number of other theatrical displays of contempt or moral disapproval. During the same period, the preplanned protest meeting, the electoral rally, the demonstration, the strike, and a number of related forms were crystallizing and becoming frequent. A great alteration in the repertoire was going on.

Was there a concomitant alteration in the structure of power? I believe there was. It included an emphatic nationalization of politics, a greatly increased role of special-purpose associations, a decline in the importance of communities as the loci of shared interests, a growing importance of organized capital and organized labor as participants in power struggles. As a consequence of these massive changes, the available means of acting together on shared interests changed as well. The same sorts of correlated transformations were occurring elsewhere in Western Europe during the nineteenth century: perhaps somewhat earlier in Great Britain, perhaps a bit later in Germany, on varied schedules according to the particular interplay of capitalism and statemaking in one region or another.

Repertoires, Social Movements, and Contemporary
Collective Action

Mapping and explaining the changes in the collective action repertoire is an important task, but it is not the task of this essay. The nineteenth-century changes connect with the previous discussion of social movements in two important ways. First, the nineteenth-century repertoire is still with us today. The strike, the demonstration, the protest meeting, and other forms of action that were novelties then are commonplaces today. As compared with the large alterations in the nineteenth century, the subsequent changes in repertoire have been relatively minor. To be sure, new forms of terrorism have arisen, demonstrations have motorized, mass media have reshaped our perceptions and our tactics. Set against the disappearance of the food riot, the withering away of satirical street theater, or the first flowering of the various forms of action based on special-purpose associations, the twentieth century's innovations nevertheless look small. The nineteenth-century repertoire comprises the basic means of action open to today's participants in national social movements.

Second, and more important, the rise of the concept and of the reality of the social movement were part of the same transformation that brought the new repertoire into being. As parties, unions, and other associations specializing in the struggle for power grew in importance, so did the idea—and the reality—of parallel streams of people, guided by shared interests and beliefs, which overflowed the narrow channels of elections or labor-management negotiations which were being dug at the same time. Those parallel streams were national social movements. Seen from the perspective of national power structures, they are coherent phenomena; they exist so long as they offer a challenge to dominant interests and beliefs. Seen from the bottom up, they are usually much more fragmented and heterogeneous: shifting factions, temporary alliances, diverse interests, a continuous flux of members and hangers-on.

National states, then, played an essential part in the creation of the modern national social movement. They play an essential part in the movement's operation today. No doubt rough equivalents of the national social movement appear any time authorities at *any* level monopolize decisions and resources which are vital to the interests of the rest of the population. The distinctive contribution of the national state was to shift the political advantage to contenders who could mount a challenge on a very large scale, and could do so in a way that demonstrated, or even used, their ability to intervene seriously in regular national politics. In particular, as electoral politics became a more important way of doing national business, the advantage ran increasingly to groups and organizers who threatened to disrupt or control the routine games of candidates and parties. State toleration or promotion of various sorts of electoral association, furthermore, provided an opportunity, a warrant, and a model for the action of associations that were quasi-electoral, semielectoral, or even nonelectoral. Signaling that you had a large number of committed supporters became an increasingly effective way to score political points. The short-run logic of the demonstration paralleled the long-run logic of the national social movement. In both cases organizers sought to display the numbers, commitment, and internal discipline of the people behind a particular set of claims on some powerful body. In both cases, the coalition mounting the action was often fragile and shifting; if from the viewpoint of the powerful the challenge was sustained and coherent, from the viewpoint of the participants it was often a hasty, temporary, and risky alliance in a common cause.

The duality of perspective accounts for the chronic puzzlement and empirical difficulty experienced by sociologists and historians who seek to study social movements systematically. From the top down, the rise and fall of a movement does normally have a sort of natural history. In the contemporary United States a frequent scenario runs like this: small, scattered sets of people begin voicing a grievance or making a demand; more people join them; the separate sets of concerned individuals start to communicate and coordinate; activists, leaders, spokespeople, and formal associations become visible; the activists make claims to speak for larger constituencies (all blacks, all farmers, sometimes all citizens); the groups involved take action to dramatize their programs, demonstrate their strength and determination, enlist new support; power holders respond variously by means of concessions, bargains, co-optation, repression, or alliances; the activists routinize and/or demobilize their action. Many protests stall in the earlier phases of this sequence. But the full sequence is roughly what observers of the contemporary United States mean by the rise and fall of a social movement. Other countries have their own standard sequences—similar, but not identical. In each country, participants, power holders, and observers customarily speak of the sequence as the history of a *group*—a fairly determinate set of people sharing a common interest who mobilize and then demobilize around that interest.

The group image is a mystification. In real social movements, involvement ebbs and flows, coalitions form and dissolve, fictitious organizations loom up and fade away, would-be leaders compete for recognition as the representatives of unorganized constituencies, leaders make deals with police and politicians. The parallels with the mounting of demonstrations are impressive. At the extreme (as John McCarthy and Mayer Zald have said) professional social movement organizations manage to keep movements going despite little or no contact with the publics on whose behalf they claim to be acting; they manage by finding elsewhere the resources to sustain a challenge.

What is more, organizers, brokers, some participants, and some authorities commonly know that they are not dealing with a group durably organized around a well-defined interest. Yet they collaborate in maintaining the illusion. Why? Because the group image is essential to a social movement's political logic: the demonstration that committed, determined citizens support an alternative to the existing distribution or exercise of power. The movement leaders threaten implicitly that the committed, determined citizens will withdraw their support from the existing power structure, devote their support to some alternative, or even attack the current system. Within a system of parliamentary representation, such a threat is often an effective way of doing political business outside the routines of parties and elections, precisely because of its possible impact on parties and elections.

Social movements do arise within churches, labor unions, schools, firms, and other settings dominated by authorities who are not managers of the national state. They differ in character from national social movements as a function of the structural peculiarities of the settings in which they develop. For example, challenges to religious authorities commonly require an extensive doctrinal justification, and play themselves out in the form of doctrinal disputes. Social movements within twentieth-century labor unions, in contrast, ordinarily settle for a modicum of doctrine, and a concerted bid to win offices and steer strategy. Yet national social movements occupy a privileged position, shaping other social movements more than other movements shape them. This is not only because the states to which national movements are oriented control more resources than other organizations do, but also because states hold an exceptional power to define actors in any arena as legitimate or illegitimate, hence to support some actors and destroy others. As a result, the sequence of actions which characterizes the national social movement within a given state tends to reappear within other settings.

The national social movement's standard sequence does not result from the internal logic of a group's development. It corresponds to the process by which a national political system shapes, checks, and absorbs the challenges which come to it. In the United States, the character of electoral politics strongly affects the course of any social movement on a national scale which passes the first stage of the standard sequence, whether or not the movement begins by challenging the national state directly. To the extent that the grievances in question promise to become electoral issues and the people concerned with those grievances an electoral bloc, every existing group which has an interest in the next round of elections responds to the movement as a potential source of competition, collaboration, or support. The American system therefore creates three main destinations for any national social movement: (1) dissolution; (2) merging of the organized activists into one of the major political parties; or (3) constitution of a durable pressure group devoted to influencing both the government and the major parties. In countries where single-constituency and single-issue parties loom larger, on the other hand, the third destination is less likely. Either dissolution or the co-optation of the activists by an existing party may well occur in such a country, but a fourth outcome is also a distinct possibility: (4) creation of a new, if usually temporary, political party. If characteristic differences in the standard paths of national social movements appear from one country or era to another, then, they are more likely to be due to differences in political contexts than to differences in the character of the people who join social movements. That domination of the paths of social movements by their political context is not easy to see; among other things, the leaders and entrepreneurs of a movement have a strong investment in making it *appear* to be continuous, coherent, and an outgrowth of its own internal logic.

From the bottom up, however, the coincidence of a particular interest, a particular population, a particular set of beliefs, and a particular program of action which characterizes a social movement turns out to be quite temporary; when the interest, the population, the beliefs, and the program move in different directions—as they inevitably do—the most active participants are generally quite aware of the change. In fact, they seek to control and disguise it at the same time. But in that case, should the student of social movements follow the interest, the population, the beliefs, or the program? So long as we mistakenly think of a social movement as a coherent group rather than as a political product, as a solo performance rather than as an interaction, the problem remains insoluble.

The solution is nevertheless at hand. The solution is (1) to study the collective action of particular groups, and then (2) ask under what conditions, from the perspective of national centers of power, that collective action appears to form part of a social movement. We look for a sustained *inter*action in which mobilized people, acting in the name of a defined interest, make repeated broad demands on powerful others via means which go beyond the current prescriptions of the authorities.

This way of proceeding shakes off the confusion between abstract definition and historically specific phenomenon. It recognizes the historical specificity of the social movement. It ties the national social movement, by definition, to the national state. Like elections and party politics, national social movements are ways of connecting particular interests to the national structure of power. As modes of interaction between citizens and authorities, they grew up with national politics. The implicit attachment of the general concept *social movement* to that historically specific reality clarifies why contemporary sociological models of social movements ring hollow when brought to bear on major conflicts and collective actions outside our own era.

We might, of course, take the opposite tack: instead of narrowing the notion of social movement to the historically specific phenomenon which brought it into being, broaden our models so they break the bounds of time and place. Suppose we think that, in and out of national states, challenges to authorities or actions in pursuit of shared beliefs have important common properties. Those common properties are, in fact, quite elusive. But if they can be shown to exist, then we need a conception of social movements which does *not* rely implicitly on the existence of national states and national politics. In that case, nevertheless, we also need recognition of the distinctive type of social movement which came to prominence in the nineteenth century: the sustained challenge to national authorities in the context of electoral politics. In either case, the renewed models of social movements should break with the old group logic and rebuild around the logic of political processes.

Implications and Conclusions

In proposing that we move away from group models of social movements and that we root our analyses in historical space and time, I am merely floating with a strong tide. Over the last ten years, in both Europe and America, students of social movements have been trying to escape the venerable assumptions (1) that movements are special sorts of groups, or groups in the making, and (2) that such groups have their own special laws of development. Analysts as disparate as Manuel Castells, Mayer Zald, Bo Öhngren, Anthony Oberschall, and Frances Fox Piven—to mention only writers who have held to the metaphor of *movement* while attempting to revise its use—have joined the effort.[14] They have moved in one or both of two directions: toward a deeper and more systematic appreciation of the connections between the durable interests and organization of the people involving themselves in social movements, on the one hand, and the character of the movements, on the other; toward a sustained treatment of the interaction between social movements and their political contexts.

On the first count, we find Michael Useem and Roberta Ash joining European Marxists in insisting that analyses of social movements begin with a specification of the material interests which are at stake in the success or failure of a given movement—or, for that matter, in the absence of a movement which could have occurred.[15] On the second count, we find Michael Lipsky and William Gamson joining collective choice theorists in attaching great importance to the organizational strategies and external coalitions adopted in the course of a social movement.[16]

At best, my proposals take a few faltering steps further along the same paths. I propose that we

1. jettison group models of social movements;
2. recognize social movements as sustained interactions between changing sets of challengers and authorities;
3. root our analyses of particular social movements in the everyday interests, organization, and collective action of potential and actual participants in those interactions;
4. include in those participants not just the aggrieved parties but the brokers, entrepreneurs, patrons, and power holders who take part in the interaction;
5. trace the historical and contemporary interdependence between social movements and national electoral politics;
6. examine how the prevailing repertoire of collective action constrains the paths of a social movement and influences its outcome.

In short, treat the social movement as an established way of doing political business rather than as a set of deviant individuals.

That agenda is mainly sociological; it is a set of recommendations for improving or understanding the connections between social movements and other forms of social behavior. There is also an overlapping historical agenda; it emphasizes understanding the connections between social movements and their settings in time and space. If the arguments of this essay are correct, the first emergence of the contemporary repertoire of collective action—including the national social movement, the sustained challenge to national authorities in the name of an unrepresented interest—deserves close examination. Its timing should tell us a good deal about the timing of more general political changes (including those we sometimes loosely call "political modernization") in different countries. Its particular path and character in a given region should help us understand what sort of power structure was coming into existence, and thereby comprehend the structure within which contention goes on in that region today. The close examination of more recent changes in the prevailing repertoire should assist us in detecting gradual alterations of the political system as a whole.

Finally, the student of the collective action of a particular group—women, farmers, regional minorities, or others—should gain plenty of insight with a systematic comparison of the repertoire of that group with the repertoires of other groups within the same national population. At this point, the history and sociology of collective action merge into a common and fruitful enterprise.

NOTES

This is an extensively revised version of "Studying Social Movements/Studying Collective Action," a paper presented to the Conference on Organizing Women (Stockholm, February 1978), and circulated as Working Paper 168, Center for Research on Social Organization (CRSO), University of Michigan. A 1979 version, under the title "Social Movements and National Politics," circulated as CRSO Working Paper 197. The present paper, however, includes yet another round of revisions of the 1979 text. The National Science Foundation supported the research which lies behind the paper. I am grateful to Bert Useem for challenges and suggestions, and to Sheila Wilder and Debby Snovak for help in producing the paper.

1. Archives Nationales, Paris (hereafter A.N.) G[7] 296; see also Archives Communales, Narbonne, BB 29, folio 144.

2. A.N. G[7] 298, 299, 300.

3. For numerous examples, see Yves-Marie Bercé, *Histoire des Croquants*, 2 vols. (Paris: Droz, 1974); René Pillorget, *Les mouvements insurrectionnels de Provence entre 1598 et 1715* (Paris: Pédone, 1975); Boris Porchnev, *Les soulèvements populaires en France de 1623 al 1648* (Paris: Mouton, 1963).

4. A.N. G[7] 296.

5. A.N. G[7] 297, October, 1686.

6. A.N. G[7] 314, July, 1710.

7. A.N. H[1] 1588[26].

8. Emmanuel Le Roy Ladurie, *Les Paysans de Languedoc* (Paris: SEVPEN, 1966), 1:629; Philippe Joutard, ed., *Journaux Camisards, 1700/1715*, "10/18" (Paris: Union Générale d'Editions, 1965), p. 19.

9. Paul Wilkinson, *Social Movement* (London: Macmillan, 1971), p. 27.

10. Félix Napo, *1907. La révolte des vignerons* (Toulouse: Privat, 1971), p. 244.

11. Napo, *Révolte des vignerons*, p. 244.

12. Rudolf Heberle, *Social Movements: An Introduction to Political Sociology* (New York: Appleton-Century-Crofts, 1951), p. 11.

13. For much more detail, see Charles Tilly, "Repertoires of Contention in America and Britain, 1750–1830," in *The Dynamics of Social Movements: Resource Mobilization, Tactics, and Social Control*, ed. Mayer N. Zald and John D. McCarthy (Cambridge, Mass.: Winthrop, 1979), pp. 126–55.

14. Manuel Castells, *Luttes urbaines* (Paris: Maspéro, 1973); John D. McCarthy and Mayer N. Zald, *The Trend of Social Movements in America: Professionalization and Resource Mobilization* (Morristown, N.J.: General Learning Press, 1973); Bo Öhngren, *Folk i rörelse. Samhallsutveckling, flyttningsmönster och folkrörelser i Eskilstuna 1870–1900* (Uppsala: Almqvist and Wiksell, 1974); Anthony Oberschall, *Social Conflict and Social Move-*

ments (Englewood Cliffs, N.J.: Prentice-Hall, 1974); Frances Fox Piven and Richard Cloward, *Poor People's Movements: Why They Succeed, How They Fail* (New York: Random House, 1977).

15. Michael Useem, *Protest Movements in America* (Indianapolis: Bobbs-Merrill, 1975); Roberta Ash, *Social Movements in America* (Chicago: Markham, 1972).

16. Michael Lipsky, *Protest in City Politics: Rent Strikes, Housing and the Power of the Poor* (Chicago: Rand McNally, 1970); William A. Gamson, *The Strategy of Social Protest* (Homewood, Ill.: Dorsey, 1975).

POPULAR INTERVENTION IN REVOLUTIONARY SITUATIONS

Rod Aya

> The ideas which are here expressed so laboriously are extremely simple and should be obvious. The difficulty lies, not in the new ideas, but in escaping from the old ones, which ramify, for those brought up as most of us have been, into every corner of our minds.
>
> —*John Maynard Keynes*

> Some readers may think that my tone of voice . . . is excessively polemical. It may comfort them to know that the assumptions against which I exhibit most heat are assumptions of which I myself have been a victim. Primarily I am trying to get some disorders out of my own system. Only secondarily do I hope to help other theorists to recognize our malady and to benefit from my medicine.
>
> —*Gilbert Ryle*

Once the national state becomes the main arena of political endeavor, and politics itself means striving to influence the distribution of power among states or groups within a state, revolution joins war as the last resort in political conflict. So much seems obvious. Less obvious is how revolutions have actually happened, and how sizable contingents of ordinary people mobilized to take part in them. Though historians have amassed a tempting wealth of fact about revolutions, including precious information on the intentions and capabilities of key participants, sociological theories of revolution hinder more than help understanding it.[1] This essay provides no theoretical master key to the riddle of why revolutions happen and how lower-class groups may intervene to influence their outcome, however. Its mission is merely to set the problem up so it *can* be solved, to frame questions for empirical inquiry, and to suggest provisional hypotheses to guide research—to devise, in short, a strategy for analyzing particular cases.

Specifically, the essay asks how the outbreak of revolutionary situations may afford politically disadvantaged groups the opportunity to press their claims in tactical alliance with one or another state-level contender—and, conversely, how these contenders may exploit the parochial rebellions of lower-class coalition partners to crash the corridors of state power. To set the problem up and outline a strategy for solving it, three steps are in order: one, rethink "revolution" to dispel confusions that hamper explaining any given instance of it; two, summarize why the most common view of revolutionary causation—the volcanic model of revolution as the eruption of outrage, an explosion of fury against unjust authority—leads analysis astray; and, three, codify an alternative argument that sets a more promising research agenda. Such is the plan of this essay.

Rethinking Revolution

There are three main ways of telling whether a revolution is afoot: by the *intentions* of its makers—whether and to what extent they seek to radically transform society; by its *outcome*—the changes of state and society that occur because of it; and by a *situation* of multiple sovereignty, in which two or more contending parties, each governing part of a populace previously subject to one sovereign authority, fight openly and violently for state power.

Identified by intentions, revolutions are attempts to seize state power and use it to "establish a new moral and material world and to impose, or evoke, radically new patterns of day-to-day conduct." The earmark of revolutions is not simply that state power is violently contested, but that at least one contending party aims to remake society. "A holy commonwealth, republic of virtue, communist society—these are the goals revolutionaries seek."

This clearly distinguishes revolutions from coups d'état that reshuffle rulers but leave property and privilege intact; fascist revolutions from the right that (while mobilizing popular support) succeed with the help of conservative elites who retain property and privilege after the "seizure of power"; rebellions that protest abuses of authority, but do not undertake to transform society; and civil wars and wars of national liberation fought to seize state power as such, rather than use it to construct a new social order. On the face of it, then, this idea of revolution makes good sense.

Three historical inconveniences arise, however, if we try to identify revolutions by the intentions of contending parties active in them. One, these aims often do not exist when the revolution begins, or emerge while the battle is on, but crystallize only later, after a new regime is established—the two greatest Latin American revolutions, Mexico and Cuba, being cases in point. Two, the political projects that make some great revolutions great are not all that revolutionary. The challengers with the most radical programs in the English and French revolutions, for example, were promptly purged, while the middle-class militants who directed the Terror in 1793 and 1794 made no attempt to transform society, but used police state methods to protect private property and public order. Three, where doctrinaire radicals seize power to enact drastic programs of social transformation, they do so (as a rule) only after other groups with different objectives overthrow the old regime. And the policies they pursue to achieve their goals mostly shape societies very different from those their theories lead them to count on living in.[4]

These objections aside, identifying revolutions by intentions raises the problem of just *whose* intentions count as revolutionary. As will be argued later in this essay, people need not have revolutionary aims to take part in revolutions. Indeed, the immediate reasons why the lower-class groups whose intervention swung the great revolutions since 1789 took action were reformist, if not conservative. But granting that radical vanguards may impose revolutionary projects, the point remains that revolutions often (1) begin without anyone intending them and (2) conclude with results that no contending party desires or expects when the shooting starts.

What, then, of the second alternative, identifying revolutions by their outcome—the changes of state and society that they help bring about? Take Samuel P. Huntington's idea of revolution as a "rapid, fundamental, and violent domestic change in the dominant values and myths of a society, in its political institutions, social structure, leadership, and government activity and policies." Seemingly clean and comprehensive, this formulation harbors serious drawbacks. It marks off an extremely narrow range of outcomes—so narrow, in fact, that depending on how we interpret "rapid" and "fundamental," it is doubtful whether a real revolution ever happened. Certainly the great revolutions cited as examples differ enormously in the extent to which they brought a "rapid, complete, and violent change in values, social structure, political institutions, governmental practices, and social-political leadership." By these criteria, the credentials of several great revolutions appear dubious indeed. Huntington is well aware that the winners of revolutions often break their promises or (by his lights, worse) fail to maintain law and order, and so proposes to gauge a revolution by the "authority and stability of the institutions to which it gives birth." But this concession compromises the original standard, according to which a true revolution is one that involves "rapid, fundamental, and violent" changes of state and society.[5]

Theda Skocpol also identifies revolutions by outcome. Rather than decree what a "real" revolution ideally consists in, however, she points to historic examples (France, Russia, China), making certain similarities between them her operational definition of a "social revolution." Thus she calls a social (as opposed to an abortive or merely political) revolution one in which "basic transformations" of a society's state and class structure are accompanied, and partly accomplished, by "class-based revolts from below." Skocpol includes *successful* change of state and society because (she argues) the "macro-structural and historical contexts" in which social revolutions have occurred differ from those surrounding either failed or merely political revolutions.⌋

— The advantage of Skocpol's idea of revolution over Huntington's is obvious: it hugs the ground of history, reminding us that no one group set social revolutions rolling or completely controlled their outcome, which emerged from the clash of several contenders, none of whom wholly desired or foresaw (in detail) what their collective actions would help bring about. Indeed, Skocpol observes, the "Big Three" social revolutions began with quarrels among ruling groups over how to manage fiscal and military crises that beset the old regime, producing a paralysis of public authority that enabled peasants and others to rebel for nonrevolutionary reasons of their own, gave previously marginal vanguard groups a crack at state power, and eventuated in the establishment of wildly hypertrophied state bureaucracies that mocked revolutionary dreams of a virtuous republic or a classless society.

Despite this advantage, however, Skocpol's proposal poses two problems. One, the historical pathways leading to rapid, basic changes of state and class structures in the twentieth century are various, only vaguely resembling (if at all) her paradigm. True, Skocpol insists that her conclusions apply only to her cases, whereas her strategy—of zeroing in on state management crises and unraveling history from there on out—will aid understanding examples beyond the Big Three she treats in detail. This is perfectly correct, making one wonder why she believes that social revolutions must have long-term causes rooted in rare types of old regimes when, plainly, such outcomes can be reached by a good many alternative routes. Two, in equating social revolution with a particular outcome, Skocpol does not distinguish the structural changes accomplished in a revolutionary situation from those achieved by government policy *after* a new regime takes power. This is no trivial semantic quibble; it concerns explanation. What enabled peasants to seize and share out landlord properties in 1917–18, for example, differs hugely from what led Stalin to collectivize agriculture after 1929. In fact, Stalin's "revolution from above" reversed the biggest result of 1917, which gave peasants control of the countryside. Social revolutions, as Skocpol explains (and not merely defines) them, entail drastic changes of state and society attended (and partly accomplished) by not only "class-based revolts from below," but *state*-based assaults from *above*. Hence to call both sorts of change a "social" revolution because they have a common set of "distinctive, long-term, structural causes" and "grow out of structural contradictions and potentials inherent in old regimes" is puzzling.

The point is worth stressing because Skocpol's definition threatens to obscure one of her clearest findings, namely, that the collapse of old regimes, the transfer of power to new rulers, and the winners' choice of social policies have different determinants. Though she insists that social revolutions were "on the agenda" once the monarchies caved in, her case studies make clear that social-revolutionary outcomes (certainly in Russia and China) required (1) the military victory of vanguard parties committed to radical change, and (2) a specific choice of development policies by top party bosses *after* they assumed state power. Neither precondition of social revolution (as Skocpol explains it) was "on the agenda" when Qing and Romanov rule came unstuck but depended—as Lenin and Mao both acknowledged in candid moments—on political intentions, organizational capabilities, and strategic opportunities having little to do with the institutional anatomy of old regimes. Needed, clearly, is a way of identifying revolutions that draws attention to the causes and consequences of contingent steps in a historical sequence, rather than tramples them under a forced march of historical inevitability.[6]

Charles Tilly makes a promising start, developing a political idea of revolutionary situations from the Bolshevik notion of "dual power," by which Lenin and Trotsky meant the standoff between the Provisional Government and the Petrograd soviet from March to November, 1917. A revolution, in this view, is a contest for state power—a "trial by battle," Trotsky called it—involving the seizure (or attempted seizure) of a governmental apparatus (i.e., the concentrated material means of coercion, taxation, and public administration in society) by one contender (or coalition of contenders) from another. The revolutionary situation itself is one of "multiple sovereignty," as Tilly terms it, in which public authority is divided between two or more power centers, each attempting to rule people and territory previously subject to a single regime. This political condition can develop in a great many ways, without any of the contenders intending it, most often through the fission of governing groups into belligerent factions. Once the polity splits, lower-class challengers may seize the opportunity to press their claims for distributive justice, exactly as happened in Skocpol's social revolutions. In any event, multiple sovereignty begins when state power comes unstuck; it ends when—by the victory of one, the defeat of another, or a settlement between warring contenders—one sovereign polity exerts a monopoly of violence, taxation, and justice.[7]

The point here is not to demand a "correct" definition, since there is no such thing. Definitions are merely conventions of consistent word usage. Unlike propositions, which state general and particular matters of fact, definitions are neither right nor wrong. They say what we mean, all right, but say nothing about it, which is why definitional disputes mostly degenerate into semantic quibbling. The point, rather, is what happens and why, not the "correct" application of labels.

While questions of words and their meanings are unimportant outside theology, confusion for want of adequate distinctions may slow solving problems of explanation. Hence, though we need not define, we must often distinguish—in the present case, between revolutionary *situations*, *intentions*, and *outcomes*. Why? Because doing so makes it easier to disentangle the threads of historical causation and see how they are interwoven. Revolutionary situations may start without benefit of revolutionary intentions, and finish without producing revolutionary outcomes. Actors who do most to start revolutionary situations and help produce revolutionary outcomes may not intend to. And those whose actions and decisions do most to transform state and society may take them only well after the revolutionary situation itself is played out. Lastly, those who initiate, provide mass support for, and chiefly benefit from revolutions may be (and usually are) very different sets of people.[8]
— To wind up this part of the argument, then, the outbreak of revolutionary situations, the victory of groups with revolutionary intentions, and the attainment of revolutionary outcomes all have different determinants, which must be opened to inquiry, case by case, not dictated beforehand by definition. Noting a distinction between revolutionary situations, intentions, and outcomes makes this first step easier to take.

Against the Volcanic Model

If we try to explain the history of revolutionary situations, however, general theories of revolution provide little help. Indeed, general theorists seldom bother with the politics of revolution, which they leave to narrative historians, but aim instead to explain the rise of a revolutionary temper that drives people to overthrow governments and transform society. Faced with any example of revolutionary violence, these theorists look for evidence of dysfunctions in the "social system" that arouse discontent, which erupts in revolution against the ruling elite. Volcanic theorists (as we may call them) seek the causes of individual discontent and, by simple extension, the aggravations of "society" as a whole.[9] Doing this, they either ignore ongoing political conflicts altogether or reduce their motivation to "social frustration," "relative deprivation," "structural strain," or "systemic disequilibrium."[10] Like the simpleton Marxism they are written to refute, volcanic theories of revolution are profoundly antipolitical.

The consequences of this theoretical default may be summarized as three fallacies.

1. *The confusion of state and society.* Whereas the events theories of revolution must explain are preeminently political—being fights over who gets what, when, and how—volcanic theorists either decline to dis-

cuss politics at all or else reduce political motives to some underlying sociopsychological compulsion. From the assumption that collective violence erupts from overheated states of mind, it follows that what needs to be discovered is the cause of mass frustration, relative deprivation, strain, or some other neologism for social resentment. Instead of examining power relations, patterns of contention, and the mobilization of belligerent parties, volcanic theorists look to the arousal of a revolutionary temper in society at large. Collective action becomes collective behavior, the abnormal, antisocial activity of disaffected persons driven to violence by pent-up frustrations with the status quo. A whole society erupts in revolution or, conversely, a revolution aims to overthrow society itself. This lack of a political focus on state institutions, power relations, and the mobilization of contending parties leads directly to a second fallacy:

2. *The strange case of the absconded actor.*[11] Because the target of theoretical attention is the revolutionary temper of a whole society—meaning simply the population living inside the borders of some national state—it remains unclear just who bears the brunt of frustration, who takes part in revolutions, and whether these are in fact the same sets of actors. Volcanic theorists seldom identify specific people acting to advance and defend their claims, if need be by violence. Instead, the individuals who form up action groups, parties, and tactical coalitions to contest power in revolutionary situations are lumped into anonymous masses whose undifferentiated hostilities discharge in collective violence. By implication, however, the prime suspects would appear to be marginal people from all walks of life, or these chronic growlers and grumblers plus a mass following recruited from the poorest and most oppressed groups—people who, living in constant anxiety and frustration, are the most desperate, unstable, and (presumably) revolutionary elements in society. Though never confirmed by competent study or successful practice, this wisdom reaches far beyond the ivied walls of academe. For with few exceptions, radicals tend to gauge revolutionary potential by, not the social power and tactical leverage of aggrieved people, but their misery and presumed discontent, on the assumption that the prize must belong, as on "Queen for a Day," to those with least reason to go on living. Which leads to a third mistake:

3. *The two-stage leap of faith*—from social change to grievances, and from grievances to revolt. Recall that volcanic theorists posit a revolutionary temper, which they believe is caused by rapid social change or by sudden adverse economic fluctuations or political turnabouts, and which erupts in violent protest, or, at minimum, renders large numbers of people susceptible to the appeals of extremist agitators.

There are two missing links in this chain of reasoning. (1) Volcanic theorists have no way of ascertaining the presence and magnitude of frustration, deprivation, or strain independently of the political conflicts they allegedly produce. These conditions are present either by definition or drastic inference from data on the pace and pattern of social development. The measures taken of relative deprivation in one famous study, for example, were not measures at all, but hypothetical projections from statistical data on social trends and conditions that were assumed to generate relative deprivation.[12] Nor do volcanic theorists, concerned with the putative emotional climate of a whole society, distinguish specific grievances, much less connect them with the political behavior of competing power groups. (2) Volcanic theories contain no credible hypothesis connecting frustration, deprivation, strain, or disequilibrium to violent politics—save the trivial truism that behind every act of collective violence lies some sort of discontent. Not only do the supposed indicators of social frustration, strain, and so forth commonly turn up in situations of stable rule, but grievances inspire collective action only under complex political circumstances (both organizational and tactical) that volcanic theories fail to encompass.[13] *Why* aggrieved people revolt in some cases but not in others remains as much a mystery as ever. And to imply, as some volcanic theorists are wont, that when the pressure of discontent is great enough, rebellion erupts, is tautologous or absurd, it being clear from comparative history that the worst abuses are mainly suffered where repression dampens protest to a whisper. Grievances motivate rebellion but do not suffice to explain it. There is no direct passage from anger to action, in other words, except by tautology.

The Political Model

About the political model of popular violence, I must make clear my assumptions: When people face a choice between alternative courses of action, in this case between violent and nonviolent strategies, they choose the one for which (as they see it at the time) the value of the expected result multiplied by the probability of success in getting it is greater. Hence, to explain why people do what they do, you make a simple model of their choice situation, including their intentions, capabilities, and opportunities to act. To make a rough and ready model of typical situations in order to explain similar and recurrent events, I codify findings from the literature that have not, thus far, been put to this purpose. Because the model is a schematic oversimplification, however, deciding whether discrepancies between prognosis and fact owe to roughness or to refutation will not always be easy. Still, tests can tell which of two competing models is the best approximation, and in social analysis such tests of situational models can be supplied by historical research.[14] That is a second aim of the exercise.

The political model is nothing new. Indeed, I only adapt and apply to revolutions and collective violence Clausewitz's view of war as a "continuation of politics by other means." Like war, revolutions and collective violence arise from struggles for power and prerogative previously conducted by diplomatic means. Like war, they entail a calculated risk and test of strength: the contenders gauge each other's intentions and capabilities, and risk collision only when the expected benefits outweigh the likely dangers. To paraphrase Clausewitz once more, war and revolution are violent extensions of normal politics, from which they differ by that fact alone. "Thus we see that war is not merely a political act, but a true political instrument, a continuation of political business, a transaction of it by other means. . . . [T]he political intention is the purpose, war is the means, and the means can never be contemplated without the purpose." Politics, he concludes, is the "womb in which war develops"; in it the lineaments of war (and revolution) lie "still hidden like the features of living creatures in embryo."[15]

Collective violence—sometimes intended, even carefully planned by rebels or rulers, often the unexpected result of runaway confrontations—relates to domestic politics as war to diplomacy. Hence "as long as the exercise of government remains a matter of dispute between various groups, the opportunity and the temptation for recourse to popular violence will remain."[16] Now if, as appears from the history of science, a theory is never defeated by facts, however damaging, but only by another explanation that looks to account more cogently for the data at risk as well as anticipate and correct further empirical findings, it behooves us to see what the political model predicts[17] in place of the three volcanic fallacies outlined above. As will be apparent, the political model confutes the volcanic model on all three scores: what sort of intentions motivate popular violence, which people have the capability to take active part, and whence they get the opportunity to act.

It is unfortunately impossible to give more than a hint of the relevant evidence. Serious documentation must await other occasions. Meanwhile, if these tentative assertions prompt others to improve or refute them with sounder research, they will have accomplished their mission.

Intentions

As collective violence is no mere eruption of rage, but a concomitant of scrambles for political advantage between counterpoised contenders, its motive lies in, not vague social frustrations, but principled complaints over recognized bones of contention. And rather than chaotic outbursts of angry people, careful study of popular violence reveals a political pattern and tactical logic—like war, diplomacy, or elections.

Consider findings published by historians of people's politics and popular violence in Europe and the Third World. These authors, after years of painstaking research into the political motives and social composition of crowds involved in riots, revolts, and a few revolutions, report abundant evidence that "behind every such form of popular direct action some legitimizing notion of right is to be found."[18] Not only did old regime insurgents appeal to "political and moral traditions" that sanctioned, even prescribed, what violence they committed, but (to preview a point sharpened below), far from being "miserable, uprooted, unstable masses," they were for the most part people with a recognized place and "stake in their community," who were "often skilled craftsmen or better," who, "even when poor and unskilled," were "respectable to their everyday neighbors," and whose violence, however cruel or unusual by present-day standards of shame and revulsion, was not "random and limitless but aimed at defined targets and selected from a repertory of traditional punishments and forms of destruction."[19]

To the discerning eye, moreover, even the most "spontaneous" and seemingly anarchic forms of collective violence—food riots, tax riots, jacqueries, *journées* (crowd actions in the French revolutions)—reveal, each of them, not only implicit theories of right and justice, as well as practical objectives—first crack at local food supply, reduced taxes (most European rebellions between 1300 and 1700 were tax revolts), a rollback of seigneurial impositions, cheap and plentiful bread—but a political anatomy, a standard operating procedure, even (most clearly visible in food riots) a veritable customary script which police and people knew by heart.[20] Like the authorities who repressed them, the food rioters, antitax demonstrators, and peasant militants knew what they wanted and had rough-and-ready methods for getting it. And if, as some argue, the common folk in preindustrial settings showed a naive, almost mystical attachment to coercion as a political panacea, it was because "violence, in one form or another—collective or private—was the only means of influencing policies and events available to the *petit peuple*."[21] This does not mean that the *petit peuple*, in France or elsewhere, never made mistakes, that they were unerringly accurate in their judgment of what went wrong and who was responsible, that they never claimed innocent victims (they plainly did, the September Massacres of 1792 being only the most notorious case), that their protest was inherently "emancipatory," that their indignation never had a repressive or reactionary component, or even that their sense of self-interest over the long run was always reliable (like voters in presidential elections, popular movements have been regularly disappointed by the parties and politicians they helped bring to power). The sansculottes, for example, as their most empathetic historian makes clear, committed major misjudgments and needless brutalities, which blunders cost them dear once the national balance of political power shifted in their disfavor.[22] All told, however, popular movements are no uglier in this regard than statesmen and generals, whose efforts to achieve political objectives through organized violence are rarely distinguished by their solicitude for defenseless civilians.[23]

What, then, to make of Lenin's overquoted dictum, "revolutions are festivals of the oppressed and the exploited," and, on the sinister side, of the observation that these festive occasions could also be "repellent, dreadful, hideous, and above all depressing," the handiwork of a popular justice that was "frequently cruel and cowardly, base and vengeful, barbaric and not at all pretty to watch"?[24] Is not all this harping on the political character of popular violence, its naive realism, its *Gesetzmässigkeit*, a lofty evasion of facts which, closely examined, become unbearable? Is it not, in short, a sociological apology for massacre? Here at least four points need mentioning. First, politics, especially people's politics, has an uproarious aspect. (Wendell Phillips once called presidential elections the "saturnalia of American life.") Second, the festivals to which Lenin compares revolutions were established parts of popular culture under the old regime, rituals that reinforced community cohesion while providing a safe occasion for vigilante criticism of public authority.[25] Third, and important to recall, the brutality of popular vengeance in revolutions owes much to the disciplinary methods of the establishment. (As Babeuf exclaimed on seeing the severed heads of two Paris notables paraded on pikes a few days after the fall of the Bastille, "Cruel punishments of every sort, quartering, the rack, the wheel, the stake, the whip, the gibbet, so many tortures everywhere have taught us such wicked ways!"[26]) Fourth, the vast majority of clashes recorded as rebellions have commenced when public authorities chose to repress collective actions that, though prohibited, were nonetheless peaceable—until police violence turned noisy but nonviolent demonstrations into insurrections.[27] (No theorist of systemic frustration, relative deprivation, or social strain as the source of civil strife has, to my knowledge, ever accused the authorities of such or similar warps of intelligence.) In short, most striking is the *continuity* of popular intentions before and during revolutionary outbreaks. While revolutions certainly accelerate the same dizzying fission and fusion of coalitions and countercoalitions, fights and truces between opposing parties, and intramural rivalries between factions and cliques that typify ordinary politics, close-up studies indicate that when mass violence attends revolutionary situations, it follows fault lines opened well before the first round of active hostilities.

A final blow to the volcanic view of intentions—which, seeing revolutionary violence as a sudden eruption of rage, reads in the perpetrators' state of mind both a bitter rejection of existing society and a mental rehearsal of radical reconstitution—is that the actual aims of popular movements have been largely conservative, even reactionary, in the literal sense of trying to preserve older economic and political arrangements under attack by the state or upper classes. From the *Bauernkrieg* of 1525 to the sansculottes of 1793 and 1794, the *communards* of 1871 to the rural rebels of 1917 who inadvertently gave Lenin's urban minority coup its indispensable boost, the words and actions of revolutionary masses give little sign that they sought to overthrow the existing order, much less replace it with a new one.[28] On the contrary, their radicalism has been tactical, their collective violence the cutting edge of defensive conservatism, and their revolutionary interventions an attempt to turn political crises to their own sectional advantage, grabbing the opportunity afforded by breakdown of state power to reclaim property or prerogatives lately usurped by dominant groups.[29] True, the spread of modern industrialism and victory of the national state over other frameworks of rule have changed the identity of players in the political game as well as its locus and immediate ends. Even so, in the few revolutions to see sizable proletarian involvement, workers have moved to remedy specific grievances—over wages, hours, working conditions, job security—affecting their particular occupations. And when they took up arms and marched under radical banners, it was to defend recent reformist gains against reactionary violence.[30]

This is not to gainsay the importance of ideology in people's politics, but only to caution that the radical projects for renovating society by which some revolutions are identified and remembered have been superimposed on popular movements by certain of their coalition partners, often (though not invariably) revolutionary intellectuals, the masses' own version of utopia being basically their experience of existing society minus its most oppressive features. The game of revolutionary ideas is thus a tricky one with at least three possible outcomes: radical projects may be rejected as irrelevant, dangerous, or both by their intended audience; the masses may adopt the ideology and organization of their coalition partners, only to bend both (at times beyond recognition) to suit their immediate objectives; or, if radical elites do gain power, the utopias of revolution may become new ideologies of rule.[31]

Capabilities

But neither ideologies nor the indignation to which they appeal explain collective action to set things right. As James Scott rightly remarks, if anger at exploitation and injustice were enough to spark rebellion, the Third World would be in flames.[32] A key question still unanswered is *which* groups with a grievance are in a position to act on it or, at minimum, lend support to parties promising redress. Here again the volcanic and political models point in different directions. If, in the volcanic view, revolutions and collective violence are eruptions of rage, then people suffering the worst grievances should make the readiest rebels. Although (as noted above) volcanic theorists seldom inquire into the social composition of action groups in revolutionary situations, they clearly imply that people who are poorest and most oppressed or, from another angle, most atomized and isolated from stabilizing community involvements will be the majority of faces in the revolutionary crowd. The political model, on the other hand, implies the opposite: that displaced, disfranchised groups will be underrepresented in the census of popular activism. Why? Because people with ostensibly the meanest grievances to fight about often have the meagerest resources to fight with. (Hence the pivotal groups in revolutionary politics are apt to be those whose economic basis, social standing, organizational networks, and political connections—including allegiances improvised according to the age-old rule that the enemy of my enemy is my friend—afford them the capability to press their claims in the political area.)

A quick scan of the literature bears this out. Popular movements have been led, staffed, and supported by not the most downtrodden and oppressed segments of society but groups that, while having plenty to fight for and against, had something to fight with. Reviewing, for example, who trooped out in medieval peasant risings (not really risings, most of them, but community self-defense actions that were substantially nonpeasant in social composition), fought the *Bauernkrieg*, stormed the Bastille, mobilized the *mouvement sectionnaire* in 1792, threw up the barricades at Lyon in 1834 and Paris in 1848, defended the Commune, and, years later, sustained revolutions from Mexico and Russia to China and Vietnam, suggests that the revolutionary masses were hardly the most miserable, desperate, disadvantaged members of society. (Far from being the unstable, disorganized, and "dangerous" classes so dear to political folklore, reactionary and radical alike, the masses were people of local standing and substance, however modest—peasant landowners, shopkeepers, artisans, journeymen—and snugly entwined in community networks. Where, with the advance of industrialism, proletarians became a political force, strike movements were spearheaded first by skilled craftsmen and, in the era of monopoly capital, by large-scale organized labor. As for "lumpen" elements, if they took to the streets at all, it was to hop a bandwagon set rolling by the hardworking little people.[33])

Eric Wolf suggests why this pattern should prevail. Observing how, "ultimately, the decisive factor in making a peasant rebellion possible lies in the relation of the peasantry to the field of power which surrounds it," Wolf notes that the political prerequisite of collective action is *tactical power*. Before peasants (or anyone else) can attempt rebellion without overwhelming risk, they must hold a social position that affords them tactical power—or else acquire this capability through coalition with outside forces powerful enough to offset their immediate enemies. "A rebellion," he writes, "cannot start from a situation of complete impotence; the powerless are easy victims."[34] Proceeding from this simple insight, Wolf identifies three sets of social conditions that endow a peasant population with tactical power. First, control over their own means of production gives middle peasants—small landowners and secure tenants farming chiefly with family labor—a margin of economic independence that, in a fight, becomes a vital political asset. Second, location in outlying areas often puts "poor but free" cultivators beyond the effective reach of landlord and official coercion. And, finally, in the case of dependent tenants and landless laborers, who to subsist must first come to terms with the lords of property, the necessary counterforce may come from the intervention of outside powers (radical parties or revolutionary armies) that crack apart established domains by superior violence. Likewise, tactical capability may come from coalitions between peasant communities and interests near the centers of power able to protect local protest with the arm of the state. With this analysis of class power balances in the countryside, Wolf makes clear that the very poor peasants who star in so much "radical" theory as the revolutionary class were no such thing and, moreover, that the practical programs (if not the rhetoric) of successful movements show that the leaders knew (or soon learned) this to be the case, regardless of what they later published for public consumption. Rather, it was the phalanx of village proprietors who supplied the first rural allies of radical power challenges in the great revolutions of our century. That these groups were themselves oppressed and threatened by current economic and political trends is obvious—the Russian villagers of 1917 being a good example. However, and this is the point, when oppressed people do manage to launch a revolt, look for special features of social organization and political opportunity that tilt the delicate balance of risk and reward to their immediate advantage. In Russia, the combination of a tight-knit rural community (whose periodic repartition of holdings to equalize tax burdens aligned rich and poor peasants in a general land hunger), an economically enfeebled landlord class (by 1917 two-thirds of landed property in European Russia was already in peasant hands), and sudden collapse of government power goes a long way toward explaining why a class notoriously oppressed could strike hard on its own behalf.[35]

Opportunities to Act

This brings us back to ask what makes people fighting mad and how their outrage induces action. Volcanic theories, recall, make two unwarranted inferential leaps—from social change to mass anger, and from mass anger to collective violence—thereby vaulting the problem of how change aggrieves various people, and how discontent activates protest. The political model, on the other hand, implies two links to span these gaps: one, an important but indirect relation between the economic and political arrangement of a social setting, the changes it undergoes over time, and the genesis of conflict; two, an organizational and tactical nexus between the advent of grievances and collective action to repair them. It suggests, in short, a political account of what aggrieves people and what they think they best can do about it.

Changes in the social structure and composition of a human setting, obviously enough, alter the identity of contending parties as well as their organizational bases of collective action—hence, too, their bargaining power vis-à-vis other groups. Note how this differs from the neo-Durkheimian wisdom, which sees revolutions and popular violence as concomitants of modernization processes that set expectations soaring faster than incumbent governments can co-opt, crush, or liquidate the groups that harbor them.[36] For the actual influence of "structural change" on political conflict, while huge, is indirect. Large-scale, long-term transformations—broadly, since 1450, the development of capitalism and formation of national states—affect social composition of groups contending for local and central power, the immediate aims of political struggle, and the repertoire of feasible stratagems—an idea Marc Bloch captured perfectly, in a single sentence, when he wrote that the "agrarian revolt is as inseparable from the seigneurial regime as the strike from the great capitalist enterprise."[37]

Jeffery Paige sharpens the point further, noting that each agricultural property system attracts its own characteristic kind of popular protest. Peasants who farm small holdings alongside large estates are apt to try and seize these properties in periods of government crisis when the landowners' power is compromised, but otherwise show little interest in national politics. Peasants who sharecrop the splintered holdings of absentee landlords whose ownership rights stand or fall with an alien regime are apt to aid revolutionary movements out to unseat that regime and redistribute property. Proletarian cultivators of business plantations, on the other hand, prefer labor strikes aimed at, not abolishing capitalism, but getting a larger share of its proceeds. Each system, in short, gets the rebellion it deserves.[38]

This again points up the organizational link between grievances and the capability to act on them. Individuals are not magically mobilized for action, no matter how aggrieved, hostile, or angry they feel. Their anger must first be set to collective ends by the coordinating, directing offices of organization, formal or informal. The habitual association of interested friends may count as organization, as may peasant communities of various types or more modern, artificial setups like labor unions or radical parties. The point, in any event, is that there must be some kind of organization on hand to orchestrate discontent and convert it into collective action. Otherwise the "unhappy merely brood passively on the sidelines."[39]

Now the question becomes, how do structural changes of society—by reshaping organizational means for acting on common claims and grievances—affect the tactical power of aggrieved groups? The issue, then, is not only how structural changes alter the identity, aims, and options of contending forces, but how they modify their respective bases of solidarity and collective effort; how, in a word, they redistribute social power chances.

As we turn our attention from rebels to rulers, finally, several questions leap to mind. One concerns the fragility of state power structures—their vulnerability to fragmentation from above and challenge from below. Here Theda Skocpol, following up Barrington Moore's pioneering labors, notes striking similarities in the political architecture of the old regimes in France, Russia, and China—like Moore, she styles them agrarian bureaucracies—and their eventual collapse into revolutionary situations. More than that, Skocpol claims a connection between the power structure of the old regime in each case, its pattern of collapse, and the options that befell contending parties once the roof caved in. This valuable approach requires two sorts of supplement to make an arrival: a careful trace of the various pathways to multiple sovereignty—in particular, the intricate rivalries, maneuvers, and realignments of governing groups whose failed consensus opened the door the revolutionaries ran through;[40] and systematic analysis of the power struggles that intercede between the crack-up of the old and establishment of a new regime. Doubtless enlightened by sociological scrutiny, these political processes do not submit to sociological reduction. There remain, as Richard Cobb writes in another well-aimed one-liner, "several principal problems to the mystery of the breakdown of government—for it is a mystery—and of that very, very fine line that separates a sedition from a revolutionary crisis."[41] Here is where political sociology rejoins political history: to sort out the social bases of contending forces and anatomize the structure of power requires sharp-eyed sociology; to see what political capital the contenders actually make of the capabilities and opportunities they have, however, demands good analytic history.

If these considerations point to any firm conclusion at all, it is that there is (and can be) no pat formula for revolutions in general which, in specific, does not reveal itself to be trivially true or plainly false. This is no cause for consternation, however. As one very shrewd theorist observes in a sensible aside on intellectual strategy tailor-made for the political sociology of revolutions, the "object of our analysis is, not to provide a machine, or method of blind manipulation, which will furnish an infallible answer, but to provide ourselves with an organised and orderly method of thinking out particular problems."[42] To this end, several pointers for sorting out and making sense of specific cases have been mentioned and may be quickly summed up. Revolutions, like collective violence generally, being the offspring of political contests, must be analyzed accordingly. A first step here is to note the difference between revolutionary situations, intentions, and outcomes (see above). The next is to jettison the volcanic model of revolution as the eruption of intolerable injury into raging violence. Once the volcanic model is out of the way, several points about political intentions, capabilities, opportunities to act come into view: (1) instead of generalized frustration as the source of political outrage, note the established rights and obligations—the prevailing terms of social contract—to which various sets of people are party and which, once violated, make for grievances; (2) note, too, with regard to capabilities and opportunities, the tactical power resources available to aggrieved groups—their economic basis, community organization, political connections with outside allies, and (most important) fissures in the power structure that may open from above. The combined result is (3) a focus on the social distribution of power chances, on tactical coalitions between various contenders, and on the occurrence of top-level power struggles that, without warning, may open the political arena to popular intervention. Thus confirmed is Plato's lasting "law" that no revolution happens without there first appearing cleavages among the incumbent power elite—cleavages that compromise both the unity of governing groups and the loyalty of their armed forces.[43] Here, again, we need sociologically informed political history able to pinpoint the intricate turnabouts that make all the difference between the coming of a revolutionary situation and the persistence of the status quo.[44]

NOTES

This essay is based on but substantially revises an article appearing under the same title in *Symposion* 1 (1979): 124–51, since republished as *Staatsvormingsprocessen in Europa en Azië na 1750*, ed. Ton Zwaan et al. (The Hague: Nijhoff, 1981). My thanks again to those whose counsel I acknowledge there, and to Gregor Benton, John Wiersma, and Ton Zwaan, who cordially excoriated one part of the present text, as well as to Hannie Hoekstra, who typed all of it.

1. My reasons for concluding this are explained in "Theories of Revolution Reconsidered: Contrasting Models of Collective Violence," *Theory and Society* 8 (1979): 39–99, esp. pp. 49–67.

2. See Michael Walzer, "A Theory of Revolution," *Marxist Perspectives* 2 (Spring, 1979): 30–44. Though this article hews to conventions I criticize, it rises beyond them to spotlight conflicts between vanguard parties and the groups they presume to benefit, suggesting that Thermidor means vanguards have been overwhelmed by the class interests their ideologies champion. The stronger the revolutionary class, the weaker the vanguard, and vice versa.

3. See Richard F. Hamilton, *Who Voted for Hitler?* (Princeton, 1982).

4. On Mexico, see John Womack, Jr., *Zapata and the Mexican Revolution* (New York, 1969); idem, "The Mexican Economy during the Revolution, 1910–1920: Historiography and Analysis," *Marxist Perspectives* 1 (Winter, 1978): 80–123, who believes the "specific contest that the victors have taught the world to call the Mexican Revolution" to be the "defeat of the first massive popular struggle against capitalism in Mexico" (p. 97); Walter L. Goldfrank, "Theories of Revolution and Revolution without Theory: The Case of Mexico," *Theory and Society* 7 (1979): 135–65; and James W. Wilkie, *The Mexican Revolution* (Berkeley, 1970), who notes that whereas most writers on revolution assume "social change . . . will take place concomitantly with political upheaval," the "real revolution in Mexican society came about mainly in times of political stability since 1940" (p. 283). In Cuba, the revolutionaries who took power in 1959 had no clear-cut ideological commitments, and determined to build a socialist economy in 1960 only after American opposition to radical reform drove them to depend on Soviet aid. Indeed, as Che Guevara remarked late in 1961, it was the United States that "made us socialists" (James O'Connor, *The Origins of Socialism in Cuba* [Ithaca, N.Y., 1970], p. 300).

For sharp accounts of the English Revolution, noting the moderate aims of its instigators, the rout of its radicals, and the conservatism of its winners, see Conrad Russell, *The Crisis of Parliaments* (Oxford, 1971), pp. 323–97, esp. pp. 339–40; Lawrence Stone, *The Causes of the English Revolution, 1529–1642* (London, 1972), esp. pp. 48–57; and Perez Zagorin, *Rebels and Rulers, 1500–1660*, 2 vols. (Cambridge, 1982), 2:130–86. On the rise and fall of the sansculottes, see Richard Cobb, *The Police and the People* (Oxford, 1970), pp. 176–211, and, on the purge of the *enragés*, idem, *A Second Identity* (London, 1969), pp. 168–76. The Terror itself was waged, not to transform society, but to rally patriots, win the war, and repress the Republic's domestic enemies. True believers in economic liberalism, the Committee of Public Safety imposed wage-price controls reluctantly as a wartime expedient; but private property remained sacrosanct and the death penalty in force against advocates of land redistribution (Norman Hampson, *A Social History of the French Revolution* [London, 1963], pp. 210–11, 228–29). "There is no evidence to suggest that the Montagnards were thinking of any radical social transformation. . . . Their main concern was victory and their principles centred round the 'moralization' of the *status quo*" (p. 229).

5. Samuel P. Huntington, *Political Order in Changing Societies* (New Haven, 1968), pp. 264, 344, 266. His great revolutions occurred in France, China, Russia, Mexico, Bolivia, Guatemala, Cuba, Vietnam, and Algeria (p. 275).

6. Theda Skocpol, *States and Social Revolutions* (Cambridge, 1979), pp. 4–5, 285–86, 295n, 287–92, 350n, 163. Note that if social revolutions require "rapid, basic transformations of a society's state and class structures" to be "accompanied and in part carried through by class-based revolts from below," scarcely half the examples Skocpol cites as cases in point—Mexico, Yugoslavia, Bolivia, Cuba, Vietnam, Algeria, Angola, Mozambique, Guinea-Bissau, and Ethiopia—meet both her criteria. The dependence of vanguard victories in China and Russia on fortuitous conditions that the communists could not control (but only exploit) and that, had they been different, would have produced different outcomes, is made clear by Chalmers Johnson ("Peasant Nationalism Revisited: The Biography of a Book," *China Quarterly* 72 [1977]: 766–85, esp. pp. 771–72) and Leszek Kolakowski (*Main Currents of Marxism*, 3 vols. [Oxford, 1978], 2:473–91, 525–27), who notes that most of Lenin's key crucial decisions were based on illusory expectations (pp. 476, 525) and that, regarding the social revolution after power, the "turning points in the evolution of Soviet Russia—War Communism, the N.E.P., collectivization, the purges—were not due to 'historical laws' but were all consciously willed by the rulers, and there is no reason to think that they 'had to' happen or that the rulers could not have decided otherwise" (3:157–58).

7. Charles Tilly, *From Mobilization to Revolution* (Reading, Mass., 1978), pp. 189–222; and Leon Trotsky, *The History of the Russian Revolution* (London, 1977), pp. 223–32. Skocpol's comparative analysis of how certain groups of ordinary people intervened in social revolutions after the fall of the old regime is by far the best available: *States and Social Revolutions*, pp. 112–54, 183–85, 187–93, 207–14, 252–62.

8. Cf. Barrington Moore, Jr., *Social Origins of Dictatorship and Democracy* (Boston, 1966), pp. 427–29, and, on definitions versus propositions, Karl R. Popper, *The Open Society and Its Enemies*, 2 vols. (London, 1966), 2:9–21, as well as idem, *Conjectures and Refutations* (London, 1974), p. 402. "'Sheer nonsense, but we do it time and again. That's why we're so . . . dreadfully wrong. We argue about *definitions* when we should be arguing about *facts*'" (John le Carré, *A Small Town in Germany* [New York, 1969], p. 121).

9. If this seems like a polemical caricature, the reader may compare Ted Robert Gurr, "The Revolution–Social-Change Nexus: Some Old Theories and New Hypotheses," *Comparative Politics* 5 (1973): 359–92, esp. pp. 364–65, 368.

10. These are the key explanatory ideas of the literature examined in "Theories of Revolution Reconsidered." The main studies criticized are James C. Davies, "The J-Curve of Rising and Declining Satisfactions as a Cause of Some Great Revolutions and a Contained Rebellion," in *Violence in America*, ed. Hugh Davis Graham and Ted Robert Gurr (Washington, D.C., 1969); idem, "Toward a Theory of Revolution," in *When Men Revolt and Why*, ed. idem (New York, 1971); Ivo K. Feierabend, Rosalind L. Feierabend, and Betty K. Nesvold, "Social Change and Political Violence: Cross-National Patterns," in *Violence in America*, ed. Graham and Gurr; Ted Robert Gurr, *Why Men Rebel* (Princeton, 1970); Neil J. Smelser, *Theory of Collective Behavior* (New York, 1962); and Chalmers Johnson, *Revolutionary Change* (Boston, 1966). Among these authors, Johnson is anomalous in having published much

excellent historical work, including a famous study of strategic conditions abetting the rise of Chinese Communism that exhibits none of the fallacies prominent in his general theory, to which it bears no discernible relation: *Peasant Nationalism and Communist Power* (Stanford, 1962). Cf. note 6 above.

11. The joke owes to Charles Tilly and James Rule, "Political Process in Revolutionary France, 1830–1832," in *1830 in France*, ed. John M. Merriman (New York, 1975), pp. 50, 54.

12. In a candid piece of scholarly self-criticism, Gurr and Duvall observe that Gurr's unexplained leap—from "social conditions and patterns of change which, *by inference*, generated varying degrees of RD" (relative deprivation)—compromised his well-known theory of civil violence as the upshot of relative deprivation. "The methodological leap of faith," they admit, "was very hard to justify" (Ted Robert Gurr and Raymond Duvall, "Civil Conflict in the 1960s: A Reciprocal Theoretical System with Parameter Estimates," *Comparative Political Studies* 6 [1973]: 138 [emphasis added]). Actually, the problem is theoretical rather than methodological, since it concerns explanation, not just testing or "verification."

13. Consider, for example, Feierabend, Feierabend, and Nesvold, "Social Change and Political Violence," pp. 634–37. In a later study elaborating the same general theory, the Feierabends say that political stability may persist despite "systemic frustration" if any of six "qualifying conditions" obtain: (1) no politically effective groups exist that can organize a revolution; (2) the government is well endowed and wise enough to improvise reforms that take the wind out of revolutionary sails; (3) the government defends itself with ruthless coercion; (4) the regime is legitimate; (5) aggression is displaced to minority groups or foreign nations; (6) individual acts of aggression are "sufficiently abundant to provide an outlet." Otherwise, in the "relative absence of similar qualifying conditions, . . . aggressive behavior in the form of political instability and violence is likely to occur as a consequence of systemic frustration" (Ivo K. Feierabend, Rosalind L. Feierabend, and Betty K. Nesvold, "The Comparative Study of Revolution and Violence," *Comparative Politics* 5 [1973]: 408). Most of these "qualifying conditions" are squarely political factors of the kind the general theory fails to encompass and, as such, provide highly elastic escape clauses which, to the extent they can be stretched to cover any observed anomaly, nullify the independent explanatory power of "systemic frustration." Thus, after grappling briefly with political conditions, the Feierabends conclude that "coerciveness at first stimulates violence until a certain point is reached. Then coerciveness, in the form of tyranny, seems probably just as apt to bring internal peace as more violence" (ibid., p. 415). Omitting to specify that "certain point," the Feierabends erect yet another tautology.

14. Cf. George C. Homans, *Social Behavior* (New York, 1974), pp. 43–47; idem, review of *Theoretical Methods in Social History*, by Arthur L. Stinchcombe, *Theory and Society* 12 (1983): 681–84; and Karl R. Popper, "The Rationality Principle," in *A Pocket Popper*, ed. David Miller (London, 1983), pp. 357–65.

15. Carl von Clausewitz, *Vom Kriege* (Bonn, 1973), pp. 210, 303.

16. Cobb, *Police and the People*, p. 85.

17. "Prediction" here does not mean forecasting tomorrow's history, but simply spelling out what empirical findings should turn up if the model is correct.

18. E. P. Thompson, *The Making of the English Working Class* (Harmondsworth, 1968), p. 73. The point is reiterated with a wealth of supporting evidence in idem, "The Moral Economy of the English Crowd in the Eighteenth Century," *Past and Present* 50 (1971): 76–136.

19. Natalie Zemon Davis, *Society and Culture in Early Modern France* (Stanford, 1975), p. 154.

20. On food riots, see Louise A. Tilly, "The Food Riot as a Form of Political Conflict in France," *Journal of Interdisciplinary History* 2 (1971): 23–57, and Charles Tilly, "Food Supply and Public Order in Modern Europe," in *The Formation of National States in Western Europe*, ed. idem (Princeton, 1975), esp. pp. 385–90. On tax revolts, Gabriel Ardant, "Financial Policy and Economic Infrastructure of Modern States and Nations," ibid., p. 194. On jacqueries, Rodney Hilton, *Bond Men Made Free* (London, 1973); David Sabean, "The Communal Basis of Pre-1800 Peasant Uprisings in Western Europe," *Comparative Politics* 8 (1976): 355–65; Norman Cohn, *The Pursuit of the Millenium* (London, 1970), pp. 104–5, 198–99, 203–4, 245–46; Zagorin, *Rebels and Rulers*, 1:175–227; Paul Avrich, *Russian Rebels, 1600–1800* (New York, 1972); Charles Tilly, "War and Peasant Rebellion in Seventeenth-Century France," in idem, *As Sociology Meets History* (New York, 1981); and Jerome Blum, *The End of the Old Order in Rural Europe* (Princeton, 1978), pp. 332–53. On *journées*, George Rudé, *The Crowd in the French Revolution* (Oxford, 1959).

21. Cobb, *Second Identity*, p. 78, and *Police and the People*, where it is asked how else ordinary "people could exercise their will and get their grievances seen to" (p. 89).

22. Cobb, *Police and the People*, pp. 118–71, 202–3, 334–35n.

23. Popular violence, writes Cobb, "is not so odious and inadmissible as that of war or of diplomacy: it was never gratuitous, nor was it ever exclusive to any one class—or any one party: all classes, all parties were enthusiastic advocates of violence when there was a good chance of using it against their immediate enemies, though they tended to discover the advantages of mercy when they looked like being on the losing side. . . . Its victims," moreover, "were, at least by modern standards, limited in number, and, as far as the violence of the common people was concerned, were more often wood and stone, glass and china, than flesh and blood" (*Police and the People*, pp. 90–91).

24. Ibid., p. 89.

25. Cf. Emmanuel Le Roy Ladurie, *Carnival in Romans* (New York, 1979) and, on the co-optation of popular festivals by the revolutionary government seeking to turn them to its own purposes of inspiring loyalty to the national state, Mona Ozouf, *La fête révolutionnaire, 1789–1799* (Paris, 1976).

26. Quoted by Jacques Godechot, *The Taking of the Bastille* (New York, 1970), p. 245.

27. The storming of the Bastille may serve as a paradigm. Not only did the defending garrison fire first, and repeatedly, on the crowd (who wanted entry to seize arms in preparation for an expected royalist attack on the city), but the casualty statistics make clear that the defenders were far more likely to survive than the attackers: of an estimated 800 to 900 besiegers, 98 were killed and 73 wounded; of the 110 defenders, 1 was killed and 3 wounded in the assault. Afterward, the crowd killed 6 of the defending garrison, as well as the commander and the acting head of the city government who had tried to avoid arming the citizenry (Godechot, *Taking of the Bastille*, pp. 229, 243, and Rudé, *Crowd in the French Revolution*, pp. 54–56). The proposition in any event may be generalized: "In Italy, France, and Germany, agents of government almost certainly did the majority of killing and wounding which occurred in the course of collective violence from 1830 onward" (Charles Tilly, Louise Tilly, and Richard Tilly, *The Rebellious Century, 1830–1930* [Cambridge, Mass., 1975], p. 243). "The substantial record of violence associated with protest movements in the United States is a record composed overwhelmingly of the casualties suffered by protestors at the hands of public or private armies" (Frances Fox Piven and Richard A. Cloward, *Poor People's Movements* [New York, 1977], p. 19).

28. Village leaders of the *Bauernkrieg* sought "no fundamental change of the peasants' position," but only a halt to increased taxation and official encroachments on rights of local self-government guaranteed under the "old law" (*das alte Recht*) (Günther Franz, *Der deutsche Bauernkrieg* [Darmstadt, 1977], pp. 100–102). The sansculottes' overriding aim was cheap and plentiful bread, and the appointment of authorities committed to assuring it (Rudé, *Crowd in the French Revolution*, p. 200). The *communards*, harkening back to 1793 rather than forward to 1917, wanted city self-government and, though they announced a number of cautious reforms (which had little anticapitalist flavor), were too preoccupied defending Paris to really enforce those they decreed (Theodore Zeldin, *France, 1848–1945*, 2 vols. [Oxford, 1973–77], 1:735–45). And the peasant rebels of the Russian Revolution simply wanted to eject parasitic squires and incorporate long-coveted estate lands into village holdings (Teodor Shanin, *The Awkward Class* [Oxford, 1972], pp. 153, 159–60; John L. H. Keep, *The Russian Revolution* [London, 1976], chaps. 12–19). Keep reports that very few people died by peasant violence, most of which was simply burning manor houses to discourage landlords from ever returning (pp. 208–9, 213).

29. "At every important stage of the Revolution the *sans-culottes* intervened, not to renovate society or to remodel it after a new pattern, but to reclaim traditional rights and to uphold standards which they believed to be imperilled by the innovations of ministers, capitalists, speculators, agricultural 'improvers,' or city authorities" (Rudé, *Crowd in the French Revolution*, p. 225). "From the beginning the movement had been a deliberate enterprise by country chiefs to restore the integrity of the state's villages, to gain local rights of participation in national progress. When Madero initiated the revolution in November 1910, Morelos rural leaders did not flock to his cause without weeks of hard reckoning and calculation. And when they did join him, it was

for conscious, practical reasons—to recover village lands and establish village security" (Womack, *Zapata*, p. 228).

30. On the essentially reformist demands of German and Russian workers in the revolutionary situations of 1918–1920 and 1917, see Barrington Moore, Jr., *Injustice* (White Plains, N.Y., 1978), pp. 340, 351–52, 362–71, 474–78; and on defensive paramilitary mobilization, pp. 374 and 478.

31. On the comparative sociology of revolutionary élites, see Alvin W. Gouldner, *The Future of Intellectuals and the Rise of the New Class* (New York, 1979), pp. 9–11, 53–57, 75–82, and, on the masses, Moore, *Social Origins*, pp. 480, 496–504, and *Injustice*, esp. pp. 351–52. Studies of the three outcomes include Isaiah Berlin, "Russian Populism," in *Russian Thinkers* (London, 1978); James C. Scott, "Protest and Profanation: Agrarian Revolt and the Little Tradition," *Theory and Society* 4 (1977): 1–38, 211–46; and Alvin W. Gouldner, "Stalinism: A Study of Internal Colonialism," *Telos* 34 (1977–78): 5–48. The clearest case study showing how little popular movements owe to the ideas of radical intellectuals is Cobb, *Police and the People*, esp. p. 206. Cf. Rudé, *Crowd in the French Revolution*, p. 225.

32. James C. Scott, *The Moral Economy of the Peasant* (New Haven, 1976), p. 4.

33. Though he filters his facts through a rigid class struggle thesis, Hilton gives tantalizing clues to the role of artisans, prosperous agriculturalists (one "peasant" rebel of 1381, for instance, had property confiscated that included two hundred acres of land, three hundred sheep, and one hundred additional livestock), and insurgent nobles and clergy (*Bond Men Made Free*, pp. 114–34, 165–213). In the German Peasant War, the "carriers of the revolt were not the village poor but, on the contrary, almost without exception the village notables, mayors and judges, innkeepers and blacksmiths, rich peasants, who later could pay [a] several hundred *Gulden* fine" (Franz, *Deutsche Bauernkrieg*, p. 287). Godechot, citing Rudé's census of the *vainqueurs de la Bastille*, notes that most were artisans and journeymen with bourgeois leaders, while Rudé points out that most *vainqueurs* were enrolled in the Paris national guard, which rigorously excluded "vagrants or social riff-raff" (*Taking of the Bastille*, pp. 221–26; *Crowd in the French Revolution*, p. 59). Cobb and Rudé also report that the sansculotte movement itself was staffed chiefly by master craftsmen (including substantial entrepreneurs), small employers of labor, shopkeepers, publicans, and wine merchants, together with a "thin sprinkling of professional men"—schoolmasters, public letter-writers, and, in the country towns, ex-priests and monks; wage earners, in fact, were rarely admitted as full members of the *sociétés populaires* (Cobb, *Second Identity*, pp. 126–27, and *Police and the People*, p. 120; Rudé, *Crowd in the French Revolution*, pp. 178, 190). In Soboul's sample of 514 sansculotte "militants" arrested by the Thermidorian regime in the year III (22 September 1794 through 22 September 1795), self-employed artisans and tradesmen outnumber wage earners nearly three to one—57 versus 20 percent of the total; including lower-grade civil servants and free professionals, "respectable" people account for almost 80 percent of all arrestees (Albert Soboul, *The Parisian Sans-Culottes and the French Revolution, 1793–4* [Oxford, 1964],

pp. 48–49). Female rioters, for their part, "were not paupers but women who in normal times could manage, proud women who were not counted among the destitute and who were fighting to remain so and to hold their families together" (Olwen Hufton, "Women in Revolution, 1789–1796," in *French Society and the Revolution*, ed. Douglas Johnson [Cambridge, 1976], p. 152). The persisting political presence of artisans and other "petit-bourgeois" elements, sometimes helped, sometimes hindered by organized wage earners, is clear from Robert J. Bezucha, *The Lyon Uprising of 1834* (Cambridge, Mass., 1974); Charles Tilly and Lynn Lees, "Le peuple de Juin 1848," *Annales: E.S.C.* 29 (1974): 1061–91; Mark Traugott, "The Mobile Guard in the French Revolution of 1848," *Theory and Society* 9 (1980): 683–720; William H. Sewell, Jr., *Work and Revolution in France* (Cambridge, 1980); and Zeldin, *France*, 1:738 (who notes that the Commune was proletarian neither in social composition nor in ideological outlook). On landholding peasants in modern revolutions, see Eric R. Wolf, *Peasant Wars of the Twentieth Century* (New York, 1969), and consider what Emiliano Zapata told a journalist in 1911: "It can't be said of me that I went off to the battlefields under the pressure of poverty. I've got some land and a stable . . . which I earned through long years of honest work and not through political campaigns, and which produce enough for me and my family to live on comfortably" (quoted by Womack, *Zapata*, pp. 127–28). The vanguard role of artisanal craftworkers in the French labor movement, and evidence that the "more organization you get, the more strikes," is explained by Edward Shorter and Charles Tilly, *Strikes in France, 1830–1968* (Cambridge, 1974). Similarly, the radical movement in German industry during World War I was centered among the labor aristocracy of highly skilled workers (Moore, *Injustice*, p. 287). On the sometime involvement of "lumpen" elements in mass action, on both sides of the barricades, see Rudé, *Crowd in the French Revolution*, pp. 186–90; Cobb, *Second Identity*, pp. 156, 276–77; and Moore, *Injustice*, pp. 319–20.

34. Wolf, *Peasant Wars*, p. 290. Cf. Anton Blok, *The Mafia of a Sicilian Village, 1860–1960* (New York, 1975).

35. Moore, *Social Origins*, pp. 475–76; Shanin, *Awkward Class*, pp. 164–69; and (for 1905) Maureen Perrie, "The Russian Peasant Movement of 1905–1907: Its Social Composition and Revolutionary Significance," *Past and Present* 57 (1972): 123–55. For details on the origin and working of the rural commune, see Jerome Blum, *Lord and Peasant in Russia from the Ninth to the Nineteenth Century* (Princeton, 1961), pp. 510–14, 522–27; on landed property distribution in European Russia on the eve of the Revolution, see Lazar Volin, *A Century of Russian Agriculture* (Cambridge, Mass., 1970), p. 133. The center of Zapatista resistance in revolutionary Mexico, Ayala, was both economically independent and the "most militant and most heavily armed rural municipality in Morelos," where most villages were legally autonomous and less than a quarter of the rural population lived on haciendas (Womack, *Zapata*, p. 62; Ronald Waterbury, "Non-revolutionary Peasants: Oaxaca Compared to Morelos in the Mexican Revolution," *Comparative Studies in Society and History* 17 [1975]: 413).

36. Huntington, *Political Order*, pp. 4–5, 36, 37, 39, 47, 56, and *passim*. How Huntington's explanation relies on loose reasoning with history to match is explained by Charles Tilly, "Does Modernization Breed Revolution?" *Comparative Politics* 5 (1973): 425–47. The Durkheimian parallels are discussed by Tilly in *From Mobilization to Revolution*, pp. 18–21.

37. Marc Bloch, *French Rural History* (Berkeley, 1966), p. 170 (translation corrected). Cf. Charles Tilly, "Getting It Together in Burgundy, 1675–1975," *Theory and Society* 4 (1977): 479–504.

38. Jeffery M. Paige, *Agrarian Revolution* (New York, 1975), pp. 40–45, 48–71, 120–22, 337–76. For doubts about part of Paige's argument, however, see Eric R. Wolf, "Why Cultivators Rebel," *American Journal of Sociology* 83 (1977): 742–50; Margaret R. Somers and Walter L. Goldfrank, "The Limits of Agronomic Determinism: A Critique of Paige's *Agrarian Revolution*," *Comparative Studies in Society and History* 21 (1979): 443–58; and Theda Skocpol, "What Makes Peasants Revolutionary?" *Comparative Politics* 14 (1982): 351–75, who notes in particular his tendency to confound sharecroppers' own objectives and organization with those of the radical parties who seek to mobilize them, as if the National Liberation Front were a kind of peasant syndicate (pp. 355–59).

39. See Shorter and Tilly, *Strikes in France*, p. 338; Joel Migdal, *Peasants, Politics, and Revolution* (Princeton, 1974), chap. 10; Samuel L. Popkin, *The Rational Peasant* (Berkeley, 1979), chaps. 5–6; and William A. Gamson, *The Strategy of Social Protest* (Homewood, Ill., 1975); and, as case studies in point, Ted W. Margadant, *French Peasants in Revolt* (Princeton, 1979); Elizabeth J. Perry, *Rebels and Revolutionaries in North China, 1845–1945* (Stanford, 1980); and Samuel Clark, *Social Origins of the Irish Land War* (Princeton, 1979).

40. "The outbreak of most revolutions has surprised the revolutionist groups and parties no less than all others, and there exists hardly a revolution whose outbreak could be blamed on their activities. It was usually the other way round: revolution broke out and liberated . . . the professional revolutionists . . . from jail, or from the coffee house, or from the library. Not even Lenin's party of professional revolutionaries would ever have been able to 'make' a revolution; the best they could do was to be around, or to hurry home, . . . at the point of collapse" (Hannah Arendt, *On Revolution* [New York, 1965], p. 263). Cf. notes 6 and 7 above.

41. Cobb, *Second Identity*, p. 277. To wit: "The Mexican Revolution happened because the high politicians of the country openly failed to agree on who should rule when President Porfirio Díaz died" (Womack, *Zapata*, p. 10).

42. "[A]nd after we have reached a provisional conclusion by isolating the complicating factors one by one, we then have to go back on ourselves and allow, as well as we can, for the probable interactions of the factors amongst themselves. . . . Any other way of applying our formal principles of thought (without which, however, we shall be lost in the wood) will lead us into error" (John Maynard Keynes, *The General Theory of Employment, Interest and Money* [London, 1973], p. 297).

43. See Diana E. H. Russell, *Rebellion, Revolution, and Armed Force* (New York, 1974). Though cluttered with untidy definitions and dubious statistical manipulations, this study is good for getting clear the centrality of control over armed force in the emergence and outcome of revolutionary situations. The determinants of armed forces politics in the several cases examined are not much clarified, however, as the author tends to pair off rebels against regimes with insufficient attention to the nuances of what Tilly terms the "polity" (see note 7 above). Cf. Jack A. Goldstone, "The Comparative and Historical Study of Revolutions," *Annual Review of Sociology* 8 (1982): 187–207, and idem, "Theories of Revolution: The Third Generation," *World Politics* 32 (1980): 425–53.

44. A superb account of one revolutionary situation, explaining historical causation (implicitly) in terms of the intentions, capabilities, and opportunities of key contenders, is Friedrich Katz, *The Secret War in Mexico* (Chicago, 1981). Cf. notes 4, 6, 7, 28, 29, 33, 35, 41, and corresponding text above.

GOVERNMENT AND THE
SUPPRESSION OF RADICAL LABOR,
1877–1918

Daniel R. Fusfeld

The political economy of the United States in the twentieth century can
be characterized as an emerging corporate state: a growing symbiosis of
big business and big government in which concentrated economic and
political power is dominated by a self-selecting elite motivated by the
twin goals of wealth and power.[1] As this pattern developed an accommodation with the emerging industrial working class was worked out that
involved union recognition and collective bargaining, ameliorative legislation to benefit workers, and restriction of imigration. Supporting this
accommodation and providing the material base that enabled it to work
was a process of economic growth that made possible continuing increases
in affluence for many. A large portion of the working class was drawn into
a junior partnership in the emerging corporate state, or at least acquiesced in the structure of power and distribution of wealth.

Radicalism in the labor movement was handled differently. An indigenous American labor radicalism grew with the working class as industrialism spread in the years before World War I. But it became politically
and economically isolated by the emerging accommodation between industrial labor and capitalist America, and was suppressed by the federal
government in 1917–18.[2]

The traditional explanation for the failure of radicalism in the American labor movement is that the American environment of political democracy, economic opportunity, and rising living standards defused radical
protest[3] and as a result business unionism and job consciousness carried
the day against radical unionism and class consciousness.[4] In these accounts the harassment and repression of radical labor by local, state, and
ultimately the federal government is largely ignored, as is the undoubted
vitality of an indigenous radical movement among workers in industrial
America.

This essay explores the economic and political forces and events that
led to the federal government's suppression of American labor radicalism
during World War I. It analyzes the growth and development of radical
labor in the forty years from 1887 to 1917, the split between radicals and
moderates within the labor movement and between moderates and con-

servatives in the business community, the early alliance between labor moderates and corporate liberals that gained the support of the federal government, and the ensuing suppression of radical labor.[5] Particular emphasis will be placed on the changing role of government as the early modern corporate state began to take form.

From Mass Strike to Haymarket, 1877–87

The mass strike came to industrial America in 1877. The strikes of that summer were upheavals of protest and rebellion involving large numbers of dissatisfied workers who were unorganized, without overall leadership and without a program of action.

The 1877 riots began among railway workers as a response to wage reductions on the major eastern railroads in the fourth year of a major depression, the worst depression in American history up to that time. Workers on the Baltimore and Ohio Railroad walked out in Martinsburg, West Virginia, on July 17. The strike spread among railroad workers in Pennsylvania, New York, and Ohio, and to Louisville, Chicago, and St. Louis. Anthracite coal miners struck in northeast Pennsylvania. In Chicago the strike spread to many industries. In St. Louis a coalition of trade unions organized a general strike and established a workers' government modeled on the Paris commune of 1871, which operated the city government for several days until ousted by police and the state militia.

There were several major riots. A mob in Baltimore set fire to the depot and attacked federal troops that had been ordered in to restore operation of the railroad. In Pittsburgh a mob of railroad and steel mill workers, unemployed youths, and underworld toughs rioted and destroyed railroad property. Yet across the river at Allegheny City there was no violence: the trainmen's union ran that section of the railroad for four days, operating passenger and mail trains but stopping freights.[6]

Order was finally restored after four to five days by the U.S. Army. The first effort to use the state militias in Pennsylvania and Maryland was ineffective: these forces would not fire on their relatives and friends. Federal troops were then used, in the first instance of the use of the army to break a strike. This tactic was effective and by July 21 the revolt was over.

The events of 1877 were new to the American experience. For the first time workers had acted as a class on a national scale, even though there was little leadership or organization and no positive program, only protest. Earlier strikes had been called by craft unions, largely on a local basis, and the largest concentrated effort was a widespread strike of local unions in New York City in 1872. But in 1877 there was an outburst that affected almost all of the industrial areas of the nation. And wherever the (strike action appeared "order" was restored by military force. It was the first great class confrontation in America, and a portent of things to come.

The events of 1877 led to a growing polarization of American society. The forces of repression began to mobilize. Many states enacted conspiracy laws directed against labor. State and federal courts revived the concept of malicious conspiracy and applied it to labor organizations. Employers took a stronger stand against union organization, using blacklists and strikebreaking. (Harassment of union organizers by local police and officials of local governments, often with the cooperation of local courts, became a common occurrence. [7]\

The state militias, which has almost disappeared after a long period of decline, were revived in 1877 for use primarily as a strikebreaking force. Established by Congress in 1792 as a compulsory national military reserve, the militias had become voluntary organizations and, where the units survived, chiefly social and honorific in function. The events of 1877 changed all that. The militia forces used in the strike had been hastily recruited from volunteers and were almost wholly untrained. They proved almost useless when used in their own localities, apparently because of unwillingness to shoot their neighbors, and elsewhere they required support from the regular army. But by and large the militia remained loyal to governmental authority and did not actively move over to support the strikers. After the revolt the states most heavily affected began to support the militia more fully. New York State began a continuing program to build armories for militia units in all large cities. Many states increased appropriations for the militia; even Iowa began such spending for the first time. All of this was done with the support of business and financial interests, whose taxes paid the bills, and with the tacit consent of military leaders, who did not want the regular army used as a police force.

In the years after 1877 the militia, which even then began to be called the National Guard (the name was officially changed in 1933) was used chiefly in breaking strikes. [8] Its voluntary organization was particularly appropriate for that purpose, for antiunion groups could be quickly recruited, mobilized, and armed, and sent to the scene of labor troubles. In some western states, particularly Colorado in 1895–1905, strikebreakers, company guards, and troops hired from the Pinkerton detective agency were organized into National Guard companies during disputes in mining areas.

The strikebreaking function of the National Guard was seldom emphasized by its advocates, but was important in practice. "Riot training" was the chief training provided in most units until about 1910. Increased congressional appropriations for the National Guard followed spectacular examples of labor unrest: in 1889 after the Haymarket bombing and trial of 1886–87, in 1897 and 1900 after the labor unrest of that decade, and in 1903 after the anthracite miners' strike a year earlier. In each case, however, the role of the National Guard as a national military reserve was emphasized, not its domestic police function.

In the late nineteenth century the United States moved more heavily into international politics, acquiring colonies, developing "dollar diplomacy" in Latin America, and building a modern navy. In keeping with this change in the nation's international posture, the National Guard was gradually transformed in the twentieth century into a more genuine national military reserve. The chief motive underlying the 1903 legislation, which reorganized the National Guard, was the organization's ineptness in the 1898 war against Spain. But the guard never lost its domestic police function. Its role in suppressing mass radical movements was enhanced by the improved training, better equipment, and tightened discipline that marked its development into a military reserve. One product of the 1877 strikes, then, was the development of a domestic police force under the command of state governments that could be used to contain further outbreaks like those of 1877.

On the other side of the class struggle, the events of 1877 brought the Knights of Labor into the open. This organization, which might have become "the fighting organization of a new class," to use Selig Perlman's descriptive phrase,[9] had been organized in 1869, but until 1878 it was a secret organization, secrecy being forced on it by employer opposition. After the 1877 upheavals secrecy was dropped and the knights sought to become a mass working-class organization open to all workers, unskilled as well as skilled, in all industries and occupations. Both the leadership and the membership learned in 1877 that national organization, a program of action, and a strike fund were necessary if economic actions by the working class were to be successful.[10]

The Knights of Labor was not a radical organization in the modern sense. It did not advocate government ownership of productive resources, or even big industry, and it did not seek to change the system of private ownership. However, its basic thrust was toward workers as a class and it advocated a more egalitarian distribution of income. The philosophy of the Knights was that workers should get a larger share of the economy's benefits, and the way to achieve that goal was for all workers to join a single organization to work actively to better the condition of all workers. In 1880 this philosophy of mass organization on a class basis was considered by many supporters of the existing order to be a dangerous threat. We should view it as the first major step toward a radical working-class philosophy following the unorganized and unfocused riots of 1877.

Radical socialist ideologies with a Marxist orientation had already spread to the United States by 1877, but they had little impact on labor unions in particular or working people in general. Nor did unity prevail among the small minority who did bear those ideas: Marxists, Lasalleans, anarchists, and syndicalists vied with each other and sought to gain footholds in labor organizations.[11] They had little success. Even in Chicago, where a vocal and vigorous group of anarchists gathered, these radical ideologies were not strong. It is a mistake to find the origins of American labor radicalism in European radical ideologies. Radicalism in the American labor movement developed slowly and painfully out of class conflict in the American economy itself. The first stage was the rioting of 1877. The second was the attempt to build a mass organization of all workers in the Knights of Labor.

Much of the activity of the Knights centered on unskilled and semi-skilled workers, such as bricklayers, tanners, and freight handlers. It was difficult to work with this segment of the working class: turnover among workers was high, strikers were easy to replace with strikebreakers, and most workers had little previous experience with organization and strikes. The result was numerous unsuccessful strikes and only a few victories.

In addition, the wide diversity of membership in the Knights included many persons who favored political action rather than strikes, around issues like monetary reform, land reform, cooperation, and various socialist and anarchist programs. Another source of weakness was opposition from existing craft unions, which took a dim view of an organization seeking to include all productive workers. Conflict between the two styles of organization became acute in the later 1880s.[12] These rivalries and internal conflicts might have been overcome if the Knights had been able to win some spectacular victories on the strike front to show that the working class could make significant advances through a class-oriented organization. But, for the most part, successes were few.

The greatest success of the Knights of Labor came in 1885 strikes on the group of railroads controlled by Jay Gould, including the Wabash, Missouri Pacific, and Union Pacific. As a result, large numbers of unskilled and semiskilled workers joined the Knights. This element in the organization had a strongly emotional antiemployer attitude and was quick to support strikes and boycotts. As its membership grew the Knights became a militant national organization representing mostly unskilled and semiskilled workers, many of whom showed a strong hatred for business and capital and were eager to use economic actions against the class enemy. The leadership, however, was more timid. Schooled in the failures before 1885, it was not prepared to use the instrument that the workers themselves presented to them.

The rapid growth of the Knights of Labor in 1885–86 was seen as a threat by many of the older craft unions. They feared that the Knights, with its stress on working-class solidarity and its organizational pattern of local and regional units, would lose sight of the interests of workers in the skilled trades. Indeed, joint economic action by all workers in the interests of all, regardless of skill, was the philosophy of the Knights. Leaders of the craft unions saw this strategy as unfavorable to the skilled workers, as it probably was in the short run. Craft unions were able to limit access to employment opportunities to a much greater extent than unions of unskilled workers, simply because of the relative scarcity of skilled workers and the relative abundance of unskilled workers. Craft unions, therefore, were able to make economic gains not open to unions of unskilled workers, and their leadership felt that this advantage would largely be lost if the policies of the Knights were followed.

As a result, the growth of the Knights of Labor was accompanied by a movement in opposition to the Knights among the craft unions, culminating in the formation of the American Federation of Labor in 1886 to provide a stronger national union of craft unions. The very success of the Knights intensified the split between unskilled and skilled workers and drove a wedge into the working class. Two national organizations now reflected two different philosophies, one job consciousness, the other class consciousness.[13]

Even at this early stage the development of industrial capitalism began to divide the working class. Skilled workers were able to make significant economic gains within the existing system of property relations. Unskilled workers, however, were unable to protect themselves from the working of competition in the labor market and the dominant position of employers. They did not have a strong vested interest in maintaining existing economic relations. Without a significant stake in the system, the unskilled turned to class militancy and radicalism.

The Knights of Labor found an issue that seemed to bridge these differences, at least temporarily—the drive to achieve a standard working day of eight hours. The movement for an eight-hour day was an old one. It arose out of the climate of opinion in the working class during the long wave of relatively prosperous times from about 1850 to the early 1870s, and was supported by many craft unions. By the mid-1880s little progress had been made. The normal working day was ten hours, and in some industries twelve and fourteen hours were common. The eight-hour day was an issue on which both skilled and unskilled workers could unite, for both groups could benefit. It was also a means for spreading work to the unemployed, thereby reducing the competition for jobs that tended to drag down wage rates. And it was an economic issue that directly affected workers' incomes and style of life. The Knights of Labor had found an issue around which the entire working class could unite. Employers saw it that way, too, and fought the eight-hour day on class lines as well as on economic and business grounds.[14]

The result was the second great confrontation of the emerging class struggle: the Haymarket "riot" in May, 1886, in Chicago. The riot grew out of the drive for shorter hours that in 1885–86 had been moderately successful throughout the industrializing northeastern states. In Chicago in 1885 an Eight-Hour Association was organized by a variety of labor organizations and several left wing political groups, and was supported by the Central Labor Union. On the Sunday before May 1, 1886, this organization sponsored a huge rally in support of the eight-hour day, and a general strike followed, starting with thirty thousand workers on May 1 and reaching about seventy-five thousand on May 4. The city was in the midst of a class-oriented mass strike like that of 1877, but one that was nonviolent and well organized.

Trouble began at the McCormick Harvester Works, which had been involved in a strike and lockout since February. Violence occurred on May 3, in which police fire killed four and wounded others. A mass meeting was organized under radical leadership for the next day at Haymarket Square. The meeting was peaceful and most had already left when police attacked the crowd. Someone threw a bomb—the first use of dynamite in a civil disorder—killing one policeman and throwing others to the ground. The police opened fire at once, shooting other policemen as well as people in the crowd. The next day, seven leaders of Chicago radical groups were arrested and charged with murder; another surrendered later to stand trial. A political trial followed. The jury was handpicked to include people who admitted prejudice against the defendants, the judge was openly biased, and the trial took place in an atmosphere of panic and hysteria. The eight defendants were convicted; seven were sentenced to death and one to imprisonment for fifteen years. The U.S. Supreme Court affirmed the verdict in the fall of 1887. One of the condemned men died of an explosion in his cell, reportedly a suicide. The sentences of two were commuted to life imprisonment (they were pardoned in 1893), and four were executed on November 11, 1887. Thus closed one of the most notorious political trials in American history. [15]

Labor and Business Strategies, 1887–1902

A wave of repression and reaction swept the United States after Haymarket. Fanned by newspaper editorials that promised a wave of destruction and violence unless anarchism was stamped out, public opinion was whipped up to support the Haymarket trial and the conviction of the defendants. Federal and state governments took no further action, but in many communities throughout the country local police raided the offices of radical groups and labor unions and arrested their leadership, many of whom were jailed. Meetings of radical groups and unions, especially those designed to assist the Haymarket defendants, were broken up by local vigilantes, often with the assistance of benign indifference on the part of local police or sheriff's deputies. Print shops for radical publications were wrecked, and offices of the publications themselves were raided. Much of this agitation seems to have originated among local business and real estate interests, and in some instances racist or anti-immigrant agitation was involved.[16] These tactics were to be perfected over the next thirty years and adopted in less violent form and with legal sanctions by the federal government in 1918–20.

The Knights of Labor, which by now was identified in the public mind with mass action by workers, was destroyed in the reaction to Haymarket, although poor leadership and a series of unsuccessful strikes in 1886–87 contributed to the organization's decline. Its membership fell from over seven hundred fifty thousand in 1886 to probably less than one hundred thousand in 1890. Most of the unskilled members had quit by the end of 1887. Whatever else may be said about Haymarket, it was instrumental in destroying the first effort to develop a class-conscious program of action out of the mass discontent of the 1887 riots.[17]

A mass-oriented labor movement did not disappear, however, but was found in a group of industrial unions that appeared in the 1890s. These unions sought to organize all workers in an industry, regardless of craft or skill level—a compromise between the one big union pattern of the Knights and the craft exclusiveness of the new American Federation of Labor (AFL). The industrial unions of the nineties appeared in the new industries of the post–Civil War industrial era: railroads, steel, coal mining, and nonferrous metal mining. Large corporations had developed in these industries, which were dominated either by leading entrepreneurs, like Andrew Carnegie in steel, or by investment bankers and other financial interests in New York and Boston, such as J. P. Morgan and Company. Except for the railroad brotherhoods, most of the craft unions, particularly the strong ones, were found in industries of a different sort, the relatively labor-intensive, more competitive, and less concentrated sectors of the economy, such as cigar manufacturing, construction, and printing. These craft unions were no threat to the management or financiers of the giant firms in the basic industries. But the new industrial unions were a threat. They confronted the dynamic leading edge of industrial capitalism, and a series of bitter struggles ensued.

The national union in the steel industry was destroyed by a union-busting corporation. The Amalgamated Association of Iron and Steel Workers was a militant, mass-oriented union. A strong thread of class consciousness ran through its policy statements, although it did not have a socialist program. It was the largest and strongest union in the country in 1892, with over twenty-four thousand members, when the great strike began against Carnegie Steel Company at Homestead, Pennsylvania.

Conflict between strikers and strikebreakers brought out the state militia, the strike spread to other Carnegie plants, and injunctions against the union were issued in local courts to protect the company's use of strikebreakers. The strike was a failure and six months later the workers were back at work without a union organization. (One of the nation's giant corporations, using strikebreakers and backed by the courts and state government, had destroyed one of the early industrial unions.[18])

A second industrial union, the Western Federation of Miners (WFM), was radicalized by class warfare. Organized in 1893 as a union of all employees in the metals mining industry of the western states, it began as an essentially job-conscious industrial union interested primarily in wages, hours, and working conditions. It faced harassment similar to that which broke the Iron and Steel Workers: refusal to bargain, strikebreakers, injunctions, use of militia, and vigilante mobs. But this union did not fold. Rather, its rank and file membership and leadership were radicalized by a series of confrontations with management throughout the 1890s. These confrontations quickly turned into class warfare. The corporations blacklisted union members and brought in strikebreakers and armed private armies. They were supported by local governments and courts, and by the local press and business interests. When necessary, state governments were called upon for National Guard units and state courts for injunctions to legalize police action against WFM organizers and strikes. The miners responded in kind, and forced expulsions of either miners or strikebreakers, depending on which side won the battle, were common occurrences in mining area conflicts. The WFM, weakened by loss of membership, was reduced to a hard core of activist radicals, and developed a socialist, class-conscious ideology. Its leadership moved in the late 1890s to form a national mass-oriented radical labor organization.[19]

A third industrial union, the American Railway Union (ARU), had been organized by Eugene V. Debs in 1892 in an effort to avoid the divisiveness of the craft union brotherhoods. In the summer of 1894 the new union went to the aid of workers striking the Pullman Palace Car Company, which refused to bargain, and ordered its members not to move trains with Pullman cars attached. There was burning and looting in some Chicago railroad yards. Railroads refused to detach Pullman cars from trains carrying mail, and the press cried out against holding up the U.S. mails. A federal court injunction was directed against the ARU and its leaders.

Debs and other leaders ignored the injunction and were indicted and arrested. When Governor Altgeld refused to call out the state militia, President Cleveland sent in army troops to enable the railroads to keep the trains running with the assistance of strikebreakers. These were tense times: the nation was gripped by the worst depression in its history, Coxey's army of unemployed was marching on Washington, and fear of insurrection was widespread. Debs appealed to the AFL for a general strike of all unions, but this effort to widen the dispute into an acknowledged mass strike of worker against capitalist failed: a conference of AFL unions decided that a general strike would be "unwise and disastrous." The strike was broken by the combination of corporations, courts, and federal government, Debs was jailed, and the union disintegrated. But Debs emerged from prison a convinced socialist, led in organizing the Socialist party, and became the foremost socialist leader of his time.[20]

The fourth important industrial union of the 1890s, the United Mine Workers (UMW), moved toward collective bargaining of the AFL type. This union was originally for coal miners only, but in 1898 it opened its membership to all employees of the coal mining companies. The broader base in the industry enabled it to achieve some important but limited successes in the bituminous coal mining sector of the industry, largely because there it faced a large number of relatively small firms rather than a few giant corporations like those the Iron and Steel Workers and American Railway Union had to deal with. But in 1902, during a titanic struggle with the highly concentrated anthracite mining part of the industry, the UMW consciously opted for business unionism and collective bargaining rather than class action. In the next section of this essay we shall examine the 1902 anthracite mining strike in some detail, for in that struggle the political and ideological alignments that ultimately led to a national labor policy of collective bargaining within the existing economic order were forged.[21]

During the 1890s, then, American workers experimented with industrial rather than craft unions in the basic industries of the country—steel, railroads, coal mining, and metal mining—contesting with some of the new giant corporations of the era and with the new centers of financial control. The result of the struggle was destruction of all union organization in steel; elimination of the industrial union in railroads, leaving a group of craft unions; the triumph of job-conscious unionism in coal; and the rise of class-conscious unionism in nonferrous metals. Homestead and Pullman showed that the large enterprises and financial giants of the time would not tolerate mass organization of workers. The instruments used to fight class organizations of working people were brought to a higher degree of effectiveness: the mass media to arouse public opinion, the courts to provide a legal basis for the use of force, strikebreakers to keep operations going and as private armies, and jail for the leaders of the workers. All of this was done under the protective umbrella of an appeal to law and order, the sanctity of private property, the United States Constitution, and "Americanism."

The federal government was drawn into the conflict in the nineties. While local courts enjoined the strikers in the Homestead strike in 1892, it was a federal court that acted against the American Railway Union in the Pullman strike of 1894, and it was a U.S. attorney general who sought the injunction. The U.S. Army rather than the national guard was used. All of this took place because the governor of Illinois refused to act, but it nevertheless marked a significant change from the state to the federal level in dealing with labor problems.

The response from the Left was varied. Socialist elements within the AFL craft unions attempted to gain control of the Federation during the 1890s, but were defeated, leaving the antisocialist Samuel Gompers and his philosophy of "pure and simple" unionism in control.[22] The Socialist Party of America was also in process of formation in the later 1890s, led by Debs, who succeeded in bringing together a wide variety of socialist political organizations to form a single party in 1901.[23]

Although the effort to turn the craft unions to the left failed, an attempt to offer an alternative to the AFL and to develop a class-conscious and united working class was made by the American Labor Union (ALU), organized in 1898 by the leaders of the Western Federation of Miners. The ALU differed from Gompers and the AFL on a number of crucial points: it wanted to organize all workers, it deemphasized craft exclusiveness by advocating free transfer from one union to another, it opposed restrictions on immigration (except Asians), and it advocated strong political action by workers as a class.

As the class war in the West accelerated in the last years of the nineteenth century, the ALU leadership became more vocal in its denunciation of capitalism and the national government that treated the repressive violence used against Western labor with benign neglect. The ALU proposed a syndicalist form of socialism: direct ownership and management of enterprises by workers. It favored industrial rather than craft unions, class solidarity of all workers, and vigorous economic action (strikes and boycotts) by the working class as a whole. Here was a further development of the mass movement of 1877 and the idea of the Knights of Labor, sharpened by the labor conflicts of the 1880s, that was to lead directly into the Industrial Workers of the World a few years later. At the time, however, the ALU made little progress against the entrenched AFL ideas and organization. It remained almost wholly an adjunct of the Western Federation of Miners.[24]

Meanwhile, the more conservative elements in the labor movement found allies among more liberal elements in the corporate community. These groups found a common ground in the "trade agreements" movement of the 1890s. In a number of industries associations of employers were organized to bargain with labor unions in order to reach agreement on wages, hours, working conditions, and other labor matters. The agreements were for specific periods of time, usually one to three years, and could be national, regional, or local in scope. Crucially, they required acceptance of the union as the representative of the workers. On the one hand, the employers acquiesced, in varying degrees, to control of access to the job by the union, although the closed shop was seldom included in the agreement. The union, in turn, gave up the right to strike for the duration of the agreement. There was some doubt that these trade agreements were enforceable in the courts, but opinion among both employers and union officials was that they involved a strong moral commitment on both sides.[25]

The growth and limited success of the trade agreements movement strengthened the position of relatively conservative labor leaders like Samuel Gompers, John Mitchell of the mine workers, and others who opposed the socialists. They could point to growing acceptance of unions by employers and concrete economic gains for workers. A middle position was emerging between the socialist ideology of left-oriented workers and the union-busting philosophy that prevailed at Homestead and Pullman.

Even among the leaders of large corporations there were some who were willing to accept labor unions as one means of achieving industrial peace. The chief spokesman for this group of "corporate liberals" was Marcus A. Hanna, U.S. senator from Ohio, who had built a large Midwest coal, iron, and lake shipping enterprise and had become an important Republican political entrepreneur as well. He was a major fund-raiser for the Republican party, managed William McKinley's campaign for the presidency, and became Republican national chairman. He was among the first to see that the new giant corporations needed labor peace to protect the security of their large investments, and that this security was best achieved by settling labor disputes in a manner acceptable to workers. He sought to avoid the threat of socialism by providing for peaceful settlement of labor-management disputes. In Hanna's own words, in a speech advocating "industrial conciliation and arbitration,"

> The large aggregations of capital feared at first by labor, may prove to be labor's best friend, in that, control of a trade being thus centralized, there is opportunity to establish friendly relations which shall make uniform conditions throughout the country, or large sections thereof, and reduce the basis of competition to the quality of the product rather than to the concessions forced from labor. . . .

> . . . The great productive capacity of this country has forced upon us the aggregation of capital and the creation of great material wealth seeking opportunity for investment. This rapidly increasing wealth must find investment, and to make the investment in industrials secure we must

have industrial peace. . . . The trusts have come to stay. Organized labor and organized capital are but forward steps in the great industrial evolution that is taking place. . . . You are well aware that there has been a tendency in this country, from the very nature of things, to what is called socialism. Everything that is American is primarily opposed to socialism. . . . There is nothing in the organization of society that can afford to permit the growth of socialistic ideas. They are un-American and unnatural to us as a people.[26]

Hanna was a pragmatist. Collective bargaining between labor and management was seen as the way to preserve private enterprise.

The National Civic Federation was born out of the trade agreements movement and the philosophy of corporate liberalism. Organized in 1900, it had its origins in the Chicago Civic Federation, a group of business leaders brought together by journalist Ralph Easley in 1894 to try to end the Pullman strike through mediation and conciliation. Failing in that attempt, Easley and his new group addressed a variety of local issues, gaining the support of much of the Chicago business leadership. One of the organization's continuing interests was arbitration and conciliation in labor disputes. Starting in 1898, the Chicago organization sponsored a series of national conferences on political reform, foreign policy, and big business, all oriented toward reform along the lines of the Progressive movement and organized around a pluralist philosophy representing business, labor, public, and other interest groups. These activities culminated in formation of the National Civic Federation (NCF) in 1900.

Although Easley was the secretary and organizer, Mark Hanna was president of the new organization and Samuel Gompers was the first vice president. This combination symbolized the approach of the NCF: reformer-publicist, corporate liberal, and labor moderate. Other well-known people who were active in the NCF included Oscar Strauss, later secretary of commerce and labor in Theodore Roosevelt's cabinet; August Belmont, New York financier; Seth Low, reform mayor of New York City and president of Columbia University; and John Mitchell, president of the United Mine Workers. Important businessmen, labor leaders, and political figures came together in an organization that sought peaceful settlement of the conflict between capital and labor based on acceptance of union organization by business and of private enterprise by unions.[27]

In the nineties, then, both workers and business interests divided. The mass unions had been largely shattered and the craft unions had rejected socialism, leaving the left with only socialist politics and one weak union. The union movement as a whole was dominated by moderate leaders like Gompers and Mitchell, who opposed radical change and political action and favored immediate economic gains within the existing economic order through collective bargaining. The business community was also dividing. One group was willing to work with the moderate union leaders for labor peace through collective bargaining and a share of the pie for workers. The business conservatives, however, remained adamantly opposed to union organization and collective bargaining, but as yet this group had no organization to act as its publicist and political arm. A contest was building that offered either class conflict or a compromise based on the coalition of labor moderates and corporate liberals. As we shall see, the resolution of this contest depended on which side was able to use the power of the state: ultimately it was liberal control of the national government that brought victory to the philosophy of collective bargaining—and repression of radical labor.

Anthracite, 1902

The anthracite coal strike of 1902 brought together all of the key issues in the struggle between labor and management.[28] It involved an industry supplying an essential commodity to millions of people (at the turn of the century anthracite coal was the chief fuel for heating urban homes) and thus aroused intense public interest and emotions. Management in the industry was opposed to negotiations and any form of union recognition. The United Mine Workers, however, was committed to collective bargaining and was willing to work with the corporate liberals of the National Civic Federation. Within the union, however, a powerful group supported a strategy of labor solidarity and class struggle. After that group was defeated, leaving a leadership that supported collective bargaining for limited goals firmly in command, the federal government interceded to force management to accept a settlement. This was the first instance of the alliance between business unionism, corporate liberalism, and state power, that, in somewhat different form a third of a century later, was to bring national legislation requiring employers to bargain collectively with unions.

The anthracite coal miners had won an earlier strike in 1900 in which they not only obtained an increase in wage rates and other improvements but also greatly strengthened their union organization. Nevertheless, only a small proportion of the anthracite miners were members of the United Mine Workers when the 1902 strike began. The employers apparently decided to try to break the union. Negotiations with the union had brought a wage increase in 1900, which was extended for a second year. The union wanted to reopen negotiations, but company managers refused to negotiate and sought to harass and weaken the union. Early in 1902 the union leadership sought the assistance of the National Civic Federation. Senator Mark Hanna was successful in setting up a meeting between four union officials, including John Mitchell, president of the UMW, with four representatives of the largest anthracite mining companies, but the companies refused to make concessions, and agreed only to a thirty-day truce. At the end of the thirty days a subcommittee of union and management representatives again failed to reach agreement.

The union demands were moderate: recognition of the union as bargaining agent, an increase in wages to a standard sixty cents per ton of coal mined, weighing of coal in the presence of union-paid checkweighmen, and an eight-hour day. The union proposed that if no agreement was reached the issues would be submitted to binding arbitration by a committee selected by the National Civic Federation, or by a committee of Catholic bishops suggested by Mitchell. Management rejected the proposal.

The strike began on May 14, 1902, timed to forestall production of coal stocks for the coming winter heating season. The companies moved to hire private police and recruited labor from outside the region, which triggered a violent reaction. By the end of July the anthracite region was in turmoil and the governor of Pennsylvania ordered two regiments of the National Guard to the area. Nevertheless, violence escalated and more troops were required. By the end of September, fourteen people had died as a result of the strike and property losses were substantial.

Meanwhile, a struggle was going on within the union between the leadership, which wanted to localize the conflict within the anthracite region, and a dissident group among the rank and file that wanted to broaden the strike by having the bituminous miners walk out in sympathy with the anthracite miners. A bituminous coal strike of any length would shut down the railroads and the steel industry, and those shutdowns would soon spread to many other industries, with effects analogous to a general strike. Many nonstriking workers would be thrown out of work. Mitchell argued that public opinion would shift against the strike and many other workers would be alienated if the bituminous miners went out to support their fellow miners. Furthermore, the bituminous miners were working under a valid collectively bargained agreement. Mitchell was also under heavy pressure from Senator Marcus Hanna of the National Civic Federation, who argued that the whole philosophy of collective bargaining and mutual recognition of each other's position by capital and labor would be jeopardized and perhaps destroyed if the bituminous miners denounced their contract.

The union opposition to Mitchell, on the other hand, argued that a bituminous coal strike would threaten the financial interests that lay behind the anthracite coal companies, because of the general economic shutdown it could bring, and thereby bring the anthracite strike to a quick and successful conclusion. This strategy was designed to win on a small front by threatening a general and devastating confrontation between labor and capital. There could hardly have been a clearer confrontation between two ideologies: class struggle versus peaceful negotiation; labor solidarity versus particularism; antagonistic versus nonantagonistic conflict.

The issue was decided at a special national convention of the United Mine Workers in mid-July, which decided not to call for a national sympathy strike of bituminous coal miners. Instead, it provided for financial assistance from the union as a whole as well as general support. Mitchell had won. The UMW decided for business unionism and collective bargaining rather than a capital-labor confrontation.

Public opinion soon moved to support of the strike, influenced by the union leadership's continuing stance of conciliation and an effective public relations program, and by an arrogant and intransigent statement by George F. Baer, president of the Philadelphia and Reading Railroad, which was the largest producer of anthracite coal, to a resident of Wilkes-Barre.[29]

The situation was serious. Coal production had fallen and failed to revive, stocks were low, and prices began to increase. A cold and expensive winter loomed ahead for the urban population of the great Eastern cities. President Theodore Roosevelt, in office for only a year and not an elected president, was caught in a dilemma. Ideologically he was a part of the liberal wing of the Republican party, where support for the position of the National Civic Federation on labor matters was strong. Marcus Hanna, U.S. senator from Ohio and president of the National Civic Federation, was probably the most important Republican politician in the country after Roosevelt himself. Hanna wore two hats as the most prominent leader of the corporate liberals and a leading political figure in the administration. On the other hand, the bulk of Republican political funds came from conservative business and financial leaders, like J. P. Morgan, who were adamantly antiunion. Indeed, Morgan and his associates were the chief investment bankers for the railroads that owned the bulk of the anthracite mines. Just as an internal struggle was going on in the union, so a similar struggle went on within the administration and the Republican leadership.

In the end, government sided with the union. Roosevelt decided, in the face of the operators' intransigence, that the federal government would have to seize the mines and send U.S. troops into the mining areas to get production started once more. With that plan as a big stick he sent Secretary of State Elihu Root to speak softly with J. P. Morgan, carrying a plan for a federal commission of inquiry whose findings would be binding on both sides in the dispute. The only concession Morgan could get was that no labor leader or former labor leader would be appointed to the commission, but even that concession was not honored, for Roosevelt appointed as a "sociologist" a member of the Interstate Commerce Commission who had formerly been president of the Order of Railway Conductors. The strikers went back to work after the operators agreed to accept the decision of the commission as binding. A cold winter was averted.

The commission held extensive hearings during the winter of 1902–3 and handed down its decision on March 18, 1903. It awarded a 10 percent wage increase and made several other recommendations. But it did not require recognition of the union as bargaining agent for the miners. That was not obtained until World War I, when the federal government required it of the operators as a means of obtaining labor peace during the war. All this was anticlimax, however. The real meaning of the anthracite coal strike of 1902 lay in the use of state power to support the coalition of conservative unions and corporate liberals around the idea of collective bargaining and peaceful settlement of labor-management disputes. The anthracite coal strike of 1902 forged for the first time the basic political alignments that were to lead to a national policy of collective bargaining.

The Crushing of Radical Labor

During the relatively strong surge of prosperity from 1897 to 1903, membership in labor unions, chiefly the craft unions of the AFL and the railroad brotherhoods, increased from about five hundred thousand to almost two million. This growth was marked by considerable strife: according to the 1907 annual report of the U.S. commissioner of labor there were 1,056 strikes at 3,809 business establishments in 1898: by 1903 those numbers had risen to 3,494 strikes affecting over twenty thousand establishments.[30] The 1902 anthracite strike was only the most spectacular of many work stoppages in that era of prosperity and union growth.

The antiunion element in the business community reacted strongly. Business firms in a number of cities began around 1900 to organize employers' associations designed to present a united front in opposition to the local organizations of trade unions. These associations were committed to the idea of the open shop, the right to hire anyone, whether a union member or not. They were opposed to all labor unions and the idea of trade agreements arrived at through union-management negotiations. By 1902 strong local employers' associations were found through the Midwest between the Appalachians and the Rockies.[31]

In 1903 this movement came to dominance in the National Association of Manufacturers (NAM), which became the chief spokesman for the open shop and the chief opponent of the collective bargaining philosophy of the National Civic Federation. From its founding in 1895 the NAM had been a rather mild organization of business firms whose chief activities were in support of tariff protection for domestic industry and expansion of U.S. exports—programs that were supported by a number of unions as well. The NAM had opposed national legislation for an eight-hour day on federal contracts and to exempt labor disputes from injunctions issued by federal courts, but these were not major elements in its program. However, in 1903 David M. Parry, president of a large carriage manufacturing company in Indianapolis, was elected president of the NAM. He was unalterably opposed to unions and was a leader of the open shop movement. At the 1903 annual meeting he attacked labor unions, including by implication the craft unions of the AFL, as "mob power" and "socialistic," and called for an employers' campaign against union "abuses" and labor-sponsored legislation. Ironically, this call to action was followed by a mild speech by U.S. Commissioner of Labor Carroll D. Wright, pleading for businessmen to understand the new relationship between capital and labor—a thinly disguised statement of the philosophy of collective bargaining that had triumphed in the recent anthracite strike. But Wright's speech was followed by passage of a resolution that set the NAM's course in opposition to labor unions and to legislation promoting collective bargaining. This action was followed later in 1903 by organization of the Citizen's Industrial Association, also headed by Parry, as a national organization to provide leadership to the local employers' associations, open to all employers and not just manufacturers. The antiunion conservative wing of the business community was now organized.[32]

The first fruit of the new militancy on the part of employers was an attack on the Western Federation of Miners in Colorado. James H. Peabody, governor of Colorado in 1903–5, organized a campaign to break the power of the WFM in the mining areas of the state. He acted in concert with the large mining corporations, most of which were dominated by Eastern capital; with the local employers' associations; and, where they were agreeable, with local government authorities. The pattern of action was as follows, with some variations due to local conditions: an industrial dispute develops between the mining company and the WFM; employer intransigence triggers a strike; local authorities ask for state assistance in maintaining order, even though there may have been little or no disorder; the governor declares martial law and sends in the National Guard, made up of volunteers recruited for that particular mission and usually paid for by the affected mining companies; the guard and local police protect strikebreakers brought in by the employers and the mines start operating again; the union leaders are arrested and either tried and jailed or deported from the area with a warning not to return. Thus, Colorado was made safe for capital investment. This pattern was repeated in one mining center after another, culminating in Cripple Creek in 1904. Within two years the Western Federation of Miners in Colorado was largely a paper organization. Colorado showed what could be done when the power of government was directed toward suppression of radical unionism.[33]

The events in Colorado, however, also helped to foster the organization of a national, class-oriented, radical labor organization, the Industrial Workers of the World. Following its 1904 defeat in Colorado, the leadership of the WFM decided to move toward "the amalgamation of the entire working class into one general organization." After preliminary meetings with like-minded labor leaders in other organizations, the Industrial Workers of the World (IWW) was organized in June, 1905.[34] It was to be a single union of all workers in all industries, with decision making in the hands of the membership as a whole, and based on the idea of irrepressible conflict between capital and labor. The chief organizers of the IWW were leaders of WFM itself and its spinoff, the American Labor Union, but it also included other socialists and a number of other left-labor people. The new organization immediately split into two factions, one interested chiefly in organization of workers, particularly the unskilled, and the other more concerned with developing a radical socialist program. After three years of struggle the "overall brigade" won out over the socialist intellectuals, who largely dropped out of the organization. By 1908 the IWW had become what its founders had intended: an instrument for organizing the working class as a whole and carrying on a class struggle against capitalism.

Just as the organization had emerged from working-class experience over more than a quarter century, so did its structure and program. The IWW was a highly democratic organization, attempting to reach out equally to all workers everywhere, with a one-person-one-vote approach to decision making by the membership as a whole (which was difficult to put into practice and sometimes quite cumbersome). Its organizational structure reflected its ideals and philosophy of democratic class action, however. Its program had a similar emphasis: the IWW envisaged a syndicalist organization of the economy, including direct worker control and management of individual enterprises, coordinated and planned at higher administrative levels by workers' representatives. The chief basis of the IWW's attraction for workers, however, was its militant action program of class opposition to employers.

The IWW appealed to the most heavily exploited groups among working people, those not represented by the craft unions of skilled workers in the AFL, bypassed by socialist intellectuals, and largely unrepresented politically (because many were migratory). In the West the IWW concentrated its efforts on mining, lumbering, and agriculture; in the East chiefly on textiles and rubber. It used new methods: organizing on the job, mass meetings in public parks and on city streets, "endless chain" mass picketing, and sitdown strikes on the job, as well as mass demonstrations reminiscent of 1877 and 1886. These methods brought major successes in 1911–13 and the organization grew both in numbers and notoriety.

Like the earlier class-oriented labor movements in the previous four decades, the IWW aroused strong emotions. Its clientele were the lowest level of workers, poorly skilled, largely propertyless with little hope of ever becoming property owners, many of them recent immigrants. Its philosophy was overtly socialist, but it was not the genteel ideology of the Socialist party, with its emphasis on democratic political action, reform, and gradualism. Much of the IWW's rhetoric was fiery, and its tactics were unsettling to many. A hostile press attacked the organization in cartoons and editorials, and news stories were often distorted, in an effort to create an impression that the IWW stood for lawlessness, destruction, and anarchy. The leadership preached nonviolence and passive resistance, but that strategy was hard to sustain when company police, strikebreakers, local police, and the National Guard attacked IWW meetings. The class warfare that the IWW advocated, when it came, was not peaceful.

The IWW was under attack from its origin. All of the methods developed since 1877 were used by a coalition of business corporations, much of the press, and local and state governments. The federal government was not involved, for the most part, until it entered the fray to apply the coup de grace in 1918.

The attack on the IWW began with a spectacular and unsuccessful show trial in 1906. Former governor Frank Steuenberg was murdered in Caldwell, Idaho, on December 30, 1905. In 1899, as governor of Idaho, he had a leading role in breaking a WFM strike in the Coeur d'Alene mining district. The murderer was quickly apprehended, one Harry Orchard, who was induced to implicate four officials of the WFM. Three of them, Charles Moyer, William D. Haywood, and George A. Pettibone (who was then no longer associated with the union) were arrested in Colorado, extradited under highly dubious procedures (which were later upheld by the U.S. Supreme Court), and taken to Idaho under guard. It amounted to legalized kidnapping. None of the accused had been in Idaho at the time of the crime, but, in a variation on the Haymarket trial, were accused of conspiring with Orchard to kill Steuenberg. A series of spectacular trials followed. The defendants were acquitted, but the trials were an expensive drain on the union treasury, the press was able to create an image of the WFM and IWW as lawless, violent organizations, and much of the leadership of the organizations was immobilized for two years. The forces of repression won a partial victory even though the trials were lost.[35]

Efforts by local governments and business-inspired vigilantes to silence the IWW led to a series of "free speech" conflicts in 1909–12. The IWW found that the best way to organize migratory and seasonal workers in industries like lumbering or agriculture was to sponsor speeches and meetings on city streets in locations where workers congregated. Success with these tactics in Spokane, Washington, in 1909 brought a city ordinance prohibiting such meetings by "revolutionists." Defiance of the ordinance led to mass arrests and jail, then to police brutality, and then suppression of the IWW newspaper and headquarters. But after two years of conflict the IWW's tactics of nonviolent opposition won: the financial cost of repression was becoming burdensome to the local government. Spokane's government agreed to allow indoor meetings, permit publication of the IWW newspaper and its sale on city streets, and to pass a satisfactory free speech ordinance; in short, to respect the U.S. Constitution. The jailed IWW leaders were released.[36]

Other free speech fights in the West were won by the IWW, but not in San Diego. There the city government worked closely with local vigilantes organized by business interests. IWW leaders and organizers were arrested by the police, taken into the desert and turned over to vigilantes, beaten, and then left to fend for themselves. A state investigation (the governor was Democratic progressive Hiram Johnson) confirmed the connivance of city officials with the vigilante guerillas. The IWW persisted in its organizing despite the brutality, and city officials finally asked for help from the federal government to destroy this organization which, they claimed, sought to overthrow the government. The U.S. attorney general refused to act, however, even though President Taft, trying to win California votes in the 1912 election, supported federal intervention. But by the end of 1912, the IWW will to resist was broken. Volunteers for continued passive resistance could not be obtained in the face of unremitting brutality on the part of vigilantes supported by local officials.[37]

A variety of police tactics were employed against the IWW during strikes. In Goldfield, Nevada, in 1907–8, at a time when the leaders of the WFM and IWW were on trial in Idaho and a growing split was developing between moderates and radicals in the WFM and IWW, the mining companies decided to reduce wages and break the local unions. But they could not rely on local government authorities for help—because the unions and workers were strong in local politics—and Nevada had no National Guard. So the companies conspired with the governor to ask for federal troops, fabricating stories of local violence to justify the action. President Roosevelt, initially deceived, complied, and even when informed of the deceit kept the army in Goldfield. This action enabled the mining companies to force a wage reduction and institute "yellow dog" contracts in which workers agreed not to join a union. Simultaneously, the AFL sent in organizers in opposition to the WFM and IWW, but made little progress.[38]

The pattern of using government police action was repeated in most of the strikes in which the IWW was active, particularly after some early successes in 1907–8 in the lumber industry in the Pacific Northwest and in eastern industrial plants in Schenectady, New York, Bridgeport, Connecticut, and Skowhegan, Maine. In 1909 at McKees Rocks, Pennsylvania, unskilled and mostly immigrant workers continued a strike at the Pressed Steel Car Company after the skilled workers had settled. At that point the IWW entered the scene and took over leadership of the strike. There had already been violence between workers and strikebreakers, and more followed after the entry of the IWW, as the immigrant workers massed to prevent strikebreakers from entering the plant. Private company police, local sheriff's deputies, and units of the Pennsylvania state police combined to support the strikebreakers. Homes were searched to confiscate weapons under a state law that forbade aliens to own weapons. But the attempt at repression did not succeed in this instance; the company quickly settled on terms favorable to the workers, largely for fear that continuation of the strike would strengthen radicalism among its workers and others in the Pittsburgh area.[39]

The tactic of using police backed by courts was soon extended. The IWW started its official publication, *Solidarity*, in Pittsburgh in 1909, following the strike at McKees Rocks; local authorities immediately arrested its entire staff. IWW-inspired strikes at New Castle and Butler, Pennsylvania, were quickly suppressed by vigorous managements in combination with local police and courts.[40] In the Southern lumbering areas of Louisiana and east Texas the companies employed their own gunmen to terrorize union organizers and the IWW—action that could continue only with benign neglect on the part of local authorities—and several IWW organizers were arrested and charged with crimes committed by company thugs (they were later acquitted).[41]

In Lawrence, Massachusetts, in 1912, where the IWW was called in to lead a strike and won an outstanding victory, much of the violence was provoked by company management and the police, and was then used as an excuse for further repression. The strike began in January. The first act of violence came when workers spontaneously smashed machinery and windows in one textile mill. This was followed three days later by a clash between strikers and local police reinforced by state militia, in which the police and militia were clearly the aggressors. Five days later the police, acting on tips, found dynamite at several locations, and a hue and cry against the strike and the IWW was raised in the press. But the dynamite was soon traced to a local businessman, who admitted he had sought to discredit the strike. He was tried and fined. Shortly afterward it was disclosed that the American Woolen Company, largest of the local firms, had arranged for the dynamite incident at the suggestion of the company president, who escaped punishment.

Late in January police interfered with an IWW parade, an officer was stabbed, and a woman striker was shot and killed. This was the incident needed by the police: the two IWW strike leaders, Joseph Ettor and Arturo Giovanetti, were charged with conspiracy in the murder, arrested, and jailed; the purpose, of course, was to deprive the strike of its leadership. But this tactic failed: the IWW sent in other leaders, including William Haywood, and ultimately Ettor and Giovanetti were acquitted. Meanwhile, the strike leadership hit on a tactic designed to arouse public sympathy and raise funds for the strike: they began a program of sending children of the strikers to foster homes elsewhere, accompanied by great publicity. The success of this program caused the local officials in Lawrence to prohibit any further movement of the children—a clearly illegal action by the authorities—and when the IWW continued the practice the police on February 24 attacked a group of women and children at the Lawrence railroad station, beating and clubbing them as they were arrested and hauled off in a National Guard truck. This stupid act of brutality, in full view of the press, brought victory to the strikers. The governor of Massachusetts, who early in the the strike had unsuccessfully tried to mediate, trying to prevent radicalism from gaining a foothold, ordered an investigation. The U.S. House of Representatives began an investigation, as did the U.S. Bureau of Labor. Many progressive political leaders expressed support for the strikers. What had started as a class war between right wing capitalists and left wing labor threatened to forge a coalition between left wing labor and reformist liberal elements. At this point the companies settled the strike on terms highly favorable to the workers.[42]

The IWW victory at Lawrence was followed by defeats at Paterson, New Jersey, and elsewhere.[43] The repressive measures that had boomeranged at Lawrence were used more successfully in those instances. Employers used strikebreakers, assisted by local police and courts, and by the state government where the National Guard was needed. IWW leaders were special targets. Police riots in which strikers and strike leaders were beaten were common occurrences. Vigilantes were organized for further violence beyond the pretense of legality while police looked the other way. IWW leaders, most of whom preached nonviolent mass action, were tried for the violence for which employers and the police were largely responsible. Among the more highly publicized incidents were the trial of Joe Hill in Salt Lake City in 1914, the "Bloody Sunday" massacre in Everett, Washington, in 1916, and the vigilante lynching of Frank Little in Butte, Montana, in 1917. In Jerome, Arizona, in July, 1917, the copper companies organized armed vigilantes who "cleared the town of agitators" by seizing Wobblies, as members of the IWW were called, and deporting them to the middle of the Mojave Desert in California. They then turned their attention to the local miners' union affiliated with the AFL and drove it out also. Inspired by this success, a similar operation on a much larger scale was carried out a week later in Bisbee, Arizona.[44] Through most of this turmoil the federal government remained neutral, state governments tended not to get involved directly, and the chief repressive measures were left to local governments and courts.

Meanwhile, there was a movement at the federal level toward legislation that promoted collective bargaining and trade agreements, and toward recognition of labor unions as the bargaining representatives of workers. Legislation in 1913 created a separate U.S. Department of Labor with full cabinet status, and established a full-time Board of Conciliation and Arbitration in the new department to deal with labor-management disputes on railroads. The Clayton Act of 1914 exempted labor unions from antitrust prosecution under the Sherman Act. In 1915 federal legislation regulated conditions of work for seamen. The Adamson Act of 1916 provided an eight-hour day and time and a half for overtime on interstate railroads, an important victory for labor. On other fronts, the cloak and suit industry in New York began to develop its machinery for arbitration of labor disputes in 1910–12; Massachusetts passed the first minimum wage law for women and minors in 1912, after the great IWW strike at Lawrence; and New York passed the first workers compensation legislation. Federal legislation in 1916 barred products of child labor from interstate commerce, but was declared unconstitutional in 1918; a new act in 1919 had a similar fate in 1922. Much other prolabor legislation failed in both Congress and state legislatures, but there clearly was activity on two fronts: ameliorative legislation to aid working people, and legislation to promote collective bargaining.[45]

During World War I promotion of collective bargaining between unions and management became federal policy. A Mediation Commission was established in 1917. In 1918 the National War Labor Board and the War Labor Policies Board were established. The first was a court of last resort to settle labor disputes; the second sought to standardize labor conditions as a means of promoting labor peace. During the war federal purchasing agencies generally insisted that suppliers bargain collectively with their employees. This policy brought large increases in union membership: AFL unions added another quarter million.[46] All of these programs were closed out when the war ended, and conservative business opinion and its antiunion policies were once more dominant, but the labor policies of 1917–18 were a forerunner of the national policies that became firmly established in the 1930s.

The IWW shared in the union growth engendered by wartime prosperity, in spite of repression. Its membership grew from perhaps forty thousand to over one hundred thousand (it claimed a quarter million) just before its suppression in 1917.[47] The organization was particularly strong among migratory farm workers of the Great Plains states, in the copper mining areas of Montana and Arizona, and in the Northwest lumber industry. It grew in spite of a renewed drive of legalized union busting. Within eight months after U.S. entry into World War I in 1917 federal troops were on duty in the mining areas of Montana and Arizona, the lumbering areas of Oregon and western Washington, and the wheat-growing territories of eastern Washington, even though there had been no violence there and no trace of foreign espionage could be found.[48]

At this time the coalition of business interests and local officials fighting the IWW in the West came to feel that the only way to get rid of the IWW was to enlist the aid of the federal government. The Espionage Act of June 15, 1917, followed by the Sedition Act of May 16, 1918, provided the legal basis for federal action; wartime patriotism provided a favorable climate of opinion. A plan suggested by former governor John Lind of Minnesota, then director of the state Commission for Public Safety, envisaged a coordinated offensive by the Justice, Labor, and Post Office departments to destroy the IWW as a functioning organization. The Department of Justice would raid IWW offices to obtain evidence of violation of wartime security statutes, and would prosecute the IWW officers responsible; the Department of Labor would detain and deport IWW aliens; and the Post Office would deny mailing privileges to IWW publications. Basically, the Lind plan would use the tactics already developed at the state and local level, under protection of federal legal sanctions, to attack radical labor on a nationwide front.[49]

This program was put into effect during the summer of 1917. In July President Wilson ordered a special investigation of IWW activities. Shortly afterward there was an unexplained break-in at the IWW's national headquarters in Chicago. In August the Post Office denied mailing privileges to two foreign-language IWW newspapers. On August 21 the U.S. attorney general informed the president of a planned full-scale assault on the IWW by the Department of Justice. On September 5 federal agents and the local police raided every IWW office and headquarters throughout the country and the homes of a number of high IWW officials, armed with extremely broad search warrants that allowed them to seize not only documents, but also the operating equipment of the offices as well. Large numbers of IWW members were arrested.[50]

The raids were expected to immobilize the IWW as a functioning organization for the duration of the war. The organization's leaders were arrested, its office equipment gone, its funds sequestered. But to make doubly sure, a second series of raids a few months later shattered the secondary leadership that had sprung up after the first few raids. Then came the trials, with public opinion whipped to almost hysterical hatred by the press. Ninety-nine IWW leaders were prosecuted in a widely publicized trial in Chicago in 1918, convicted on flimsy evidence, and given long prison sentences. Forty-seven secondary leaders were tried in Sacramento later in the year, and twenty-five in Kansas City in 1919.[51] This federal action was supplemented by many arrests of local IWW leaders under state criminal syndicalism laws.

Meanwhile, the U.S. Department of Labor was active in two ways. On the one hand, it deported numerous alien IWW members. On the other hand, it sought to replace the IWW with AFL unions in the lumber and mining districts where the IWW had been strong, and to develop collective bargaining there. This effort was assisted by Samuel Gompers of the AFL and by Ralph Easley, who for many years had been with the National Civic Federation. The War Labor Board and the War Labor Policies Board supported these tactics unofficially. These efforts were unsuccessful, however, and the open shop prevailed. Nevertheless, it was the policy of the Wilson administration to encourage unionization and collective bargaining by job-conscious unions while it destroyed class-conscious unions.[52]

The methods used by the federal government against the IWW were also used against the Socialist party. Socialists had often supported the IWW, particularly in its spectacular Lawrence and Paterson strikes and the free speech battles in the West. Both the IWW and the Socialists had opposed U.S. entry into the war and gave at best lukewarm support to the war effort. The Socialist party was the next logical target for suppression of radicalism, particularly after the Bolshevik seizure of power in Russia in 1917 aroused increased fear of communism. Socialist periodicals were denied use of the mails, socialist leaders were jailed under the wartime security laws, and party offices were raided. The attack on left wing political organizations culminated in the notorious "Palmer raids" of 1919–20, planned by Attorney General A. Mitchell Palmer and directed by the young J. Edgar Hoover.[53]

Federal suppression of the IWW also coincided with passage of criminal syndicalism legislation by a number of state legislatures. These laws were directed at the IWW, although that organization was not specifically named in any of the laws. The usual pattern included a press campaign attacking the IWW on patriotic and ideological grounds, and organized support for the legislation by trade associations and other business groups. Starting with Minnesota in 1917, most of these laws were passed in 1918 and 1919, and they were the basis for criminal prosecution of radicals in general, Wobblies in particular, and even some liberal activists. Widely publicized show trials and long prison terms were common outcomes.[54]

Other events added to the atmosphere of hysteria, fear, and class conflict: the Russian revolution in 1917 and seizure of power by the Bolsheviks under Lenin's leadership; the bitter 1919 strike in the steel industry; the NAM's intensified drive for the open shop starting in 1919–20. The federal government's suppression of the IWW and drive against radicals was part of a larger economic, political, and ideological confrontation between capital and labor in which capital was generally successful.

Epilogue

Workers in industrial America between the Civil War and World War I worked out several alternative paths toward solutions to their problems. Two were allowed to develop: job-conscious business unionism of the AFL type; and political action within the framework of existing political institutions. Both of these approaches accepted the existing economic order and offered no serious challenge to patterns of income distribution, the ownership of wealth, or the locus of economic and political power. A "fair share" within the existing structure was their theme.

Two other adaptations were not allowed to exist: a labor movement emphasizing mass action, class consciousness and a radical ideology; and radical political action directed toward socialism. Here we have examined in detail only the repression of radical labor. Yet radicalism in the labor movement was as American as baseball, hot dogs, and apple pie. It developed out of the American experience with industrialization, starting with the disorganized mass protests of 1877 and leading through the Knights of Labor in the 1880s and the industrial unionism of the 1890s to the IWW in the early decades of the twentieth century. It was not a radicalism imported from Europe, nor did it have its roots among the intellectuals or the urban middle class. Radicalism of those sorts was present in the half-century between the Civil War and World War I: Marxism and anarchism from central Europe, utopian socialism, Bellamy's nationalist movement, for example. But the radicalism of the IWW was different, arising out of the reality of an industrial society and sharpened by both the opposition of moderate unions and the attacks of business interests and their allies in local and state governments, the courts, and the press. This indigenous labor radicalism showed tremendous vitality, resurging strongly after each setback. Ultimately, the federal government suppressed it.

We should not think of that repression in the simplistic terms of a capitalist state single-mindedly serving the interests of the capitalist class.

Capitalists, as a class, were divided on the issue of how to deal with class conflict, just as were workers. Similarly, labor leaders were obviously trying to work their way through a difficult situation in which a variety of pressures were at work. Gompers, for example, felt that in the long run his union could not survive if it took a radical stance, and he may well have been right. Complex political forces created a coalition of labor conservatives and corporate liberals around a policy of collective bargaining and ameliorative legislation as an alternative to class warfare. The suppression of labor radicalism followed, almost as if the progressive-liberal coalition was trying to mollify the conservatives by destroying their chief enemy.

Furthermore, government action against radical labor evolved and developed over the years as the role of government itself changed. In the 1870s and 1880s government action against radical labor was taken chiefly by local and state governments. The National Guard, the chief instrument of force in addition to local police and hired strikebreakers, was an agency of the states. The U.S. Army was used only when the guard was ineffective (as in 1877), when state governments refused to act (in the Pullman strike of 1894), or when there were no guard units in the state (Goldfield, Nevada, 1907–8). Even as late as 1912 federal intervention against the IWW in San Diego was denied on the ground that the state government was the proper instrument.

As the industrial economy spread across the nation and penetrated more deeply into the fabric of the economy, the question of how to deal with the growing class of industrial workers became a national issue. An accommodation between corporate liberals and labor moderates began to emerge, while the conflict between the business right and labor left escalated. The federal government was drawn into the conflict as it became a national issue. A national policy emerged, based on collective bargaining and ameliorative legislation. Another part of the policy entailed repression of radicalism.

Governmental repression was facilitated by the isolated political position of radical labor. It was probably a minority within the labor movement itself, among rank and file workers, although this is far from clear. Certainly the great majority of the leaders of organized unions were opposed to radical transformation of property relationships along the lines advocated by the IWW. Furthermore, while the IWW represented a high point in the economic organization of mass radical movements in American labor, an associated radical political movement had not appeared. The Socialist party was itself divided among divergent factions and its political program was not closely articulated with the class-conscious radicalism and emphasis on economic action of the IWW. Radical labor was in an exposed position, isolated from other sectors of the working class and without a supporting radical political organization. It could readily be offered up as a sacrifice to conservative business interests by the coalition of corporate liberals and conservative union leadership.

The final victory of the supporters of collective bargaining and ameliorative legislation as an alternative to the class struggle did not come until the New Deal years of the 1930s. And victory did not come without turmoil. At that time the labor radicalism of the years before 1918 had disappeared as an effective force and even the revived industrial unionism of the 1930s was molded by business unionism. Without the older labor radicalism to worry them, employers took a largely unified stand in opposition to trade unions, and a somewhat different coalition of economic and political interests developed around the issues of labor legislation. But that is another story.

NOTES

1. Daniel R. Fusfeld, "The Rise of the Corporate State in America," *Journal of Economic Issues* 6, no. 1 (March, 1972): 1–22.
2. Daniel R. Fusfeld, *The Rise and Repression of Radical Labor, U.S.A.—1877–1918* (Chicago: Charles H. Kerr, 1980).
3. John H. M. Laslett, *Labor and the Left: A Study of Socialist and Radical Influences in the American Labor Movement, 1881–1924* (New York: Basic Books, 1970); John H. M. Laslett and Seymour M. Lipset, eds., *Failure of a Dream? Essays in the History of American Socialism: Its Conspicuous Absence in American Politics* (Stanford, Calif.: Hoover Institution on War, Revolution and Peace, 1977); Gerald Rosenblum, *Immigrant Workers: Their Impact on American Radicalism* (New York: Basic Books, 1973); Alan Dawley, *Class and Community: The Industrial Revolution in Lynn* (Cambridge, Mass.: Harvard University Press, 1976).
4. Selig Perlman, *A History of Trade Unionism in the United States* (New York: Macmillan, 1922) and *A Theory of the Labor Movement* (New York: Macmillan, 1928).
5. John R. Commons and associates, *History of Labor in the United States*, 4 vols. (New York: Macmillan, 1918–35); Philip S. Foner, *History of the Labor Movement in the United States*, 4 vols. (New York: International Publishers, 1947–65); Louis Adamic, *Dynamite: The Story of Class Violence in America*, rev. ed. (New York: Viking Press, 1934); Jeremy Brecher, *Strike!* (San Francisco: Straight Arrow Books, 1972); Sidney Lens, *The Labor Wars: From the Molly Maguires to the Sitdowns* (Garden City, N.Y.: Doubleday, 1973); Merl E. Reed, "Lumberjacks and Longshoremen: The I.W.W. in Louisiana," *Labor History* 13, no. 1 (Winter, 1972): 41–50; Robert J. Goldstein, *Political Repression in Modern America: 1870 to the Present* (Cambridge, Mass. and New York: Schenkman Publishing and Two Continents Publishing Group, 1978).
6. Robert V. Bruce, *1877: Year of Violence* (Indianapolis: Bobbs-Merrill, 1959);

Commons, *History of Labor*, 2:185–94; Foner, *History of the Labor Movement*, 1:464–74; Brecher, *Strike!*, chaps. 1, 7–9; Adamic, *Dynamite*, chap. 3; Samuel Yellen, *American Labor Struggles* (New York: Harcourt Brace, 1936), chap. 1; Lens, *The Labor Wars*, chap. 3; Joseph A. Dacus, *Annals of the Great Strikes in the United States* (Chicago: L. T. Palmer, 1877); David T. Burbank, *City of Little Bread: The St. Louis General Strike of 1877* (microprint, 1957; condensed version published as *Reign of the Rabble*, New York: Augustus Kelley, 1966); Rosa Luxemburg, *The Mass Strike* (Detroit: Marxist Educational Society, 1925; New York: Harper and Row, 1971).

7. Commons, *History of Labor*, 2:190–91; Foner, *History of the Labor Movement*, 2:158–59, 161–72; Adamic, *Dynamite*, pp. 36–37; Yellen, *American Labor Struggles*, pp. 33–38.

8. William H. Riker, *Soldiers of the States: The Role of the National Guard in American Democracy* (Washington, D.C.: Public Affairs Press, 1957), esp. chap. 4; Jerry M. Cooper, "Federal Military Intervention in American Labor Disputes, 1877–1900," Ph.D. diss., University of Wisconsin, 1971, and idem, "The Army as Strike-breaker—the Railroad Strikes of 1877–1894," *Labor History* 18, no. 2 (Spring, 1977): 179–98; Burton C. Hacker, "The United States Army as a National Police Force: The Federal Policing of Labor Disputes, 1877–1898," *Military Affairs* 33 (1969): 255–64.

9. Commons, *History of Labor*, 2:420.

10. Norman J. Ware, *The Labor Movement in the United States, 1860–1895: A Study in Democracy* (New York: Appleton, 1929); Commons, *History of Labor*, vol. 2, pt. 6, chaps. 1, 8–10; Foner, *History of the Labor Movement*, 1:433–38, 405–512, and vol. 2, chaps. 3–5, 11; Terrence V. Powderly, *Thirty Years of Labor 1859–1889* (Columbus, Ohio: Excelsior, 1889; New York: Augustus Kelley, 1967), and idem, *The Path I Trod* (New York: Columbia University Press, 1940).

11. Commons, *History of Labor*, vol. 2, pt. 6, chaps. 2, 6; Foner, *History of the Labor Movement*, 2:32–44; Adamic, *Dynamite*, chap. 4; Yellen, *American Labor Struggles*, pp. 44–50.

12. Commons, *History of Labor*, 2:395–413; Ware, *The Labor Movement*, chaps. 8–9. See also the citations in note 14, below.

13. Foner, *History of the Labor Movement*, vol. 2, chaps. 9, 12–13; Samuel Gompers, *Seventy Years of Life and Labor*, 2 vols. (New York: E. P. Dutton, 1925), vol. 1, chaps. 11–13; Stuart B. Kaufman, *Samuel Gompers and the Origins of the American Federation of Labor, 1848–1896* (Westport, Conn.: Greenwood Press, 1973), esp. chaps. 6–7; Philip Taft, *The A.F. of L. in the Time of Gompers* (New York: Harper and Brothers, 1957), chaps. 2–3; and Lewis L. Lorwin, *The American Federation of Labor: History, Policies, and Prospects* (Washington, D.C.: Brookings Institution, 1933), pp. 18–31.

14. Foner, *History of the Labor Movement*, 1:363–69, 371, 377–82, 500–504, 2:93–101; Commons, *History of Labor*, vol. 2, passim (see "eight hour day" in index). Also, Lemuel Danryid, *History and Philosophy of the Eight-Hour Movement* (Washington, D.C.: American Federation of Labor, 1899), pp. 4–7.

15. Henry David, *The History of the Haymarket Affair*, 2d ed. (New York: Russell and Russell, 1958); Commons, *History of Labor*, 2:386–95; Foner, *History of the Labor Movement*, vol. 2, chap. 7; Adamic, *Dynamite*, chaps. 4–6; Yellen, *American Labor Struggles*, chap. 2; Lens, *The Labor Wars*, chap. 4; Philip Foner, ed., *The Autobiographies of the Haymarket Martyrs* (New York: Humanities Press, 1969).

16. Brecher, *Strike!*, pp. 46–50; Foner, *History of the Labor Movement*, 2:116–19, 161–62; Commons, *History of Labor*, 2:504–5; Goldstein, *Political Repression*, pp. 40–42; Lens, *The Labor Wars*, pp. 64, 66–67.

17. Foner, *History of the Labor Movement*, vol. 2, chap. 11; Commons, *History of Labor*, 2:482–95.

18. Leon Wolff, *Lockout, The Story of the Homestead Strike of 1892: A Study of Violence, Unionism and the Carnegie Steel Empire* (New York: Harper and Row, 1965).

19. Vernon Jensen, *Heritage of Conflict: Labor Relations in the Nonferrous Metals Industry up to 1930* (Ithaca, N.Y.: Cornell University Press, 1969); See also Adamic, *Dynamite*, chaps. 12–15; Foner, *History of the Labor Movement*, 2:230–34; Laslett, *Labor and the Left*, chap. 7; Lens, *The Labor Wars*, chap. 7.

20. Almont Lindsey, *The Pullman Strike* (Chicago: University of Chicago Press, 1942); United States Strike Commission, *Report on the Chicago Strike of June–July, 1894* (Washington, D.C.: Government Printing Office, 1895); William H. Carwardine, *The Pullman Strike* (Chicago: Charles H. Kerr, 1894); Adamic, *Dynamite*, chap. 11; Brecher, *Strike!*, pp. 78–96; Foner, *History of the Labor Movement*, vol. 2, chaps. 17–18; Lens, *The Labor Wars*, chap. 6; Yellen, *American Labor Struggles*, chap. 4; Ray Ginger, *The Bending Cross: A Biography of Eugene V. Debs* (New Brunswick, N.J.: Rutgers University Press, 1949); Eugene V. Debs, *Writings and Speeches* (New York: Hermitage Press, 1948); Donald L. McMurray, *Coxey's Army: A Study of the Industrial Army Movement of 1894* (Seattle: University of Washington Press, 1968); Felix Frankfurter and Nathan Greene, *The Labor Injunction* (New York: Macmillan, 1930).

21. Harold W. Aurand, *From the Molly Maguires to the United Mine Workers: The Social Ecology of an Industrial Union, 1869–1896* (Philadelphia: Temple University Press, 1971); William A. McConaghan, "The History and Progress of the United Mine Workers of America," Ph.D. diss., University of Illinois, 1925; David J. McDonald and Edward A. Lynch, *Coal and Unionism: A History of the American Coal Miners' Unions* (Silver Spring, Md.: privately printed, 1939); William J. Walsh, "The United Mine Workers as an Economic and Social Force in the Anthracite Territory," Ph.D. diss., Catholic University of America, 1931, chap. 2.

22. Commons, *History of Labor*, 2:514–20; Foner, *History of the Labor Movement*, vol. 2, chap. 19; Taft, *The AFL*, pp. 74–75, 125–28; Gompers, *Seventy Years*, vol. 1, chaps. 17–19; Lorwin, *The American Federation of Labor*, pp. 30–31, 38–40; Louis S. Reed, *The Labor Philosophy of Samuel Gompers* (New York: Columbia University Press, 1930); Will Chasen, *Samuel Gom-*

pers: Leader of American Labor (New York: Praeger, 1971); Bernard Mandel, *Samuel Gompers: A Biography* (Yellow Springs, Ohio: Antioch Press, 1963), esp. introduction by Louis Filler, "Samuel Gompers, Labor Statesman or Labor Fakir"; Kaufman, *Gompers and the American Federation of Labor.*

23. Howard H. Quint, *The Forging of American Socialism* (Indianapolis: Bobbs-Merrill, 1953), chaps. 10–11; Foner, *History of the Labor Movement*, vol. 2, chap. 25.

24. Foner, *History of the Labor Movement*, vol. 3, chap. 16; Melvin Dubovsky, *We Shall Be All: A History of the Industrial Workers of the World* (Chicago: Quadrangle Books, 1969), pp. 64–76.

25. United States Industrial Commission, *Report* (Washington, D.C.: Government Printing Office, 1900–1902), vol. 17, chaps. 13ff.; Commons, *History of Labor*, 2:479–82; John R. Commons, "Trade Agreements," in *Trade Unionism and Labor Problems*, ed. John R. Commons (Boston: Ginn and Co., 1905), pp. 1–12.

26. Marcus A. Hanna, "Industrial Conciliation and Arbitration," *Annals of the American Academy of Political and Social Science* 20, no. 1 (1902): 21–26.

27. Marguerite Green, *The National Civic Federation and the American Labor Movement, 1900–1925* (Washington, D.C.: Catholic University Press, 1956); William E. Akin, "Arbitration and Labor Conflict: The Middle Class Panacea: 1887–1900," *Historian* 29 (1967): 565–83; Foner, *History of the Labor Movement*, 2:384–87, and vol. 3, chaps. 3–4; James Weinstein, *The Corporate Ideal in the Liberal State: 1900–1918* (Boston: Beacon Press, 1968), chap. 1.

28. Robert J. Cornell, *The Anthracite Coal Strike of 1902* (Washington, D.C.: Catholic University Press, 1956); U.S. Anthracite Coal Strike Commission, *Report to the President on the Anthracite Coal Strike Commission of May–October, 1902* (Washington, D.C.: Government Printing Office, 1903); Mary A. Merrick, *A Case Study in Practical Democracy: Settlement of the Anthracite Coal Strike of 1902* (Notre Dame, Ind.: University of Notre Dame, 1942); Walsh, "The United Mine Workers," chaps. 3–6; Commons, *History of Labor*, vol. 4, chap. 4; Foner, *History of the Labor Movement*, 3:86–102; Lens, *The Labor Wars*, pp. 138–44.

29. *The Independent*, August 28, 1902, p. 2043.

30. U.S. Department of Commerce and Labor, Commissioner of Labor, *Twenty-First Annual Report* (Washington, D.C.: Government Printing Office, 1907), pp. 12–15.

31. Foner, *History of the Labor Movement*, vol. 3, chap. 2; Commons, *History of Labor*, vol. 4, chap. 13.

32. Albert K. Steigerwalt, *The National Association of Manufacturers, 1895–1914: A Study of Business Leadership* (Ann Arbor, Mich.: Bureau of Business Research, Graduate School of Business Administration, University of Michigan, 1964); National Association of Manufacturers, *Proceedings of the Ninth Annual Convention* (New York: National Association of Manufacturers, 1903); David M. Parry, "Is Organized Labor Right? The Only Question," *Bankers' Magazine* 67 (November, 1903): 668–72; Albion G. Taylor, *Labor Policies of*

the National Association of Manufacturers (Urbana: University of Illinois Press, 1928).

33. George H. Suggs, Jr., *Colorado's War on Militant Unionism: James H. Peabody and the Western Federation of Miners* (Detroit: Wayne State University, 1972).

34. Dubovsky, *We Shall be All;* Foner, *History of the Labor Movement,* vol 4; Joyce Kornbluh, ed., *Rebel Voices: An I.W.W. Anthology* (Ann Arbor: University of Michigan Press, 1964); Robert L. Tyler, *Rebels of the Woods: The I.W.W. in the Pacific Northwest* (Eugene: University of Oregon Press, 1967); Patrick Renshaw, *The Wobblies: The Story of Syndicalism in the United States* (New York: Columbia University Press, 1932); John S. Gambs, *The Decline of the I.W.W.* (New York: Columbia University Press, 1932); Joseph R. Conlin, *Bread and Roses Too: Studies of the Wobblies* (Westport, Conn.: Greenwood Press, 1969); Paul F. Brissenden, *The I.W.W.: A Study of American Syndicalism,* 3d ed. (New York: Columbia University Press, 1957); Justus Ebert, *The I.W.W. in Theory and Practice* (Chicago: I.W.W. Publishing Bureau, 1921); Vincent St. John, *The I.W.W., Its History, Structure and Methods* (Chicago: I.W.W. Publishing Bureau, 1917); Fred Thompson, *The I.W.W.: Its First Fifty Years* (Chicago: Industrial Workers of the World, 1955); *Proceedings of the First Convention of the Industrial Workers of the World* (New York: New York Labor News, 1905); William D. Haywood, *Bill Haywood's Book: The Autobiography of William D. Haywood* (New York: International Publishers, 1929); Joseph R. Conlin, *Big Bill Haywood and the Radical Union Movement* (Syracuse, New York: Syracuse University Press, 1969).

35. Foner, *History of the Labor Movement,* vol. 4, chap. 2; Dubovsky, *We Shall be All,* pp. 95–105; Commons, *History of Labor,* vol. 4, chap. 19; Adamic, *Dynamite,* chap. 15; Lens, *The Labor Wars,* pp. 152–55.

36. Dubovsky, *We Shall Be All,* pp. 175–84; Foner, *History of the Labor Movement,* vol. 4, chap. 7.

37. Dubovsky, *We Shall Be All,* pp. 189–97; Foner, *History of the Labor Movement,* vol. 4, chap. 8.

38. Dubovsky, *We Shall Be All,* pp. 120–25; Russell R. Elliott, "Labor Troubles in the Mining Camp at Goldfield, Nevada, 1896–1908," *Pacific Historical Review* 19 (November, 1950): 369–72.

39. Dubovsky, *We Shall Be All,* pp. 202–8; Foner, *History of the Labor Movement,* 4:282–95.

40. Dubovsky, *We Shall Be All,* pp. 208–9.

41. Dubovsky, *We Shall Be All,* pp. 209–20; Foner, *History of the Labor Movement,* vol. 4, chap. 10; Reed, "Lumberjacks and Longshoremen."

42. Dubovsky, *We Shall Be All,* chap. 10; Foner, *History of the Labor Movement,* vol. 4, chaps. 13–14; Commons, *History of Labor,* 4:266–73; Lens, *The Labor Wars,* chap. 10; Yellen, *American Labor Struggles,* chap. 6.

43. Dubovsky, *We Shall Be All,* chap. 11, pp. 307–11, 337–41, 391–392; Foner, *History of the Labor Movement,* vol. 4, chaps. 15–16, 23.

44. Dubovsky, *We Shall Be All,* pp. 384–87.

45. Commons, *History of Labor*, 3:403–50, 461–95, 506–22, 541–59, 616–23, 661–85; Weinstein, *The Corporate Ideal*, chap. 2; Edward Berman, *Labor and the Sherman Act* (New York: Harper, 1930).
46. Commons, *History of Labor*, vol. 4, chap. 32; Weinstein, *The Corporate Ideal*, chap. 8; Goldstein, *Political Repression*, pp. 121–25; Taft, *The AFL*, chap. 22; Lorwin, *The American Federation of Labor*, chaps. 6–7; U.S. Department of Labor, Bureau of Labor Statistics, *National War Labor Board: A History of Its Formation and Activities* (Washington, D.C.: Government Printing Office, 1922).
47. Dubovsky, *We Shall Be All*, pp. 349–50.
48. Ibid., p. 402.
49. Ibid., pp. 394–95.
50. Ibid., chap. 16.
51. Ibid., chap. 17.
52. Ibid., pp. 414–22.
53. William Preston, Jr., *Aliens and Dissenters: Federal Repression of Radicals, 1903–1933* (Cambridge, Mass.: Harvard University Press, 1963); Horace C. Peterson and Gilbert C. Fite, *Opponents of War, 1917–1918* (Madison: University of Wisconsin Press, 1957); Robert K. Murray, *Red Scare: A Study in National Hysteria, 1919–1920* (Minneapolis: University of Minnesota Press, 1955); Edwin P. Hoyt, *The Palmer Raids, 1919–1920: An Attempt to Suppress Dissent* (New York: Seabury Press, 1969); Harry N. Scheiber, *The Wilson Administration and Civil Liberties, 1917–1921*, Cornell Studies in American History, Literature and Folklore, No. 6 (Ithaca, N.Y.: Cornell University Press, 1960); Frank L. Grubbs, Jr., *The Struggle for Labor Loyalty: Gompers, the A.F. of L., and the Pacifists, 1917–1920* (Durham, N.C.: Duke University Press, 1968).
54. Eldridge F. Dowell, *A History of Criminal Syndicalism Legislation in the United States*, Johns Hopkins University Studies in Historical and Political Science, vol. 17, no. 1 (Baltimore: Johns Hopkins Press, 1939).

RECONSTRUCTING ORDER
THROUGH ACTION
Jim Crow and the Southern
Civil Rights Movement

Susan Harding

Jim Crow was a complex of laws, social practices, and cultural ideas that segregated and stratified blacks and whites in the American South for most of this century. For the most part, blacks and whites did not live, work, eat, drink, sleep, play, pray, or die together. They did not go to the same schools. They sat in separate sections of restaurants, theaters, and stadiums. They were born and doctored in separate hospitals. They were mourned and buried in separate funeral homes and cemeteries. According to the prevailing white rationale, blacks were biologically and morally inferior to whites and any form of interaction between them would degrade whites. Behind the fear of social contact was the fear that any "mingling" of black and white bodies and blood would "pollute" the white race and destroy white civilization. This reasoning also justified a racial etiquette that engaged blacks in public rituals of subordination and humiliation, a racial economy that assigned blacks the lowest order jobs and excluded them from any possibility of advancement, and a racial polity that disenfranchised blacks, banned them from government, judged them without due process, and punished them arbitrarily.[1]

During the 1960s, the civil rights movement challenged the whole system of Jim Crow racial segregation and stratification through a series of intense, often massive, and sometimes violent political conflicts that ultimately eliminated Jim Crow's most overt features in many Southern towns and cities. The movement emerged from a long tradition of organized black protest against Jim Crow, and few of the forms of protest were actually invented during the 1960s, but during that decade the magnitude and extent of protest escalated to the point of substantially altering the system of Southern race relations.[2]

The literature on the civil rights movement is immense, and we know a good deal about its origins, its dynamics, and its accomplishments.[3] We also have memoirs of individuals and histories of organizations active in the movement, accounts that tell us how persons and groups became involved and the course of movement encounters in many towns and cities. We know that hundreds of laws and regulations requiring segregation were repealed, that many prohibiting it and other kinds of racial discrimination were passed, and that integration and fairer treatment actually came about in many places. Federal interventions, sought by civil rights leaders and organizations in their conflicts with state and local governments, were crucial to the movement's course and outcome, and we know a good deal about those interventions and failures to intervene, and their effects on the movement.

Much more elusive, both historically and theoretically, is the story of how the social experience and cultural understandings of blacks and whites were remade by the civil rights movement. The movement not only brought about institutional changes, it *was* a process of change. We know something of the worldviews of blacks and whites before the movement, and something of them since then, but how did the movement remake their worldviews? This is a historical query about the civil rights movement, and a theoretical one about movements more generally: how are shared understandings reconstructed in the course of the collective actions that compose a movement? This essay provides a partial answer to both queries as it traces shifting patterns of shared interpretation during the course of movement events in two Southern towns. It proposes that the cultural change wrought by civil rights movement encounters consisted less in an invention of new ways of thinking than in a reorganization of existing ways of thinking, a reorganization that involved and affected whites as much as blacks. More specifically, the actions of the civil rights movement rendered black definitions of reality visible in the white world and reconstructed the white worldview into one in which those definitions had more validity and efficacy. The change thus represented a shift in the relative power of respective interpretations of reality, or a remaking of white hegemony.

In its original sense, *hegemony* describes the political predominance of one state, or government, over another.[4] Marxists, following Antonio Gramsci, have extended the meaning of hegemony to refer to the political predominance of the bourgeoisie over other classes in capitalist societies. Here I am using *hegemony* to refer to the political predominance of whites over blacks in the South. Political predominance means much more than political control. It refers to a complex interlocking of political, economic, social, and cultural forces that sustains a public definition of the world, of human nature, and of proper social relationships that, in effect, renders one worldview dominant over others in a society. Hegemony is not a state of affairs that, once established, survives on inertia. It is continuously reproduced, and it is continuously challenged. A hegemonic system is reproduced through its capacity to define certain challenges as unwise, impolite, illegitimate, illegal, or treasonous, and to punish transgressors. Its viability rests equally on authority, on widespread acceptance of the dominant group's right to rule, and on power, on the dominant group's ability to enforce its interpretation of events when it is challenged.

This essay proposes that social movements are one mode through which hegemonic worldviews are challenged and, to the extent a movement is successful, shifted. In this context, a movement is a prolonged series of conflictful interactions between individuals and groups challenging and those defending a hegemonic worldview.[5] A movement, or a particular series of movement encounters, begins when challengers protest hegemonic constraints on behavior and attitude and proceeds through an escalating series of interactions which includes breaches of conduct by challengers and repressive efforts by authorities. Usually after considerable polarization on both sides, the series of encounters culminates in some form of realignment of the forces of control and domination, either retrenching the authorities or giving way to challengers.[6] Legal restrictions and customary behavior are called into question, and so are the prevailing understandings that define the social identity of, and power relations between, the contending groups. Shared patterns of thought and feeling are altered along the way on both sides, but a movement victory, culturally speaking, is more of a shift in which a preexisting way of thinking prevails—a shift in hegemony—than it is a replacement of an old by a new way of thinking.

Jim Crow was not the only worldview in the South before the 1960s. Most blacks shared a different construction of reality, and many whites subscribed to a more egalitarian understanding of racial relations. However, Jim Crow was hegemonic in the sense that virtually every facet of public life was organized in its terms. It was hegemonic in the sense that it was a worldview that everyone participated in, however unwillingly, while other, more egalitarian worldviews were known only to those who believed in them—*publicly, they did not exist*. Again, this was the outcome of a complex interlocking of state, culture, and society; so too then was the process, the movement, that would challenge it. Blacks had been protesting Jim Crow segregation rules by violating them ever since they were instituted around 1900, and over the century blacks had evolved a culture and an infrastructure with which to resist and sometimes defy white domination, but the process of escalation and polarization that transformed protest and resistance into a movement was triggered in 1960 by the lunch counter sit-ins in Greensboro, North Carolina. By the end of the decade the civil rights movement had not replaced white domination with a regime of complete racial equality, and many forms of discrimination, inequality, and injustice remained intact, but in much of the South, it was no longer acceptable to advocate publicly racial stratification and segregation. Racist and paternalistic images of blacks did not disappear, nor were they entirely suppressed, but they were forced to give way, to make room for more egalitarian images in public discourse and behavior. Overt racism was no longer legitimate; Jim Crow had lost hegemony.

This essay traces how white hegemony was transformed in one city and in one county in the South. The task of opening up white hegemony to more egalitarian understandings was an enormous one, as testified by the course of events everywhere the civil rights movement emerged. Within those dimensions, there was much variation in the course of the movement across the South. I have chosen to trace movement events in Greensboro, North Carolina, and in Neshoba County, Mississippi, partly because they illustrate the main lines of variation.

In the upper South and in cities such as Greensboro, the rules applied more loosely, racial relations were more paternalistic, and whites accepted the ultimate authority of the federal government. What happened in Greensboro illustrates the classic forms and phases that the civil rights movement assumed—a sustained unfolding of public, collective actions carried out by blacks demanding changes in the racial status quo. In the deep South and the countryside such as Neshoba County, Jim Crow rules were strictest, white supremacist beliefs were fierce, and, for many whites, the Civil War was not quite over. The story of Neshoba County illustrates the process of coercing change where Jim Crow was so powerful there was little room for public collective action on the part of blacks, and the primary challenge took place inside the chambers of the federal judiciary.

Another reason for selecting these two cases is that their consequences extended well beyond their local boundaries. Events in both Greensboro and Neshoba County were tracked by regional and national media, and they re-etched the mind of the nation as well as the mental life of local blacks and whites. In examining events in Greensboro, I focus on how movement actions progressively challenged the prevailing white worldview. In examining events in Neshoba County, I stress how the consequences of civil rights movement actions reordered shared patterns of interpretation among whites.

Greensboro

Before the civil rights movement in Greensboro, although overt forms of segregation and discrimination were widespread, white terrorism was virtually nonexistent and blacks had been gradually allowed to register and to vote in elections. During the 1940s, the black community developed its electoral potential and in 1951 elected the first black to the Greensboro city council. However, it was the ideological trappings of the predominant political faction, which was moderate on issues of race relations, that most distinguished Greensboro's Jim Crow from that of the deep South. In *Civilities and Civil Rights*, a detailed narrative of movement events in Greensboro, the historian William Chafe describes the prevailing ideology as a progressive mystique.[7] Chafe uses the word *mystique* because he is not referring to a political system with rigid regulations and procedures, but to "a series of assumptions, nuances, and modes of relating that have been all the more powerful because they are so elusive."[8] Its cornerstone was civility, "a way of dealing with people and problems that made good manners more important than substantial action."[9] The idea of civility combined three elements: first, a belief that conflict was inherently bad and that voluntary consensus was the only basis for action; second, a courtesy toward and tolerance of new ideas, as long as they were not acted on; and third, "a generosity toward those less fortunate than oneself,"[10] which sustained a sense that those less fortunate than oneself had nothing to complain about.

What all this added up to was prohibition against collective action on the part of blacks, a prohibition which reflected and guaranteed their continued subordination to whites. Given the etiquette of race relations, whites saw blacks as clients, or they did not see them at all. Hidden from whites by their own hegemony was an array of black organizations and institutions in Greensboro—churches, schools, colleges, voluntary organizations, and the largest chapter of the National Association for the Advancement of Colored People (NAACP) in the state—that produced a consciousness of racial equality and eventually a capacity to fight for it. Whites did not know this world existed because "they took ritualistic deference as an authentic expression of black attitudes toward them. . . . Yet it was this world that in the 1950s and 1960s gave rise to the black part to the dialectic that would be the civil rights movement in Greensboro."[11]

The history of the civil rights movement in Greensboro may be divided into three periods. During the first, from 1954 to 1960, blacks worked largely through legal and legitimate channels toward racial equity in general, and for the desegregation of schools in particular, in the wake of the 1954 Supreme Court decision which outlawed segregated schools. In the second period, between 1960 and 1968, Greensboro blacks challenged the overt forms of discrimination, the face of Jim Crow, through collective actions that were illegal or illegitimate in white eyes. During the third period, from 1968 to 1972, blacks challenged white hegemony at its core by redefining the rules of interracial discourse, mainly through community organizing that enlarged the independent bases of black power, and by contesting all forms of white control of black life.

Before 1954, segregation had been challenged with some minor successes in Greensboro. For example, biracial teams had quietly removed Jim Crow signs all over the city. The 1954 Supreme Court decision, however, mobilized the defenders of Jim Crow in Greensboro. The initial, official reaction of the school board was to announce its acceptance and endorsement of the decision, in keeping with the city's reputation for progressivism. It shortly became clear, though, that "acceptance" did not mean the board endorsed integration, but only acknowledged that the legal sanction of segregation had been eliminated. While token transfers of blacks to white schools would be allowed to prevent federal intervention, no effort would otherwise be made to alter the racial status quo in the schools. Paralleling these maneuvers on the local level, the governor and the legislators of North Carolina prepared an arsenal of legal, administrative, and ideological weapons to resist desegregation, again with enough of a progressive veneer to avert federal intervention. So, although blacks made considerable efforts to have the Supreme Court decision implemented, they made only token gains during the late 1950s.

Greensboro blacks saw that there would be no voluntary compliance on the part of whites with any substantive challenge to Jim Crow through legal and legitimate channels. These lessons were behind the decision of the four Agricultural and Technical College (A&T) students to sit in at the Woolworth's lunch counter in 1960, and behind the immediate mobilization of other black students and the black community in general to support the sit-ins and other forms of active protest. After six months of sit-ins, marches, pickets, intermittent negotiations, and an economic boycott, the three downtown stores with lunch counters agreed to desegregate. Subsequently, blacks returned to "normal political channels" to redress their grievances, some perhaps thinking that white leaders would be more open to hearing them and more willing to respond positively. White leaders were not, and in 1962 a new series of protests against Jim Crow practices in the city produced the same pattern of white retreat and retrenchment and black escalation, until a final confrontation in the summer of 1963. For two weeks there were mass marches nearly every night, leading to mass arrests, with fourteen hundred blacks incarcerated at one point. The mayor of Greensboro, faced with calling in the National Guard, finally gave in to black demands and ordered the full desegregation of public places in Greensboro.

Again in the aftermath, whites, instead of approaching interracial communication with a new spirit of respect, shored up their defense of the vestiges of Jim Crow. Black requests for a comprehensive busing plan to desegregate schools, for an open housing ordinance to correct the residential segregaton, and for a ward system of representation in city council were rejected. Blacks saw, when they dismantled the facade of Jim Crow, a substructure of arrangements and understandings in the city and in its government that reproduced racial inequality covertly. These forms of racial discrimination did not provide public forums in which blacks could demonstrate an injustice, as did segregated facilities, and it was clear once again by the end of the 1960s that unless blacks found a way to coerce white compliance, there would be no justice, no equity, forthcoming.

By the late 1960s new leaders and new forms of organizing had developed in the black community, ones which in the name of black power overcame the progressive mystique by operating outside of it, shaping new rules, agendas, language, and culture, in order to take power. Through community organizing—of tenants, of workers, of welfare recipients, of neighbors, of young people in high schools and colleges—they built an independent base of operations that enabled blacks to act more in their own interest, free of white influences and definitions. By assuming more militant stances in both their rhetoric and behavior, black power systematically rejected the code of white civility. Some moderate black leaders were critical of these developments, and virtually all white leaders reacted to them with contempt and fear and, finally, massive repressive force.

The first major confrontation with police occurred in the wake of Martin Luther King's assassination. Several hundred students marched into downtown Greensboro the day of his murder, chanting "black power," and when they began to smash car windows and throw rocks, police responded with tear gas and shotguns. The mayor called in the National Guard; there was another major battle the next evening on the A & T campus which resulted in six injuries. The mayor imposed a curfew for the next four days, with National Guard units occupying the campus and rooftops of major downtown buildings. Blacks noted the violent overreaction of police, the fact that the mayor did not consult any black leaders before calling in the guard and imposing the curfew, and the pleasure with which white papers described both sorts of action. Early in 1969, there were more explosive moments: one barely averted under the guidance of black negotiators, and another that mobilized the entire student body of A & T and resulted in a mass march that dispersed with demonstrators throwing stones and police firing guns and tear gas.

The final confrontation was in May of 1969. Black school officials, acting under orders of the city's white-controlled school board, invalidated the election of Claude Barnes as student council president of Dudley High School. Barnes was active in community organizing in Greensboro's black community and an advocate of black power in the schools. A walkout of students and picketing resulted in a melee with police. The school was closed, and students fled to the A & T campus. The National Guard was called in to occupy the campus, and there were two nights of high tension and gunfire. On the first night, a black student, Willie Grimes, was shot in the head and killed. The next night, some policemen were injured, and the following morning, National Guardsmen swept through the dormitories, shooting doors open and evacuating students, who were sent home, and the campus was shut down.

Blacks saw what they had seen before, only amplified and more vicious. They saw white recalcitrance in the face of a legitimate grievance; they saw white leaders bypass black leaders and entrench in the face of further protest; finally, they saw whites willing to apply massive force, to injure and to kill, in order to defend their control over the situation. In the initial aftermath, there were no concessions to blacks, but a few months later, for the first time, major factions of leadership in the white community began to actively support and even promote substantial changes in the racial status quo of Greensboro. Political hegemony had shifted, at least temporarily, from the white moderates to the white liberals. In the next two years blacks increased their representation on city council and were appointed to major offices in city government. Campaigns to meet the grievances of tenants and workers won major concessions, and community organizing among blacks in Greensboro continued to develop. In 1970, Claude Barnes was allowed to run for office at Dudley High School, and a new student group committed to black unity was approved. In 1971, the city school board finally capitulated to pressures from the movement and from the federal government and ordered the full and complete desegregation of the city's forty-seven public schools. A massive program of preparation was carried out over the summer by biracial committees and the school system was fully integrated with very few disruptions in the fall. The process that had begun seventeen years before, in 1954, was finally complete, and marked the end of the civil rights movement in Greensboro.

It was clear by the end of the 1950s that challenges through "normal channels" would bring about no real changes in the racial status quo. In the movement proper, beginning in 1960, the initial challenges came directly from the black community of Greensboro and they took the form of breaches of civility that forcefully articulated alternative black worldviews, first a more moderate one of racial equality and integration, then a more militant one of black power and autonomy.

Of all the actions, the sit-ins were the most cogent and comprehensive violation of Jim Crow and perhaps the most compelling expression of the black worldview. As one demonstrator in Charlotte, North Carolina, put it, the sit-ins were a "means of expressing something that had been on our minds for a long time."[12] In one simple action, blacks could demonstrate to themselves and to whites that they did not consider themselves inferior, that they considered themselves equal, that they would not cooperate with ritual segregation that reproduced racial stratification, and that they would behave according to their own understanding of how things should be: integrated, equally open to blacks as to whites. It was a breach that not only requested and demanded change; it also asserted the change. Picketing, marching, and demonstrating likewise represented a change in that blacks were acting publicly and collectively in their own interests. While in their content these actions were requesting change rather than asserting it, in their form they were also punctiliously civil ritual assertions of the collective rights of blacks to spaces hitherto defined as white, and in which white definitions were formulated and enforced, such as main streets and courthouse squares. Their effect was to make visible, in an unexpected and (to the whites) incongruous place, the collective presence of a black society that was a basis for an alternative, and equally civil, worldview. The major breaches of the subsequent period of the movement were community organizing and the rhetoric of black power. Like earlier forms of protest, both asserted a change rather than demanded one, but it was a change much more threatening to white hegemony than desegregating public places, hence the reaction was much more violent.

Breaches of white hegemony provoked crisis periods consisting of escalating breaches on both sides until some final showdown when one side or the other capitulated. The escalation of the movement corresponded precisely to a process of escalating retrenchment on the part of white elites. Movement actions forced white progressives into ever more reactionary corners until they had to choose between forsaking their "civility," in order to repress the activists with brute force, or opening up to change. This at least was the dialectic of events during the earlier phase in Greensboro. During the later phase, black power activists challenged the progressive mystique itself, refusing to deal with whites on their terms at all, and, with their rhetoric of militance and their small attacks on white property, provoked whites to abandon civility completely. For blacks, and ultimately for many white liberals, the repression leveled against the students and the killing of Willie Grimes revealed the real racist core of white hegemony.

The earlier, civil disobedience, phase and the later, black power, phase of the Greensboro movement were characterized by marked differences in the nature of actions and goals. They also represented separate phases in the attack on white hegemony. In both, issues of the content of race relations and the form of interracial discourse were at stake. However, in the earlier phase, from 1960 to 1968, when blacks attacked the most overt rituals and rules of discrimination, issues of content were primary. In conceding those issues, whites reasserted the progressive mystique which obscured white control of the definition of what was real and unreal, permissible and impermissible, in a veil of civilities and delegitimized further black demands. In the later phase, from 1968 to

1969, white control over the definition of interracial relations was the main subject of contention. This is seen in the triviality of the issue that triggered the final confrontation between black students and police forces—whether or not Claude Barnes's election as student council president was valid. This was the tip of an iceberg. The real fight was over who would control the definition of what was real and unreal, permissible and impermissible—whites or blacks. In the immediate contest for control, whites won, not only in the streets, but ideologically, and for months afterward they produced astonishing conspiracy theories, charging that the Dudley events were part of an elaborate plot by the Black Panther party to start a race war and overthrow the U.S. government. However, winning had transformed white moderates into racist reactionaries, hence, delegitimized them in their own terms. Their victory was also a defeat, as it gave license and legitimacy for the first time to other whites willing to forsake some control over the racial status quo.

The success of the black challenge to Jim Crow and the progressive mystique in Greensboro depended on blacks acting collectively, publicly, and eventually illegally and uncivilly—outside the so-called normal channels of political discourse—over and over again, until whites were driven to the point of great financial losses, of invoking massive repression, or of submitting to intervention by state and federal armed forces. At these moments, new coalitions gained power and the authority to make compromises and concessions. Left unconstructed were huge chunks of institutional racism, countless hard-core racists, and some of the old etiquette of race relations, but the absolute segregation of public places and of housing and schools was broken, and blacks had gained considerable political power, in the offices of government and in the form of community, cultural, and political organizations. On the one hand, rituals and practices reproducing castelike inequalities had been eliminated, and on the other, new bases of black consciousness, power, and action had been generated. Both constituted real durable changes in the organization of white domination in Greensboro, North Carolina.

Neshoba County

I have described hegemony as a combination of political, social, economic, and cultural forces supporting the domination of one group over another. Both a state of affairs and a state of mind, a set of practices and a moral climate, hegemony is at once imposing and elusive.

A full interpretation of shifting hegemony would also include detailed descriptions of the *experience* of white hegemony in motion, of how blacks and whites experienced their worlds before, during, and after the movement. The following discussion of events surrounding the murder of three civil rights workers comes to us via Florence Mars, a white moderate, resident of Neshoba County, and participant in and observer of many of the events. Mars took it upon herself to record and, with the assistance of Lynn Eden, write up all she could about the events.[13] Her white moderate view is partial in both senses of the word, but it does give us a subjectively real understanding of what white hegemony was in Neshoba County and how its shifts affected the social experience of whites. The Neshoba case also illustrates Jim Crow at its reactionary extreme, in its most absolute and vitriolic form, and the nature of the struggles against Jim Crow as they were carried out not in the streets but inside the state, specifically in the judicial process of indicting, trying, and convicting the white men who murdered the civil rights activists.

Let me begin the story of the events in Neshoba County in the words of Florence Mars.

> On June 16, 1964, three young men, civil rights workers, disappeared from the Neshoba County jail in Philadelphia, Mississippi. Their decomposed bodies were eventually dug out of a twenty-foot earthen dam. Three and a half years later, eighteen men, most of whom were either known or assumed to be members of the White Knights of the Ku Klux Klan of Mississippi, went on trial for conspiracy to deprive these three men of their federal rights of life, liberty, and the pursuit of happiness. The eighteen defendants included the sherriff, deputy sheriff, former sheriff (and sheriff-elect) of Neshoba County, a Philadelphia city policeman, and the imperial wizard of the White Knights.[14]

The murders of Michael Schwerner, James Chaney, and Andrew Goodman, the trial of their killers, and surrounding events were the main site of the ideological, political, and social struggle over white hegemony in Neshoba County. The following review of events leading up to the murders in 1964, to the trial in 1967, and the trial's aftermath, focuses on the evolving white interpretation of events, on the twists and turns of the white hegemonic perspective in the world of Neshoba County.

In 1960, some twenty thousand people lived in Neshoba County, of whom five thousand were black. Blacks and whites lived in segregated sections of the county's major town, Philadelphia, and in small segregated communities in the surrounding countryside. Segregation and the racial code of conduct were strictly adhered to, and blacks were completely excluded from the political structures of the county. As elsewhere in the South, there were indigenous bases of black power in the form of churches, schools, businesses, and a chapter of the NAACP. The NAACP chapter was formed in the late 1940s and worked diligently to add blacks to the list of registered voters. Blacks, however, were turned away by the registrars with equal diligence, and in 1964 there were still only ten registered to vote in the county. Except for ongoing unsuccessful efforts on the part of blacks to register, whites saw no sign of the civil rights movement in Neshoba County until 1964. Political elites in the county, and in the state of Mississippi, unrestrained by a progressive mystique, responded rapidly and resolutely to the 1954 Supreme Court decision outlawing segregated schools. White citizens' councils and political leaders mobilized white supremacist sentiment and an arsenal of legal weapons against *any* deseg-regation. White moderates were silent; all middle ground disappeared.

Trials with black defendants, or of whites for crimes against blacks, had traditionally been occasions for ritual displays of white hegemony in the deep South. In effect, in cases involving blacks and whites, the issue was not so much what happened, or who did what, but whether a black could dispute a white, and whether white supremacy would prevail. At-torneys representing whites invariably argued at some point to their white juries that "our way of life rests on the decision in this case."[15]

Thus, when a white killed a black in Mississippi it could not be seen as an isolated act between persons, but was always interpreted in the light of Jim Crow race relations, which did not even recognize the killing as murder. After 1954, racial murders and the workings of the judicial sys-tem in relation to those murders acquired even greater symbolic import. The most publicized case was the trial and acquittal of two white men who killed a black teenage boy, Emmet Till, in 1955. According to Mars, the case "polarized resistance and made it clear that Mississippi would fight any moves toward integration and equality with an emotional intensity not felt since the Civil War."[16] Mars was not surprised by the verdict in the Till case, but she was by "the emotional outburst it provoked. The glare of publicity and the threat of intrusion into Mississippi's way of life opened up old wounds and exposed racist attitudes in the *most* genteel whites, attitudes I had never seen and never knew existed in my then thirty-two years."[17] Other less well publicized racial murders took place in the late 1950s and early 1960s in Mississippi, and the guilty whites were either never identified, exonerated without a trial, or tried and acquitted. Equal justice for all was not being weighed in the scales of Mississippi's judicial system in these cases; white hegemony was. The verdict was that whites had total control not only over the definition of real and unreal, permissible and impermissible, but also of life and death, truth and untruth, as far as blacks were concerned.

White resistance to the challenges of the black movement in Mis-sissippi during the early 1960s was largely out in the open and much of it in clear violation of federal mandates. Not only was the white population resisting aggressively, but so were local and state political elites and police forces. In the words of one civil rights activist, it was clear early on that white Mississippi "lacked the moral resources to reform itself," and that extraordinary federal intervention would be required to bring about any racial reforms.[18] Registering blacks to vote in rural Mississippi was especially dangerous. Movement leaders in charge of that project on the state level decided to recruit Northerners, white and black, to work alongside Mississippi blacks during the summer of 1964 on voter registration and the training of local blacks for movement action in Freedom Schools. They did so knowing that behind Northerners, at least behind Northern whites, was the strong arm of the federal government, and they anticipated that the participation of Northern whites would bring greater federal pressures to bear on Mississippi whites.

The immediate effect of the voter registration project, called the Mississippi Summer Project, was to provoke a rearming of white supremacy. Mississippi legislators passed laws expanding police powers of arrest and facilitating the pooling of police resources. They made it a felony to circulate material that encouraged boycotts; they prohibited picketing of public buildings; and they made it a crime to operate a school without permission of the county clerk. The governor doubled the size of the state highway patrol, and the mayor of Jackson doubled his police force, bought 250 shotguns, three more paddy wagons, and a Thompson tank.

The Ku Klux Klan spread through Mississippi in early 1964, and by the spring, crosses were burning on weekends in many Mississippi communities. Klan leaders and literature intensified the ideological struggle considerably by arguing that behind the blacks, the Northerners, and the agents of the federal government was a Russian, Cuban, "Jewish Communist" conspiracy to destroy the Southern way of life and urging whites to defend it with their lives. Indeed, the summer was to be one of great violence, much of it committed by Klan members, all of it committed by white supremacists.

In 1963, Lawrence Rainey was elected Neshoba County sheriff by a landslide vote. Rainey's campaign promise was to "take care of things," and he had a reputation for being "hard on Negroes," having killed two under dubious circumstances as deputy sheriff.[19] A few months later, the Ku Klux Klan organized in the county, burning crosses and leafleting houses, and Rainey and his deputy, Cecil Price, were among its leaders. Events moved swiftly in June, 1964. Black parishioners of the Mt. Zion Methodist Church not far from Philadelphia had been meeting with Mississippi Summer Project staff about using the church as a Freedom School that summer. In mid-June, Klansmen confronted and beat up parishioners as they left a meeting one evening and burned the church to the ground. They were looking for Michael Schwerner, a project staff member, whom they considered a ringleader and whom they had targeted to kill. Schwerner was not there that evening. Shortly after the incident,

Schwerner went with James Chaney, another project staff member, and Andrew Goodman, one of the new volunteers, to investigate the church burning. As they were leaving the county, Deputy Sheriff Cecil Price arrested them for speeding and on suspicion of having burned the church themselves in order to attract publicity and raise money. He held them for several hours, and released them around 10:30 P.M. after fining them twenty dollars. Three cars full of white men, including the deputy sheriff, intercepted them outside of Philadelphia and took them to a side road just off the highway. First Schwerner and Goodman, both Northern and white, were taken out of the car and shot and killed, then Chaney, a black from Meridian, was riddled with bullets and his body mutilated. Their bodies were stuffed into their station wagon, driven to a nearby dam construction site and buried beneath a mound of dirt.

For the six years between the murders and the incarceration of the murderers, Neshoba County whites battled over how to define the killings of Schwerner, Chaney, and Goodman. The question was whose construction of reality would prevail, the white supremacists', for whom the killings were not murders and the killers were not criminals, or the white moderates', for whom the Klansmen were criminals who had murdered three innocent men. The larger questions were, would reactionary Jim Crow prevail over a more paternalistic, or moderate, version of white domination, and would a local definition of reality that exonerated the Klan prevail over the federal government's definition of law and justice.

The interpretative shift over the six-year period did not reflect, but rather constituted, a process of hegemonic realignment. It was not the exclusive signal, but, for the white community, how the killings were defined would be the central symbolic indicator of Jim Crow's fate in the county. Until the trial, the prevailing interpretations were those of the white supremacists. For the first six weeks after the killings, until the bodies were found, the disappearance of the civil rights workers was treated as a hoax staged by them in order to get publicity and raise money. A similar theory prevailed about the burning of the Mt. Zion church, which occurred a few days before the disappearance. The images were sufficiently powerful that even whites who did not believe them looked for evidence to disprove them.

Note here that whose interpretation requires proof is an indicator of who has and who lacks hegemony. Florence Mars did not think the disappearance was a hoax, but she was not completely convinced until the burned-out station wagon was found. "When the boys' wagon was found I knew they were dead. Even if they had wanted to stage a disappearance they would not have burned their only means of escape."[20] Later, when the bodies were found and the fact of murder incontrovertible, the supremacists argued that the Federal Bureau of Investigation planted the bodies there as part of a conspiracy with black activists to invade the county and destroy its racial order. Most whites saw the civil rights workers as "the enemy and whatever happened to them was justified and deserved."[21]

The organization of silence, in addition to the assignment of the burden of proof, is a powerful indicator in discourse of where hegemony lies. Defenders of the Klansmen counseled everyone in the county not to talk to federal agents about anything. The Klan defenders did not want anyone to talk for very practical reasons, of course, because winning the judicial battle depended on withholding evidence from their opponents. Silence and noncooperation also validated the white supremacist interpretation that they were united against outsiders in their defense of Jim Crow. But their ability to maintain and enforce silence was also a direct measure of their hegemony because hegemony, in part, is defined by the ability of a dominant group to construct reality and to render alternative versions invisible and inaudible. So a major activity of white supremacists between the murders and the trials was a continuous campaign of intimidation, harassment, and punishment aimed against anyone, black or white, who articulated any piece of an alternative construction of reality.

Still, white supremacists lost ground over the three-year period before the trial. Within a year after the killings, Neshoba County blacks had become a force to be reckoned with, and it showed in both their behavior and their discourse with whites. After the killings, civil rights activists continued to help blacks in the county register to vote, and hundreds of blacks finally succeeded in the wake of the Voting Rights Act of 1965. Blacks also won court cases ordering that Jim Crow signs be removed in the courtroom and the first four grades of Neshoba County schools be desegregated in 1965. Although attacked by angry white mobs, blacks carried out memorial marches on the first two anniversaries of the murders, hence establishing their right, literally and publicly, to demonstrate their construction of reality. These were limited victories, but in Neshoba County, where blacks traditionally had *no* political voice, they were remarkable. In addition, moderate whites made some tentative forays into the public eye during the time between the murders and the trial. While moderate whites were turned back by Klan threats in their attempt to help raise funds to rebuild the Mt. Zion church, they stood by the school superintendent's decision to cooperate with limited school desegregation. Gradually, they began to speak out in public against the Klan and the murders, especially after each new set of indictments was handed down. In doing so, the white moderates did not effectively challenge the hegemony of the white supremacists, but they broke the illusion of its unity and began to develop a sense of collective voice.

When the trial finally began in 1967, it galvanized the attention of the county. This was the great showdown between the forces for and against white supremacy and the verdict would symbolize which side won. In effect, the murdered activists as well as their killers, the civil rights movement and the Klan, racial equality and Jim Crow, federal jurisdiction and states' rights were all on trial. How the trial was conducted mattered almost as much as who won because that was the process by which the competing versions of reality were constructed. Everything would make a difference in the outcome: the judge, the demeanor of the defendants and the witnesses, the lawyers' motions, questions, and summations, the tone of the courtroom, and the media coverage.

Judge Harold Cox, who presided in the Federal District Court in Meridian where the trial was held, had a reputation for being hostile to blacks in the courtroom. The defendants were relaxed and joked with each other throughout the trial, betraying no sense of guilt or expectation of punishment. Their mood might have gained sway had not the judge unexpectedly set a different tone early in the trial. One of the Klansmen's lawyers asked a witness, a black minister, a question passed to him by one of the defendants: "Now, let me ask you if you and Mr. Schwerner didn't advocate and try to get young male Negroes to sign statements agreeing to rape a white woman once a week during the hot summer of 1964?"[22] Judge Cox asked the lawyer his basis for asking that question. Unsatisfied and irritated with the answer, Judge Cox said: "I'm not going to allow a farce to be made of this trial and everybody might as well get that through their heads including every one of the defendants right now. I don't understand such a question as that, and I don't appreciate it."[23] According to Mars, the lawyer was startled by the judge's reaction, "which was not what he expected," and "the style of the Neshoba County bar was cramped for the rest of the trial."[24] We do not know what motivated Judge Cox to rule as he did at this moment in the trial. It was not likely a change in conscience; more likely, he was submitting to the scrutiny of the entire federal judicial system and the nation's media. The significance of his ruling, whatever his motivation, was to place limits on the defense's capacity to elaborate the supremacist construction of reality.

Most of the prosecution's case, conducted by Assistant U.S. Attorney General John Doar, consisted of straightforward testimony from local blacks and whites about events that led up to the murders of Schwerner, Chaney, and Goodman, and about the murder itself. The defense's case did not attempt to refute any of this evidence, except by establishing alibis for the defendants and by casting aspersions on the characters of the informants. Much of their case was testimony about the good reputations of the defendants.

In summation, government and defense lawyers articulated the worldviews in peril. John Doar stressed the strength of the evidence and the importance of equal justice. He also alluded to the significance of the verdict for Jim Crow.

> If you find that these men or that each of them is not guilty of this conspiracy it would be as true to say that there was no night-time release from jail by Cecil Price, there were no White Knights, there were no young men dead, there was no murder. If you find that these men are not guilty you will declare the law of Neshoba County to be the law of the state of Mississippi.[25]

According to Doar, a not-guilty verdict would mean that killing civil rights workers was not a crime in Mississippi. When defense lawyers summed up their case, they portrayed the murder charge as unreal, attacked the role of the federal government in the investigation, and proclaimed the unity of all whites in the face of outside threat. Their summation articulated Jim Crow ideology at its extreme. According to one defense lawyer,

> The government must prove that these three people who are said to have been killed, I say they ain't even proved who's been killed beyond a reasonable doubt, but if they are they must prove that they are citizens of the United States of America before you could return a verdict of guilty and I haven't heard a single witness to get up on the stand and say that Schwerner, Goodman or Chaney were citizens of the United States of America, and if there is any reasonable doubt in your minds to that effect, you should find them not guilty.[26]

According to another defense lawyer,

> Ladies and gentlemen, you are fellow Mississippians, the same blood that flows through the veins of your county flows through the veins of Neshoba County. In Neshoba County, we have white people, we have Negroes, we have Choctaw Indians, and they all live side by side in harmony and peace and prosperity. . . . You don't need a Washington attorney to come down and tell you what to do, tell your hearts and your soul what you should do, you know what to do, you know liberty, freedom, honor and trust will say to you not guilty, not guilty, eighteen times. Then Ladies and Gentlemen of the jury, we'll lift up our heads, look on ahead to tomorrow, hold our heads high, look everybody in the eye and say Neshoba County is honorable, these defendants are innocent.[27]

After two days of deliberation, the jury reported it was unable to reach a verdict, and the judge made another fateful decision. Instead of declaring a mistrial, he issued a "dynamite charge," ordering the jury to reconsider the evidence and make every effort to reach a verdict. The next day the jury returned with convictions for the seven men who were most directly associated with the killings.

A thread of suspense persisted after the trial, until the Klansmen were actually sent to prison three years later, but the drama that had mesmerized the county after the murders was resolved as the jury foreman read the verdict. Again, the drama was not so much whether the Klansmen had committed murder—most people had long made up their minds about what they believed—but whether it was a crime for Klansmen to kill civil rights workers in Neshoba County and whether the worldview in which it was not a crime would prevail. The trial was mesmerizing because the outcome was unpredictable, because it depended very much on what individuals said and did—what charges the judge made to the jury, for example—and because it would alter the moral and political climate of the county.

The guilty verdict, in effect, passed hegemony from white supremacists to white moderates in Neshoba County. For Mars and her elated friends, it meant they no longer had to restrain their speech in public, they could speak out with a new ease and authority. They no longer had to couch their beliefs and interpretations in relation to a prevailing white supremacist consciousness, but could speak freely as if the world were the one in which they believed. Most county whites, of course, were shocked, not elated. No one had expected a guilty verdict and most were not prepared to accept it. For some time they continued to speak of the trial as part of a conspiracy against Neshoba County and to spin countertheories about what really happened. These people did not change their minds much about what happened, but before long it was they, not the moderates, who had to couch their interpretations in relation to a worldview that denied them. Admissions of guilt and acknowledgment of defeat crept into their statements. One former defender of the Klan in the county and a critic of integration expressed the experience of losing hegemony exquisitely when he said: "We resent this forcing, but there's no way to resist it. It's like looking down the barrel of a cannon— you can't fight back with a peashooter."[28]

A shift in hegemony involves a reordering of cultural conceptions and authority relations so that formerly strong conceptions languish and opposing conceptions gain visibility and legitimacy. The reordering affects the experience and behavior of both the winners and the losers in the contest. In the case of the Neshoba County murder trial, the implications were multiple. It altered discourse among whites and tipped the balance of authority in the county from right to center, and it also represented a shift in the terms of Jim Crow, in the balance of race relations in the county. The use of unrestrained violence and terror in defense of white supremacy was checked. It broke the illusion of white unity and removed fierce pressures against coalitions between blacks and moderate whites to carry out even the mildest reforms. It lent legitimacy to the work of civil rights activists and to black demands in general. It robbed the white supremacists of their judicial monopoly and demonstrated the capacity of the federal government to intervene effectively in the face of systematic defiance on the local level. Whites as well as blacks understood that the legal victory over the Klan meant a corner had been turned in the struggle against Jim Crow. The shift was not absolute or irreversible, nor did it cause events that followed so much as create a context in which new things could happen, and some old things could not. According to Mars,

> Two years after the trial ended, the climate had changed in Neshoba County. No longer could one yell "civil rights" and "outside interference," as had once been possible, and mold resistance to almost anything. The confrontation had taken place; emotions reached an intensity that was difficult to recall, and men were waiting to go to prison for their part in putting three "integrationists" underneath twenty feet of dirt. [29]

When the Supreme Court ordered Neshoba County public schools fully integrated in 1969, the white community complied with no organized opposition and only a few parents sent their children to private schools. The editor of the Philadelphia paper, who had been outspoken in defense of the Klansmen in 1967, wrote

> The school integration has gone smoothly and this is a great achievement. It's gone more smoothly here than many places. People knew they didn't want anything resembling [the Klan killings] to happen again. The futility of making such a stand is very clear, and the community is gradually changing. [30]

New factories that moved into the area abandoned overt practices of discrimination, and several federally funded projects were integrated. By 1972, two thousand of the county's thirteen thousand registered voters were black and elections were reflecting the change in the electorate and in the political climate.

Accounts of the trial and its aftermath, including that of Florence Mars, tell us very little about the subjective experience of the black community in Neshoba County and how collective perceptions of blacks changed as a result of the murders, the trial, and surrounding events. It seems that the abuse and violence that whites heaped upon blacks in the county after 1954, and which escalated in 1964, was for them as important as the trial in mobilizing them to challenge Jim Crow in the county. The black community held memorial marches on the first two anniversaries of the deaths of Schwerner, Chaney, and Goodman, and in 1976 blacks dedicated a monument to the slain activists. The monument's plaque describes the connection between the deaths and changes in the world and worldview of Neshoba County blacks.

> Out of one blood God hath made all men. This plaque is dedicated to the memory of Michael Schwerner, James Chaney, and Andrew Goodman, whose concern for others, and more particularly those of this community, led to their early martyrdom. Their death quickened men's consciences and more firmly established justice, liberty, and brotherhood in our land.[31]

Conclusion

Events in both Greensboro and Neshoba County revealed two phases of challenge to Jim Crow hegemony. In the first phase, some of Jim Crow's features were attacked and changed, and blacks publicly articulated an alternative worldview to that of Jim Crow. The forms of white domination were altered, but the underlying assumptions did not change. During the second phase, the polarization between the competing worldviews reached new extremes, then began to reverse direction as the forces of culture, society, and state that had held Jim Crow together gave way to an emerging "middle ground." This phase actually constituted the shift in white hegemony through which blacks gained some measure of access to the means and ends of domination.

The course of these two phases was very different in Greensboro and in Neshoba County. In Greensboro, the two phases were successive. During the first, from 1960 to 1968, blacks launched two campaigns of collective, public protest against forms of discrimination. The protests were a mixture of legal and illegal actions, but the illegal ones generally violated specific Jim Crow regulations. They were challenging manifestations of Jim Crow, and victories resulted in piecemeal concessions, not a change in the organization of white hegemony, so that in their wake whites invariably behaved as if it were time for blacks to return to their invisible, inaudible station in society. The second phase was much shorter, from 1968 to 1969, but crucial in actually shifting white hegemony, as blacks attacked the code of white civility itself, refusing to follow even its ostensibly neutral constraints on behavior. With more militant actions and rhetoric, they challenged Jim Crow's underlying assumptions, the substructure of arrangements and understandings that sustained white hegemony more covertly, and provoked increasingly repressive responses from the white power structure. Finally, they drove white moderate leaders to breach their own code with the murder of Willie Grimes, and, as the legitimacy of moderate leadership drained away, room opened up for white liberals to form coalitions that linked both sides in the conflict and enabled them to assume the reins of civic power.

In Neshoba County, where Jim Crow ideology assumed the form of white supremacy rather than white civility, the two phases were overlapping. In the summer of 1964, blacks were only beginning to mobilize for public challenges to white domination in the county, when, in rapidly escalating anticipation of such challenges, whites wielded their ultimate repressive instrument by killing Schwerner, Chaney, and Goodman. Not only did whites bypass the phase of making concessions and absolutely polarize the conflict in their lethal response to the mere suggestion of a breach of conduct by local blacks, but prevailing white opinion in the county was not chagrined by the action, which was interpreted instead as a legitimate exercise of white authority. Neshoba County, in other words, was a place where a breach of black conduct was equivalent to a challenge to the whole racial system, and where internal constraints on white behavior were so weak that nothing whites might do to blacks would lead them to reform themselves. Although the first phase was not completely eclipsed and collective protests by blacks did occur in the county subsequent to the killings, the system of Jim Crow was at stake from the beginning. Moreover, given the virulence of white hegemony in the county, it was clear that it could be shifted by civil rights supporters only in alliance with federal officials, by moving the contest to a higher level of state and bringing the encapsulating system of justice to bear on local officials. Once the verdict was rendered and the killers were judged murderers, hegemony shifted, the "middle ground" opened up, more moderate governing coalitions assumed power, and race relations began to change in Neshoba County.

There was nothing inevitable about the progression of events in either Greensboro or Neshoba County, and the same general ends came about by other means in other Southern cities, towns, and counties. However, I would argue that, whenever the local system of white domination was changed by civil rights actions, the two phases I have described may be distinguished in some manner, and that it is important to distinguish them in order to recognize the crucial moment of hegemonic change. According to this analysis, the symbolically charged encounters between blacks and whites of the first phase of movement action did not, in themselves, suffice to transform social reality by overturning white hegemony.[32] The ultimate authorities in the case of Jim Crow hegemony were political power holders, agents of state, and it was only when their internally defined legitimacy was effectively diminished that hegemony shifted.

In general terms, the encounters of the first phase—the public, collective actions which breach a prevailing code of conduct—challenge the forms of hegemony and may win concessions, but they do not open up the hegemonic system, much less overturn it in and of themselves. In this phase, corrective actions taken by authorities reinforce their legitimacy rather than undermine it, and new governing coalitions are unable to assume leadership and power. Shifts in hegemony are an outcome of the second phase of contest in which corrective actions are perceived, immediately by some and ultimately by most within ruling circles, as illegitimate, hence delegitimizing. Unity is broken and there is a realignment of governing forces, often involving several branches and levels of state, which results in substantive changes in society and state. It is this realignment which constitutes the shift in hegemony, not the challenges to it, no matter how public, how large, or how successful they are in bolstering participants or in winning concessions.

Civil rights movement actions culminating in the death of Willie Grimes in Greensboro, and in the convictions of the murderers of Schwerner, Chaney, and Goodman in Neshoba County, brought about realignments within the structures of governance and a reorientation of the shared patterns of thought, feeling, and action of whites in both places. Among the changes that demonstrated a significant realignment was the full desegregation of public schools without major disruptions and with the vocal support of many who had been silent or opposed to it. In addition, there were manifold changes in the organization of normal public discourse—in the assumptions people made about who was likely to be right and wrong, in the visibility and communality of shared self-images, and in the ability to engender voluntary consensus and public initiative. These actions did not occur directly as a result of movement encounters but because movement actions provoked encounters inside the state structures that eventually delegitimized the coalition of forces defending Jim Crow and legitimized more liberal or moderate coalitions. It was not the movement encounters themselves, but their political consequences, that transformed Jim Crow hegemony in the South.

Social movements challenge and, when successful, constitute shifts in the relative power of particular ways of thought to govern public and, though less effectively, private life. The state is a target of movement action, in part, because it is the ultimate arbiter of social hegemonies. It is not a monolithic, absolutely autonomous arbiter, however, but a contentious, internally divided arena in which competing perspectives are continuously ranked via the laws, policies, procedures, actions, factions, and personalities of state. Politicians are central mediators of this process, and they are particularly sensitive to social movements because they reflect potential shifts in their bases of governance. This is especially true in democratic polities because those bases are also voting blocks. A major movement indicates a new pattern of cleavages growing beneath the feet of politicians, and they may ignore it, deny it, resist it, or accommodate to it by adjusting their language, actions, and alliances. Politicians thus become part of the process of reasserting an old or defining a new hegemonic order, or they miscalculate and fall between the cracks of the order which is coming or going. Major governing realignments signal the completion of a shift in a hegemonic order, by no means irreversible, but indicating that state authorities will now interpret certain events, practices, policies, and ideas differently.

All movements, by definition, transform their participants' conceptions of self and the social order, and are thus mechanisms of sociocultural change internally. When they succeed in altering the way state authorities perceive a matter, they become, through their reverberations of state, broader mechanisms of sociocultural change as they reshape the worldviews of a nation.

NOTES

For help with my concepts, facts, writing, and morale while working on this essay, I am grateful to Sam Bowles, Charles Bright, Bill Christian, Lynn Eden, William Gamson, Tom Holt, Skip Rappaport, Rebecca Scott, and Charles Tilly.

1. My general sources on the social relations of Jim Crow were Charles S. Johnson, *Patterns of Negro Segregation* (New York: Harper and Row, 1943); C. Van Woodward, *The Strange Career of Jim Crow* (New York: Oxford University Press, 1974); and Pauli Murray, *States' Laws on Race and Color* (Women's Division of Christian Service of the Methodist Church, 1951). Also see William Percy, *Lanterns on the Levee: Recollections of a Planter's Son* (New York: Alfred A. Knopf, 1941), and Tom P. Brady, *Black Monday* (Jackson, Miss.: Citizen's Councils of America, 1955).

2. See August Meier and Elliott Rudwick, *Along the Color Line* (Bloomington: Indiana University Press, 1976), and idem, *CORE: A Study in the Civil Rights Movement 1942–1968* (New York: Oxford University Press, 1973); Aldon Morris, "Black Southern Student Sit-in Movement: An Analysis of Internal Organization," *American Sociological Review* 46 (December, 1981): 744–67; and Richard Kluger, *Simple Justice: A History of Brown v. the Board of Education and Black America's Struggle for Equality* (New York: Alfred A. Knopf, 1976) on the civil rights movement's prehistory.

3. In addition to Woodward, *The Strange Career of Jim Crow*, Meier and Rudwick, *CORE*, and Morris, "Black Southern Sit-in Movement," see Howell Raines, *My Soul is Rested: Movement Days in the Deep South Remembered* (New York: Putnam, 1977); Howard Zinn, *SNCC, The New Abolitionists* (Boston: Beacon Press, 1964); Frances Fox Piven and Richard Cloward, *Poor People's Movements* (New York: Vintage, 1977); and Carl

Brauer, *John F. Kennedy and the Second Reconstruction* (New York: Columbia University Press, 1977).

4. Antonio Gramsci locates hegemony in civil society, whereas I describe it as the intersection between processes of state and society. See Perry Anderson, "The Antinomies of Antonio Gramsci," *New Left Review* 100 (November 1976/January 1977): 5–78; and Raymond Williams, *Marxism and Literature* (Oxford: Oxford University Press, 1977).

5. My major conceptual sources on political and social movements are Charles Tilly, *From Mobilization to Revolution* (Reading, Mass.: Addison-Wesley, 1978); William A. Gamson, Bruce Fireman, and Steve Rytina, *Encounters with Unjust Authority* (Homewood, Ill.: Dorsey, 1982); and E. P. Thompson, *The Making of the English Working Class* (New York: Vintage, 1963). Also see Charles Tilly's essay in this volume, and Susan Harding, "Family Reform Movements: Recent Feminism and Its Opposition," *Feminist Studies* 7, no. 1 (Spring, 1981): 57–75, for some elaboration of the concept of a movement as a series of interactions between challengers and authorities, explicitly in Tilly's essay and through a case study in my own.

6. Victor Turner, *Dramas, Fields, and Metaphors* (Ithaca: Cornell University Press, 1974), pp. 78–79.

7. Oxford: Oxford University Press, 1980. Chafe's analysis of movement dynamics and white ideologies in particular make it a theoretically as well as historically rich book.

8. Ibid., p. 7.

9. Ibid., p. 8.

10. Ibid.

11. Ibid., p. 9.

12. Ibid., p. 86.

13. The Neshoba County account is largely from Florence Mars, with Lynn Eden, *Witness in Philadelphia* (Baton Rouge: Louisiana State University Press, 1977). My other sources on the civil rights movement in Mississippi were Tom Hayden, *Revolution in Mississippi* (Students for a Democratic Society, 1962); Len Holt, *The Summer That Didn't End* (New York: William Morrow and Co., 1965); Meier and Rudwick, *CORE; Anne Moody, Coming of Age in Mississippi* (New York: Dell Publishing, 1968); Woodward, *The Strange Career of Jim Crow;* and Zinn, *SNCC.*

14. Mars, *Witness in Philadelphia*, p. xv.

15. Ibid., p. 51.

16. Ibid., p. 65.

17. Ibid., pp. 68–69.

18. Holt, *The Summer That Didn't End*, p. 197.

19. Mars, *Witness in Philadelphia*, pp. 76–77.

20. Ibid., p. 88.

21. Ibid., p. 103.

22. Ibid., p. 235.

23. Ibid.

24. Ibid.

25. Ibid., p. 257.
26. Ibid., p. 258.
27. Ibid., pp. 258–59.
28. Ibid., p. 272.
29. Ibid., p. 269.
30. Ibid., p. 278.
31. Ibid., p. 181.
32. I am grateful to Charles Tilly for posing this problem to me.

CONTRIBUTORS

ROD AYA teaches at the Anthropology-Sociology Center at the University of Amsterdam. He is the author of *The Missed Revolution: the Fate of Rural Rebels in Sicily and Southern Spain, 1840–1950,* and an editor of *Theory and Society.*

SAMUEL BOWLES is Professor of Economics at the University of Massachusetts, Amherst. He is coauthor, with Herbert Gintis, of *Schooling in Capitalist America,* and, with David Gordon and Thomas Weisskopf, of *Beyond the Wasteland.*

CHARLES BRIGHT teaches history and politics at the Residential College, the University of Michigan. A specialist in European political and military history, he has moved toward American history and is currently at work on a study of Michigan politics in the twentieth century.

ELIZABETH M. BRUMFIEL is Assistant Professor in the Anthropology-Sociology Department at Albion College. She is currently at work on a book on *The Aztec Economy, 1350 to 1521.*

KENNETH FINEGOLD is Assistant Professor of Political Science at Vanderbilt University. His current research is on progressive reform in early-twentieth-century New York, Cleveland, and Chicago.

DANIEL R. FUSFELD is Professor of Economics at the University of Michigan. He is the author of *The Age of the Economist* and, with Timothy Bates, *The Economics of the Urban Ghetto.*

LYNN EDEN is completing her Ph.D. in sociology at the University of Michigan. Her essay in this collection is drawn from her dissertation. She is the author of *Crisis in Watertown* and, with Florence Mars, of *Witness in Philadelphia.* She is currently a fellow at the Center for Science and International Affairs at the John F. Kennedy School of Government at Harvard University.

MICHAEL GEYER is Associate Professor of History at the University of Michigan. A specialist in German studies, especially military and economic history in the twentieth century, he has written widely on the German military and the history of the Third Reich.

HERBERT GINTIS is Professor of Economics at the University of Massachusetts, Amherst. He is coauthor, with Samuel Bowles, of *Schooling in Capitalist America,* and of *Inequality* with Christopher Jencks et al.

RAYMOND GREW is Professor of History at the University of Michigan and editor of *Comparative Studies in History and Society.* A specialist in nineteenth-century European social history, he is author of *A Sterner Plan for Italian Unity.*

SUSAN HARDING is an Associate Professor in the Residential College and the Department of Anthropology at the University of Michigan. She is author of *Remaking Ibieca: Rural Life in Aragon under Franco.*

ROBERT A. SCHNEIDER is Assistant Professor of History at Brandeis University. A specialist in early modern France, he recently completed a dissertation on "Urban Sociability in the Old Regime: Religion and Culture in Early Modern Toulouse" at the University of Michigan.

THEDA SKOCPOL is Associate Professor of Sociology and Political Science and Director of the Center for the Study of Industrial Societies at the University of Chicago. She is the author of *States and Social Revolutions: A Comparative Analysis of France, Russia, and China,* and the editor of *Vision and Method in Historical Sociology.* She is at work on a book about the political formation of the American welfare state.

CHARLES TILLY is Professor of Sociology and History and Director of the Center for Research on Social Organization at the University of Michigan. His books include *The Vendee, The Formation of National States in Western Europe,* and *From Mobilization to Revolution.*